From Politics to the Pews

Chicago Studies in American Politics

A SERIES EDITED BY BENJAMIN I. PAGE, SUSAN HERBST,

LAWRENCE R. JACOBS, AND ADAM J. BERINSKY

Also in the series:

Additional series titles follow index

From Politics to the Pews

How Partisanship and the Political Environment Shape Religious Identity

MICHELE F. MARGOLIS

The University of Chicago Press
Chicago and London

The University of Chicago Press, Chicago 60637

The University of Chicago Press, Ltd., London

© 2018 by The University of Chicago

Published 2018

Printed in the United States of America

27 26 25 24 23 22 21 20 19 18   1 2 3 4 5

ISBN-13: 978-0-226-55564-5 (cloth)

ISBN-13: 978-0-226-55578-2 (paper)

ISBN-13: 978-0-226-55581-2 (e-book)

DOI: https://doi.org/10.7208/chicago/9780226555812.001.0001

Library of Congress Cataloging-in-Publication Data

Names: Margolis, Michele F., author.

Title: From politics to the pews : how partisanship and the political
    environment shape religious identity / Michele F. Margolis.

Other titles: Chicago studies in American politics.

Description: Chicago : The University of Chicago Press, 2018. |
    Series: Chicago studies in American politics

Identifiers: LCCN 2018004882 | ISBN 9780226555645 (cloth : alk. paper) |
    ISBN 9780226555782 (pbk. : alk. paper) | ISBN 9780226555812 (e-book)

Subjects: LCSH: Religion and politics—United States. | Partisanship—Political
    aspects. | Identity politics—United States.

Classification: LCC BL65.P7 M37 2018 | DDC 201/.720973—dc23

LC record available at https://lccn.loc.gov/2018004882

For my parents, Peter and Wendy Margolis
For Adam

CONTENTS

ACKNOWLEDGMENTS

As a senior at UC Berkeley, I decided to write a thesis on how members of different religious traditions vote. I was terrified when I approached Jack Citrin to ask if he would be my thesis advisor. Convinced that he would say no, I almost didn't ask him. But I mustered the requisite courage, and I am so glad I did. With Jack as my advisor and mentor during my senior year, I discovered a love of doing research and my fascination with religion and politics in America. My sincerest thanks go to Jack for starting me down this path.

Once in graduate school at MIT, my advisors—Adam Berinsky, Gabe Lenz, and Charles Stewart—helped me transform my general interests and vague intuitions into a research agenda. Adam's natural skepticism and probing questions forced me to refine my arguments and think through the theoretical and empirical implications of each of my claims. I knew when I had convinced Adam of something that I had made progress. I also thank Adam for his financial generosity; much of the early data collection for this book would not have been possible without the Political Experiments Research Lab at MIT. I benefited tremendously from Gabe's thorough and constructive reading of my work; he offered critical input on issues of research design, analysis, and framing, while simultaneously being the consummate cheerleader. Gabe's willingness to provide feedback and support made it easy for me to forget that he was not actually living in Cambridge for a good deal of my graduate school career. Charles's knowledge about religion proved invaluable as this book project took shape. On numerous occasions, he pointed me toward useful data sources on religion about which I would not have otherwise known. In graduate school, I had the good fortune to be part of vibrant intellectual communities in both Cambridge and Chicago, where I received thoughtful feedback and useful advice on my research. In particular, I thank Dan Altman, Steve Ansolabehere, Jon Blake, John Brehm, Andrea Campbell, Devin Caughey, Justin de Benedictis-Kessner, Anthony Fowler, Allison Harris, Joyce Hodel, Alisha Holland, Krista Loose, Ethan Porter, Miranda Priebe, Mike Sances, Betsy Sinclair, and Chris Warshaw.

Much of this book was written and rewritten while I was at the University of Pennsylvania, where I received continuous support, constructive criticism, and practical advice from my colleagues. I am enormously indebted to Dan Hopkins, Matt Levendusky, and Marc Meredith. By virtue of working with their office doors open, Dan, Matt, and Marc ended up being my go-to people for questions and quick feedback. Their help with everything ranging from reading parts of (or whole) chapters and giving their thoughts on a recent iteration of a graph to sharing LaTeX code and offering professional advice not only improved the quality of the book but also made the experience of writing it easier. I am also grateful to Diana Mutz for always being eager to help in any way possible and generously using her own resources to provide data for this project, John Lapinski for providing several research assistants, and Dan Gillion for his advice on the publishing process. Deep thanks also go to John DiIulio. Though John's university obligations keep him very busy, he nevertheless found time to read and provide insightful comments on the entire manuscript. John also graciously gave me an opportunity to present my work to some of the country's most important religious scholars and leaders and brought me on as a fellow at the Program for Research on Religion and Urban Civil Society (PRRUCS).

I also thank Bethany Albertson, Vin Arceneaux, Jon Blake, Louis Bolce, Avery Goldstein, Julia Gray, Guy Grossman, Allison Harris, Mike Horowitz, Yue Hue, Cindy Kam, Dorothy Kronick, Shana Kushner-Gadarian, Ed Mansfield, Rogers Smith, Jessica Stanton, Dawn Teele, and Melissa Wilde for helpful conversations, feedback, and professional advice. In particular, Vin Arceneaux, Louis Bolce, Guy Grossman, Allison Harris, Dorothy Kronick, and Adam Ziegfeld read various chapters, and their comments helped refine the book's argument and improve its readability. Another thank you goes to Adam Berinsky and Gabe Lenz, who have continued to provide guidance on the project as well as the publishing process even after I was no longer officially their student.

The book benefited tremendously from a one-day book conference in April 2016. I am deeply thankful to Ed Mansfield—the department chair when I arrived at Penn and who started the tradition of supporting junior faculty book conferences—as well as to Anne Norton, the current chair who continued this tradition. I extend a heartfelt thank you to the four external participants—Vin Arceneaux, Paul Djupe, Taeku Lee, and Bob Shapiro—who took the time to engage closely with my manuscript. Their chapter-by-chapter feedback helped me structure and frame the book and brought to light underdeveloped themes and implications stemming from my research. In addition to the external participants, I am grateful to those from the Philadelphia political science community who read my manuscript and took part in the daylong event: Nyron Crawford, Allison Harris, Dan Hopkins, Jay Jennings, Matt Levendusky, and Marc Meredith. Also, my thanks go out to Naya Blackwell for helping to organize the conference and Adam Ziegfeld for taking notes during the conference.

I further benefited from the comments of seminar participants at Harvard, Yale, and Vanderbilt, as well as the detailed feedback and probing questions I received during a presentation at a National Capital Area Political Science Association meeting. Jacob Ausubel, Erin Farrell, Nikki Lin, Kareen Movsesyan, and Veronica Podolny provided valuable research assistance. Their close readings of and thoughtful questions about the manuscript undoubtedly improved the final product, and I appreciate their willingness to help with some of the less exciting parts of book writing and editing. John Tryneski, Chuck Myers, Holly Smith, and two anonymous reviewers helped turn a book manuscript into an actual book. I am grateful for how seamless the publication process has been; one would never have known that Chuck took over for John as my editor at the University of Chicago Press between submission of the manuscript and its eventual publication. My thanks also go to the University of Chicago Press for allowing me to publish portions of chapters 3, 4, and 5 in a paper titled "How Politics Affects Religion: Partisanship, Socialization, and Religiosity in America" in the *Journal of Politics* (2018) prior to this book appearing in print.

The research for this book would not have been possible without the financial support of several institutions. While a graduate student, I received a grant from the National Science Foundation (SES 1219787) as well as an opportunity to collect data through Time-Sharing Experiments for the Social Sciences. My thanks also go to David Kinnaman for sharing data that the Barna Group had collected. Since arriving at Penn, I have received support from PRRUCS and the Program on Opinion Research and Election Studies.

The professional debts I have accrued while writing this book are nothing compared to the personal debts I have amassed. Since beginning this project, I gained a father- and mother-in-law. Richard, whose enthusiasm for my research is second only to his enthusiasm for his own son's research, always asked with genuine interest how my work was progressing. And, whereas most people thank family and friends solely for their emotional support during the book-writing process, I am grateful to my mother-in-law, Paulette, for additionally contributing to this book with her fast and thorough copyediting. Dan and Debbie, my brother and sister-in-law, make my trips to California less productive, but far more fun. Keeping my professional deadlines and milestones in her calendar, learning and adopting political science jargon, helping me formulate game plans, and reminding me to cut myself some slack are just a few of the many things for which I am forever indebted to Rebecca Graff. Everyone needs a Becca in his or her life while writing a book. I am also grateful to my grandmother, Mema, not only for being a constant source of support and encouragement, but also for being Professor Judith Margolis, a professional role model and pioneer who paved the way, not just for me, but for many women in academia. Thanks also go to Mort Margolis (Gramps) and Rhoda Pashkowitz (Nana). They are not here to see my book in print, but they both had an indelible impact on my life.

My deepest thanks go to my parents, Peter and Wendy Margolis. My dad's nonchalance at my successes ("Of course you got a book contract, you are a rock star") and genuine disbelief at my setbacks ("I don't understand how anyone could reject your paper") provided much needed encouragement during the long and exhausting process of writing this book. My mom's uncanny ability to know exactly what I need—a listening ear, a metaphorical kick in the rear, or a care package with gluten-free flour tortillas—has made this arduous process seem a little more manageable. I am incredibly fortunate to have parents who are both my role models and friends, and I am profoundly grateful for their love and support.

Finally, words cannot express my gratitude to my husband, Adam Ziegfeld. Not only is Adam an incredibly supportive and encouraging partner, but he has also contributed a great deal to this project, from giving feedback on half-baked ideas and taking notes at my book conference to testing surveys before they went into the field and line editing most of the manuscript. Our wonderful son Rafael arrived just as I needed to begin the revisions on my book manuscript. Adam gave me the time and space to revise the book, which meant doing the lion's share of the childcare and doing less of his own research in the process. None of this would have been possible without him.

ONE

Group Identities and Politics
in the United States

Karen's religious community is at the center of her life.[1] She attends church each Sunday without fail and participates regularly in Bible study sessions; she takes great comfort in knowing that God is watching out for her; and it was important for her that her children be baptized. In addition to supporting Republican candidates at both the national and local levels, Karen is quite open about her conservative political views. For example, Karen shared her excitement on Facebook when a congressman introduced the Life at Conception Act (H.R. 1091), which declares that the unborn are "persons" under the Fourteenth Amendment to the Constitution. Karen also believes that marriage should be between one man and one woman, federal aid programs—such as food stamps—create a culture of dependency, and political correctness has gone too far.[2]

Fran, in contrast, is not very religious. Although she continues to observe a few cultural traditions associated with her religious upbringing, she is not particularly devout and worries that organized religion does more to pull people apart than bring them together. Fran is also a strong and vocal Democrat. She supported Barack Obama in both 2008 and 2012 and took her young child to the polls to vote for Hillary Clinton in 2016; she has donated money to progressive organizations associated with abortion rights and the protection of immigrant communities; and she is concerned that religion plays too large a role in politics. In fact, a sticker she posted near her desk at work reads: "The only wall we need is between church and state."

Karen and Fran each resemble millions of Americans and are emblematic of one of the "most important and enduring social cleavage[s]" in the electorate (Bolce and De Maio 2014: 48). Today, the highly devout and frequent churchgoers tend to identify with and support the Republican Party, while religious nonidentifiers and infrequent attenders generally support the Democratic Party. These religious differences between Democrats and Republicans, often referred to as the "God gap" or "religiosity gap," correspond to some of the largest electoral blocs and most stable constituencies in the American party system.

Conventional wisdom suggests that religion has produced this God gap, with religious voters sorting into the Republican Party and secular and less religious voters joining the Democratic Party's ranks. This explanation presumes that Americans have responded to the changing relationship between religion and politics over the past five decades. For much of American history, political parties differed along denominational lines, each drawing disproportionate support from Americans belonging to different religious traditions. But beginning in the 1970s and 1980s, denominational differences between the parties increasingly gave way to new partisan coalitions based on religiosity, or level of religious involvement. Democratic and Republican elites staked out divergent positions on moral issues, used religious faith to varying degrees when reaching out to voters, and debated religion's role in the public sphere. Politically oriented religious groups also emerged on the scene with the hopes of influencing public policy. This new political environment, according to many scholars, prompted a mass restructuring of party allegiances. Voters, for the first time, relied on how deeply felt their religious identities were and how entrenched they were in their faiths and communities when forming political preferences, thereby uniting previously politically dissimilar voters—Catholics, mainline Protestants, and evangelical Protestants—under the umbrella of religiosity. According to this explanation, Karen's identification with the Republican Party likely reflects her religious involvement whereas Fran's lack of religious commitment increased her likelihood of becoming a Democrat.

However, a second process—one that is not often considered—could also produce the God gap and explain why Karen is a religious Republican and Fran is a far less religious Democrat. According to this second explanation, politics drives the God gap, with partisans selecting into (or out of) organized religion based on their partisan identities. Whether people choose to identify with a religious faith and the extent to which they are involved in a given religious community are, in part, responses to their political surroundings. Instead of religiosity driving political attitudes, the shifting political landscape—in which Republicans have become associated with religious values and cultural conservatism to a greater extent than the Democrats—could have instead changed partisans' involvement with their religious communities. This explanation, in which Karen's Republican leanings led her to become more religious and Fran's affiliation with the Democratic Party pushed her away from religion, changes our understanding of politics' role in shaping social communities and group attachments. The political factors that produce contemporary electoral politics in America can also alter the makeup of the relevant social groups presumed to be the parties' key constituencies. Which explanation accounts for the current religious-political landscape in the United States? Does religion push voters in the direction of certain parties, as is commonly assumed? Or might politics explain voters' levels of religiosity and commitment to religion? Answering these questions is the main goal of this book.

Main Argument

The pages that follow argue against the widespread assumption that religion, particularly the strength of religious affiliation and involvement in a religious community, is itself impervious to politics. Rather, this book shows that partisan identities can profoundly shape identification with and engagement in the religious sphere.

A novel theory that draws on what we know about Americans' religious and political socialization experiences generates predictions about when partisanship can affect religious affiliation and involvement. In brief, the distinct timings of the religious and political socialization processes create a window during which partisanship can influence decisions related to religion. Partisan identities typically crystallize in adolescence and early adulthood, which is the very time when many people have distanced themselves from religion. As young people reach adulthood, however, they must decide whether and how involved they want to be in a religious community. At this juncture, partisan identity, which has already solidified for many, can shape religious attachments. Further, because religious identification and practices are often stable after these initial decisions are made, partisanship's impact on religious decisions can persist for decades.

Why does partisanship affect levels of religiosity? The life-cycle theory, described briefly above and in more detail in chapter 3, identifies a life stage during which partisanship and politics can influence religious attachments. However, the life-cycle theory on its own does not predict how members of a particular party will behave. Instead, the political environment in which people are situated informs specific expectations about how partisanship influences religious attachments. The 1970s saw new political issues and electoral strategies emerge that resulted in the parties becoming distinct along a religious dimension that did not previously exist. Once the parties and party elites diverged on questions related to religiosity, Americans could draw on their partisan identities when making religious choices. Elite cues provide information to voters as they transition from young adulthood into adulthood about how people "like them" engage with religion. Empirical tests presented throughout the book corroborate the life-cycle theory: Partisanship influences religious decision making at a certain life stage, and these partisan-driven religious choices are evident for many years to come. All told, the elite-led changes to the parties' positions and strategies not only affected how religious people came to view the parties but also how partisans came to view religion.

Why Does It Matter If Politics Affects Religion?

This book focuses on the political origins of social groups. How do social identities develop, and why do some people more strongly identify with certain social groups—such as racial, religious, or gender groups—than others? American politics scholars often ignore these questions because they do not think that politics influences social identities or the extent to which individuals identify with certain social groups. Having assumed that group attachments take root outside the political sphere, researchers have found ample evidence that group-centered politics is alive and well in the United States, shaping how Americans engage in politics. But what if politics plays a role in the formation of these social identities? The book focuses on religious identities to answer this question. In doing so, it explores whether politics helped create the strong bonds between Americans' religious and political attachments that are widely analyzed and discussed during each election cycle. Identifying a reciprocal relationship in which religious attachments both affect and are affected by politics changes how we think about the last forty-five years of American political history, religion's ability to influence politics, the power of partisanship, and identity in general.

If we fail to recognize that partisanship can shape religious attachments, our understanding of recent political history is woefully incomplete. The chapters that follow offer an alternative—and, I would argue, far more complete—account of the dramatic change in the composition of American electoral coalitions over the past forty-five years, during which time a strong and enduring cleavage has developed that pits religious Republicans against more secular Democrats. Moreover, the life-cycle theory helps make sense of the decades-long time lag between changing strategies and rhetoric at the elite level and the emergence of the religiosity gap among voters. If partisanship affects the religious choices of only a subset of individuals, rather than the population as a whole, then many years should need to pass before changes at the elite level become evident in the religious and political attitudes among the broader population. Whereas researchers pinpoint the 1990s as the beginning of the God gap, change had been under way for decades.

Although the argument advanced in this book does not preclude religion from influencing politics, it nevertheless raises questions about how and when religion plays a role in the political sphere. For example, conventional wisdom is that religious voters select into the Republican Party. One implication of this is that campaigns can win support using religious appeals. Conversely, these same campaigns imbued with religious themes and rhetoric should alienate nonreligious voters. If, however, such religious appeals and campaign strategies also changed the religious makeup of the United States, then these tactics will appear far more successful in shaping political preferences than they actually are.

Moving beyond how the results reshape our understanding about religion and politics, the alternative narrative presented in this book also suggests the need to reevaluate our understanding of social group influence in politics. Research focusing on social groups takes as a starting point that being part of a group, or holding a specific identity, provides members with "a place in the social world" (Simon and Klandermans 2001: 320), which generates a common worldview and shared priorities among members (Abdelal et al. 2009; Campbell et al. 1960). This outlook can, in turn, shape how group members respond to events and interpret the world around them, including politics. Indeed, when political differences emerge among groups within society, many assume that these "distinctive [political] patterns are produced, in one fashion or another, by influence of the group" (Campbell et al. 1960: 295). Moreover, researchers have found that strong identifiers—those who are more attached to a particular group—are the most likely to behave politically like others in the group (Berelson, Lazarsfeld, and McPhee 1954; Campbell et al. 1960; Conover 1988, 1984; Gurin, Miller, and Gurin 1980; Shingles 1981; Tate 1994), while nominal affiliates, or members who are "psychologically peripheral" to the group, are the most likely to deviate from the group's norm (Campbell et al. 1960: 309). Scholars frequently attribute any difference in political outlooks between strong and weak identifiers to the influence of the social group. If, however, we choose identities along with how strongly we associate with them, researchers must consider whether politics plays a role in that process of identity acquisition. In fact, "this ability to recreate and refashion one's identity many times over is arguably at its extreme in contemporary American society" (Huddy 2001: 137). The theory and empirics from this book offer a critical first step in understanding how politics influences group identification and when an identity becomes politically consequential in the United States.

Politics' ability to affect identification with and participation in a religious community also changes how we should think about partisanship's power to influence, and possibly divide, Americans. Even though voters are politically unaware (Berelson, Lazarsfeld, and McPhee 1954; Campbell et al. 1960; Converse 1964; Delli Carpini and Keeter 1996) and many Americans hesitate to call themselves strong partisans (Klar and Krupnikov 2016), partisanship cleaves the electorate by changing who belongs to and participates in the country's largest social institution. The findings from this book demonstrate that by creating social divisions, partisanship's impact on average citizens extends far beyond the political sphere.

This book focuses on how partisanship can influence seemingly nonpolitical decisions related to religion; however, politics' impact on religion has important political implications as well. If partisans select into or out of religious communities, in part, based on their political outlooks, they will find themselves in more politically homogeneous social networks where they encounter less diverse political information. Rather than churches being places where people with different political viewpoints come together, religious communities may become more like echo chambers populated by likeminded partisans. Politically homogeneous social groups and an associated absence of countervailing information not only encourage the creation of durable bonds between religious and partisan identities but may also fuel further political animosity toward the opposing party. As partisans become even less likely to interact with politically dissimilar people and increasingly come to see the out-party as differing both politically and socially, it is likely that the political biases and partisan hostility that currently exist in American politics (Huddy, Mason, and Aarøe 2015; Miller and Conover 2015; Iyengar, Sood, and Lelkes 2012) will continue to grow.

Finally, the power of partisanship and the origins of social group membership also matter for democratic accountability. In a democracy, we often think that politicians respond to voters' preferences. Voters have the power to keep politicians in office or kick them out. Voters' power, therefore, relies on people's ability to make political decisions consistent with their preferences. Scholars have shown that this is easier said than done (Kinder 1983; Kuklinski and Quirk 2000; Sniderman 1993). Though voters reward or punish candidates based on performance issues—such as the economy or perceptions of honesty—voters have more difficulty choosing candidates based on policy preferences. Moreover, politicians often "lead" on matters of public opinion; voters frequently update their attitudes to be consistent with their parties' positions rather than changing their views of the parties to match their political attitudes (Lenz 2012). Findings such as these suggest a pessimistic view of democracy because voters cannot hold politicians accountable on the basis of policy. That said, voters may be able to reward or punish politicians based on their group interests.

By looking to other group members and leaders for guidance on how to act, being part of a group or holding a specific social identity can help voters overcome informational deficits that make it difficult for them to hold elected officials accountable. Group ties can therefore enable voters to act in their best interest politically even when they would not otherwise be able to do so on their own. The findings from this book, however, cast doubt on this optimistic claim that group membership offers a collective solution to citizen ignorance. When social identities develop in response to politics, it calls into question whether group identities enable Americans to vote in accordance with policy preferences or whether their policy preferences are being shaped alongside group membership.

Definitions

Since the book's main focus is on the origins and consequences of religious and partisan identities, it is prudent to consider what these identities mean in this context. The sections below discuss different conceptualizations of partisan and religious identities and offer definitions and examples that will appear throughout the book.

What Does Partisan Identity Mean?

Political identities can be conceptualized in multiple ways, including party identification, political ideology, and policy positions. Although the exact wording of partisanship questions varies, most surveys elicit a respondent's partisanship by asking something along the lines of: "Generally speaking, do you usually think of yourself as a Republican, a Democrat, an Independent, or what?" In contrast, political ideology questions ask whether people think of themselves as politically "liberal, conservative, or moderate," and questions on policy stances gauge individuals' opinions on specific policy issues and proposals. The three types of measures, while distinct and representing different facets of a person's political identity, are related and have become increasingly aligned in recent years. Democrats are more likely to identify as liberal and take liberal positions on salient political issues, while Republicans have become increasingly conservative in both their stated ideology and policy positions (Abramowitz and Saunders 1998; Bafumi and Shapiro 2009; Baldassarri and Gelman 2008; Layman and Carsey 2002; Levendusky 2009).

Throughout the book, references to partisan identities, allegiances, and affiliations refer to a person's partisanship. I make this decision for three reasons. First, party identification is highly stable, even over long periods of time (Converse 1964; Converse and Markus 1979; Green, Palmquist, and Schickler 2002). In comparison, individuals' ideologies and issue positions are more inconsistent and malleable. Converse (1964) finds that most voters do not have a coherent ideology, and many voters simply do not think about politics enough to form "well-developed abstract belief systems" (Levendusky 2009: 110). Similarly, many people's attitudes change regularly (Converse 1964). They frequently hold multiple, possibly conflicting opinions on a topic (Zaller and Feldman 1992), and many are willing to offer opinions on topics they know very little about (Benson 2001) or on policy proposals that do not exist (Bishop et al. 1980; Bishop, Tuchfarber, and Oldendick 1986).

A second reason to look specifically at party identification is that partisanship can be thought of as a social identity. Party identification is similar to identifying with other social groups or joining a political team in which individuals identify with fellow partisans, root for their chosen party, and attach affective ties to political leaders and groups (Green, Palmquist, and Schickler 2002). In doing so, partisans prefer members of their own party while denigrating out-party members: Democrats' (Republicans') dislike for Republicans (Democrats) has increased in recent decades (Iyengar, Sood, and Lelkes 2012), and partisans routinely favor copartisans in both political and apolitical situations (Alford et al. 2011; Huber and Malhotra 2017; Iyengar and Westwood 2015). Partisans, although many are ideologically centrist and hold moderate policy positions (Fiorina, Abrams, and Pope 2006), draw on their partisan identities when thinking about themselves and evaluating others.

And third, whereas partisanship today is more closely associated with political ideology and policy positions than in previous decades (Bafumi and Shapiro 2009), party identification drives these related political outlooks. Partisans adopt political positions that are consistent with those of their party leaders (Layman and Carsey 2002; Lenz 2012), and the tighter association between party identification and ideology occurred because Democrats became liberal and Republicans became conservative (Levendusky 2009). People do not choose their party affiliations to be consistent with a set of political beliefs or specific attitudes; rather they use their partisan identities when adopting ideologies or policy preferences.

Given partisanship's stability and strength, it is perhaps unsurprising that it is currently the single best predictor of vote choice. Ninety percent of partisans vote for their party's candidate (Erikson and Tedin 2007; Jacobson 2010), and split-ticket voting has declined since the 1970s (Hetherington 2001). All told, partisanship represents a strong and stable affiliation with a political party that operates much like other social identities. In contrast, political ideology and individual policy positions are more likely to be ephemeral or stem from a person's partisanship.

This book, therefore, focuses on partisan identification. That does not mean, however, that ideology or policy positions cannot influence religious decision making. Thus, statistical models will include ideology and relevant policy preferences as control variables. The influence of these variables is usually quite small and their inclusion never changes partisanship's effect. Empirically, the analyses use a three-point party identification scale that distinguishes among Republicans, Independents, and Democrats. I treat partisan leaners—those who lean toward one party but do not readily identify with a party—as partisans because their behaviors look similar to partisans, not Independents, in this context.

What Does Religious Identity Mean?

Organized religion is made up of many large institutions that hold unique philosophical and theological outlooks and have long historical traditions that have evolved over time in response to changes in society and interactions with others. Religion offers its members a structured worldview, social norms, and expectations about appropriate beliefs and behaviors (Leege and Kellstedt 1993). In short, religion at its broadest includes "belief systems, congregations (sets of people), houses of worship (locations), attachments to people and things (psychological factors), collections of symbols, labels, identities, or something" (Djupe and Calfano 2013: 20). From this starting point, both religion's breadth and its emphasis on divine beings and communication make it difficult to conceptualize and measure a person's individual relationship with religion. Instead, social scientists focus not on the otherworldly aspects of theology but on the more tangible outgrowths of religion, such as personally held beliefs and involvement with religious institutions. In particular, within the social sciences, scholars tend to think of religion as either a mental phenomenon that is personal in nature or as a social phenomenon that is group-oriented in nature. While both mental and social aspects of a person's religious identity will be addressed in the book, the theory and empirics largely adopt the latter—religion as a social phenomenon—framework.

Religion as a mental phenomenon includes "fundamental beliefs, ideas, ethical codes, and symbols associated with a religious tradition, including what others call a theology or belief system" (Wald 1992: 27). This approach corresponds to a personal-subjective understanding of religion (Roof 1979), which focuses on an individual's private faith and piety (Wald and Smidt 1993). Religion, according to this framework, is a purveyor of overarching religious belief systems that guide day-to-day living. Examples of these beliefs include orthodoxy, fundamentalism, and biblical literalism (Stark and Bainbridge 1985) as well as beliefs about communitarianism (Mockabee, Wald, and Leege 2011), which according to this perspective, can influence opinions and behavior (Barker, Hurwitz, and Nelson 2008; Kellstedt and Smidt 1993; Leege and Kellstedt 1993; Mockabee, Wald, and Leege 2011). This conceptualization of religion is frequently operationalized in political science through a survey question on biblical literalism that measures whether people believe that the Bible is the literal word of God, inspired by God but written by men, or a book written solely by men.[3] These privately held religious beliefs become politically consequential if voters apply them to broader societal issues, which has occurred throughout American history.[4]

Religion as a social phenomenon, in contrast, takes as its starting point that religion is "born and nurtured among groups of people" (Iannaccone 1994: 1183). This perspective recognizes that privately held religious beliefs, despite having the potential to be both strong and powerful, do not develop in isolation. Rather, "religion finds expression within social entities" (Wald and Smidt 1993: 33) as religious institutions and communities provide the necessary context and information for an individual to develop personal beliefs (Smidt et al. 2010). This conceptualization of religion focuses on group identification and community involvement. In particular, being part of a religious community offers the mechanism through which religion successfully imparts group norms for its members to follow.

Belonging to a particular faith creates a shared identity among members, and this public affiliation operates in much the same manner as other social identifies. Group members attach positive affect to others in the group and favor members of their group over nonmembers (Tajfel 1981). Religious identities can therefore be thought of as expressions of social membership—"a declaration, both to themselves and to others, of their social identity" (Wald and Smidt 1993: 40). Importantly, these identities gain relevance through social interactions with others.

Churches and other houses of worship are communities that "are well suited to the transmission and maintenance of group norms" (Wald, Owen, and Hill 1988: 532). Learning about others' viewpoints and beliefs can help people form their own values and develop their own opinions. Religion's influence on attitudes therefore comes about as group members engage with others in the community. Religious communities provide opportunities for members to interact both at religious services (Crawford and Olson 2001; Djupe and Gilbert 2002) and through study, community, or social groups frequently organized by churches. All told, religious identities gain relevance through social interactions with others and become internalized through both formal and informal networks within religious congregations (Djupe and Gilbert 2009; Wald, Owen, and Hill 1988).

Thinking about religion as a social phenomenon means that "political thought and behavior of religious group members are not necessarily derived from their specific religious beliefs, experiences, or practices" (Wald and Smidt 1993: 33–34) but instead come from other sources. For example, a congregant's moral and political conservatism is more strongly associated with her congregation's average theological conservatism than her own personal theological conservatism (Wald, Owen, and Hill 1988). In other words, the theological position of the group is more important in determining a person's views on moral issues than her personally held religious beliefs. According to this conceptualization of religion, being part of a community that hears similar messages is what produces a common interpretation of beliefs and symbols. Take, for instance, the evolution of evangelical theology. In the nineteenth and early twentieth centuries, the social gospel, which emphasized improving social conditions, was a major component of evangelical Protestantism. An emphasis on otherworldliness and political withdrawal, however, then became the dominant biblical interpretation. It was not until the 1970s that moral order and traditional values became a central focus of religious teachings in evangelical churches. Despite evangelicals abiding by a literal interpretation of the Bible and holding on to other orthodox beliefs throughout the centuries, the changing evangelical leadership and community upended evangelicals' beliefs and how evangelicals applied these beliefs to the world around them. The emphasis on distinct religious teachings at different points in time corresponds to evangelicals valuing and acting on certain religious teachings over others (Clark 1976; Hammond 1983; Moberg 1977). Taken together, individuals' social experiences within religious communities shape their private beliefs and imbue these beliefs with social and political relevance. Social institutions and arrangements therefore enable religious beliefs—even extremely orthodox beliefs—to remain accepted by large groups of people (Berger 1967). To understand private religious beliefs, it is therefore best to start by looking at the religious communities within which people participate.

A person's religious identity is a complex web of theology, beliefs, self-categorization, and behavior. In conceptualizing religion as a social phenomenon, the empirics of this book will emphasize two frequently measured aspects of a person's religious identity that fit within this framework: willingness to identify with a religious faith and attendance at religious services, although other measures of religious identity will be used at certain points.[5] Identifying with a religious faith—particularly in an era in which nonidentification rates have skyrocketed—measures a willingness to be part of a community that people are increasingly opting out of. This self-categorization represents a first measure when considering religion as a social identity. The second measure, church attendance, is a proxy for involvement in a religious community. While there are admittedly many ways a person can be involved, worship attendance is closely associated with other forms of religious engagement, including support for religious organizations and volunteerism within the religious community (see Green 2010). Moreover, church attendance "stands out as a behavior practiced and viewed as normative across many traditions" (Mockabee, Monson, and Grant 2001: 677) unlike reading scripture or holding specific beliefs, which are more associated with certain religious denominations than others. Church attendance therefore measures religiosity in a manner that is applicable to many religious faiths while also being a stronger predictor of political attitudes and behaviors than religious beliefs (Putnam and Campbell 2010).[6]

Importantly, a person's private religious identity differs from how religion is frequently conceptualized in the public sphere. A person's religious identity—described above—is unique to each individual. A person can subscribe to certain tenets while ignoring others or be very (un-)involved in a theologically liberal or conservative church. In contrast, public religion has taken on a specific interpretation in the United States. Religion, particularly in today's political sphere, commonly refers to conservative Christian traditions and their values. The conservative interpretation of Christian doctrine within American politics and, in particular, its link to the Republican Party may have different effects on different types of people. Just as today's God gap is most pronounced among white Christians and Catholics (Green 2010; Putnam and Campbell 2010), the emphasis on conservative Christianity in the public sphere may have more of an impact on white Americans who affiliate with or were raised in Christian or Catholic traditions. A longer discussion of this possibility appears in chapter 3.

Although this book conceptualizes individual-level religious identity in a manner that is similar to that of other political science research on religion, the pages that follow tell a very different story about the relationship between a person's religious involvement and his or her politics. Whereas previous research has focused on how the messages received in church, either from religious leaders (Nteta and Wallsten 2012) or more informally from other congregants (Djupe and Gilbert 2009; Wald, Owen, and Hill 1988), inform a person's politics, the main argument of this book is that an individual's partisan identity may inform his or her religious decisions. Politics therefore changes a person's environment that is thought to be a driver of both political opinion and action. Moreover, these politically induced religious changes have important consequences by changing the makeup of religious communities and altering how partisans respond to religion being used in politics. Therefore, although this book starts from the same point as many other books examining the intersection of religion and politics, it provides a new perspective on the correlation between religious and political attitudes and an alternative explanation to the generally held finding that religiosity shapes political preferences. The section below describes what is to come in the following chapters.

What Is to Come

Chapter 2 provides an overview of religion's recent role in American politics. In the 1970s and 1980s, Democratic and Republican elites for the first time staked out divergent positions on moral issues and used religious faith to varying degrees when reaching out to voters. At the same time, voters shifted from being politically divided along mainly denominational lines—for example, most Catholics were Democrats and most mainline Protestants were Republicans—to being divided along lines of religiosity—with devout Catholics and Protestants being Republicans and less religious Catholics and Protestants being Democrats. The chapter then describes the received wisdom on how this so-called God gap came about: Religious individuals sorted into the Republican Party and the less religious became Democrats. The chapter concludes by explaining why this explanation is intuitively appealing, yet ultimately unsatisfactory. While many scholars assume religious affiliation and involvement to be strong and stable aspects of a person's identity, religiosity waxes and wanes over the course of a person's life and is, at times, susceptible to external influences. One such external influence is a person's partisan affiliation, which is also a strong and stable identity.

When might partisan identities influence decisions associated with religious identities? Chapter 3, the book's core theoretical chapter, describes the life-cycle theory, which builds on two well-established ideas in political science and sociology. First, the "impressionable years" hypothesis from political science states that outside influences and events shape one's long-term political outlook, including partisan identity, during adolescence and young adulthood. After this period, the resulting partisan identity is a stable, powerful identity in its own right. Second, sociologists of religion have shown that although teenagers and young adults tend to distance themselves from their parents' religions and religious practices, they must then decide whether to remain on the outskirts of religion or to reenter the religious realm as they emerge into adulthood. Those who return to religion must then also decide (1) to what degree to be involved in religion and (2) what religious beliefs to accept and reject. Bringing these two strands of research together yields a theory about the effect partisanship can have on religion. The timings of the religious and political socialization processes mean that partisan identities form at the very time when religion is a peripheral concern for many people. Then, when individuals must decide if and how to engage in the religious world, their partisan identities—solidified earlier in young adulthood—may exert an important and lasting influence on their religious identifications and practices.

With the necessary background and testable expectations drawn from the theory, chapter 4 offers the first empirical test of the life-cycle theory. Two sets of panel data collected decades apart offer three trends consistent with the life-cycle theory. First, partisanship affects religious decisions among those individuals moving from being unmarried and childless to starting a family. This is precisely when, after a natural hiatus from religion, most people are confronted with a decision about whether and how to renew their religious involvement. Second, religious choices made during a particular life stage are often long lasting, and partisanship's effect is evident many years later. And third, church attendance is unrelated to changes in partisanship and vote choice among those whose position within the life cycle predicts that partisan identities are more solidified than religious identities. These findings establish patterns consistent with the life-cycle theory, but they do not account for how the political environment gives rise to long-term changes.

Chapter 5 explicitly tests how the political environment can shape partisans' religious behaviors and outlooks. The elite-level link between the

Republican Party and organized religion allows voters to associate the parties with different levels of religiosity. Two survey experiments show that the close relationship between the Republican Party and organized religion affects Democrats and Republicans alike, but in opposite ways: Republicans' religious identities become stronger while Democrats' religious identities become weaker. Panel data additionally show how partisans respond when the linkages between religion and the Republican Party become more salient. Party identification corresponds with changing religious practices after gay marriage became a more salient political issue. Democrats (Republicans) reported lower (higher) rates of religiosity in 2004 than they did in 2000 and 2002. And, consistent with the life-cycle theory, this relationship is strongest among respondents who were most likely making decisions regarding their levels of religious involvement. A final survey experiment explores whether this response pattern is unavoidable by testing how partisans respond when religion is linked with policies on the political left. The results show that Americans pay attention to the political content of the message; the Democratic exodus from religion disappears when religion is brought into left-leaning politics.

Chapter 6 explores how political knowledge helps create the religiosity gap and shows that religious involvement and political engagement covary but in opposite directions for Republicans and Democrats. First, respondents with medium and high levels of political knowledge drive the findings from the previous chapters. In contrast, partisans with little political knowledge did not update their religious attachments to be consistent with their partisan identities. Next, a political knowledge gap, in addition to a partisan gap, exists within churches. If more knowledgeable Republicans select into religion and more knowledgeable Democrats select out of religion, then Americans affiliated with different religious currents should differ both in terms of partisanship and political knowledge. The results show that while Republicans who are politically engaged are also more likely to be involved in religion, Democrats who are politically engaged are less likely to be involved with religion. Republicans, therefore, not only attend church more often than Democrats, but churchgoing Republicans are also more politically engaged than churchgoing Democrats. Partisan differences in political knowledge and engagement, in turn, change the likelihood that campaigns can successfully mobilize supporters through churches.

Chapter 7 tests the life-cycle theory on African Americans and explores the political consequences of their unique constellation of identities—as both ardent Democrats and frequent churchgoers. Because black Protestant theology focuses on social justice and equality, two themes that align with

Democratic economic messages, African Americans may not feel pressure to update their religious or political attachments in the same way that white Americans might. The data show that while African Americans undergo a similar transition away from religion just as white Americans do, African Americans' partisan identities operate differently when making religious decisions as adults. The chapter then considers the political consequences of African Americans' religious and political attachments. The results from two experiments show that although African Americans are comfortable with religion and politics mixing, as one might expect from a highly religious group, they are not open to religion entering the political sphere when the Republican Party is doing the mixing. This occurs because the political values valorized in black Protestantism differ from those emphasized by religious denominations and groups associated with the Republican Party.

Chapter 8 applies the life-cycle theory to a different political context. The expectations tested throughout this book stem from the contemporary political environment, but the life-cycle theory does not rely on any particular relationship between religion and the political parties. The theory should therefore be a useful guide as new issues emerge, new groups form, and the parties change their policy positions and electoral strategies. The chapter offers one example of this by looking at the 1960 presidential election and shows evidence of the life-cycle theory at work in an environment in which religion and the political parties were linked in very different ways than they are today.

Chapter 9 concludes by discussing the implications of the book's main findings and prospects of continued sorting in the future. First, the chapter considers how politically driven religious sorting has fundamentally transformed American politics and politicians' ability to mobilize support. The Republican Party can directly target voters who are likely responsive to religious rhetoric and faith-based politics through churches and religious organizations. Democrats, in contrast, increasingly spend their Sundays outside of church and are less interested in religious justifications for public policies. Together, these results highlight not only that politics and partisanship have altered the religious makeup of the United States but also that these changes dramatically alter our understanding of electoral politics. Second, the chapter addresses how the findings impact how we think about identity politics. Identities do not form in a vacuum but rather develop and change over time in response to outside influences. In light of these findings, scholars may have previously overestimated social groups' influence on public opinion. And third, the chapter draws on recent demographic and political trends to make predictions about partisan-driven religious sorting in the future.

But before jumping into the theory and findings, the next chapter provides helpful background on religion's role in American politics over the last half century.

TWO

Putting Things in Context: Religious and Political Attachments over Time

The 2012 presidential contest between Barack Obama and Mitt Romney produced distinct religious factions supporting the candidates. While only 20% of white evangelicals voted for Obama, 70% of the religiously unaffiliated, or religious "nones," did so. Whereas 39% of weekly church attenders voted for Obama, 62% of nonattenders did so (Pew Research Center 2012). These results are not an anomaly. In 2008, 75% of religious "nones" and 67% of nonattenders supported Obama over McCain, while only 26% of white evangelicals did so (Pew Research Center 2008). And even though pundits wondered whether religious voters would support Donald Trump given his personal life and style, the 2016 election produced little change in religious-political alignments (Pew Research Center 2016a). These electoral coalitions reflect the recent political reality in which party support is divided according to both religious affiliation and religiosity. Public opinion data show that Democrats, compared to Republicans, are not only more likely to be religious nonidentifiers—that is, those who do not identify with a religious tradition—and less likely to attend religious services, but they are also less likely to pray and believe that the Bible is the direct word of God. In contrast, Republicans, relative to Democrats, consider themselves more religious and are more likely to report that religion plays a guiding role in their everyday lives.

Subsequent chapters will show that partisan identities, which people develop when involvement in religion is not a top priority, can influence their religious decisions in later stages of life. Before developing and testing the life-cycle theory, however, this chapter first describes today's religious-political environment and explains how the current landscape came to pass, providing background to readers unfamiliar with the way scholars think about religion in American politics. After laying out four stylized facts about the role of religion in American politics over the past fifty years, the chapter describes how these facts form a common explanation for why religious Americans are more likely to be Republicans while their less religious counterparts are more likely to be Democrats. The chapter concludes by offering an alternative account, which will be tested in later chapters.

1. Democrats Are Less Religious and Republicans Are More So

Religion plays a large role in Americans' lives, and recent survey data can help illustrate the relationship between religion and politics today. Scholars can measure a person's religious identity in a number of different ways—behaviors, beliefs, or self-categorization—although the corresponding relationships with politics are largely similar. More religious Americans, however defined, are more likely to identify as Republicans and support Republican candidates than their less religious counterparts.

Figure 2.1 shows this strong association between religious and political variables. Using data from the General Social Survey (GSS) and American National Election Study (ANES), the graphs present the change in probability that a respondent identifies as a Republican based on different sociocultural measures. The first set of bars, gray for the full sample and white for the white subsample, compares Americans based on their reported church attendance levels. Comparing a weekly church attender to a person who does not attend church, the probability that the church attender is a Republican increases by about 0.20 in the GSS sample and 0.24 in the ANES sample. The probability increase is 0.30 in both data sets when only white respondents are considered. The larger gap among the white subsample occurs because many ethnic and racial minorities in the United States—for example, Hispanic Catholics and black Protestants—generally identify as Democrats and are also relatively religious. Consequently, when people discuss the "religious gap" in American politics, the trend is most pronounced among white Americans. The second set of bars compares the one-third of Americans who believe that the Bible is the literal word of God with the approximately one-fifth of Americans who believe the Bible is a book of fables. Here again, biblical literalists have a significantly higher probability of identifying as Republicans, particularly among white respondents. The third set of bars compares Americans who do not identify with a religious faith and those who do. The distinction here is not between denominational affiliations but rather between those who claim no affiliation versus those who identify with a religious tradition. Religious nonidentification rates have risen over recent decades, and roughly 25% of Americans claimed

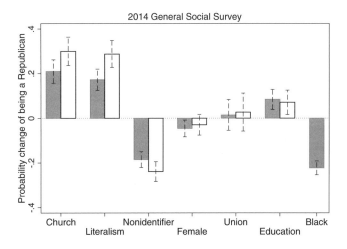

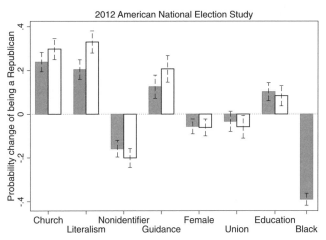

2.1. Religiosity and religious involvement are correlated with being a Republican. Gray bars represent the full sample of respondents; white bars represent the white subsample.
Source: 2014 General Social Survey and 2012 American National Election Study.

they were "nothing" when asked their religious affiliation in the 2012 ANES, whereas 20% did so in the GSS sample. Religious nonidentifiers are not equally dispersed across the parties, however. The probability of being a Republican is much lower for religious nonidentifiers compared to those who report identifying with a faith (−0.18 and −0.13 in the full samples, −0.23 and −0.20 in the white subsamples). The ANES also asks a question about how much guidance religion provides in the respondent's daily life.

Importantly, this question is asked only if a respondent initially reported that religion is an important part of her life. Whereas the previous measures include staunchly secular respondents, everyone answering the religious guidance question agrees that religion is important. Even within the more religious subsample, those reporting that religion provides "a great deal" of guidance in day-to-day life are much more likely to identify as Republicans compared to those who report only "some" guidance. Other scholars have noted these trends (e.g., Claassen 2015; Green 2010, 2007; Green and Silk 2004; Olson and Green 2006; Putnam and Campbell 2010; Smidt et al. 2010), and these gaps remain even in statistical models that include extensive demographic and socioeconomic control variables, exclude religious nonidentifiers, and look at respondents in the South and non-South separately.

How does this political gap based on religious involvement and beliefs compare to other well-known "gaps" in American politics? Previous research has looked at the relationship between party identification and gender (Bendyna and Lake 1994; Box-Steffensmeier, De Boef, and Lin 2004; Kaufmann and Petrocik 1999; Kenski 1988; Miller 1991; Norrander 1999, 1997), living in a union household (Hojnacki and Baum 1992; Miller 1991; Stanley, Bianco, and Niemi 1986; Stanley and Niemi 1991; Zuckerman, Valentino, and Zukerman 1994), and education levels (Dalton 2007; Miller and Shanks 1996; Shively 1979); however, each of these relationships is noticeably weaker than the various religious indicators. The GSS and ANES data show that females are less likely to identify as Republicans than males and that respondents with college degrees or higher are more likely to identify as Republicans compared to respondents with high school degrees or less. There is also some evidence that people from union households are less likely to be Republicans than individuals from nonunion households, although the evidence is weaker than the gender and education results. Race is the only indicator that has a stronger association with partisanship than religiosity: African Americans are far less likely than whites to identify with the Republican Party.

All told, involvement in a religious community is strongly associated with partisan identity in the United States, and the religious differences between Democrats and Republicans either rival or surpass other well-known sociodemographic differences in American politics today. Importantly, however, one religious tradition is not responsible for the pattern.

2. This Religiosity Gap Appears within Religious Traditions

Religious involvement is correlated with partisanship across the major religious traditions in the United States today.[1] One explanation for the

Table 2.1 Church attendance is correlated with partisan identification across religious traditions

	Mainline Protestants		Evangelical Protestants	
	% Democrats	% Republicans	% Democrats	% Republicans
Seldom attend	48	44	34	53
Attend a few times a year	39	51	34	56
Attend a few times a month	38	48	23	67
Attend weekly or more	33	57	16	79
	Catholics		Undifferentiated Christians	
	% Democrats	% Republicans	% Democrats	% Republicans
Seldom attend	51	32	34	47
Attend a few times a year	53	33	27	55
Attend a few times a month	43	41	32	54
Attend weekly or more	30	61	19	78

Source: 2012 American National Election Study.

religiosity results above may be that one religious tradition produces the gap found in the population. Alternatively, a greater number of nonidentifiers in the Democratic Party might explain the gaps in church attendance and biblical literalism. This religiosity gap, however, appears within large religious traditions. Table 2.1 shows the partisan breakdown based on church attendance for mainline Protestants, evangelical Protestants, Catholics, and undifferentiated Christians. Undifferentiated Christians are individuals who identify with Christianity but who cannot be neatly classified as mainline Protestant, evangelical Protestant, or Catholic. Although there is some variation across traditions—for example, evangelical Protestants are on average more Republican than members of other religious traditions—frequency of church attendance is related to partisan identification in each case. Higher levels of church attendance correspond with higher rates of Republican identification. The results are noteworthy even among mainline Protestants who have the weakest relationship between church attendance and political affiliation. Democrats have a slight numeric advantage among mainline Protestants who rarely or never attend church, whereas the Republican Party enjoys more support among weekly attending mainline Protestants. These relationships also extend beyond party identification to presidential vote choice (Green 2010; Layman 1997). Importantly, these trends are most pronounced among white Americans, and political differences across religious traditions are still present (Guth et al. 2006; Kellstedt and Green 1993; Kohut et al. 2000; Layman 2001; Leege et al. 2002). For example, white Protestants are more likely than Catholics to be Republicans whereas black Protestants and Jews support the Democratic Party more than members of other traditions (results not shown). While religious affiliation is still associated with partisanship, the data show a consistent relationship between religiosity and politics across the major religious traditions.

These within-tradition divisions along the lines of religiosity have given rise to coalitions across religious traditions. For instance, religious evangelicals and religious Catholics have come together in their opposition to abortion (Boorstein 2016). This was seen most recently at the 2017 March for Life rally in Washington, DC, an annual demonstration that takes place on the anniversary of the *Roe v. Wade* decision. Although Nellie Gray, a Catholic, organized the first March for Life demonstration and the rallies have traditionally been attended by religious Catholics, religious evangelicals have begun participating as well. This includes influential evangelicals, such as Jim Daly, president of Focus on the Family, one of the largest evangelical organizations in the country. A few generations ago, it would have been hard to imagine evangelicals and Catholics joining forces. Members of both groups previously disliked, distrusted, and sought to distinguish themselves from the other (Curry 2015; Kaylor 2011; Kellstedt 1988; Wilcox 1988). But today, religious members of both traditions routinely come together to advance their common social and political goals.

An important feature of the religiosity gap is that it appears across religious traditions. More frequent attenders, from various religious families, are more likely to identify with the Republican Party, and no one religious tradition accounts for the differences found between Democrats and Republicans. This relationship between religiosity and partisanship, however, has not always existed. Rather, it developed during the latter part of the last century.

3. This Religiosity Gap Is Relatively New

The political gap between the religious and secular, those who attend church and those who do not, did not always exist; the gap developed over the past five decades. The *ethnoreligious* model—which argues that shared ethnic, cultural, and racial factors within religions produce political differences across religious families—accurately describes the relationship between religion and politics prior to the middle of the twentieth century. Catholics, Jews, black Protestants, and southern white evangelicals traditionally supported the Democratic Party. The Republican Party, on the other hand, garnered support from white mainline Protestants (Berelson, Lazarsfeld, and McPhee 1954; Green 2007; Kellstedt et al. 1996). These differences, which were key fixtures of the Republican and Democratic parties until the 1950s, began to give way in the latter part of the twentieth century. The political distinctiveness of religious groups waned alongside declining social and economic differences among religious traditions. These shrinking differences, in turn, gave rise to differences between the religious and secular, the highly committed and weakly committed.

The *restructuring* principle (Wuthnow 1989, 1988) and the *culture wars* perspective (Hunter 1991) argue that people are no longer divided based on group membership but rather based on religious beliefs and behaviors. Religious modernists and traditionalists are now pitted against each other within society. Those who are religiously orthodox and religiously progressive hold competing moral philosophies, with the former believing in a single moral authority based on a higher power and the latter allowing for the meaning of moral authority to change in response to experience, context, and judgment. One political implication of this new cleavage is that voters also cohere politically based on their religious worldviews rather than on group memberships alone. In other words, religious *beliefs* now matter a great deal.

While academic debates surrounding the existence, or lack thereof, of a culture war are still ongoing (e.g., Hunter 2006; Wolfe 2006), researchers are fully aware that these religious beliefs do not become politically relevant in isolation. *Belonging* to a religious community and taking part in religious *behaviors* shape religious beliefs and imbue them with political importance (Jelen 1991; Kellstedt et al. 1996; Putnam and Campbell 2010; Smidt, Kellstedt, and Guth 2009; Stark and Bainbridge 1985; Wald, Owen, and Hill 1988). Scholars have therefore found that across measures of the 3 B's—belonging, behaving, and believing—a political gap emerged between those who are more and less devout (Brewer and Stonecash 2007; Green and Dionne 2008; Leege et al. 2002). This empirical relationship, however, is relatively new. For example, Layman (1997) shows that religious commitment—measured through frequency of church attendance—became an important predictor of vote choice in the 1980s and 1990s for the first time. Higher levels of church attendance, within any religious tradition, have become increasingly predictive of Republican support. Similarly, religious traditionalists became more likely to support Republican candidates for president

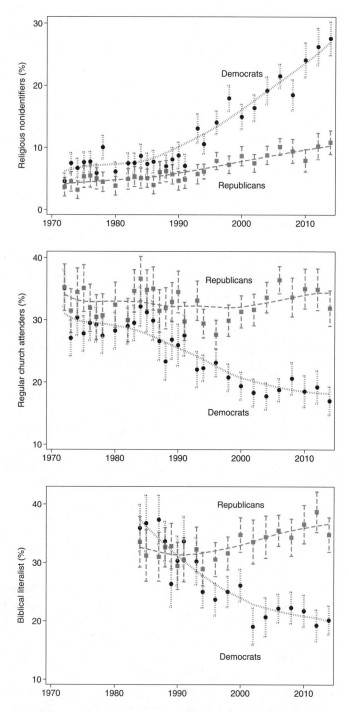

2.2. Today's relationship between partisanship and religiosity developed over time. The top panel presents the percentage of religious nonidentifiers over time; the middle panel presents the percentage of regular church attenders (weekly or more) over time; and the bottom panel presents the percentage of biblical literalists over time. In all panels, gray squares represent Republicans and black circles represent Democrats.
Source: General Social Survey.

between the 1960s and 2000s compared to religious centrists and modernists. Important and consistent with the discussion from the previous section is that a religious-modernist gap emerges among evangelical Protestants, mainline Protestants, and Catholics alike (Kellstedt et al. 2007).

Figure 2.2 offers an example of the types of trends about which scholars have been writing over the past few decades. The top panel shows the percentage of Democrats and Republicans who identify as religious nonidentifiers or "nones" over time. Religious nonidentification rates have risen over the past forty years; however, Democrats account for virtually all of the increase. In 2014, about 25% of Democrats did not identify with a religious tradition, up from less than 5% in 1972. In contrast, nonidentification rates among Republicans increased from roughly 4% to 8% over the same time period. While a doubling of the number of Republican nonidentifiers should not be dismissed, the Republican increase pales in comparison to the huge increase found among Democrats. The middle panel shows the percentage of Democrats and Republicans who report attending church on a regular basis over time. Church attendance rates remained relatively stable among Republicans and actually increased slightly during the first decade of the twenty-first century. In contrast, the percentage of Democrats attending regularly has steadily declined. The bottom panel shows the percentage of partisans who believe the Bible is the word of God, and the patterns echo the identification and church attendance gaps. Taken together, these results demonstrate that while there was virtually no religiosity gap between the parties in the not-so-distant past, a gap has emerged in recent years. Today, nonreligious voters are in the Democratic camp while their more religious counterparts have sided with the Republican Party. One of the central contributions of this book is offering an alternative explanation of how religious nonidentification, behaviors, and beliefs became associated with partisanship during the latter part of the last century. This relationship developed in response to religion's changing role in politics.

4. The Political Landscape Changed Dramatically

Religion has always been politicized in the United States. Examples include religiously motivated abolitionist sentiment during the Civil War (Carwardine 1993), debates over Prohibition pitting Protestants against Catholics (Munger and Schaller 1997; Wasserman 1989), views about morality and purity affecting perceptions of women's proper role in the public sphere (Morone 2003), and the presidential campaigns of both Alfred E. Smith and John F. Kennedy that elicited anti-Catholic sentiment (Carleton 1964;

Dumenil 1991; McGreevy 1997; Perl and Bendyna 2002). While acknowledging that religion has been important since America's founding—after all, Puritan teachings influenced revolutionaries (Bercovitch 1976; Morgan 1967) and morality politics undergirds American political history (Morone 2003)—religion's role within society generally and particularly in politics changed dramatically during the second half of the twentieth century. Beginning in the 1960s, America saw a dramatic shift in societal values, the emergence of new political issues, the entry of religious elites into politics, and the adoption of new religious strategies by politicians. While it is nearly impossible to understand each change's independent effect on society, as they are inextricably linked, together these changes constitute a reshaping of how religion and religiously tinged policy issues were addressed in the political sphere.

Societal values change. The postwar calm of the 1950s gave way to social upheaval in the 1960s. So much changed during the sixties that entire books can be, and have been, written on the subject. Putnam and Campbell (2010) succinctly describe that decade's impact on American culture:

> The Sixties represented a perfect storm for American institutions of all sorts—political, social, sexual, and religious. In retrospect we can discern a mélange of contributing factors: the bulge in the youngest age cohorts as the boomers moved through adolescence and into college, the combination of unprecedented affluence and the rapid expansion of higher education, "the Pill," the abating of Cold War anxieties, Vatican II, the assassinations, the Vietnam War, Watergate, pot and LSD, the civil rights movement and the other movements that followed in its wake—the antiwar movement, the women's liberation movement, and later the environmental and gay rights movements. (91)

During this time, many—especially younger—Americans eschewed traditional values and institutions in favor of more radical beliefs and unconventional lifestyles. Americans challenged the standard way of looking at and engaging with the world, and this had dramatic effects on both political and social organizations, including religion. Whereas piety and religious involvement were previously ubiquitous in American life, religious institutions were hard hit. Many Americans' changing ideologies were no longer compatible with churches' conservative outlooks on sex, marriage, and family roles. The dramatic shifts over such a short period of time produced a society that looked unrecognizable from the way it appeared just a decade earlier during Eisenhower's presidency: "Where once two-thirds of the state legislatures were willing to vote for prohibition, there was open campaigning for the legalization of marijuana. Where divorce once caused considerable social stigma, there were single parent, lesbian, and male homosexual 'families'" (Bruce 1988: 32).

The 1960s disrupted American society not only by changing American political culture but also by giving rise to a reactionary movement for "family values" in the 1970s (Hartman 2015; Leege et al. 2002; Putnam and Campbell 2010). Religious conservatism in the 1970s and 1980s emerged as a response to the earlier wave of cultural liberalism. If the 1960s represent a cultural "earthquake," then the religious response represents an "aftershock" (Putnam and Campbell 2010). The dramatic changes in society during this time period created cultural conflict that involved "disagreement about what society should or does prescribe as the *appropriate way of life*. It is not just about preference ordering; it deals with what is perceived as right and wrong, us versus them" (Leege et al. 2002: 26, emphasis in original). While the debate about whether and to what extent America is embroiled in a so-called culture war is still ongoing (Fiorina, Abrams, and Pope 2006; Hunter 1991; Hunter and Wolfe 2006), the 1960s and 1970s set the stage for new discussions and debates about morality and religion in the public sphere.

New political issues emerge. A new crop of policy issues became salient during the 1960s and 1970s. These issues, sometimes described as "morality politics," created a new and substantively different political dimension on which the parties could differentiate themselves. Legal protections for gays and lesbians, equality for women, access to abortion, and legalization of marijuana are a few issues that previously had not been discussed at length in politics but were hotly debated during the 1970s (Fejes 2016; MacCoun et al. 1993; McBride and Parry 2016; McCaffrey 2000; Wald, Button, and Rienzo 1996). These new policies not only relate to many of the changing societal values described above but have either direct or indirect links to religious values and teachings. Church-state relations also became salient in the 1960s. The Supreme Court, which previously upheld prayer in schools so long as no denomination was given special treatment, reversed its position. The 1962 *Engel v. Vitale* and 1963 *Schempp v. Murray* cases established the current prohibition on prayer in state-sponsored schools, disallowing prayer or Bible readings even when nondenominational or optional (Brown 1963; Bruce 1988; Kauper 1968). These new and salient issues changed the political landscape by expanding the debate as well as the number of relevant considerations available to Americans making political decisions.

Religious elites enter the political sphere. Another important change during the latter part of the twentieth century was the direct role conservative religious elites began to take in politics. Between the 1920s and 1970s, conservative

Christians largely remained out of politics, believing that the focus should be on higher-order priorities related to faith and salvation rather than the impure world of politics (Boyer 2008; Reichley 1986). Alongside the other changes in society, religious elites' involvement in politics also began to change in the 1970s. New Christian Right organizations began forming, the two most important of which—the Christian Voice and the Moral Majority—were founded in 1978 (Wilcox 1992a).[2] While the organizations' names, leaders, and membership changed over time (Wilcox, Rozell, and Gunn 1996), they shared a common purpose of bringing conservative religious values out of the churches and into public policy (Jelen 1993; Lassiter 2008). The creation of these large-scale organizations provided a national platform to religious conservatives for the first time.[3]

Religious broadcasting, which grew increasingly popular in the 1970s and 1980s, allowed religious elites' messages to reach a wide audience of conservative Christians (Hadden 1987). As televangelist Billy Graham succinctly said, "I can preach to more people in one night on TV than perhaps Paul did in his whole lifetime" (Littell 1976: 16). His statement was accurate; an Annenberg/Gallup report estimated that over 13 million Americans watched religious broadcasting each week in 1984 (Abelman and Neuendorf 1987). Religious elites therefore had a broad audience at their disposal as they sought to generate support for their causes. Moreover, the number of political discussions taking place on religious television programming increased over the course of the 1970s and 1980s (Abelman and Neuendorf 1987) providing some evidence that religious broadcasting politicized its viewers (Frankl 1987).

These large national organizations coupled with the megaphone that religious broadcasting provided helped forge public linkages between religious values and the Republican Party. For example, the Religious Roundtable, a sister organization of the Moral Majority led by prominent evangelical clergy, held large rallies for Ronald Reagan in 1980 and invited ministers from across the country to attend and speak (Green and Guth 1986; Liebman and Wuthnow 1983). Jerry Falwell, a vocal supporter of Reagan in both the 1980 and 1984 elections, became a household name during this time—he appeared on the covers of both *Time* and *Newsweek*, was named among the top twenty-five most influential people in America by *U.S. News & World Report* in 1983, and regularly appeared on national broadcasts to discuss politics. Reverend Pat Robertson's candidacy for the Republican presidential nomination in 1988 further made clear which party better represented cultural conservatives' positions (Green et al. 1996; Green and Guth 1988; Johnson, Tamney, and Burton 1989). Using the *700 Club*, the most popular television show on the Christian Broadcasting Network (CBN), Robertson appealed directly to religious voters and, in doing so, informed viewers of his partisan leanings. By pushing a conservative agenda rooted in religious values, the New Christian Right movement helped bring religion into partisan politics. Assessing the successes, failures, and impact of religious political organizations is not the purpose of this book; however, the creation of these organizations and their mobilization attempts ushered in a new political era in which religious conservative elites speak out on political issues and have a seat at the Republican table.

Political elites change their strategies. Finally, political elites and political parties began to separate themselves along religious and cultural lines beginning in the early 1970s. Whereas many equate the Republican Party with religion and conservative religious values, it was the Democratic Party that made the first move along the religious and cultural dimension. George McGovern, the Democratic nominee for president in 1972, favored more lenient penalties for marijuana use and opposed calls to ban abortion at the national level, earning him the tagline as the "Acid, Amnesty, and Abortion" candidate (White 1973). Also during the 1972 election, secularists became a visible thread in the Democratic fabric, with secularists and cultural liberals making up a significant presence among Democratic activists and convention delegates for the first time (Kirkpatrick 1976; Layman 2001). The Democratic Party platform also contained liberal stances on cultural issues, including sections titled "The Right to Be Different," "Rights of Women," and "Family Planning" (Layman 2001: 114), signaling the party's stances on these newly salient issues.[4]

Republicans, in contrast, did not immediately adopt a religiously conservative strategy. Secular leaders on the political right took note of Jimmy Carter's victory in 1976 and realized the electoral advantage a candidate who openly talks about his or her religious faith has. Seeing the potential power of this, these political elites began strategizing about how to mobilize evangelical voters around Republican causes (Himmelstein 1983; Oldfield 1996; Reichley 1987). In fact, Falwell formed the Moral Majority only after leaders of the secular New Right approached him and "promised support in the form of direct-mail lists, organizational support, and training of state and regional leaders" (Wilcox 1992a: 12). Religious conservatives, therefore, did not enter politics by happenstance; Republican political elites helped religious elites enter the political sphere.

The Republican elites, most of whom were not religious themselves, thought they could draw support from these religious voters by focusing on politics relating to religion and morality. This strategy, embodied by

Ronald Reagan in the 1980 election, was successful. Reagan emphasized issues that religious voters cared about, such as abortion, prayer in public school, subsidizing private religious education, and gay rights (Hartman 2015; Layman 2001; Miller and Wattenberg 1984; Oldfield 1996). Reagan also actively reached out to evangelical Christians and Jerry Falwell's newly formed Moral Majority during the 1980 presidential campaign (Brudney and Copeland 1984; Green et al. 1996; Reichley 1986). He visited Falwell's Liberty Baptist College and expressed his support for prayer in the classroom, and his address to the Religious Roundtable's National Affairs Briefing used rhetoric that was virtually identical to the language used by Falwell, who also spoke at the briefing:

> Reagan presented evangelicals with a litany of complaints about anti-Christian policies that federal agencies had passed. "Federally funded textbooks" Reagan said, "taught grade school children [moral] relativism," while the Federal Communications Commission tried to restrict the "independence of religious broadcasting." The Department of Labor "tried to exert regulatory control over church employees" at the same time that the IRS launched an "unconstitutional regulatory vendetta" against Christian schools. Reagan's administration, in contrast, would restore "parental rights" to the proper primacy and would limit the intrusion of "big government" into church and family life. (Williams 2010: 141–42)

Carter, despite being an evangelical Christian who spoke candidly about his personal faith, adopted an "inclusive perspective that balanced his reliance on biblical teachings with a respect for separation of church and state" (Kaylor 2011: 50). Moreover, Carter criticized Reagan's close ties with religious Christians, highlighting that "this nation was not founded just on the Christian religion" and even mocking Reagan by saying "the Bible doesn't say whether there is one or two Chinas, the Bible doesn't say how you balance the federal budget. And the Bible doesn't say what causes pollution." Reagan and Carter's diverging strategies marked the point after which politicians would use religion differently.

Reagan's strategy of appealing to religious voters continued throughout his first term as president—declaring 1983 the "Year of the Bible," contributing an article to the *Human Life Review*, and releasing a memo suggesting ways in which public schools officials could encourage voluntary student prayer that was constitutionally permissible (Miller 2014). Reagan also used religion as a political threat. During the 1984 campaign, Reagan derided those on the political left who opposed prayer in school: "The frustrating thing is that those who are attacking religion claim they are doing it in the name of tolerance, freedom, and open-mindedness. Question: Isn't the real truth that they are intolerant of religion? They refuse to tolerate its importance in our lives." Across the aisle, Walter Mondale—the 1984 Democratic presidential nominee—tried to use Reagan's religious rhetoric and close ties with religious conservatives to his advantage. Mondale, during his speech at the Democratic National Convention, asserted that the Republican platform was prepared under the leadership of Jerry Falwell and ran a television ad suggesting that the Christian Right had taken over the Republican Party (Miller 2014). And while Michael Dukakis—the 1988 Democratic presidential nominee—similarly took a secular approach in his rhetoric and strongly supported a strict separation of church and state (Kaylor 2011), more recent Democratic presidential nominees have spoken about their personal faith and connected religious beliefs to policy positions (Domke and Coe 2010; Kaylor 2011; Smidt et al. 2010). These changes in Democratic strategy, however, have not resulted in Democratic and Republican politicians utilizing religion to the same degree, as Republican politicians routinely support policies that directly bring religion and morality into the political sphere, even advocating policies "that cross the church-state line" (Kaylor 2011: 118). Even though the Democratic Party has not taken up the secular torch, the Republican Party remains more closely associated with religion and religious values.

In addition to rhetoric and campaign strategies, the parties' policy positions also changed during this time. Abortion represents a clear example of the parties diverging on an issue closely associated with religion and morality. Whereas neither party mentioned abortion in their 1972 party platforms, the 1973 *Roe v. Wade* decision catapulted abortion from the state level to the national stage. Initially, the parties were internally divided on the issue; supporters and opponents of abortion rights were found among both Democratic and Republican elites. Over time, however, the political parties along with party leaders began to separate themselves into the camps we see today (Adams 1997; Carmines and Woods 2002). Differences in how abortion was discussed in the party platforms illustrate the evolution of the parties' positions. For example, the 1976 Republican platform recognized the diversity of opinion within the Republican Party and took a weak pro-life stance.

> The question of abortion is one of the most difficult and controversial of our time. It is undoubtedly a moral and personal issue but it also involves complex questions relating to medical science and criminal justice. There are those in our Party who favor complete support for the Supreme Court decision

which permits abortion on demand. There are others who share sincere convictions that the Supreme Court's decision must be changed by a constitutional amendment prohibiting all abortions. Others have yet to take a position, or they have assumed a stance somewhere in between polar positions.

We protest the Supreme Court's intrusion into the family structure through its denial of the parents' obligation and right to guide their minor children. The Republican Party favors a continuance of the public dialogue on abortion and supports the efforts of those who seek enactment of a constitutional amendment to restore protection of the right to life for unborn children.

By 1980, however, the position had been strengthened: "While we recognize differing views on this question among Americans in general—and in our own Party—we affirm our support of a constitutional amendment to restore protection of the right to life for unborn children. We also support the Congressional efforts to restrict the use of taxpayers' dollars for abortion" (1980 Republican Party platform). And by 1984, the party had removed discussion of the pro-choice position as a valid stance and invoked religious trope for the first time.

The unborn child has a fundamental individual right to life which cannot be infringed. We therefore reaffirm our support for a human life amendment to the Constitution, and we endorse legislation to make clear that the Fourteenth Amendment's protections apply to unborn children. We oppose the use of public revenues for abortion and will eliminate funding for organizations which advocate or support abortion. We commend the efforts of those individuals and religious and private organizations that are providing positive alternatives to abortion by meeting the physical, emotional, and financial needs of pregnant women and offering adoption services where needed.

We applaud President Reagan's fine record of judicial appointments, and we reaffirm our support for the appointment of judges at all levels of the judiciary who respect traditional family values and the sanctity of innocent human life. (1984 Republican Party platform)

In contrast, the Democratic Party's platform took a firmer pro-choice position over time. While both the 1976 and 1980 platforms "recognize the religious and ethical nature of the concerns which many Americans have on the subject of abortion," the 1980 platform also underscored "the belief of many Americans that a woman has a right to choose whether and when to have a child." And whereas the 1976 Democratic platform said it was "undesirable to attempt to amend the U.S. Constitution to overturn the Supreme

Court decision in this area," by 1980 the Democratic platform actively supported "the 1973 Supreme Court decision on abortion rights as the law of the land and opposes any constitutional amendment to restrict or overturn that decision." These changes reflect elite-level polarization taking place on a salient issue.

The large-scale shifts in official party positions, candidate rhetoric, and the salience of moral issues mark the first instances in which the parties became known for being on opposing sides of the religious and cultural aisle. Looking at the parties in the 1960s, it was not obvious whether and how they would diverge. Instead, responses to broader cultural shifts, individual leaders' decisions, and specific events created the strategy of "cultural politics" (Leege et al. 2002) that has continued to the present day.

These changes to the political environment set the stage for producing a religiosity gap. With the parties diverging along religious, cultural, and moral lines, Americans are able to bring their religious and partisan identities into alignment, either by updating their partisan or their religious attachments.

How Did We Get Where We Are? The Current Explanation

These societal and political changes over the past forty years give rise to an intuitive explanation for how the current religious gap emerged. As religion moved from the private into the public sphere, Americans relied on their religious identities and involvement (or lack thereof) in religious communities in forming political judgments. By this logic, a hypothetical person who attends church weekly becomes a Republican. Perhaps this churchgoing voter likes Republicans' conservative stances on moral issues, prefers Republican candidates because they speak openly about faith, or is influenced by messages from clergy or fellow congregants. On the other side of the religious spectrum, another hypothetical voter's distance from religion pushes him or her to support the Democratic Party. In this case, the nonreligious voter may gravitate toward the Democrats because the party takes a stricter stance on the separation between church and state and feels alienated when Republicans use religious justifications for taking a particular policy position, or has similarly nonreligious friends who are Democrats. In both examples, religion drives identification with one of the parties by endowing voters with political attitudes that more closely align with one party or another. This explanation is naturally appealing for three reasons.

First, religion is often thought of as a hereditary trait, one that is passed down through the generations. Scholars have noted that the religious environment in which a person is raised has long-term effects on his or her religious affiliation and practices as an adult (Green and Guth 1993; Wilson and Sherkat 1994). If an individual "inherits" religious attachments, religion can be thought of as an ascriptive trait similar to age, race, and gender. Although recent research has shown that religious identification and practices now represent concerted choices (see Putnam and Campbell 2010, chap. 5), many still treat religion as a characteristic outside a person's own choosing. If religion is a stable trait that develops separate from the political sphere, then religion can reasonably be classified as a driver of public opinion.

Second, at its core, "religion is in the business of indoctrination" (Campbell, Layman, and Green 2012: 170). Religion provides members with formal rules, rituals, authority structures, and beliefs promoting a particular worldview. Religious institutions shape fundamental outlooks and priorities by providing direction on nearly every aspect of a person's life. With religion affecting all manner of a member's behavior in his or her search for eternal salvation, it would be surprising if religion's influence did not reach the world of politics. Identifying with a religious faith also draws a person into a social world, with expectations, group norms, and standards created by others who share the same identity (Wald and Smidt 1993). The high salience of religion for many people makes it likely that this identity may help shape their political outlooks.

Third, politics is tangential to many citizens' lives. Many Americans do not pay close attention to politics (Lenz 2012), have relatively low levels of political knowledge (Delli Carpini and Keeter 1996, 1991), and are not able to distinguish between the major parties on key policy issues (Berelson, Lazarsfeld, and McPhee 1954; Campbell et al. 1960; Fowler and Margolis 2014). With politics being a low priority, citizens instead utilize shortcuts to develop policy preferences (Lupia 1994; Mondak 1993; Popkin 1991; Schaffner and Streb 2002). Being part of a religious community and interacting with others from that community can reduce the costs of forming political decisions. When cues highlight linkages between social groups and politically relevant information, group members can form an attitude that aligns with their group interest without much cognitive effort.

These assumptions lead to a reasonable interpretation of how religious people have come to be Republicans while less religious people have ended up as Democrats. As voters were given an expanded set of choices on which to make their political decisions, they began relying on their levels of religious commitment. Whereas religiosity was uncorrelated with party identification prior to the changing social and political landscapes described earlier, the creation of new considerations has given rise to a correlation between religiosity and partisan identification, particularly among white Americans of

Christian faiths.[5] Scholars have built on this explanation to show how re-
ligiosity influences attitudes on the environment (Boyd 1999; Eckberg and
Blocker 1989; Greeley 1993; Guth et al. 1995), immigration (Daniels and Von
Der Ruhr 2005; Knoll 2009; Nteta and Wallsten 2012), the death penalty
(Miller and Hayward 2008; Young 1992), abortion (Fawcett, Andrews, and
Lester 2000; Jelen 1988, 1984; Valenzuela 2014), social service provision
(McKenzie and Rouse 2013), gay marriage (Valenzuela 2014; Whitley 2009),
and many other political issues. Although the citations presented here represent a small proportion of the research done on the political consequences
of religiosity, each study takes as its starting point that individuals act politically based on some aspect of their religious involvement. While religion
undoubtedly affects politics, the obvious explanation for religious gaps in
public opinion overlooks the complexity of religion and underestimates the
strength of partisan identities.

How Did We Get Where We Are?
The Less Obvious Explanation

Religious voters are disproportionately Republican and secular voters are
overwhelmingly Democrats today. This result is indisputable. The question is how this gap came to pass. The conventional explanation, described
above, suggests that voters aligned their partisan identities with their preexisting religious identities. But if the reverse also occurred—people aligned
their religious involvement and commitment with their preexisting partisan
identities—the end result we see today would be identical.

At first blush, it might seem far-fetched to think that a person's partisan
identity may affect his or her involvement in organized religion. After all,
partisan identity may be nothing more than a response given on a survey
or a forced choice when registering to vote. Conversely, religion can represent fundamental beliefs governing a person's daily life, and large amounts
of time are devoted to religious communities. But thinking more deeply
about political and religious attachments highlights the limits of these
generalizations.

Religious identities are not as stable as many political scientists assume,
and partisan identities are routinely shown to be quite strong. First, religious
identities and practices are not static; they are open to influence and change
over time. Scholars of religion have found that affiliation and practices do not
remain stable over the course of one's life (Arnett 2000; Putnam and Campbell 2010; Roof 1993; Wilson and Sherkat 1994; Wuthnow 2007), and religious change occurs in response to shifts in socioeconomic status (Newport

1979), familial roles (Chaves 1991; Stolzenberg, Blair-Loy, and Waite 1995) and geographic residence (Smith, Sikkink, and Bailey 1998; Stump 1984). In short, religious identities—including affiliation, involvement within a community, and personal beliefs—are not determined in a vacuum, and they are not immutable. Second, partisan identities in America are quite strong and affect how partisans view the economy (Bartels 2006) and government (Keele 2005; Sances and Stewart 2015); spend their money (Gerber and Huber 2010, 2009); feel about and treat members of their own party as well the other party (Iyengar, Sood, and Lelkes 2012; Iyengar and Westwood 2015; Munro, Weih, and Tsai 2010); participate in politics (Huddy, Mason, and Aarøe 2015); and develop ideologies (Levendusky 2009) and policy positions (Lenz 2012). If religious identities are vulnerable to an array of outside influences, could it be that the Republican described above attends church more frequently *because* he or she is a Republican, or that being a Democrat pushes a voter to disavow religion altogether? Despite the strong influence that religion seems to have in many people's lives, is it possible that politics actually affects religion? Answering this question is one main goal of the book. The theory and the data together show that partisan identities can influence whether someone identifies with a religious faith and the extent to which a person is involved in a religious community. In doing so, the results illustrate why social-political coalitions in American politics are particularly sticky; namely, because they are self-reinforcing. Religion and politics are tightly linked in Americans' minds not only because religious ideologies and teachings influence political attitudes but also because partisans actually update core parts of their religious identities to reflect their political outlooks.

For partisanship to influence religious identification and engagement, a person's partisan identity must be stronger or more salient than his or her religious identity. It is unlikely that this assumption holds true for all people at all times, leaving us to consider when partisan identities are most likely to impact religious identities. Chapter 3, which considers the religious and political socialization literatures together, develops a theory aimed at understanding just that.

THREE

A Life-Cycle Theory of Religion and Politics

For many, religion is a family activity; it is easy to conjure up images of moms and dads sitting with their children in the pews during church services, parents picking up their kids from Sunday school, and families coming together to celebrate religious holidays. These mental snapshots often consider a family at a single point in time and therefore give the illusion that the family members' religiosities have been and will always be the same: the parents were religious before having children, the parents will remain religiously involved once their kids are grown, and the children will retain the levels of religiosity with which they were raised as they transition from childhood into adolescence and adulthood. But is this necessarily the case?

The scholarly literature tells us that the answer to this question is likely no. Individuals' religious identifications and levels of religious involvement change over time, raising questions regarding what outside factors might affect these religious identities. One goal of this book is to show how and when partisan identities are strong enough to influence religious decision making. This chapter lays the groundwork by detailing when and why we might expect to see politics operating as a consideration when people make choices related to their religious identities.

Implicit in the claim that partisanship can influence religious identification and engagement is that a person's partisan identity is stronger, more salient, or more stable than the individual's religious identity. While this is likely not the case for all people, the religious and political socialization literatures identify a period in one's life when this is more likely to be true. Religious involvement and strength of religious identification wax and wane over a lifetime for many people, and these natural fluctuations provide opportunities for external influences to impact religious decisions. One stage during which this is particularly likely to happen is when people are making religious choices affecting themselves and their families. At this point, many decide whether, and to what extent, religion will be a part of their lives. It is during this time that partisanship is most likely to exert influence on religious choices, as partisan identities are more likely to be salient and stable than religious identities.

The next sections begin laying out the theory by describing the religious and political socialization processes found in the United States. Generalized expectations about when partisanship may influence individuals' religious attachments stem from considering these two literatures together, while specific expectations as to the direction of partisanship's impact on religiosity relies on the current political landscape. With the theory and expectations described, the final part of the chapter discusses how the theory will be operationalized and tested in the subsequent chapters.

Religious Life Course

The claim that partisanship can influence religious attachments and engagement relies on research describing how people's membership and involvement in religious institutions change throughout their lives. Sociologists, developmental psychologists, and scholars of religion have noted that religious identification, behaviors, and beliefs are dynamic, not static; people's affiliation with and engagement in formal religious institutions ebb and flow over the course of a lifetime (Argue, Johnson, and White 1999; Chaves 1991; Hoge, Johnson, and Luidens 1993; Ingersoll-Dayton, Krause, and Morgan 2002; Roof 1993; Wilson and Sherkat 1994).

An Exodus from the Religious Sphere

The religious life-cycle theory in sociology begins with the observation that teenagers and young adults have weak religious attachments. Religion and its corresponding practices are frequently a peripheral concern among adolescents (Arnett and Jensen 2002; Brinkerhoff and Mackie 1993; Desmond, Morgan, and Kikuchi 2010; Gallup and Castelli 1989; Hoge, Johnson, and Luidens 1993; Hunsberger and Brown 1984; Roof 1993; Smith 2009; Uecker, Regnerus, and Vaaler 2007; Willits and Crider, 1989; Wuthnow 2007). For example, after interviewing teenagers when they were between 13 and 17 years old and then again five years later, Smith (2009) found that the number who did not identify with a religious tradition doubled between interviews. Researchers similarly found that as individuals move from their teenage years into their twenties church attendance declines (Desmond,

Table 3.1 Demographics of church dropouts (%)

	Have you ever gone through a period in your life when you dropped out of attending church?
Full	57
Reported religious identification as a child	
White evangelical Protestant	57
White mainline Protestant	62
White Catholic	53
Reported church attendance as a child	
Rarely	27
Sometimes	55
Frequently	66
Family structure	
Parents still married	57
Parents not still married	60
Present-day party identification	
Democrat	58
Republican	63

Source: 2010–2011 Faith Journey Survey privately commissioned by the Barna Group.
Note: Question reads: "Have you ever gone through a period of life when you dropped out of attend-ing church after having regularly gone to church?" Asked only of respondents who (1) identified as Christian or Catholic at the time of the survey or (2) attended a Catholic or Christian church before the age of 18 or (3) considered themselves Christian or Catholic before the age of 18.

Morgan, and Kikuchi 2010; Koenig, McGue, and Iacono 2008; Smith 2009; Smith et al. 2002; Willits and Crider 1989), as does the rate of prayer (Smith 2009; Smith et al. 2002) and the importance placed on faith (Desmond, Morgan, and Kikuchi 2010; Smith 2009).

Consistent with previous research, the top row of table 3.1 shows the percentage of young adults (aged 18–29) who reported having ever stopped attending church. The question read: "Have you ever gone through a period of life when you dropped out of attending church after having regularly gone to church?" It was asked of respondents who reported identifying as Christian or Catholic at the time of the survey or reported having attended a Christian or Catholic church while growing up.[1] In total, 57% of these 18- to 29-year-olds responded that they stopped attending church for a period of time.[2]

When does this move away from religion likely take place? Desmond, Morgan, and Kikuchi (2010) used data in which individuals were first interviewed between the ages of 13 and 19 and then subsequently interviewed four additional times over the next seven years. Respondents ranged between 21 and 27 at the time of the last interview. Although the authors found that church attendance rates declined among respondents of all ages, the change was most pronounced among the youngest respondents who were teenagers during most of the seven-year period. Koenig, McGue, and Iacono (2008) found similar trends when looking at changes in religiosity for two cohorts at two points in time. The first cohort was interviewed when respondents were 14 and 18 years old, while the second cohort was interviewed at ages 20 and 25. The authors found a significant decrease in church attendance between ages 14 and 18 but no change in church attendance between ages 20 and 25. Moreover, church attendance rates among the 18-year-olds in the younger cohort are similar to those reported by the older cohort at both interview periods. The authors therefore concluded that the trend found among the younger cohort is likely a maturational effect, not a cohort effect. These results comport with Smith et al.'s (2002) analyses that compared eighth, tenth, and twelfth graders and show that attendance at religious services decreases during high school years. Taken together, the natural falling away from religion occurs during a person's teen years and continues into his or her twenties.

Who moves away from religion? While there are differences in youth religiosity based on denominational affiliation, race, and region of residence (Smith et al. 2002), the empirical trend of moving away from organized religion is not specific to a particular generation, religious tradition, or home-life situation. First, across multiple generations and indicators of religious involvement, young adults are the least likely to be religious (Gallup and Castelli 1989; Roof 1993; Smith 2009). Figure 3.1 provides a visual illustration of these over-time trends. The top panel graphs the percentage of religious nonidentifiers over time, separately for different age groups. The graph not only shows that religious nonidentification rates have increased dramatically in recent years but also that young adults—those between 18 and 25—are consistently the most likely to report having no religious affiliation. The bottom panel presents similar trends but shows the percentage of regular church attenders. Again, there is a consistent gap in which younger respondents, across time, are less likely to attend church regularly. Second, the move away from organized religion in young adulthood is not unique to one religious tradition. The second set of results in table 3.1 shows a fair amount of consistency in church dropout rates based on respondents' reported religious traditions as children.[3] These results corroborate other studies finding that those raised in the Catholic, Presbyterian, or Mormon traditions are far more likely to fall away from religion during late adolescence and early adulthood than at any other period (Albrecht, Cornwall, and Cunningham 1988; Hoge 1981; Hoge, Johnson, and Luidens 1993). Additionally, Uecker, Regnerus, and Vaaler (2007) show that approximately three-

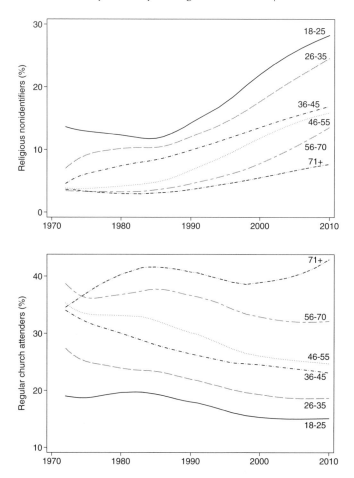

3.1. Younger Americans are consistently less religious than older Americans. The top panel presents the percentage of religious nonidentifiers over time for different age groups, while the bottom panel presents the percentage of regular church attenders (weekly or more) over time for different age groups. *Source*: General Social Survey.

quarters of mainline Protestants and Catholics report declining rates of church attendance, and 63% of evangelical and black Protestants attend religious services less frequently as young adults compared to earlier in their lives. Although there is some variation across religions, no religious tradition is immune from these declines in religiosity.

Importantly, coming from a religious and close-knit family does not insulate adolescents and young adults from moving away from religion. The third set of results in table 3.1 corroborates research showing that attendance decreases most dramatically among young adults who attended religious services regularly as children and who have parents who regularly attend (Myers 1996; Petts 2009; Sharot, Ayalon, and Ben-Rafael 1986). Similarly, teenagers with stronger moral beliefs experienced a greater decline in believing religion is important upon reaching young adulthood (Desmond, Morgan, and Kikuchi 2010) and being "close to parents" in adolescence only weakly predicts religiosity in young adults (Smith 2009). The bottom of table 3.1 shows similar evidence when comparing different family structures. Whether respondents' parents are still married and living together has very little bearing on whether respondents ever stopped attending religious services. Even those raised in religious households with a traditional family structure and good parent-child relations demonstrate this general shift away from religion.

Why do young adults have weak ties to organized religion? Sociologists offer several explanations, many of which are related to adolescents' and young adults' changing life circumstances. First, disruptions that occur during this life phase, including leaving home, changing peer groups, adopting new roles and responsibilities, and achieving financial independence, often lead people to cut ties with their childhood religious institutions (Goldscheider and Goldscheider 1999; Hoge, Johnson, and Luidens 1993) in order to focus on personal and professional successes (Smith 2009). As Smith (2009) notes:

> Learning to stand on one's own involves concerns that most view as this-worldly: finishing education, skills training, job experience, career development, paying bills, balancing bank accounts, setting up new households, buying cars, developing one's own social networks, and so on. Relating to God, going to religious services, reading scripture, getting involved in a religious community, praying regularly, growing in faith, and such concerns are rarely in American culture considered relevant to or important for achieving identity and financial independence. So investing wholeheartedly in the former can be thought of as having the effect of neglecting the latter. (76–77)

Such disruptions place young adults on the outskirts of organized religion until they actively seek out new spiritual homes. Second, young adults often wish to assert their independence from their parents, which includes distancing themselves from their parents' religious beliefs and practices (Arnett and Jensen 2002; Smith 2009). This desire for independence helps explain findings that even those raised in religious households drift away from religion. Third, young adults who engage in behavior that is incongruous with religious teachings have lower levels of religiosity (Bryant, Choi, and Yasuno 2003; Uecker, Regnerus, and Vaaler 2007). Smith (2009) argues that the cognitive dissonance that comes from young adults' exposure to and experimentation with binge drinking (Perkins 1987), drug use (Engs and Mullen 1999), and premarital sex (Zaleski and Schiaffino 2000) pushes young adults away from religion. Fourth, if religious participation helps teach morality and values, young adults who have already learned these lessons may feel as though they do not need to be religiously active. When religion is considered as a means of imparting life lessons, it makes sense that adolescents who become less involved, or even uninvolved, in organized faith are not opposed to religion and even report wanting to return after having children (Dean 2010; Smith 2009). A final, more passive, reason for decreased religiosity among young adults is that they simply lose interest or are too busy with other activities. For many, the decline in religiosity is not a conscious decision but rather an unintended eventuality once they are given free rein over their time (Dinges et al. 1998; Smith 2009).

The sociological explanations given for decreased religiosity suggest that the changes in outward displays of religious participation and identification correspond more generally to weak religious attachments. Adolescents and young adults do not hold strong nonreligious identities, meaning they do not derive self-esteem from being religiously uninvolved or unaffiliated. Instead, "the vast majority of U.S. teens view religion in a benignly positive light" (Dean 2010: 17). Teenagers are not hostile toward religion because they don't care much about it: "People fight over things that matter to them—but religion barely causes a ripple in the lives of most adolescents" (Dean 2010: 17–18). In other words, religious identities during this life phase are generally weak and not very salient. Individuals may retain certain religious beliefs during this period, such as views of the afterlife (Smith 2009), but religion does not play an important role nor does it warrant extensive thought. Although "American adolescents harbor no ill will toward religion," they "tend to approach religious participation, like music and sports, as an extracurricular activity: a good, well-rounded thing to do, but unnecessary for an integrated life" (Dean 2010: 6). This relative indifference toward religion explains not only why religious participation decreases but also why religion does not play a guiding role nor is faith seen as important during this time in people's lives (Desmond, Morgan, and Kikuchi 2010; Smith 2009).

Taken together, adolescents and young adults have weak religious identities, measured by their religious behaviors as well as their religious self-identification and views about religion. And while decreases in religiosity during adolescence do not preclude changes at other times in people's lives—for example, figure 3.1 shows that religious nonidentification rates have increased across all age groups—it is younger respondents who are regularly the least religious within society. Moreover, although the literature does not claim that everyone will experience a move away from religion, the trend occurs across a diverse set of people. If religion were to become a peripheral concern, adolescence and young adulthood would be the most likely time this would take place. And finally, despite the general move away from religion during young adulthood, people do not necessarily remain on the outskirts of religion indefinitely. The next section discusses the research exploring determinants of religious involvement in adulthood.

For Some, a Return to the Religious Fold

Although religiosity and religious participation often decline in adolescence and remain low in young adulthood, many people undergo life changes that encourage them to participate in religious communities as they become adults. Getting married (Becker and Hofmeister 2001; Hadaway and Roof 1988; Roof 1993; Sandomirsky and Wilson 1990) and having children (Argue, Johnson, and White 1999; Arnett and Jensen 2002; Chaves 1991; Gallup and Castelli 1989; Ingersoll-Dayton, Krause, and Morgan 2002; Ploch and Hastings 1998; Wuthnow 2007) are strongly and positively correlated with attendance at religious services and participation in religious organizations. Marriage and children also both decrease the likelihood of becoming a religious nonidentifier and increase the likelihood of adopting a religious identification among those who previously dropped out of religion (Wilson and Sherkat 1994). In particular, married individuals with school-aged children are the most likely to be affiliated with religious institutions and to participate in religious communities (Argue, Johnson, and White 1999; Becker and Hofmeister 2001; Rotolo 2000; Schleifer and Chaves 2017; Stolzenberg, Blair-Loy, and Waite 1995). Moreover, recent research has shown that having young children in school—not simply getting married or having children— is the most important driver of increased religious participation (Schleifer and Chaves 2017).

Scholars have offered numerous related explanations for why religious participation goes up in response to family formation. Parents may increase their rates of religious involvement because they see religious communities as a way to provide children with a religious upbringing (Roof 1993; Wuthnow 2007), teach children core values (Ingersoll-Dayton, Krause, and Morgan 2002), socialize with other parents (Stolzenberg, Blair-Loy, and Waite 1995), learn new parenting strategies (Alwin 1986; Wilcox 1998), and take part in a conventional social and cultural system (Smith 2009; Wilcox and Wolfinger 2007; Wuthnow 2007). These explanations share a common social element; religious involvement offers families community and support. Even self-labeled atheist parents attend religious services more frequently than atheists who do not have children (Ecklund and Lee 2011). Importantly, the literature also consistently finds that the relationship between family formation and increased religious participation is directly tied to being part of a "traditional family," meaning two parents and children (Chaves 2011). These results are intuitive when we consider that the main tenets of most religions center around traditional family life. Further strengthening this relationship, many congregations reach out to and design programs aimed at families (Wilcox and Wolfinger 2007; Wuthnow 2007).

Marriage and children are an important impetus for returning to the religious fold, but it is not guaranteed that people return to their childhood beliefs and practices. Many never return to religion after leaving in young adulthood and instead become religious "dropouts" (Roof 1993). And even those who return to organized religion are not bound to bring up the next generation in the same way they were raised. Instead, individuals accept and reject religious beliefs and practices that suit their needs and are consistent with their preexisting identities (Arnett and Jensen 2002; Sherkat and Blocker 1997; Wilson and Sherkat 1994). For example, Newport (1979) finds evidence of denominational switching based on socioeconomic status, and Stump (1984) shows how migrants' religiosities increase and decrease in conjunction with the average religious commitment of their new geographic homes. Rather than replicating their religious upbringings, parents create new religious environments for their children based on their current situations, outlooks, and beliefs. All told, the literature shows that—whether parents ultimately decide to increase their levels of religious involvement, adopt particular religious practices, or remain on the outskirts of religion—parents are making religious choices both for themselves and their children during this life phase. And in making these decisions, religious attachments—which were weak and unimportant in young adulthood—solidify.

Researchers find that older adults have relatively stable levels of religious identification and religiosity (Dillon and Wink 2007). Of those who changed religious faiths, a majority report joining their current religion before reaching the age of 36 and very few report switching religions after 50 (Pew Research Center 2009). And while religious participation increases in response to having younger, school-aged children, participation rates are more stable among parents of teenagers (Schleifer and Chaves 2017), as

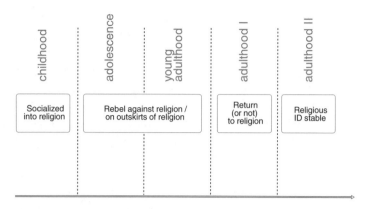

3.2. Religious socialization process.

these parents likely have already made religious decisions for themselves and their families. And although certain life events can influence religious participation (Ingersoll-Dayton, Krause, and Morgan 2002), religious practices are less likely to change in later adulthood.[4]

Figure 3.2 presents a visual illustration of the sociological religious life-course model. This socialization process creates a window in adolescence and young adulthood when many are less involved with and less attached to organized religion. After getting married and having children, however, these newly minted adults must decide (1) whether to return to the religious sphere and (2) to what extent to become involved. Consistent with the definitions laid out in chapter 1, the religious socialization and family formation literatures conceptualize religion as a *social-collective* identity, measured by a person outwardly identifying as a member of a religious community and being involved in a religious organization. Attachment to and participation in a religious community are not the only ways to measure religious identity, but they represent external indicators of being part of a social group and holding a social identity. While the literature described identifies how changing positions within the life cycle can affect levels of religious participation, we know less about the preexisting identities, attitudes, or preferences that may impact religious decision making at this life stage. The next section shows that while religion is a peripheral concern for adolescents and young adults, other aspects of their identities continue to develop. In particular, partisan identities develop at the very time when religion happens to be on the back burner for young adults. The stable party identification that often emerges during young adulthood is one influence that can affect individuals as they make decisions about returning to religion.

Political Life Course

The political socialization literature, which describes how partisan identities form and crystallize, provides additional background that will help us understand how partisanship might come to affect religious identities. Scholars largely accept the premise that core dispositions, including party identification (PID), are stable over the course of one's adult life (Abramson 1979; Alwin, Cohen, and Newcomb 1991; Green, Palmquist, and Schickler 2002; Sears 1983; Sears and Funk 1999, 1990). Even those who believe attitudes are based on a "running tally" of evaluations recognize that certain outlooks are "sticky" and slow to change (Fiorina 1981). What is less clear is the point at which people have "well-formed, crystallized attitudes toward the important objects of the day" (Sears and Valentino 1997: 46). This process does not happen overnight but occurs as individuals age, learn, and engage with the political sphere.

The "impressionable years" hypothesis claims that adolescence and young adulthood are the periods when people are most impressionable. During this time, influences and events shape adolescents' long-term political outlooks, most notably influencing partisan identification (Abramson 1979; Sears 1990, 1983, 1975).[5] One key driver in the political socialization process comes from the home. The family unit provides a "social identity and a location within the social structure," both of which can affect a child's political orientation (Glass, Bengston, and Dunham 1986). Scholars using data from the 1960s and 1970s found that parents' political leanings influence adolescents' partisanship (Jennings and Niemi 1981, 1974; Niemi and Jennings 1991), especially in cases when politics is salient in the household (Beck and Jennings 1991; Tedin 1974), and that the parental influence is still present after these adolescents become adults. Jennings, Stoker, and Bowers (2009) have further replicated these findings in a younger generation. The authors found similar socialization trends among a cohort that came of age in the 1990s, demonstrating that the intergenerational transmission of partisan identities is not cohort specific. Partisanship, however, is not wholly a hereditary trait; outside factors can affect it.

A second key influence in the political socialization process is the broader political environment (Alwin, Cohen, and Newcomb 1991; Firebaugh and Chen 1995; Giuliano and Spilimbergo 2014; Green, Palmquist, and Schickler 2002; Nteta and Greenlee 2013; Osborne, Sears, and Valentino 2011; Stewart, Settles, and Winter 1998). Few people are insulated from the political world; however, adolescents and young adults are particularly susceptible to their surroundings impacting their political outlooks (Beck

1974; Niemi and Jennings 1991; Dinas 2013). Both large-scale events, such as war or scandal (Dinas 2014, 2013), and regularly occurring events, such as elections, can affect individuals in this life stage. The event-driven political socialization theory contends that the extensive media coverage of these highly visible political events provides information about politics, allowing adolescents to engage with and learn about the political realm (Sears and Valentino 1997; Valentino and Sears 1998). Elections are a time when many are tuned into politics (Lenz 2012), and campaigns boil down complex issues into simple, digestible ideas. Coverage of and information from political events allow adolescents to sort out their political leanings as they become partisans (Sears and Valentino 1997; Valentino and Sears 1998).[6]

Party Identification in Adulthood

The resultant partisanship from this socialization process is a stable affiliation that often lasts a lifetime. Green, Palmquist, and Schickler (2002) find that partisanship measured in 1965 among a group of high school seniors remained a strong predictor of partisanship and vote choice years later when these same respondents were 35 and 50 years old. Despite the long gap, only 6% of high school seniors who called themselves a Democrat or Republican switched parties in the seventeen-year window between 1965 and 1982. Even in the face of a political party's misfortunes, which may cause a partisan to evaluate his or her own party less favorably or even vote for the opposing party, partisanship rarely swings in a dramatic fashion. Watergate did not produce an exodus from the Republican Party, nor did the Lewinsky scandal change rates of Democratic identification (Green, Palmquist, and Schickler 2002).

Partisanship is not just a stable political affiliation that is correlated with vote choice; partisans of different stripes view and respond to the political world differently. Partisans differ in their evaluations of the economy (Bartels 2006), trust in the government (Keele 2005), and confidence that votes were counted properly (Sances and Stewart 2015). In all three cases, partisanship and the political landscape—measured by the party of the president, which party controlled Congress, or which party won an election—together impacted reported political evaluations. Gerber and Huber extended this line of research by showing that partisanship also drives consumption behavior as measured by taxable sales at the county level (2009) and self-reported spending decisions (2010). The correlations between partisanship and economic evaluations are not confined to survey responses; they translate into actual spending decisions. Finally, partisanship is a driver of Americans' ideologies (Levendusky 2009) and policy positions (Lenz 2012), not the other way around. All told, partisan attachments—which can deepen over time in response to voting and supporting candidates (Mullainathan and Washington 2009)—have political consequences that go beyond choosing a candidate to support.

The strength of partisanship indicates that party identification is likely more than a political identity; it can also be considered a social identity in its own right (Greene 2004, 1999; Huddy, Mason, and Aarøe 2015; Mason 2015; Miller and Conover 2015). For example, Greene (2004, 1999), using the Identification with a Psychological Group (IDPG) scale (Mael and Tetrick 1992), showed that partisans express feelings of shared identity and experiences. The scale measures agreement with statements about, for example, how respondents feel when someone criticizes their political group, whether respondents view the group's successes as their own successes, and whether respondents use "we" or "us" when speaking about the group.[7] Partisans do not just vote along party lines; they also see themselves as members of a group and derive self-esteem from their political identities. Borrowing Green, Palmquist, and Schickler's (2002) analogy that one's partisan identity is like being a member of a team, partisans root for their teams, have positive affect for their teams, dislike their teams' competitors, and have team loyalties that are slow to change.

One result of joining a political team is the creation of an "us" versus "them" mentality, which psychologists generally find produces in-group favoritism and out-group hostility. Social Identity Theory finds that people have warmer feelings toward members of their own groups while ascribing negative evaluations to members of out-groups (Tajfel 1970; Tajfel and Turner 1986). Even in instances when the group assignment is trivial or random, identifying with a group in a competitive environment produces negative out-group sentiments (Billing and Tajfel 1973). Both political scientists and psychologists have recently built on this strand of research to show that partisans make in-group and out-group distinctions in their political evaluations. Partisan dislike for the political out-group has risen dramatically since the 1960s (Haidt and Hetherington 2012), partisans are more likely to believe that out-group politicians have ulterior motives for their actions (Munro, Weih, and Tsai 2010), and Implicit Association Tests (IAT) reveal the subconscious in-group biases held by partisans even surpass in-group biases along racial lines (Iyengar and Westwood 2015).

These in-group out-group distinctions, in turn, have large political and social consequences. First, the social aspects of partisanship—identifying as a partisan and with copartisans—play a stronger role in political participation

(Huddy, Mason, and Aarøe 2015; Mason 2015; Miller and Conover 2015), partisan bias (Mason 2015), and political hostility and anger (Mason 2015; Miller and Conover 2015) than the instrumental aspects of partisanship based on ideological views and policy preferences. In other words, affect and social ties are more important to certain aspects of politics than the relevant issues of the day. Second, partisanship's reach is evident outside the political sphere. Partisans are more likely to give a scholarship to a student with whom they share a partisan identity and are more generous (stingy) toward members of the political in-group (out-group) in economic games (Iyengar and Westwood 2015). Partisanship even impacts dating and marriage, as mate selection along political lines explains political similarities among spouses (Alford et al. 2011; Huber and Malhotra 2017), and a sizable number of partisans (49% of Republicans and 33% of Democrats) report that they would disapprove if their child married someone of the opposing political party (Iyengar, Sood, and Lelkes 2012). All told, the partisan identification that develops in adolescence and young adulthood is quite stable throughout adulthood and can produce meaningful changes in partisans' attitudes and behaviors, both political and not. Figure 3.3 presents a visual illustration of the political socialization process.

Figure 3.4 reveals that partisan identities are being formed and internalized at the very time when religion is not a salient concern and religious attachments are more likely to be weak. Upon reaching adulthood, individuals have solidified partisan affiliations as they make choices associated with their religious identities. Just as elite cues encourage partisans to adopt specific attitudes (Cohen 2003; Lenz 2012), individuals at this point in their lives may draw on their partisanship, elite cues, and their political

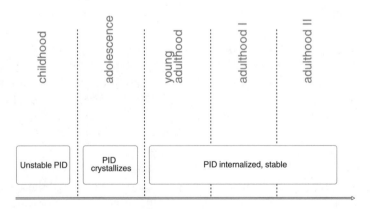

3.3. Political socialization process.

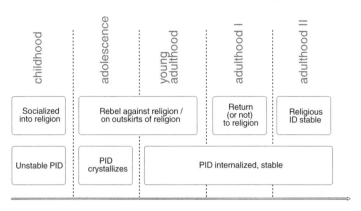

3.4. Religious and political socialization processes.

surroundings when making religious decisions. Once religious identities have solidified, however, they are quite stable over long periods of time. Therefore, partisanship's effect on religion should be relatively muted for those squarely in adulthood—that is, those who have already made religious decisions for themselves and their families. The two socialization literatures together identify a particular life-cycle window in which partisan identities may be more solidified and salient than religious identities, thereby offering a testable hypothesis as to when partisanship is most likely to influence religious identity.

Religious and Partisan Identities in the American Context

Campbell et al. (1960) noted in *The American Voter* that "as proximity between the group and the world of politics increases, the political distinctiveness of the group will increase" (311). Just as the authors assumed that an individual's social identity should exert more political influence as that identity becomes more relevant to politics, proximity should similarly correspond to the amount and type of influence a partisan identity exerts on a social identity.

Chapter 2 described large-scale changes in the political landscape beginning in the 1960s. The Republican Party has aligned with organized religious groups and become associated with religious values while the Democratic Party has been linked to morally liberal positions and less religious organizations. In explaining the individual-level responses to these elite-level changes, scholars follow Campbell et al.'s (1960) lead in assuming that as religiosity became relevant to politics, religious voters became

Republican supporters and less religious and secular voters began to support the Democratic Party. But the changing relationship between religion and politics at the elite level may have also activated partisan-driven change in religious involvement. While the life-cycle theory is agnostic about the direction of partisanship's influence on religious identities, religion's changing role in American politics since the 1960s generates a testable hypothesis about the direction of religious movement: *Republicans should become more religious and Democrats should become less so over time.*[8]

What exactly do *more religious* and *less religious* mean? In conceptualizing religion as a social phenomenon, religion is an institution that, first and foremost, brings people of a shared identity together. Scholars who think about religion within a social framework look at an individual's religious affiliation as an indication of her willingness to identify with the group as well as her involvement in a religious community, often measured by church attendance. The empirical chapters follow suit, operationalizing "religious" to relate to religious identification and attendance at religious services. While a reader can easily think about religion as a mental phenomenon, which would include a person's private religious beliefs and values, it is more reasonable to assume that a social identity like partisanship would have a direct effect on the social aspects of a person's religious identity rather than on privately held beliefs or activities performed alone. Moreover, if partisanship affects more personal aspects of a person's religious identity—such as beliefs about the Bible, views about the afterlife, or private devotion—it likely operates indirectly through religious involvement and being surrounded by others with similar viewpoints (Berger 1967; Wald, Owen, and Hill 1988) and who engage in similar actions.

Perceiving differences between the parties, candidates, or constituencies along religious lines is a necessary condition of both a religious-driven explanation of political change and a partisan-driven explanation of religious change. People can bring their religious and partisan attachments into alignment only if they perceive a clear delineation between the parties and religion. Importantly, the data show that average Americans have become aware of the religious gap in politics and have internalized differences across the parties and their members. Campbell, Green, and Layman (2011), for example, asked survey respondents to classify groups of individuals as "mainly Republicans," "mainly Democrats," or "a mix of both." Among the respondents, 46% reported that they believed "religious people" are mainly Republicans and another 45% reported that they are a mix of Democrats and Republicans, leaving only 5% reporting that religious people are mainly

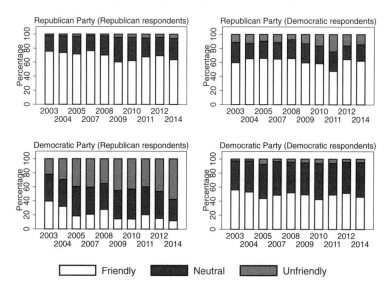

3.5. Partisans view the parties as having different relationships with religion. Respondents answered two questions that asked, "Do you feel that the [party name] is generally friendly toward religion, neutral toward religion, or unfriendly toward religion?" The top two panels present responses about the Republican Party over time, separately for Republican (left) and Democratic (right) respondents. The bottom two panels present the same results asking about the Democratic Party. *Source:* 2003–2014 Pew Research Center.

Democrats. The results flip when respondents were asked about the political leanings of nonreligious people: 48% reported they are mainly Democrats, 45% reported that they are a mix, and only 3% reported that nonreligious people are mainly Republicans. Additionally, Patrikios (2013) found evidence of a composite evangelical-Republican identity in which Americans associate the two identities to such an extent that they have become a single fused identity.[9]

In addition to knowing about the God gap at the individual level, Americans also perceive the parties' as having different relationships with organized religion. The Pew Research Center has regularly asked survey respondents to rate the parties' friendliness toward religion since 2003. For each party, respondents can answer that the party is friendly toward religion, neutral toward religion, or unfriendly toward religion. Admittedly, this is an imperfect measure because a partisan may be hesitant to say that his or her party is unfriendly toward anyone or anything. Even so, the data reflect reasonable partisan responses. Figure 3.5 presents the distribution of responses regarding the Republican Party (top two panels) and the Democratic Party (bottom two panels) separately for Republican respondents (left panels) and Democratic respondents (right panels).

Partisans generally view the Republican Party as friendlier toward religion than the Democratic Party, but the Democratic Party is not viewed as being overwhelmingly unfriendly toward religion. Averaging the years together, roughly 70% of Republicans reported that the Republican Party is friendly toward religion, with yearly rates ranging between 60% in 2009 and 76% in 2007 (top left graph). The overwhelming majority of remaining Republican respondents reported that the Republican Party is neutral toward religion; only about 3% of Republicans reported that the party is unfriendly toward religion. The top right graph presents Democratic respondents' evaluations of the Republican Party. Sixty percent of Democrats also reported that the Republican Party is friendly toward religion. A majority of Democratic respondents provided the "friendly" response in every year except 2011, when the percentage dipped to 40. Even among Democrats, "friendly" is the modal response across the decade of data. While the percentage of unfriendly responses is much higher among Democratic respondents than Republican respondents, "unfriendly" is still the least common response option throughout the entire period. Democrats and Republicans both report that the Republican Party is friendly toward religion.

The bottom two panels present results for the question asking whether the Democratic Party is friendly, neutral, or unfriendly toward religion. Republicans are generally split in their views. Pooling together Republican respondents across the entire time period, an equal percentage of respondents reported that the Democratic Party is unfriendly and neutral toward religion (39% each), with 23% reporting that the Democratic Party is friendly toward religion. Republicans' views also changed, with rates of "friendly" responses steadily decreasing and unfriendly response rates increasing over time. In the most recent survey, a majority (56%) of Republicans reported that the Democratic Party is unfriendly toward religion and only 11% reported that the Democratic Party is friendly toward religion. Although there is not wholesale acceptance among Republicans that the Democratic Party is unfriendly toward religion, the Democrats are certainly perceived as significantly less friendly toward religion than the Republican Party. The final graph in the quadrant presents Democratic respondents' evaluations of the Democratic Party. Here, Democratic respondents generally feel that the Democratic Party is either neutral or friendly toward religion. Perceptions of the Democratic Party illustrate that the linkage between the Democratic

Party and religion is less clear than the relationship between the Republican Party and religion. While the Republican Party is more closely associated with religion than the Democratic Party, the Democratic Party is not perceived as a strongly secular force or hostile toward religion (see Bolce and De Maio 2002 for a more detailed discussion). This might be because Democratic politicians have recently employed religious rhetoric (Domke and Coe 2010; Kaylor 2011) and outreach (Smidt et al. 2010) to appeal to religious voters. While the Democratic Party is not seen as being unfriendly toward religion, the Republican Party is consistently seen as being friendlier toward religion among Republicans and Democrats alike. Not only is there a religious divide in American politics today, but Americans know about it.

Why might partisans feel compelled to bring their religious identities into alignment with their partisan identities? One explanation, cognitive dissonance, comes from the field of psychology. Cognitive dissonance theories contend that individuals want consistency among their cognitions (i.e., beliefs and behaviors). Dissonance arises when elements of cognition do not fit together, motivating a person to reduce or eliminate the dissonance, "just as, for example, the presence of hunger leads to action to reduce the hunger" (Festinger 1957: 18). A common example of dissonance includes people who smoke despite knowing the associated health risks. Smokers can reduce the psychological discomfort stemming from the dissonance by downplaying the quality of research on smoking's effects, emphasizing the innumerable unavoidable health perils in the world, considering the potential drawbacks of quitting, and remembering that the enjoyment of smoking is worth the risk (Festinger 1957). Extending this line of reasoning, people want their behaviors and identities to be aligned. For example, when Democrats hear Republican candidates espousing religious values and principles or when they read about the Republican Party's close relationship with religious organizations, Democrats may take the information as a cue about how partisans "should" act with respect to religion. And if these Democrats are in the process of making decisions associated with their religious identities, not being religious may reflect a desire to minimize cognitive dissonance. Republicans, on the other hand, may internalize the same political landscape differently. Sensing that the Republican Party is closely associated with religious values while the Democratic Party supports culturally liberal policies, Republicans' ties to organized religion may grow stronger. In both examples, elite behaviors play an important role in determining whether and in what direction partisan identities should affect religious decision making. Political issues, rhetoric, and campaign strategies that differentiate the parties along religious lines enable Americans to perceive their religious and partisan identities as either in concert with or in opposition to each other, thereby making cognitive dissonance possible.

A second, more indirect, explanation for why partisans change their religious involvement relates to partisan homophily, or the tendency to sort socially along political lines. If partisans socialize with, date, and marry copartisans (Alford et al. 2011; Huber and Malhotra 2017; Iyengar, Sood, and Lelkes 2012), then politics may influence religious choices through partisans' social networks. In this case, partisans may not look at the political environment when making religious decisions but instead look at what their friends, family, and neighbors are doing. Even weak or unengaged partisans can become religiously sorted over time by following the lead of others in their social networks—some of whom may be politically engaged and attuned to elite-level cultural and religious differences. While this explanation offers a slightly different route to religious sorting, the end result of Republicans opting into and Democrats selecting out of organized religion, along with the associated consequences, are the same.

The life-cycle theory builds on and contributes to previous research exploring politics' effects on religion. Hout and Fischer (2014, 2002) opened the door to this line of microlevel research when they used cross-sectional data to argue that the close relationship between Republican elites and religious conservatives has pushed liberals and moderates out of religion. This change in the political environment, according to the authors, helps explain the increased number of religious nonidentifiers, even among those who retained personal religious beliefs. Patrikios (2008) built on this finding and used panel data to show that partisanship has become correlated with changes in church attendance in recent years among white evangelicals. This research demonstrates that politics "may be able to 'construct' religious communities" (Patrikios 2008), but it raises questions about how, why, and under what conditions partisanship can shape an individual's religious choices.

Religion is a strongly held and, at times, quite stable identity. How then might we expect to see politics exerting an influence? The life-cycle theory serves as a theoretical underpinning for generating testable hypotheses and offers an explanation for why this unexpected relationship exists when, as Putnam and Campbell (2010) note, it seems "implausible that people would hazard the fate of their eternal soul over mundane political controversies" (145). Based on the theory, we should not think religion is always vulnerable to the influence of politics, but rather its vulnerability changes over the course of a person's life. The life-cycle theory, therefore, identifies when politics is most likely to influence a person's religious identity. The findings also extend previous research by considering the effect that politics may have on Republicans. The emphasis to date has been on Democrats responding to the political environment by viewing evangelicalism and Republicanism as a single fused identity and opting out of or moving away from organized religion (Campbell et al., forthcoming; Hout and Fischer 2014, 2002; Patrikios 2013, 2008). The empirics supporting the life-cycle theory, on the other hand, show how the political environment can pull Republicans deeper into the religious fold as well. Finally, the individual-level theory also complements recent work focusing on religious change at the organizational and denominational level. Smith (2015) argues that religious leaders and denominations respond to the changing cultural and political milieus in which they find themselves. When this happens, as Smith shows, religious institutions, and the principles and values they profess, are not impervious to outside influences, including politics. The results presented here extend Smith's overarching argument to include how average citizens respond to the surrounding political environment.

Testing the Life-Cycle Theory

The religious and political socialization literatures create testable expectations regarding politics' ability to influence religion. These literatures also guide decisions about how to operationalize the theory and test the general predictions. First, the theory applies most directly to those born in the United States. Individuals raised in another country experience different socialization processes. Thus, the same theoretical expectations may not apply. Second, we may wonder whether individuals of all religious faiths respond in the same manner. The political linkage between the Republican Party and Christian conservatism may matter a great deal for white Americans raised in Christian households but may not matter to non-Christians. The political landscape in which Christian conservatism plays a large role in the public sphere, therefore, may not influence everyone to the same degree. Due to the limited number of respondents from religious minority groups in public opinion surveys, it is difficult to empirically test the life-cycle theory on smaller religions (e.g., Jews, Hindus, Muslims). And while the data are better suited to explain trends among white members of large religious families (mainline Protestants, evangelical Protestants, and Catholics), the empirical results are the same regardless of whether members of these small religious traditions are included in or excluded from the models. Moreover, consistent with previous findings that there is a religiosity gap within each of the large Christian traditions in America today (Green 2010; Kellstedt et al. 2007), the data show that partisanship influences religiosity among respondents within these larger religious traditions.[10]

Additionally, a reader knowledgeable about political-religious coalitions may have wondered about whether the analyses should focus on all Americans or specifically white Americans. African Americans, for example, are the single most loyal constituency to the Democratic Party and are also more religious than white Americans. This pattern stands in contrast to everything discussed up to this point. African Americans have maintained a strong racial linkage with the Democratic Party over time, even as the ties of other "ethnic" groups to the Democratic Party, such as white Catholics, waned. This raises an important empirical question of whether nonwhites, particularly African Americans, should be included in the analyses that follow. On the one hand, it is important to include nonwhite Americans in order to make generalizable statements about the magnitude of religious change in the United States. On the other hand, minority groups' unique religious and political histories mean that group members might not follow the same religious trajectory as their white copartisans. Including nonwhite respondents, therefore, may produce slightly smaller estimates and noisier results as these are individuals for whom we may have different theoretical expectations. The results that follow include the full sample of respondents, unless specifically noted, to give readers a better overall understanding of the size of the politically driven religiosity gap in American politics. Importantly, however, analyses that limit the sample to self-identified white respondents produce substantively and statistically similar results. Readers can therefore be assured that this coding decision does not produce the findings presented in the subsequent chapters. Finally, just because the inclusion of nonwhite respondents in the sample produces similar results does not mean that nonwhite partisans respond to the political environment in the same manner as white partisans. Chapter 7 looks at African Americans and addresses how their life-cycle experience differs from that of the white majority and the political consequences of African Americans' religious and political attachments.

Scholars can conceptualize and measure religious identity in numerous ways; however, as discussed in chapter 1, the empirical chapters will focus on religious identification and church attendance. More specifically, religious identification will measure willingness to identify with a religious community and the strength of that identification rather than with which specific religious tradition a person identifies. This strategy has three distinct benefits. First, looking at willingness to identify helps uncover whether there are political causes of secularism and explains whether politics has had something to do with the increased rates of religious nonidentification in recent decades.

Second, strength of social group identification, including religion, is correlated with adhering to group norms and looking politically like others in the group (Berelson, Lazarsfeld, and McPhee 1954; Campbell et al. 1960; Conover 1988, 1984; Gurin, Miller, and Gurin 1980; Shingles 1981; Tate 1994). Understanding how politics affects the depth of religious identification therefore reveals how these strong statistical associations come to pass. And third, willingness to identify and strength of identification sidestep problems associated with religious classification schemes. There is a great deal of diversity both between denominations that make up a religious tradition as well as between congregations of the same denomination (see Djupe and Calfano 2013 and Djupe and Gilbert 2009 for a more detailed discussion of this critique). In the same way that it would be a mistake to make assumptions about a person's religious community based solely on his or her religious tradition, it may also not be appropriate to look for evidence of politics affecting selection decisions into these broad religious families. Additionally, researchers should be concerned about measurement error when classifying respondents based on their reported religious denominations. For example, the American Baptist Association is an evangelical denomination while the American Baptist Churches USA is a mainline denomination. While measurement error is generally difficult to identify because denominational questions are usually not repeated in panel studies, the GSS panel asked about religious denomination in both 2006 and 2008. Approximately 30% of self-identified Protestants changed their denomination in a two-year period. While some of this movement may reflect real changes in affiliation, many of these changes are between denominations with similar names. By focusing on willingness to identify with a religious tradition and identification strength, the empirical results avoid the pitfalls commonly associated with traditional measures of religious affiliation.

Church attendance acts as the second main dependent variable in the chapters that follow. Attendance at church is highly correlated with other forms of religious involvement (Green 2010), an important vehicle through which interactions take place within a religious community (Crawford and Olson 2001; Djupe and Gilbert 2002), and viewed as an integral aspect of many different religious faiths (Mockabee, Monson, and Grant 2001). Also, questions about church attendance are routinely asked in public opinion surveys and exit polls. Consequently, when journalists and pundits discuss the God gap after each election, they are usually referring to the political gap in attendance at religious services. So, while reported church attendance seems like an obvious place to look for evidence of partisan-induced change in religiosity, there is a lingering question of how to interpret reported church attendance on a survey. Changes in church attendance can be interpreted in one of two ways. First, changes in church attendance can be thought of as real changes in partisans' behaviors. This interpretation, however, poses a problem if people cannot accurately recall their behaviors when asked (Tourangeau, Rips, and Rasinski, 2000) or if they respond with their "ideal self" rather than their "actual self" in mind (Brenner 2011). To accommodate this issue, a second interpretation is to think of reported church attendance as a subjective measure. In this case, reported church attendance indicates ideal levels of religious involvement or feelings of closeness to the religious community (Brenner 2011; Chaves 2011). This interpretation more broadly reflects partisans' feelings about the religious world while also being correlated with actual religious behavior. Although substantively distinct, both interpretations of church attendance capture how partisans feel toward and engage with the religious realm.

With the sample and main variables of interest established, the next step is to operationalize the theory. Testing the life-cycle theory requires categorizing individuals based on where they are within the life cycle. This becomes tricky quite quickly, as the demarcations between periods of a person's life are fuzzy. The classification of people within life-cycle windows depends on the type of data collected. In some instances, panel data are gathered over many years. When information is collected on the same individuals throughout their adult lives, the analyses can test how their religious involvement changed as they moved from one life stage to another. In other instances, the data are collected over a short period or even at a single point in time. With these data, the analyses focus on two groups: those who are married with children living at home (under 18) and those who are married with grown children (over 18). The former should be in the process of making religious decisions, while the latter should have a relatively internalized religious identity and stable rates of participation. Additional analyses take the age of the children into account when the survey and sample size permit.

Importantly, the analyses focus on individuals who are part of a "traditional family" structure because the sociology of religion literature finds that religious involvement is highest for people who are married and have school-aged children (Argue, Johnson, and White 1999; Schleifer and Chaves 2017; Stolzenberg, Blair-Loy, and Waite 1995). Many religious communities do not condone divorce or having children out of wedlock, so parents of children in these circumstances would not necessarily see the children as an impetus to come back to religion (Schleifer and Chaves 2017; Stolzenberg, Blair-Loy, and Waite 1995; Taylor and Chatters 1988). By looking at married people with children, the analyses focus on those whom sociologists have previously found to be increasing their religious participation. Additionally, family structure may not only be correlated with rates of religious participation but with partisanship as well. If so, variations in family structure—not politics—may be the cause of changes in religious participation. Holding family structure constant rules out this possibility. Finally, and reassuringly, although looking at married respondents with children is most faithful to the sociology literature, classifying respondents simply by parental status produces substantively similar results.

The religious life-cycle model does not have much to say about individuals who make the active choice to forgo having children. The theory is silent, in part, because religiosity is tied to having children in the first place (McQuillan 2004). With that caveat in mind, it is still the overwhelming norm to plan on having children. Newport and Wilke (2013) found that 87% of individuals aged 18 to 40 without children plan to have them in the future.[11] Therefore, while this theory applies only to those who plan to have or have had children, this categorization encompasses most Americans today. The active decision to not have children raises a related concern about selection bias. What if some people are predisposed to have children and return to religion? This is not only a distinct possibility but a likely reality. This selection bias, however, should make it more difficult to find evidence of partisan-induced religious differences between Republicans and Democrats. By focusing on people who selected to have children, we can be confident that the results do not occur because certain types of people are both less likely to be religious and less likely to have children.

An alternative to this life-stage classification would be to categorize individuals based on their ages. This strategy poses both theoretical and empirical problems. From a theoretical standpoint, the religious socialization theory emphasizes that life-cycle transitions are important drivers of religious change. Regardless of whether a person is 30 or 45 when his or her child reaches school age, the parent often makes decisions related to the child's religious upbringing at that point. Age and position in the life cycle are certainly correlated, but they are not interchangeable. Using age also poses an empirical problem as variation in the age that people have children has increased in recent decades. People could easily be miscategorized based on age alone. Chapter 5 offers one example of this. After social issues became politically prominent in early 2004, partisans with children at home diverged in their rates of church attendance. Because the age range of parents is large, however, there is a fair amount of age overlap between parents with young children living at home and parents with older children who are out of the house. It turns out that life-cycle status, and not age, explains over-time changes. Older parents of young children looked virtually identical to their younger counterparts, while parents with grown children look similar to one another regardless of whether they had their children early or late in life.

Having laid out the theory's expectations, categorizations, and limitations, the next chapter offers the first empirical evidence testing the theory.

FOUR

Tracking Religious Trajectories over a Lifetime

The religious and political socialization literatures explore how identities develop and change over the course of a lifetime. Identities do not develop in isolation nor are they immutable. And when taken together, the two socialization processes provide insight into when and how partisanship may influence religious choices. This chapter offers the first empirical tests of the life-cycle theory by looking for individual-level change as partisans transition from one life-stage window to another. Such analyses require data that follow the same people over long periods of time. Two such data sources fit the bill. The first, the Youth-Parent Socialization Panel Study, followed a single cohort from 1965 when respondents were 18 years old until 1997 when they were 50, interviewing cohort members four times over the thirty-two-year period. In the first part of the chapter, these data show that while religious identification and involvement declined in young adulthood, participation rates increased after many from this cohort got married and had children. Religiosity and religious involvement did not increase uniformly across the board, however; Republicans were more likely than Democrats to increase their rates of religious participation.

The second data source is an extension of the 2008 National Annenberg Election Study. The Annenberg study, which interviewed respondents five times over the course of the 2008 presidential election, asked questions about religious identification and involvement once in 2007 at the panel's outset. The Institute for the Study of Citizens and Politics then reinterviewed a random subsample of the initial Annenberg respondents multiple times during subsequent campaigns. In doing so, respondents answered the same questions about religious identification and involvement again in 2014, seven years later. Using these data, the second part of the chapter shows that partisans who had babies in 2007, and therefore had school-aged children in 2014, diverged in both their levels of church attendance and rates of religious identification over time. By 2014, Republican parents had become more likely than Democratic parents to attend church and identify with a religious faith. Although the two data sources differ on a host of dimensions, together they test the life-cycle theory and show when partisanship plays a role in religious decision making. The chapter concludes by discussing how these results change our understanding of recent political history.

The Youth-Parent Socialization Panel Study

The first test draws on panel data from the Youth-Parent Socialization Panel Study (YPSP). The YPSP, initially collected by M. Kent Jennings and Richard Niemi, first interviewed a national sample of high school seniors as well as their parents in 1965. Follow-up surveys in 1973, 1982, and 1997 reinterviewed the same individuals three more times.[1] The data have three features that lend themselves to testing the life-cycle theory presented in the previous chapter. First, the researchers interviewed cohort members at key points in their lives: 18, 26, 35, and 50. At 18, high school seniors live at home. By 1973, however, these same individuals have moved out of their parents' houses and started down the road of adulthood, including higher education for some and full-time employment for many. The 1965 and 1973 survey waves can test the religious socialization theory, which predicts that these young adults should distance themselves from religion during this period. The third wave of data, collected in 1982 when the student generation was 35, allows for a direct test of the life-cycle theory laid out in the previous chapter. As a reminder, the theory predicts that partisanship is most likely to exercise influence on religious decision making as individuals get married and have children. This transition into adulthood had occurred for most in this cohort by the 1982 survey. Finally, the data from 1997 can test whether any evidence of partisan-driven religious change found between 1973 and 1982 was still present fifteen years later when respondents were 50 years old.

A second useful feature of the YPSP data is the survey's timing. Between 1973 and 1982 morality politics became more salient, conservative religious organizations entered politics, politicians began courting religious voters, and the parties became divided along religious and moral lines. In other words, members of the YPSP student generation were making religious decisions during a time when religion and politics had recently become linked in new and different ways. If politics and partisanship can influence religious decisions, this should be when we find the first evidence of this taking place. A third feature of the YPSP data is the extensive sociodemographic

variables available, including information from the parent-generation surveys. These measures serve as control variables that help rule out alternative
explanations derived from the literature. For example, religious upbringing
is an important predictor of adulthood religiosity, but these measures are
not often available on surveys or they rely on adults' retrospective evaluations. Surveying the parent generation therefore provides details about the
students' relevant childhood experiences that may affect both their partisan identities and their religiosities in adulthood. Additionally, data from
the parent generation can address two alternative explanations and bolster
confidence in the main findings. First, the parent-generation data show that
not everyone in the country experienced the same changes in religiosity
found among the student generation. These results comport with the life-
cycle theory's predictions that the parent generation's religious engagement
should remain relatively stable over time, even in the face of a changing political environment. And second, data from the parent generation alleviate
concerns about omitted variables that may correlate with both partisanship
and religiosity, as any omitted variable must affect the student generation
but not the parent generation. Although the data have limits and cannot
rule out every alternative explanation, they are well suited to test how partisanship and religiosity change as individuals transition from one life-cycle
window to another.

1965–1973: The Natural Exodus from Religion

This section traces the student generation's levels of religious involvement
as the students moved from being teenagers living with their parents to being in their twenties living on their own. Between 1965 and 1973, church
attendance declined among the student cohort. More than half (58%) of
respondents reported attending church at a lower rate in 1973 than in 1965,
another 33% reported the same level of attendance, and only 9% reported
an increase in church attendance. Moreover, although only 3% of students
reported that they never attended church in 1965, 21% reported never attending in 1973, and regular church attendance (almost weekly or more)
dropped from 65% in 1965 to 30% in 1973.[2]

Table 4.1 shows the general trend away from religious involvement
among young adults using raw data. The first two columns of table 4.1 report the average rate of attendance at religious services (generally referred
to as "church attendance") for respondents in 1965 and 1973, respectively.
Church attendance ranges between 0 (never attend services) and 1 (attend
services almost every week or more), so that higher numbers indicate more

Table 4.1 1965–1973: Student generation decreased their rates of church attendance

	Church attendance		
	1965	1973	1973–1965
Student sample	0.82	0.51	−0.31
1965 religious identification			
Mainline Protestant	0.74	0.46	−0.28
Evangelical Protestant	0.88	0.60	−0.28
Catholic	0.95	0.50	−0.45
Black Protestant	0.89	0.52	−0.37
1965 parents' church attendance			
Never	0.64	0.44	−0.20
A few times a year	0.65	0.43	−0.21
Once or twice a month	0.85	0.50	−0.35
Almost every week	0.94	0.57	−0.37
1965 region of residence			
Northeast	0.74	0.44	−0.30
Midwest	0.84	0.52	−0.32
West	0.80	0.51	−0.29
South	0.88	0.54	−0.34
1965 educational trajectory			
College preparatory curriculum	0.82	0.52	−0.30
Non-college preparatory curriculum	0.82	0.50	−0.32
1965 partisanship			
Democrat	0.82	0.51	−0.31
Republican	0.83	0.50	−0.33

Source: Youth-Parent Socialization Panel Study.
Note: Cells represent averages. Church attendance ranges between 0 (never attend) and 1 (attend almost every week). N = 1,440.

frequent church attendance. The third column of the table calculates the difference between 1973 and 1965 church attendance. A positive difference indicates that the average rate of church attendance increased between the two waves, while a negative difference indicates that the average reported church attendance decreased. The first row of results corresponds to the full student cohort. Consistent with the sociology literature, church attendance dropped by over 30% of the scale over the eight-year period.[3] Importantly, this trend is not unique to a particular demographic group.

The movement away from religion occurred irrespective of one's religious up-bringing and personal characteristics. Large religious declines occurred among mainline Protestants, evangelical Protestants, Catholics, and black Protestants. Despite different starting positions—for example, Catholics attended religious services more frequently than members of the other religious traditions in 1965—average rates of religiosity declined sharply among all four religious groups. The next set of results presents religious change based on parents' reported church attendance in 1965. Religious attendance of the parent generation is a good proxy for whether the students were raised in religious households. Again, church attendance rates dropped across the board. In fact, the dramatic decrease in church attendance among those raised in the most religious households shrinks the 1965 attendance gap based on religious upbringing. Similarly, there are not large differences based on students' 1965 region of residence or educational trajectory (third and fourth set of results). Although regional variation in religiosity has been widely noted (Newport 2014; Smith et al. 2002; Smith, Sikkink, and Bailey 1998; Stump 1984), coming from a more religious part of the country, such as the South, did not insulate these young adults from becoming less religiously active. Additionally, although early sociologists of religion thought that higher education was a "breeding ground for apostasy" (Caplovitz and Sherrow 1977: 109; Funk and Willits 1987; Hadaway and Roof 1988; Hunter 1983; Sherkat 1998; Wuthnow 1988), there is no difference in the trend away from church between those who did and did not take part in a college preparatory curriculum in 1965.[4]

The bottom of table 4.1 shows that religious decline occurred among Democrats and Republicans alike. Looking at the data in a different way, the top panel of figure 4.1 plots the raw percentage of the student generation who reported attending church almost weekly or weekly in 1965 and 1973, separately for self-identified Republicans and Democrats (measured in 1965). While roughly 67% (64%) of Republicans (Democrats) reported attending church nearly every week in 1965, that percentage plummeted to 30% (29%) in 1973.

Similar trends emerge for religious affiliation and biblical literalism. Whereas only 1.7% of the 1965 student generation reported that they did not belong to any religious denomination or faith (making up twenty-eight students in total), this percentage increased to over 13% in 1973. Here, the comparison is between those who identify with a religious tradition—irrespective of what that tradition is—and religious nonidentifiers. This provides a straightforward measure of whether people categorize themselves as members of religious groups or whether they shed this identity altogether. While there is some variation in rates of disaffiliation based on childhood religious tradition—evangelical Protestants were less likely to disaffiliate than mainline Protestants or Catholics—nonidentification rates increased among each of the major faiths. And similar to the church attendance rates, this decrease is seen among Democrats and Republicans alike. By 1973, 13% of Democrats and 16% of Republicans were religious nonidentifiers.[5] Finally, whereas just under half of the sample (46% Democrats and 43% Republicans) reported believing that the Bible is the word of God in 1965, the percentage dropped to 26% and 29%, respectively, in 1973.[6]

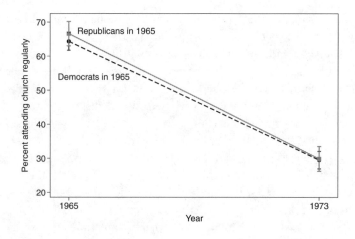

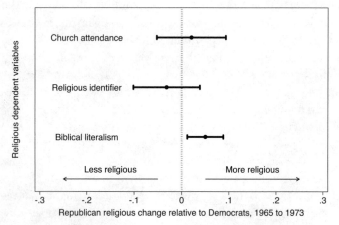

4.1. 1965–1973: Partisanship is uncorrelated with declining levels of religiosity in young adulthood. The top panel presents raw changes in the percentage of regular church attenders over time. The bottom panel presents partisan differences in changing levels of religiosity between 1965 and 1973. Estimates come from change models that include a lagged dependent variable and control variables described in the text. Positive estimates indicate that Republicans became relatively more religious than Democrats between 1965 and 1973. Negative estimates indicate that Democrats became relatively more religious than Republicans between 1965 and 1973. Estimates near zero indicate that neither group became relatively more religious than the other between 1965 and 1973.

Source: Youth-Parent Socialization Panel Study.

The three religiosity variables together illustrate the religious life cycle. On the one hand, the rate of religious disaffiliation is striking, rising from basically zero to more than one in ten. This marks a definitive shift in the less religious direction. On the other hand, the overwhelming majority of this generation retained at least a nominal affiliation with a religious tradition. These results are consistent with existing literature showing that religiosity often declines without a full repudiation of one's religious identity (Smith 2009). These findings also highlight that religious identities have multiple facets. Even among those who remained nominally affiliated with a faith in 1973, the percentage of respondents attending church nearly every week dropped to 32% (down from 66%) and the percentage of biblical literalists dropped from 48% in 1965 to 32% in 1973. All told, young adulthood is a time during which individuals' religious identifications, behaviors, and beliefs change.

In contrast to the general weakening of religious attachments, party affiliation is more stable and there does not seem to be a trend in changing partisan loyalties over the eight-year period. First, whereas one-third of this generation maintained the same level of church attendance between 1965 and 1973, nearly two-thirds had the same partisan affiliation. Second, the changes in church attendance were more marked than changes in partisan identification. For example, more than 50% of regular attenders in 1965 reported attending church a few times a year or less in 1973 whereas only 20% of the student generation flipped from being a Democrat to a Republican or vice versa between survey waves. Third, there was no general trend toward or away from one party or another. Of those individuals whose partisan identities flipped, the Democratic and Republican parties lost and gained members in roughly equal proportions. Additionally, about three-quarters of Independents in 1965 came to identify with a party by 1973, and these one-time Independents headed into the Democratic and Republican camps at the same rate. And fourth, the various religious measures from 1965 are not correlated with changing partisan identifications between 1965 and 1973. Consistent with the political socialization literature, partisanship is relatively stable over time and does not show any systematic shifts between 1965 and 1973. That said, partisan affiliation did change for some. The empirical sections below address this and discuss how changing partisan identities might affect the results presented throughout the chapter.

Corroborating These Results with Formal Tests

Rather than assessing how partisans' religiosities differ at a particular point in time, the panel data allow us to assess how well partisanship—measured years beforehand—corresponds with *changing* religious responses over time.

The top panel of figure 4.1 presents the intuition behind the models. The figure uses the first two waves of data collected in 1965 (when students were 18) and 1973 (when students were 25) and plots church attendance for both years based on party identification from 1965. In the same vein, statistical models can capture whether Democrats and Republicans behaved in similar or different ways over time.

The results presented throughout the chapter come from a series of change models that include a lagged dependent variable while also controlling for individuals' religious and socioeconomic backgrounds.[7] In a traditional regression framework, a coefficient represents the effect that an explanatory variable has on a dependent variable. For example, if a coefficient for an explanatory variable is 2, the correct interpretation is "a one-unit increase in the explanatory variable produces a two-unit increase in the dependent or outcome variable." Including a lagged dependent variable changes the interpretation slightly. When an explanatory variable has a coefficient of 2 in a change model, the correct interpretation is "a one-unit increase in the explanatory variable produces a two-unit change in the dependent variable over time."[8] Though a subtle difference, models that include a lagged dependent variable test whether partisanship is correlated with *changes* in religious responses. A change model can statistically corroborate what we glean from looking at the top panel of figure 4.1: Democrats and Republicans decreased their levels of church attendance at roughly the same rate.

The most obvious benefit of panel data is that reverse causation is less of a concern. Traditional regressions looking at the relationship between religious and political attitudes often use cross-sectional data in which the independent and dependent variables are measured at the same time. This strategy poses an estimation problem if religious variables both affect and are affected by political variables. A main strength of panel data is that variables at time t can predict outcomes at time $t + 1$. Concerns surrounding reverse causation are mitigated as the explanatory variables of interest are measured prior to the outcome variables. Because church attendance comes from the 1973 survey wave while the partisanship measure comes from 1965, the analysis more strongly indicates that partisanship is correlated with a change in church attendance, not the other way around. Although having multiple waves of data has advantages, later sections address the limitations as well as alternative explanations.

Statistical models can also include control variables, which can test whether other factors that are correlated with the explanatory variable of interest (partisanship) actually explain changes to the dependent variable (religious involvement). Panel data, which include measures for the same individuals over time, reduce concerns about alternative explanations and the need for control variables to a certain extent. This is because individuals, along with their personal traits and qualities, are held constant in the models. Therefore, characteristics that make individuals likely to participate in religion or return to religion after a hiatus are less likely to explain the statistical findings. That said, individuals change and the effect that certain traits have on religious participation may also change. Statistical controls that affect both an individual's partisanship and changing religiosity are therefore important to include in the models. First, the models control for student's religious affiliation, region of residence, gender, race, type of high school curriculum (college preparatory track or not), and stated closeness with parents in 1965. Second, measures from the 1973 survey wave control for whether the student had attended college, gotten married, had children, or served in the Vietnam War between 1965 and 1973 as well as controlling for income in 1973. And third, responses from the parent interviews serve as control variables related to how students were brought up. The models include parent responses regarding average church attendance, mother's and father's party identifications, education of the household head, and family income in 1965. These control variables help rule out explanations commonly associated with religious change, including education and social mobility (Newport 1979; Smith 2009), religious upbringing (Carroll and Roof 1993; Myers 1996; Petts 2009; Sharot, Ayalon, and Ben-Rafael 1986; Sherkat 1998), and family dynamics (Myers 1996; Smith 2009; Wilson and Sherkat 1994).[9]

The parametric tests confirm the previously described results. The bottom panel of figure 4.1 shows the relevant graphical results from the change models.[10] The models include binary variables for Republicans and Independents, excluding Democrats as the reference category. This strategy allows for a direct comparison between Republicans and Democrats and does not assume that the relationship between partisanship and changing religiosity is linear. The first result plots the average difference in changing levels of church attendance for Republicans as opposed to Democrats (black circle with solid black 90% confidence interval). A positive point estimate indicates that the church attendance gap between Republicans and Democrats grew between the first and second survey waves, with Republicans becoming more frequent church attenders relative to Democrats. The raw data, however, clearly show that many respondents—Republicans and Democrats alike—stopped attending church frequently. So a positive coefficient would not mean that Republicans became more religious over time, but rather it would indicate that Republicans' church attendance rates declined to a lesser extent than those of Democrats. Negative coefficients indicate the opposite:

Republicans became less frequent church attenders between 1965 and 1973 relative to Democrats. And a coefficient close to zero indicates that Republicans' and Democrats' religious trajectories were similar over time. Whatever gap existed (or did not exist) in 1965 is still present (or absent) in 1973. The null result on the Republican coefficient means that while church attendance declined dramatically between 1965 and 1973 (shown in the top panel of figure 4.1), this decline occurred among Democrats and Republicans to the same extent (0.02; p-value = 0.65).

The subsequent results show a similar story for religious identification and biblical literalism.[11] For consistency, higher numbers correspond to greater levels of religiosity. Religious identifiers, therefore, receive a code of 1 whereas religious nonidentifiers have a code of 0. The coding scheme is the same for distinguishing biblical literalists (1) from those who do not believe the Bible is the literal word of God (0). Even though religious identification rates dropped between 1965 and 1973, the decrease occurred at roughly equal rates for Democrats and Republicans (−0.03; p-value = 0.46). There are some differences, however, when comparing Republicans and Democrats' beliefs about the Bible. Republicans became about 5% more likely to remain biblical literalists than Democrats (p-value = 0.03). Despite this gap, both Republicans and Democrats were less likely to be biblical literalists in 1973 compared to 1965, and there is not a large absolute difference in rates of biblical literalism in 1973 (26% versus 29%).

This biblical literalism gap likely occurs because literalist beliefs are more closely tied with certain religious traditions than others, and members adhering to different religious traditions make up different percentages of the parties. Mainline Protestants were less likely to be biblical literalists in 1965 (34%) compared to Catholics (44%) and evangelical Protestants (66%). So, while mainline Protestants were less likely to be biblical literalists in 1973 than 1965, the decline was less steep among mainline Protestants given their lower starting position.[12] Mainline Protestants were also disproportionately Republicans in 1965, making up nearly half of the Republican subsample but just over a quarter of the Democratic subsample. Mainline Protestants therefore had relatively low rates of literalism in 1965 and correspondingly smaller changes in beliefs while also being disproportionately represented in the Republican Party.[13] Importantly, however, rates of biblical literalism declined among all major religious traditions and there are no partisan differences in biblical beliefs within religious traditions. Republican and Democratic Catholics decreased their rates of biblical literalism at roughly the same rate, as did Republican and Democratic evangelical Protestants and Republican and Democratic mainline Protestants.[14]

   While these results support the religious socialization theory claiming that religious attachments weaken in young adulthood, they do not rule out the possibility that religiosity declined across all age groups in the United States. As discussed in chapter 2, societal values changed dramatically during the 1960s on issues related to sex, drugs, alternative lifestyles, civil rights, and war. It is possible that the previous results are not indicative of a life-cycle explanation of young adults pulling away from religion but rather an example of Americans generally moving away from religion in response to broader changes in American culture.

   The parent data can address this possibility. As a brief reminder, the average church attendance score among the student generation was 0.82 in 1965 and 0.51 in 1973 (on a 0–1 scale) and regular attendance dropped from 65% in 1965 to 30% in 1973. In contrast, the average attendance score for the parent generation declined from 0.70 in 1965 to 0.68 in 1973, and whereas 51% of the parent generation attended church regularly in 1965, 49% reportedly did so in 1973. Religious identification rates also remained relatively stable, with 1.7% and 3% of the parent generation not identifying with a religious faith in 1965 and 1973, respectively. And finally, whereas 50% of the parent generation believed the Bible was the literal word of God in 1965, 47% reported believing this in 1973. Consistent with the sociological literature on religion, the religious involvement, identification, and beliefs of the parent generation remained relatively stable over time, particularly when compared to their children.[15]

   These data demonstrate a broadly global trend: young adults decreased their levels of religious involvement and commitment after graduating from high school and leaving home. This shift occurred among young partisans of all stripes, whereas their parents' levels of religiosity remained stable over time even in the wake of a cultural upheaval. The next section explores what happens as this cohort moves from their twenties into their thirties.

1973–1982: For Some, a Return to the Religious Fold

Members of the student cohort were approximately 35 years old during the third data-collection effort. By 1982, most of this cohort had completed their education, married, had children, and settled into a community. Cohort members were therefore making decisions about their religious involvement between the second and third waves of the panel. Prior to their making these religious decisions, however, many individuals' partisan identities had solidified through exposure to and participation in the political sphere. It is at this point—when partisan identities are stable and people are making decisions about religious involvement—that partisanship is most likely to be associated with changing levels of religiosity. For partisanship to influence religious choices, however, people must perceive an association between the political parties and organized religion. If the parties do not differ in their relationships with religious constituencies and religious political groups or if the parties take similar positions on policies linked to religious values, citizens cannot draw on their partisan identities when making decisions about religiosity and religious involvement. As it turns out, the political landscape began shifting in the 1970s, and both political elites and the parties themselves began separating on important religious questions. The large-scale shifts in official party positions, campaign rhetoric, and the salience of moral issues that took place in the 1970s and 1980s mark the first instance in which the parties became known for being on opposing sides of the religious and cultural aisles.

By the third wave of the panel, collected in 1982, seculars and nonreligious people had become prominent within the Democratic Party and the party had taken liberal positions on cultural issues. On the other hand, conservative Christian leaders had a visible role in the Republican Party, and Republican politicians espoused culturally conservative policy positions (Guth 1983; Guth et al. 1997; Kaylor 2011; Layman 2001; Shupe and Stacey 1983). If partisanship can influence religious decisions, it is against the backdrop of the 1970s and 1980s when this relationship might have first taken form.[16] Based on the life-cycle theory presented in chapter 3, the changing religious-political landscape that occurred between 1973 and 1982 should have affected Republicans and Democrats of the student cohort differently. While both Republicans and Democrats became less religious in young adulthood, Republicans should have been more likely to return to religion between 1973 and 1982 relative to Democrats.

Members of the high school class of 1965 represent one of the first cohorts who were "becoming adults"—that is, getting married and having children—in this new political environment. Religion and politics were not linked in this way while they were growing up. The students' parents may have been devout Democrats or less religious Republicans. The YPSP generation therefore is the first group whose members, as newly formed adults, may have experienced a tension between their political affiliations and religious upbringings.

Testing Whether Partisanship Is Related to Religious Decision Making

The 1973–1982 analyses take a similar approach to the previous ones. Church attendance, religious identification, and biblical literalism again serve as dependent variables. The YPSP also asked an additional religious participation question in both 1973 and 1982. The survey asked whether respondents were involved in "church-connected groups, like a church men's club or ladies' society." The yes (1) or no (0) coding offers another measure of church involvement. As scholars have found that small-group membership within the church is important for developing civic skills, political recruitment, and discussing politics informally (Djupe and Gilbert 2009, 2006), understanding whether partisanship influences small-group participation is particularly consequential for politics. The empirical strategy, just as before, first looks at the raw data—in order to avoid making any modeling assumptions—and then uses change models that include statistical controls. Here, the change models assess how partisanship, measured in 1973, is related to changing levels of religious involvement between 1973 and 1982.

The models also control for demographic characteristics, including the student generation's region of residence, education, income, marital and parental status, gender, race, and service in Vietnam—all measured in 1973—as well as religious affiliation, church attendance, and high school curriculum (meaning whether students took college preparatory classes) from 1965. The demographic controls account for baseline differences across the students that may correlate with partisanship and changes in religiosity. For example, controlling for religious affiliation takes into account that certain religious traditions may emphasize specific behaviors or beliefs more than others (Mockabee, Monson, and Grant 2001). If, for example, people raised as evangelical Protestants came back to church at a higher rate than those in other religious traditions and were also disproportionately Republican, we might misattribute evangelicals' greater tendency to return to religion as evidence of the effect of politics.[17] Additionally, a variable from 1973 measuring how close students feel to their parents helps rule out the possibility that parent-child relationships affect both the development of partisan identities and religious decisions in adulthood (Myers 1996; Wilson and Sherkat 1994). The models also include the same parent-level control variables from the 1965–1973 analyses and also incorporate students' attitudes on important policy issues of the day.[18] Including respondents' opinions about the Vietnam War, school busing, marijuana legalization, government aid to minorities, equal rights for women, and economic liberalism (all measured in 1973) helps stave off concerns that the real culprits behind religious change were the great social upheaval and changes to broader societal attitudes that took place during the 1960s and 1970s (Sherkat and Blocker 1997).[19] Parametric results both with and without various controls are in the appendix.

One final concern with the panel approach is that both partisanship and religiosity may change over time. Major events such as war or political scandal, both of which occurred between 1973 and 1982, could influence partisan identities (Dinas 2014, 2013). Even though the literature notes that partisanship is quite stable, even over long periods of time and in the wake of political turmoil (Green, Palmquist, and Schickler 2002), partisanship is not permanently fixed. Although a valid critique, the use of time lags is more likely to mask an effect than exaggerate one. For example, a non-church-attending Democrat in 1973 might become a frequently attending Republican by 1982. In this case, it is impossible to say whether partisanship affected church attendance, church attendance affected partisanship, or a third variable affected both partisanship and church attendance at the same time. Instead, the data will show a Democrat in 1973 becoming a more frequent church attender between 1973 and 1982, which goes against the theoretical expectation. In other words, changes to partisanship over time make it harder to detect a relationship. Finding evidence that partisanship affects church attendance despite this methodological obstacle, rather than because of it, should increase our confidence in the results.

Two additional checks of robustness can further ameliorate concerns about the time lag problem. First, replicating the results using a restricted sample of respondents whose partisanship remained the same across the two survey waves produces comparable findings. Although the resultant sample is no longer representative of the high school class of 1965, changing partisanship between the two survey waves is no longer a concern. Second, using previous measures of partisanship (X_{t-1}) as an instrument for the present-day partisanship (X_t) also produces statistically and substantively similar results. This model specification, however, raises concerns about the exclusion restriction, as 1973 partisanship could affect 1982 church attendance indirectly and not solely through 1982 partisanship. Although neither strategy is perfect, these alternative specifications produce results very similar to the main findings presented in the chapter, offering some assurances that the main findings are, in fact, capturing partisanship's effect on changing religiosity. The appendix presents the results using these alternative specifications.

Partisan-Driven Religious Changes Take Place between 1973 and 1982

The top panel of figure 4.2 presents the raw changes in church attendance between 1973 and 1982 separately for Democrats and Republicans. If Democrats and Republicans "returned" to church at the same rate, the lines that connect the points would have the same slope. But this is not

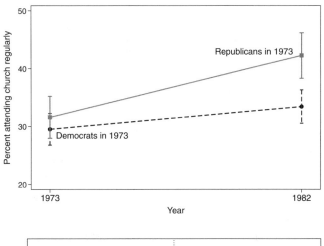

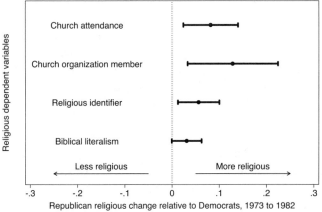

4.2. 1973–1982: Partisanship is correlated with religious decisions upon reaching adulthood. The top panel presents raw changes in the percentage of regular church attenders over time. The bottom panel presents partisan differences in changing levels of religiosity between 1973 and 1982. Estimates come from change models that include a lagged dependent variable and control variables described in the text. Positive estimates indicate that Republicans became relatively more religious than Democrats between 1973 and 1982. Negative estimates indicate that Democrats became relatively more religious than Republicans between 1973 and 1982. Estimates near zero indicate that neither group became relatively more religious than the other between 1973 and 1982.
Source: Youth-Parent Socialization Panel Study.

the case. Despite the similar appearance of Democrats and Republicans in 1973 (30% of Democrats and 32% of Republicans), the Republican slope is steeper than the Democratic slope. By 1982, 42% of Republicans reported regularly attending church compared to 33% of Democrats. While the overall increase is consistent with the religious socialization process, the magnitude of the increase is not the same for Democrats and Republicans. Republicans were more likely to become regular attenders between 1973 and 1982 relative to Democrats. While there was no church attendance gap between Democrats and Republicans in 1973, a 7% gap emerged by 1982 in the raw data.[20] The bottom panel of figure 4.2 presents the results from the change models. Just as before, the coefficients represent the changes over time among Republicans relative to Democrats, with partisanship measured in 1973. A model that includes control variables corroborates the raw results; Republicans "returned" to the pews to a greater extent than Democrats (0.08; p-value = 0.02).

Two comparisons provide necessary context for interpreting this eight-point change between Republicans and Democrats. First, religious upbringing is an important predictor of religiosity in adulthood (Chaves 1991; Wilson and Sherkat 1994), and church attendance among the parent generation in 1965 serves as a good proxy for the religious environment in which students were raised. The four-point response scale options for church attendance include never, a few times a year, once or twice a month, or almost every week or more. Members of the student generation who were raised in households where the parents were regular churchgoers were the most likely to increase their church attendance between 1973 and 1982. Those raised in churchgoing households shifted 0.13 on the church attendance scale compared to those raised in homes where the parents did not attend church (p-value = 0.05), 0.07 compared to those raised in homes where the parents attended a few times per year (p-value = 0.09), and 0.08 compared to those who were raised in homes where the parents attended once or twice a month (p-value < 0.01). These results corroborate what we already know; those raised in religious households are more likely to be religious themselves when they become adults. And while it is not surprising that the partisan gap is smaller than the gap between people raised in the least versus most religious households (0.13 religious upbringing gap versus 0.08 partisan gap), the relative magnitude highlights the strength of partisan identity. Moreover, that the partisan gap is roughly equal to the gap between students raised in not-very-religious households (attend services a few times a year) or somewhat religious households (attend once or twice a month) and those raised in homes where their parents attended church regularly (0.07 and 0.08, respectively) offers further evidence that partisanship's relationship with decisions associated with church attendance is substantively meaningful.[21]

A second way to contextualize the relationship between partisanship and changing levels of religiosity is to look at partisanship's relationship with another changing attitude. The YPSP asked students about their views on economic policy in both 1973 and 1982 using a common question about whether the government should provide a job and good standard of living or whether people should get ahead on their own. While this question measures attitudes related to economic liberalism, a key feature that distinguishes the Democratic and Republican parties, there was no correlation between party identification and this view in 1973. A correlation, however, emerged by 1982: Republicans were more likely to hold the view that people should get ahead on their own while Democrats were more likely to report that the government should ensure that people have a job and good standard of living.[22] Moreover, this relationship came about because respondents changed their economic policy preferences to match their 1973 partisanship rather than changing their partisan affiliations based on their 1973 policy views. In a basic change model in which economic policy preference in 1982 is the dependent variable and partisanship and economic policy preference from 1973 are the independent variables, Republicans became 0.15 more economically conservative than Democrats on a 0–1 scale (p-value < 0.01). Even in a model that includes the extensive list of demographic, background, and attitudinal control variables, a partisan gap of 0.10 (p-value < 0.01) appears between Republicans and Democrats.[23] These results not only comport with research demonstrating that partisanship is a powerful determinant of politically relevant attitudes and behaviors (e.g., Bartels 2006; Huddy, Mason, and Aarøe 2015; Lenz 2012; Levendusky 2009), but they also show that partisanship's relationship with changing levels of religiosity is substantively meaningful by comparison.

The second measure of a person's participation within a religious community comes from the question asking about participation in a smaller group or organization within a person's church. Although about 45% of the student generation attended church with some frequency in 1973, only 18% were members of a church group in 1973. And even among those who reported attending church weekly or more, less than half responded that they are part of a church group (48%).[24] By 1982, however, roughly 30% of the student generation reported being a member of a church group, representing a 66% increase in membership rates across the two survey waves. Similar to the church attendance rates, however, Republicans were more likely to become group members relative to Democrats. In the raw data, Democrats' participation in these groups increased by about 10 percentage points between the two waves, while Republican membership increased by roughly 18 percentage points. This eight-point difference found in the raw data is slightly smaller than the full parametric model that includes control variables, which finds that the probability of becoming a group member is 0.12 higher for Republicans than for Democrats (p-value = 0.03). The second estimate in the bottom panel of figure 4.2 represents this result. And just as with the church attendance result, the magnitude of the effect becomes substantively meaningful when it is compared to the relationship between religious upbringing and joining a church group. The partisan gap in church-group membership is more than half the size of the church-group gap that emerges between those raised in households where the parents attended church frequently and those raised in households where the parents never attended church (0.20; p-value = 0.04) and about the same size of the gap between those raised in households where the parents attended church frequently and those raised in households where the parents attended infrequently (0.10; p-value = 0.11) or somewhat frequently (0.07; p-value = 0.27).

The next result looks at religious identification, or willingness to identify with a religious faith rather than identify explicitly as nothing. Republicans and Democrats were similarly likely to disaffiliate between 1965 and 1973. Although less than 2% of 18-year-olds claimed to have no religious affiliation in 1965, this number jumped to 13% in 1973. This is not surprising, as nonidentification rates are routinely higher among young adults than other age groups (Smith 2009). While religious identification and religious behavior are no doubt correlated, nominal identification with a religious faith often persists even in the absence of engaging in traditional behaviors. For example, while 56% of the survey's 25-year-olds rarely attended church in 1973 (measured by reportedly attending a few times per year or never), only 17% of these respondents were religious nonidentifiers. Although there was no partisan component in the disaffiliation process between 1965 and 1973, partisanship played a role in the decision to reaffiliate. Religious identification rates increased between 1973 and 1982, and Republicans were approximately 5% (p-value = 0.04) more likely to reaffiliate relative to Democrats over the time. In addition to denominational differences between Republicans and Democrats, there is now a general identification gap as well. And finally, the biblical literalism measure shows a similar, albeit smaller, response pattern: Republicans compared to Democrats became about 3% more likely to believe that the Bible is the actual word of God during this time period (p-value = 0.10). The smaller partisan change reflects the relatively stable nature of biblical literalism rates over time. Whereas

27% reported believing the Bible was the word of God in 1973, 31% did so in 1982. Despite people's returning to church and joining church organizations, views about the inerrancy of the Bible remained comparatively static over the nine-year period.[25] And here, unlike the other measures of religious involvement, religious upbringing is much more strongly related to biblical literalism in adulthood relative to partisanship. Individuals raised in households where the parents went to church regularly were much more likely to become biblical literalists relative to those raised in households where the parents never attended church (0.15; p-value = 0.08). Partisanship has a weaker relationship with changing views about the Bible relative to other, more outward, measures of religious identity.

The results presented above do not occur solely because of non-identification. It is reasonable to assume that religious nonidentifiers—who are much less likely than nominal affiliates to attend church, be part of a church organization, or believe the Bible is the word of God—explain the overarching findings. If Republicans became relatively more likely to identify with a religious faith between 1973 and 1982, then it is possible that the other gaps appear because there are fewer nonidentifiers in the Republican Party. This does not seem to be the case, however, as similar partisan gaps are present in analyses that include only religious identifiers in 1973. Even among partisans who retained their nominal religious affiliations, Republicans became more religiously involved than Democrats.

Moreover, one religious denomination does not account for the results. While other work has focused on evangelical Protestants as a group ripe for having partisanship influence religious decision making (Djupe, Neiheisel, and Sokhey, forthcoming; Patrikios 2008), the evidence suggests that similar changes are taking place—to varying degrees—among Catholics, evangelical Protestants, and mainline Protestants. This trend appears even on the biblical literalism measure, which is a belief more closely tied to evangelical traditions (Mockabee, Monson, and Grant 2001). Partisanship explains some of variation in biblical views among Catholics and mainline Protestants despite the overall lower rates of biblical literalism among these groups. Although smaller sample sizes that result from looking at religious groups separately make the findings suggestive rather than definitive, they point to a political explanation for changes in religious participation across multiple religious faiths.

Taking the 1973–1982 results together, religious participation and identification increased between the 1973 and 1982 survey waves. Individuals became more involved in organized religious life as they married and had children, corroborating findings from the religious socialization literature. The changes, however, were not the same for Democrats and Republicans.

Republicans were more likely than Democrats to report reengaging in the religious world. These results are striking in light of the political landscape. The relationship between religious and political elites had just started to form, and it was unclear how enduring these bonds would be. And yet, meaningful differences in partisans' identification with and involvement in organized religion appear.

The results also bring to light an important distinction between the social and personal dimensions associated with religious identities. Partisanship's influence on religious decision making is most evident in analyses that use religiosity measures that conceive of religion as a social identity, including participating in a religious community and self-categorizing as a group member. Personal beliefs about the Bible, by contrast, remain relatively stable between 1973 and 1982, and partisanship has only a weak association with changing biblical beliefs. Looking at the four dependent variables together, partisanship—a social identity—has a stronger influence on the social, as opposed to the personal, aspects of religion.

The trends among political Independents are also worth discussing, particularly given the attention scholars have paid to Independents in this generation. The social upheaval of the 1960s produced an increase in political independence, leading some scholars to say that the era of political parties had come to an end (Wattenberg 1986). There has been debate about whether this statement is true or overblown. Nearly half—48%—of this cohort reported not identifying as either a Republican or Democrat, indicating a great deal of political independence. After a follow-up question, however, four out of five of those Independents reported feeling closer to one party over another. Despite cohort members' initial reluctance to identify with a party, many self-reported Independents still retain partisan loyalties.

Partisan leaners—that is, those who initially report being politically independent but lean toward one of the parties—look virtually indistinguishable from those who readily identify as partisans in the data. The gap that emerges between partisan identifiers that excludes partisan leaners and the gap that emerges between partisan leaners look very similar. While analyses looking exclusively at partisan leaners produce more uncertainty around the point estimates due to the smaller sample size, the substantive result is the same: Republicans (and Republican leaners) became more religious over time relative to Democrats (and Democratic leaners). These results are consistent with Keith et al.'s (1992) findings that partisan leaners often behave like partisans. These findings additionally point out that religious sorting is not reserved for the strongest partisans but can also occur among weak partisans and partisan leaners.

What about pure Independents, those 20% who do not identify with either party? The life-cycle theory does not offer a concrete expectation for these individuals, and the small number of pure Independents makes it difficult to provide a definitive answer; however, two empirical results are noteworthy. First, Independents were less religious, across the board, than both Democrats and Republicans before religion became salient in the political sphere. Thinking about political parties and religious institutions as two groups that people can join makes it unsurprising that political Independents are also more religiously independent. These individuals may simply not be joiners. Second, Independents' religious trajectories between 1973 and 1982 are distinct from those of both Democrats and Republicans. While Independents returned to church at a slightly higher rate than Democrats, they look similar to Democrats with respect to their changes in religious identification, biblical literalism, and membership in a church organization.[26] What explains Independents' religious choices is not clear from the data, but given their lower levels of religiosity in 1973, the answer may not be political.

Having shown that partisanship from 1973 is correlated with changing levels of religiosity between 1973 and 1982 among the student generation, the next sections ask and answer a series of questions that further test the life-cycle theory and shed additional light on partisanship's relationship with religious decision making.

Further Tests of the Life-Cycle Theory

An underpinning of the life-cycle theory is that partisanship is able to influence religious decisions at a certain period in people's lives because individuals' partisan identities have solidified and are stable while they are still sorting out where they fit into the religious sphere. This explanation generates two additional testable expectations. First, within a certain period in the life cycle, partisanship should be a driver of religious involvement and not the other way around. And second, older individuals should have more stable religious attachments that are less open to outside influence.

What about Religion Affecting Politics?

While the data show that members of the student generation made religious choices consistent with their preexisting partisan identities between 1973 and 1982, it is also possible that church attendance affected political attitudes during this time. If religiosity influenced political decisions between 1973 and 1982, then the life-cycle theory would be incomplete. A reciprocal

86 / Chapter Four

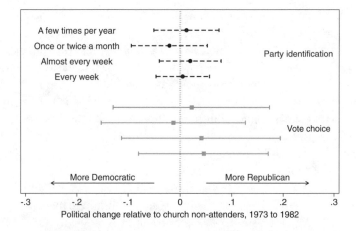

4.3. 1973–1982: Church attendance is unrelated to changing partisan attachments. The figure presents changes in seven-point party identification (black circles) and vote choice (gray squares) between 1973 and 1982 based on church attendance in 1973. The coefficients represent the difference between each level of church attendance and nonattenders, who serve as the reference category. Estimates come from change models that include a lagged dependent variable and control variables described in the text. Positive estimates indicate that people with a given level of church attendance became relatively more Republican or more likely to support a Republican presidential candidate relative to nonattenders. Negative estimates indicate that people with a given level of church attendance became relatively less Republican or less likely to support a Republican presidential candidate relative to nonattenders. Estimates near zero indicate that neither group became more Republican or more likely to support a Republican presidential candidate than the other.
Source: Youth-Parent Socialization Panel Study.

relationship, in which partisanship both affects and is affected by religiosity, would be a more appropriate categorization.

Figure 4.3 tests this possibility using two measures of political change. The top part of the figure presents the results of a model testing how individuals' 1973 church attendance correlates with changes in seven-point party identification between 1973 and 1982, ranging between 0 (strong Democrat) and 1 (strong Republican). Similar to the previous analyses, the model includes lagged partisanship and sociodemographic control variables.[27] The main independent variable of interest is church attendance in 1973, which appears in the model as a series of binary variables with "never attend" serving as the reference category. While partisanship is correlated with changes in church attendance between 1973 and 1982, the reverse is not the case. And because partisanship is a strong identity that is difficult to move, the bottom portion of figure 4.3 replicates the results looking at whether church attendance is correlated with changes in the likelihood of voting for the Republican candidate between the 1972 and 1980 presidential elections (measured in 1973 and 1982, respectively). Here again, church attendance is not correlated with changing political support between 1973 and 1982.

These findings hold even when the model specifications increase the likelihood of finding an effect. First, analyses that look only at individuals whose church attendance did not change between 1965 and 1973 produce the same results. If there is anyone for whom religiosity should affect political variables, it would be those whose levels of religious commitment did not wane during a time when most members of this cohort experienced a decrease in religiosity. Yet even within this subsample, there is no evidence that church attendance influenced politics during this time. Second, the influence of church attendance may differ across religious families, giving rise to the overall null results. Of the three traditions that are large enough to look at individually—Catholics, mainline Protestants, and evangelical Protestants—church attendance does not correspond to changes in partisanship or vote choice between 1973 and 1982.[28] While partisanship affected religious decision making among the student generation, religious involvement appears uncorrelated with political decisions.

Is This Happening to Everyone?

The main results are consistent with the life-cycle theory; partisanship affects religion at a particular point in people's lives. These results, however, do not rule out the alternative explanation that partisans of all generations underwent the same changes between 1973 and 1982. If people of all cohorts updated their religious attachments and practices to be consistent with their preexisting partisan identities, then the argument that there is a specific life stage when politics can influence religious choices would be wrong. Instead, a more appropriate interpretation would be that politics is always a potential driver of religious change. Fortunately, the parent generation was also interviewed in 1965, 1973, and 1982, making it possible to test whether this is the case.

Figure 4.4 replicates the main results using only data from the parent generation. The control variables are slightly different from those used with the student data, but the intuition about what we want to take into account remains the same. The models include controls for region of residence, gender, education, household income, marital status, religious identification, and policy attitudes. The only major difference between the models using the parent and the student data is that there are no measures of the parents' upbringings. In contrast to the student cohort results in which Republicans and Democrats diverged over time, there is no such divergence among the

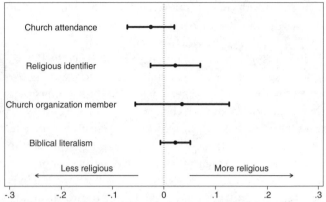

Republican religious change relative to Democrats (parent generation), 1973 to 1982

4.4. 1973–1982: Partisans in the parent generation have stable religious attachments. The figure presents partisan differences in changing levels of religiosity between 1973 and 1982 among respondents in the parent generation. Estimates come from change models that include a lagged dependent variable and control variables described in the text. Positive estimates indicate that Republicans became relatively more religious than Democrats between 1973 and 1982. Negative estimates indicate that Democrats became relatively more religious than Republicans between 1973 and 1982. Estimates near zero indicate that neither group became relatively more religious than the other between 1973 and 1982. *Source*: Youth-Parent Socialization Panel Study (parent generation).

parent generation. The results in figure 4.4 corroborate the raw data that show that religiosity remained stable among both Democrats and Republicans in the parent generation and reduce concerns that everyone experienced partisan-driven religious change.

1973–1997: Does This Religiosity Gap Remain?

What are the long-term consequences of the main findings presented above? Perhaps Democrats are simply a bit slower in their return to religion, but they eventually catch up. In this case, the partisan-produced religious gap would be merely a temporary difference between Democrats and Republicans that closes over time. The gap that appears at this critical juncture, it turns out, remains for many years to come. By 1997, Democrats' religiosities had not "caught up" with Republicans. On all four religious measures, Republicans—as measured in 1973—were reporting that they were more religious than their Democratic counterparts in 1997. While the partisan-driven gap that emerged between 1973 and 1982 narrowed on church organization membership, Democrats did not wholly close the gap, and the religious gap on church attendance and identification remained completely intact fifteen years later when respondents from this cohort reached middle age.

Alternative Explanations

The results have thus far provided evidence in support of the life-cycle theory. Evidence in support of a theory, however, does not rule out alternative explanations. This section presents and discusses a series of plausible explanations that, if true, would undermine the life-cycle theory and main empirical findings.

Is This Only a Religious Thing?

The religious socialization theory, which finds that getting married and having children serve as an important impetus for increased religious involvement, is specific to religious participation. But perhaps Republicans and Democrats began to differ on all sorts of civic and political engagement measures. What would it mean if Republicans simply are joiners while Democrats choose to be less involved? If this were the case, the evidence above would not support a religious life-cycle theory but rather a broader life-cycle trend of societal engagement. A series of questions asking about political and civic participation serve as placebo tests to rule out this explanation. Figure 4.5 plots changes in Republicans' behaviors relative to Democrats between 1973 and 1982. The top two points measure political participation. Presidential turnout measures change in a partisan's propensity to vote between 1973 and 1982. For both Democrats and Republicans, individuals became more likely to vote over time. While only 8% of respondents who reported voting in the 1972 election (measured in 1973) reportedly did not vote in the 1980 election (measured in 1982), 27% of nonvoters in the 1972 election reported voting in the 1980 presidential election. Despite the general increase in participation, there is no partisan element to the change over time. The second estimate measures whether individuals contacted an elected official to express an opinion. The 1973 version asks whether the respondent had ever contacted an elected official, while the 1982 version asks whether the respondent had contacted an elected official any time since 1973. Again, the partisan difference is right around zero, indicating that Republican and Democratic behaviors did not change in different ways over time.

The bottom six measures look at other forms of civic and social involvement. Similar to the question that asked whether respondents were members of a church organization, the survey also asked about membership in fraternal organizations (such as Elks or Knights of Columbus), informal

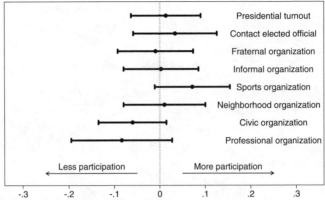

Republican change in secular participation relative to Democrats, 1973 to 1982

4.5. 1973–1982: Partisans do not diverge in nonreligious societal participation. The figure presents partisan differences in changing levels of secular participation between 1973 and 1982. Estimates come from change models that include a lagged dependent variable and control variables described in the text. Positive coefficients indicate that Republicans became relatively more involved than Democrats between 1973 and 1982. Negative coefficients indicate that Democrats became relatively more involved than Republicans between 1973 and 1982. Coefficients near zero indicate that neither group became relatively more involved than the other between 1973 and 1982.
Source: Youth-Parent Socialization Panel Study.

social groups (such as sewing circles, poker clubs, or bridge clubs), sports organizations, civic organizations (such as Rotary), and professional groups. Whereas Republicans were more likely than Democrats to join a church group between 1973 and 1982, they were not more likely to join any other sort of group.[29] These results together assuage concerns that Republicans are simply joiners or became more participatory in all aspects of societal life during this time period.

Is This Occurring Because of the South?

Another set of tests explores whether respondents living in the South differ from the rest of the sample and how the main results look for southerners and nonsoutherners separately. During the 1970s and 1980s, the solidly Democratic South was beginning to shift toward the Republican Party. In particular, these shifting partisan allegiances at the aggregate level are most prominent among white southerners. If young, white southerners were disproportionately likely to become Republican and more likely to return to religion after a hiatus, then southerners would drive the main findings. The data do not support this explanation.

First, southerners were no more likely than nonsoutherners to become Republicans between 1965 and 1973. Southerners have, and continue to be, more religious than the rest of the country. Consequently, if these white southerners moved from the Democratic to the Republican Party and are more likely to be religious, this could explain the main results. This, however, does not seem to be the case as there was not a wholesale shift to the Republican Party among white southerners between 1965 and 1973. Although Republican identification increased from 23% to 29% between the first two survey waves among white students who lived in the South in both 1965 and 1973, just under 55% of white respondents living in the South identified as Democrats in 1973. Moreover, southerners were no more likely to become Republicans between 1965 and 1973 than individuals living in other parts of the country.[30]

Second, the religious trajectories of southerners did not differ from those of people living in the rest of the country. Southerners, compared to nonsoutherners, were no more likely to fall away from religion between 1965 and 1973 and were no more likely to return between 1973 and 1982.[31] Southerners and nonsoutherners looked quite similar both in their likelihood of becoming Republicans by 1973 and in their likelihood of returning to religion between 1973 and 1982. And finally, the main results look similar after dropping southerners from the analysis; nonsouthern Republicans and Democrats diverged in their religious behaviors, identifications, and beliefs between 1973 and 1982 (results in the appendix).

Is It All in the Genes?

Researchers have documented the genetic underpinnings of both religious and political behaviors and attitudes (Alford, Funk, and Hibbing 2005; Friesen and Ksiazkiewicz 2015; Hatemi et al. 2009a; Kendler and Myers 2009; Koenig et al. 2005; Settle, Dawes, and Fowler 2009; Vance, Maes, and Kendler 2010), raising the question of whether certain people are predestined to be both Republicans (Democrats) and (not) religious.[32] If this is indeed the case, a shared genetic path may explain what seems to be evidence of partisan-driven religious change as young adults enter adulthood. In fact, given that genetic influences on social behaviors and attitudes are often stronger once people leave home (Hatemi et al. 2009b; Hatemi and McDermott 2012; Kendler and Myers 2009), genetics offer a straightforward explanation for why certain people return to the pews at a higher rate than others.

In assessing the potential for a genetic explanation, it is worth discussing a relevant debate in the literature regarding genetics and party identification. While scholars have noted genetic influences on policy attitudes (Alford, Funk, and Hibbing 2005) and ideology (Hatemi et al. 2010; Smith et al. 2011), the evidence is mixed on party identification. Both Hatemi et al. (2009a) and Settle, Dawes, and Fowler (2009) find little evidence that genes play a role in party identification using data from the 1980s and mid-2000s, respectively. Settle, Dawes, and Fowler (2009) explain that party identification represents an attachment to a group whose principles may change over time, making it an unlikely object of genetic influence.[33] Fazekas and Littvay (2015), on the other hand, find a genetic component to party identification using data from 2008. Fazekas and Littvay argue that the more recent politically sorted landscape—one in which liberals are overwhelmingly Democrats and conservatives are quite likely to be Republicans—allows for the genetic component of partisanship to be expressed. Fazekas and Littvay (2015) therefore respond to Settle, Dawes, and Fowler's (2009) claim that the parties' changing positions are what make it unlikely that there would be a genetic predisposition toward a party; they argue that it is precisely these changing contexts that allow genes to be expressed under certain circumstances.

The YPSP data are well suited to rule out a genetic explanation due to the timing of the data collection. Setting aside whether there is or is not a genetic component to partisanship, it does not seem likely that this party gene would have been expressed in 1973. The parties did not differ as dramatically as today, nor were voters well sorted (Levendusky 2009). Therefore, the political landscape does not meet Fazekas and Littvay's (2015) criteria of when the party gene would be expressed. Additionally, if genetics came to play a role in party identification between 1973 and 1982, it would be more difficult to find evidence of partisan-driven religious change. This is for the same reason described earlier in the chapter. Imagine that the changing political environment activated a shared political and religious genetic path (see Friesen and Ksiazkiewicz 2015) and encouraged some Democrats to become Republicans and to become more religious. These individuals, however, appear in the data as Democrats becoming more religious, which goes against the theoretical expectations coming from the life cycle.

Does Some Other Unobserved Variable Explain These Findings?

Omitted variables pose a constant threat when trying to make inferences using observational data. While the structure of panel data and extensive control variables rule out many alternative explanations, it is easy to conjure up omitted variables that may explain the findings. By way of an example, imagine that extraverted people are more likely to be both Republicans and religious. The personality trait of extraversion would therefore be an omitted variable, and the findings that had previously been attributed to partisanship would have actually come about because the extraversion trait affected both partisanship and religiosity.

The dynamic component of the life-cycle theory, however, makes this possibility less likely. As a reminder, the life-cycle theory produces different expectations for individuals at different points within the life cycle, and the data support these expectations. First, partisanship is not correlated with changing levels of religiosity as individuals move from adolescence into young adulthood. Second, partisanship is correlated with changing levels of religiosity as individuals move from young adulthood into adulthood. And third, partisanship is not correlated with changes in religiosity once individuals are squarely in adulthood. Given the theoretical expectations from the life-cycle theory and the corresponding empirical findings, not only must the omitted variable be correlated with partisanship and changing religiosity over time, but the omitted variable's relationship with partisanship and changing religiosity must also vary systematically based on position within the life cycle. Returning to the extraversion example, this omitted variable must be positively correlated with Republican partisanship and increasing levels of religiosity at a certain point in a person's life, but not at others.

One omitted variable whose relationship to partisanship and religiosity may give rise to results that are consistent with the life-cycle theory's predictions is the norms and expectations of different religious communities. Members of certain strict religious denominations may become very involved in their religious communities because their denominations require it. In other words, people's social networks and communities may push them to be more religiously involved. If members of strict religious denominations are also Republicans, the relationship between partisanship and changing religiosity may actually be the result of different participation expectations that manifest during this period within the life cycle. Controlling for religious tradition in the models and finding similar relationships across the major religious families does a great deal to alleviate concerns surrounding this alternative explanation; however, the large amount of religious heterogeneity within religious traditions means that these tests alone do not fully eliminate the possibility. As a result, this plausible alternative explanation must remain unanswered until chapter 5, which uses data that are better suited to ruling out this possibility completely.

Selection bias is similarly a concern in these data. After all, some people may be predisposed both to want children and to return to religion, and this would affect the empirical results. While these data cannot directly address this possibility, the presence of selection bias likely underestimates the partisan effects presented so far. This predisposition, which should affect Democrats and Republicans alike, would mean that Democrats with children should be more likely to return to religion than they would in the absence of this predisposition.[34] Consequently, the partisan-driven religious gap would be larger if the decision to have children was random and unrelated to religious predispositions.

Other Unanswerable Alternative Explanations

Two additional alternative explanations that the YPSP data cannot address relate to cohort and aging effects. First, the graduating class of 1965 has unique characteristics, which raises the possibility that the results found above do not apply to other generations in other periods. Men from this cohort could have been (and were) drafted, and this cohort came of age squarely in the middle of the "culture shock" of the late 1960s and 1970s (Putnam and Campbell 2010) that included liberalizing attitudes toward drugs and sex. Although the data from the parent generation mitigate concerns about a period effect, looking only at the student cohort makes it difficult to say whether the same result would appear in a different context. Second, the results also comport with an aging explanation, not a life-cycle explanation. It may be that getting married and having children is not what allowed partisanship to influence religious decisions but would have occurred naturally as the students aged. The YPSP data cannot adjudicate between these explanations because the student cohort is the same age and virtually everyone underwent these life-cycle changes. Instead, replicating the main findings using a different sample collected at a different time period helps address these alternative possibilities.

2007–2014: Another Case of Partisan-Driven Religious Divergence

The second empirical test draws on dual data-collection efforts. The National Annenberg Election Study (NAES) conducted a large five-wave panel over the course of the 2008 presidential election, and the Institute for the Study of Citizens and Politics (ISCAP) then continued to reinterview a random subsample of the initial respondents during subsequent election years. The NAES survey captured church attendance and religious identification once in 2007, before the NAES survey began, and the ISCAP survey captured the same measures for the same respondents seven years later in 2014.

The political backdrops against which the YPSP and NAES/ISCAP data were gathered differed substantially. The YPSP student cohort was among the first to make religious decisions in this new religious-political sphere, but the relationship between the parties and religion continued to develop during the latter part of the twentieth century. Parents in the NAES/ISCAP sample therefore came of age against this political backdrop, and this different socialization experience may change expectations regarding the younger generation. Since politics and religion are closely linked—and have been closely linked for the majority of these individuals' lives—then it may be difficult to detect changes in religiosity because (1) religious attachments influenced party identification or (2) partisanship influenced rates of religious "withdrawal" in adolescence and young adulthood. Both scenarios are possible, and both scenarios would make it more difficult to find evidence of partisanship exerting influence on religious choices in adulthood.

The empirical strategy is similar to the analyses presented above. Church attendance and religious identification serve as the two dependent variables. Church attendance ranges between 0 (never attend) and 1 (attend weekly) and religious identification distinguishes between identifiers (1) and nonidentifiers, or religious "nones" (0). Change models that include the lagged dependent variable test whether partisanship, measured in 2007, is correlated with changes to religious identities over the seven-year period. And as before, the models include socioeconomic control variables that may affect both changes in partisanship and changes in religiosity over time.[35] In contrast to the YPSP survey that interviewed a national sample of a single age cohort, the NAES/ISCAP survey interviewed a nationally representative sample. This means that not everyone in the sample was making decisions about their religious involvement between 2007 and 2014. Fortunately, each respondent with a child living at home in the 2007 wave provided age categories for his or her oldest: younger than 2, between 2 and 5, between 6 and 12, and between 13 and 18. Respondents with children younger than 2 or between 2 and 5 in 2007 would have children between 7 and 13 in 2014. The intervening seven years would have been crucial for these respondents, as their children went from being babies to starting school. It is during this time, according to the literature, that these parents were most likely to be making decisions about their own, as well as their children's, religious involvement. The life-cycle theory predicts that partisanship should have the largest influence on these people. By comparison, partisanship should have a smaller influence among respondents whose children were older (between 6 and 12) or grown in the first wave of the study.

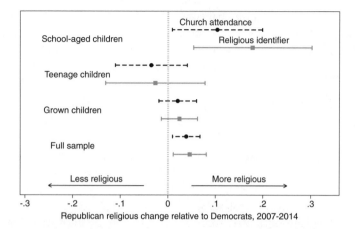

4.6. 2007–2014: Partisan-driven religious changes occur among respondents with school-aged children. The figure presents partisan differences in changing levels of church attendance (black circles) and religious identification (gray squares) between 2007 and 2014 for respondents at various points in the life cycle. Estimates come from change models that include a lagged dependent variable and control variables described in the text. Positive coefficients indicate that Republicans became relatively more religious than Democrats between 2007 and 2014. Negative coefficients indicate that Democrats became relatively more religious than Republicans between 2007 and 2014. Coefficients near zero indicate that neither group became relatively more religious than the other between 2007 and 2014.
Source: National Annenberg Election Study/Institute for the Study of Citizens and Politics.

Figure 4.6 presents the main set of results. Just as before, the *x*-axis represents difference in religiosity change between Republicans and Democrats. Positive coefficients indicate that Republicans became more religious relative to Democrats between 2007 and 2014, negative coefficients indicate that Democrats became relatively more religious compared to Republicans, and coefficients near zero indicate that there was no change in the size of the relative gap. The black circles and dashed lines represent the change in church attendance levels while the gray squares and solid lines represent the change in probability of being a religious identifier, that is, identifying with a religious tradition as opposed to being a religious nonidentifier. The top set of results looks at respondents with young children in 2007 and who therefore would have at least one school-aged child by 2014. The positive coefficients for those with school-aged children show that not only did the religious gap between Republicans and Democrats grow between 2007 and 2014 but also that the gap emerged in such a way that Republicans were more religious than Democrats in 2014 compared to 2007. The church attendance gap grew by 0.10, representing one-half of one response option and nearly doubling the 2007 church attendance gap.[36] Rates of religious identification also changed between 2007 and 2014, and Republicans became 17% more likely to be religious identifiers relative to Democrats.

In contrast, there is no partisan-induced change in church attendance or identification among respondents whose children were already in school in 2007 and were therefore teenagers or in their twenties in 2014. While Republican parents in this category are more religious than their Democratic counterparts, the gap did not change during the seven years between survey waves. These individuals likely made their religious choices prior to the 2007 wave of the study. There is also some evidence of partisan-driven change among respondents who had grown children in 2007. For example, a statistically suggestive 4% gap emerges between Republicans and Democrats on the religious identification measure (p-value = 0.12); however, the size of the partisan gap is significantly smaller than the 17% gap found among those respondents with school-aged children (difference between groups = 0.13; p-value = 0.03).[37] These statistically marginal results point out that religious participation and identification should never be assumed to be completely stable, despite becoming more stable in adulthood. The final set of results presents the divergence among the full sample of respondents. These results, while substantively small, are statistically significant. Republicans and Democrats diverged in their religiosities between 2007 and 2014. These full results, however, mask important differences across people based on where they are in their lives, as parents of school-aged children drive these results.[38]

Is This Really about the Life Cycle, or Is It Just about Aging?

The NAES/ISCAP data also can address the alternative explanation that the results are not a function of the respondents' changing positions in the life cycle but are simply a function of people getting older. If an aging explanation is better suited than the life-cycle theory to explain the results, respondents within narrow age brackets should look similar to each other irrespective of life stage. If, however, the evidence supports a life-cycle explanation, religion should be a peripheral concern for respondents without children, and politics should therefore not be correlated with religious change over time. While politics may exert influence on the religious outlooks of these individuals in the future, religious activity—or inactivity—should be relatively stable at this stage. While comparing respondents with and without children is generally a problematic strategy, as these groups likely differ on

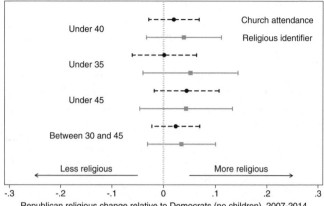

4.7. 2007–2014: Partisan-driven religious changes are not a function of aging. The figure presents partisan differences in changing levels of church attendance (black circles) and religious identification (gray squares) between 2007 and 2014 for respondents without children. Estimates come from change models that include a lagged dependent variable. Positive coefficients indicate that Republicans became relatively more religious than Democrats between 2007 and 2014. Negative coefficients indicate that Democrats became relatively more religious than Republicans between 2007 and 2014. Coefficients near zero indicate that neither group became relatively more religious than the other between 2007 and 2014.
Source: National Annenberg Election Study/Institute for the Study of Citizens and Politics.

a host of dimensions, the analysis can rule out the possibility that aging accounts for the changes seen over time.

Figure 4.7 presents the results for models that use the same dependent and control variables as the main findings but use subsamples of people of varying age ranges who do not have children. The four age classifications produce the same general evidence: there are no partisan-driven changes evident among respondents without children.[39] While there are many differences, both observable and unobservable, between those with and without children, these null results offer evidence that the main findings are not attributable to the aging process alone.

Discussion

When the parties diverged along religious and cultural lines in the 1970s, they presumably hoped to gain the votes of those who supported the parties' positions. This chapter shows that such elite-level changes also had unintended consequences on individual-level religious attachments. More specifically, the longitudinal results from this chapter offer five empirical takeaway points. First, having children represents a critical juncture during which individuals make decisions about their religious identities. After a large drop in religiosity between 1965 and 1973, many increased their religious participation between 1973 and 1982 when most of the student cohort had children of their own. These increases in religiosity and religious involvement stand in contrast to the YPSP parent generation, whose levels of religious activity remained stable over time. Although scholars have looked at what factors influence religious decision making at this point, none have explored whether partisanship is a key driver in the decision.

The second empirical point that can be taken from this chapter is that partisanship plays a role when people make decisions related to religious engagement. Analyses using two data sources collected decades apart show that Republicans' and Democrats' religiosities diverged when partisans had school-aged children at home. There is evidence that not only is partisanship correlated with religious change but also that the changes are consistent with the life-cycle theory's prediction about *when* partisanship is likely to exert influence. Third, religious choices made during a particular life stage are often long lasting, which means that the effect of partisanship is evident many years later. The partisan-driven gap that appears between 1973 and 1982 is still present in 1997. Fourth, church attendance does not influence partisanship and vote choice among respondents whose partisan identities are theoretically solidified but who are still sorting out their religious attachments. While many assume that religiosity—frequently measured by church attendance or biblical literalism—can bring about political change, this is not the case for everyone. And fifth, partisanship does not correspond with religious change among individuals who have theoretically stable religious attachments, nor does partisanship correspond to changes in other forms of social and political engagement. These negative cases, or placebo tests, rule out important alternative explanations for the empirical results. Taken together, the chapter's results comport with the life-cycle theory's predictions that during a particular life stage, partisan identities may affect choices related to religion.

The YPSP Study has multiple strengths that make it well suited to test the life-cycle theory. Most important, individuals are followed throughout much of their lives. Additionally, information about the students' religious upbringings, backgrounds, and family relationships addresses existing sociological explanations of religious change (Carroll and Roof 1993; Myers 1996; Sharot, Ayalon, and Ben-Rafael 1986; Sherkat 1998; Wilson and Sherkat 1994). The drawback of the YPSP data is also its strength—the survey

looks at only a single cohort. This leaves open the question of how generalizable these findings are and whether the same trends exist in different time
periods. The NAES/ISCAP data show that the experience of the high school
class of 1965 reflects a more general pattern that is evident in the present
day. When the time comes to make religious decisions for themselves and
their families, partisans behave in distinct ways. The result is an increasing
religiosity gap between Republicans and Democrats that occurs, in part, because partisans select into or out of religious communities based on politics.

These results put some of the recent trends about religion and politics into
perspective. Much of the research that links individual-level religiosity to political variables such as partisanship and vote choice do not see a strong relationship until the 1990s and onward. For example, Layman (1997) finds that
religious commitment—such as church attendance—was not correlated with
partisanship and vote choice in the 1970s and early 1980s but became an important correlation in the late 1980s and 1990s. Green (2010) similarly shows
that a church attendance gap did not always exist in presidential voting, emerging for the first time in the 1990s. In line with these findings, scholars point to
1992 as the time when the God gap became present in the mass public, decades after elite-level shifts began to take place. If religion and politics became
noticeably intertwined beginning in the 1970s, why did aggregate correlations
between religiosity and partisanship not emerge until the 1990s? While the
YPSP data show that partisanship influenced religious decisions as far back
as the late 1970s and early 1980s, these younger cohorts made up a small percentage of the electorate. Moreover, both partisan and religious identities
were quite stable among the parent generation. If the older generations maintained similar religious and political identities over long periods of time, large
aggregate changes should not have appeared overnight. Instead, as younger
cohorts' relative size within the electorate increased, the correlation between
individual-level religiosity and political measures should also have increased.

The 1980 ANES shows evidence of this. Whereas there is a positive correlation between church attendance and Republican identification in the
full sample, the relationship is much stronger among those between 30 and
35. Reported church attendance—rescaled to range between 0 and 1—was
about 0.07 higher among Republicans compared to Democrats in the full
sample and 0.09 in the white subsample. Among those in the YPSP age
range, however, Republicans' average level of church attendance was much
higher than Democrats' average attendance rate: 0.17 and 0.21 in the full
sample and white subsample, respectively. Looking at younger generations
would have foreshadowed the development of a religiosity gap years before
social scientists identified the relationship in the full electorate. This type of

time lag has implications for researchers interested in voters' reactions to the changing political environment. If, for example, the political parties stake out new policy positions or electoral coalitions change, scholars should not just look at nationally representative data to learn whether voters responded to the elite-level shift. Instead, the focus should be placed on individuals for whom the changing political landscape is most likely to exert influence. In this way, scholars can better predict whether large-scale changes in the aggregate are likely to appear.

The YPSP findings also help make sense of recent research exploring the religious determinants of political attitudes. Partisanship's relationship with changing levels of religiosity is most pronounced among outward measures of religiosity and is more modest when biblical literalism is examined. Attendance at religious services, willingness to identify with a religious faith, and participation in church organizations all correspond to social aspects of religiosity. Biblical literalism, in contrast, measures a privately held belief.[40] These findings encourage us to revisit recent religion and politics research showing that religious behaviors and affiliation matter more in shaping political attitudes than religious beliefs (Mockabee, Monson, and Grant 2001; Putnam and Campbell 2010; see Friesen and Wagner 2012 for an overview).

Why might the religion and politics literature find that religious behaviors and identification are stronger predictors of political outlooks than religious beliefs? While the results from this chapter show that partisanship is correlated with changes in religiosity at certain life stages, these results do not preclude religiosity from also affecting political attitudes and behaviors at other times. In fact, if politics influences religion in early adulthood, this likely increases the possibility that religion can influence politics later in life. If Republicans returned to religion on account of their partisan identities, then religious messages, congregational communities, and political mobilization strategies should all be more effective in appealing to voters in church, particularly in support of Republican candidates and causes. If partisanship first influences the extent to which individuals return to religion after a hiatus, politics helps set the stage for religion to play an important political role later on. With liberal Democrats not returning to the religious fold, they are not hearing—and potentially rejecting—conservative religious messages. Instead, those who select back into church should be more persuadable than those who remain on the outskirts. This is precisely what Michael Tesler (2015) found using the YPSP data when cohort members were adults: Church attendance influenced vote choice between 1982 and 1997. The ability of religious involvement to change vote choice occurred, in part, because partisanship influenced religious decisions earlier. In the same vein, the correlation between religious beliefs and politically relevant attitudes and behaviors may be weaker because partisanship plays a smaller role in shaping these beliefs in the first place. Taken together, partisanship's differential influence on religious identities helps explain why correlations between religious beliefs and political attitudes are weaker than the corresponding correlations using religious behaviors and identification.

The results from this chapter also offer an additional pathway explaining why Democrats are less religious than Republicans. Research examining the effect of politics on religious identities (Hout and Fischer 2014, 2002) and church attendance (Patrikios 2008) assumes that politics is pushing Democrats away from religion. More specifically, Hout and Fischer's explanation of the rising religious nonidentification rates revolves around liberals opting out of religion because of politics. This is certainly happening, and there is evidence in support of this explanation in chapter 5. But the YPSP data show that Democrats also end up being less religious than Republicans on account of returning to religion at lower rates than Republicans. Therefore, it is not only the case that Democrats stop identifying with a religion because of politics, as Hout and Fischer suggest, but they are less likely to reaffiliate after having been unaffiliated in adolescence and young adulthood, which is a common time for apostasy.

This chapter details how partisanship is related to religious decision making as individuals move from one life-cycle window to another. Tracking the same individuals as they transition between life stages, however, requires using observational data collected many years apart. These data, despite careful analyses and attention paid to alternative explanations, allow for the possibility that something other than partisanship and the political environment influences individuals' religious choices. Chapter 5 addresses this lingering concern by testing how partisans respond to short-term changes in the political environment, using experiments and panel data with shorter windows between waves.

FIVE

Partisans' Religious Responses to the Political Environment

The 2004 presidential election prompted extensive discussion about whether Americans had voted based on moral issues, such as gay marriage and abortion, or on the economy and the ongoing war in Iraq. While researchers have since found the claim that moral issues dominated voters' decisions to be overblown, the 2004 campaign was unique in that moral issues, particularly gay marriage, became salient, and the media extensively covered the religious-secularist divide between the Republican and Democratic parties. As a result, voters were able to learn how the parties differed along religious and moral lines. The political landscape led some observers to claim that voters relied heavily on their religious commitment when casting their ballots in the 2004 election. Another explanation, however, is that the salience of moral issues and media coverage of the parties encouraged partisans to bring their religious attachments into line with their partisan identities. This chapter not only disentangles these two explanations to make sense of how morality politics mattered in 2004, but it also answers a more general question that arises from the 2004 case: What kinds of circumstances bring about partisan-driven changes in religious attachments? In doing so, this chapter tests whether Americans interpret their surroundings through a partisan lens and use relevant political cues when making religious choices.

Chapter 4 showed that Republicans and Democrats have different religious trajectories over the course of their lives. Religious decisions made upon entering adulthood leave Republicans more religiously involved and engaged than Democrats. The assumption underlying these findings is that the political landscape, one that linked the Republican Party to religious groups and values and the Democratic Party to culturally liberal policies, affected partisans' decision making as they moved from one life stage to another. The data, however, do not show how partisans respond to information about the political landscape and instead show only the end result—that Republican and Democratic adults have different religious profiles. This chapter tests how these long-term changes come about by seeing how partisans at different points in the life cycle respond to information linking religion and politics.

The life-cycle theory predicts that at a particular life stage—namely, as partisans' children reach school age—partisan identities are more stable than religious identities. We might therefore expect religious decisions to be open to political influence at this point. Over time, however, religious identities solidify and we should expect the influence of politics to wane. Knowing the groups for whom politics is most likely a powerful influence allows predictions as to whether religious-political coalitions—the presumed source of partisan-driven changes in religiosity—impact religious identification and involvement. Individuals with children still at home should respond to short-term changes in the political or informational environment, bringing aspects of their religious identities in line with their partisan identities. Those with grown children, however, should be less responsive to the same environmental changes. Whereas chapter 4 emphasized individual-level change as partisans progressed through the life cycle, this chapter focuses on partisans' more immediate religious responses to the political environment. Moreover, while the findings from chapter 4 show that Democrats may be less likely to return to religion after a hiatus, the findings in this chapter show that the political environment may also alienate Democrats who might otherwise be open to being religiously involved.

The next sections offer evidence from two survey experiments demonstrating that the close relationship between Republicans and organized religion has pushed Democrats out of the organized religious sphere and brought Republicans deeper into the religious fold. Panel data then provide additional verification of this finding by testing how partisans respond when the linkages between religion and the Republican Party become more salient. The data show that, in response to the increasing importance of gay marriage as a political issue in 2004, party identification influenced subsequent religious practices: Democrats (Republicans) reported lower (higher) rates of religiosity in 2004 than they did in 2000 or 2002. Whereas the first three sets of results test how the Republican Party's close relationship with religious conservatives influences partisans, the final part of the chapter shows that different political-elite linkages—in this case, religion being used to promote liberal policies—affect partisans differently. Exploring how the political landscape shapes religious identities offers an additional test of the life-cycle theory and details why we see partisans updating their religious attachments.

What Happens When We Prime Partisan Identities?

A priming experiment offers a direct test of partisanship's influence on reported religious identities. Researchers can circumvent the problem that identities are not randomly determined by instead measuring attitudes (Jackson 2011; Johnson, Rowatt, and LaBouff 2012; Klar 2013) and behaviors (Dijksterhuis and van Knippenberg 1998; McLeish and Oxoby 2009; Shariff and Norenzayan 2007; Shih, Pittinsky, and Ambady 1999) after randomly assigning whether or not a particular identity has been primed, or made salient. This strategy allows researchers to uncover what role specific identities and categorizations play in attitude development. For example, Hogg and Turner (1987) found that increasing the salience of gender encouraged respondents to think of themselves in gender-stereotypic terms. Study participants for whom gender had been made salient adopted prototypical attributes associated with their genders. In a similar way, priming partisan identities can test whether partisan typicality is associated with religious identification. If partisans believe Republicans to be religious and Democrats to be less so, primed partisans may adopt religious identities that are more closely aligned with perceptions of the parties' relationships with religion.[1]

The two-wave experiment took place in August 2013 using a diverse national sample.[2] Respondents answered a standard set of party identification questions in the first wave, and the experimental portion took place two weeks later using 1,230 respondents. In the beginning of the second wave, respondents were randomly assigned to a treatment or control condition. Respondents in the treatment condition received the following introductory screen:

> This part of the study is concerned with how people respond to advertisements for community events. On the next few screens you will be asked to judge different flyers advertising an event by the Ohio Voters' Council. For each comparison, we want to you look at both flyers and decide which flyer you prefer. There will be a brief pause on each screen so that you can look at the flyers closely.

To prime partisan identities, treated respondents rated the aesthetics of three flyers advertising a voter registration and political engagement drive put on by the fictitious Ohio Voters' Council. Self-identified Democrats and Democratic leaners in wave 1 rated flyers for a Democratic event while self-identified Republicans and Republican leaners rated flyers for a Republican version of the event. Through random assignment, treated Independents either received the Democratic or Republican prime. Respondents compared three sets of flyers, evaluating two flyers at a time. For each comparison, respondents chose which flyer was easier to read, which flyer made the event seem more attractive, and which flyer the respondent preferred overall. The Democratic flyers are available in the appendix.

The experimental stimulus is subtle. The purpose of the treatment is only to remind individuals of their partisan identities, and therefore the flyers do not refer to specific policies, politicians, or groups that might be associated with one of the parties. Consequently, any link respondents make between their partisan and religious identities is made on their own. After answering a final question about voter registration drives, respondents moved on to the next part of the study, which asked a series of attitudinal and behavioral questions. The main dependent variable—religious identity—appears at the end of the survey along with other demographic questions.

The dependent variable is a four-point measure of religious identification strength based on two questions. Respondents first answered a standard religious identification question and then one follow-up question. If respondents identified with a religion, they received a follow-up asking whether they identify strongly or not strongly with the religion. For example, if a respondent self-identified as Catholic, the follow-up would read: "Do you identify strongly as a Catholic or not very strongly as a Catholic?" For respondents who identified as an "other" religion, the religion specified in the open-ended box was carried over to the follow-up question. Approximately 40% of religious identifiers classified themselves as "weak" identifiers while 60% considered themselves "strong" identifiers. Respondents who did not identify with any religion, making up approximately 23% of the sample, were asked: "Do you think of yourself as closer to one particular religion over another?" and were given the same response options as the initial identification question along with an option that they do not feel any closer to one particular religion. A full quarter of respondents who initially said that they did not identify with a religious tradition "leaned" toward one religion. The resultant four-point scale of religious identification ranges from 0 (strong nonidentifier) to 1 (strong identifier).

What types of people might respond to a partisan prime by changing their reported strength of religious identification? According to the life-cycle theory, individuals whose partisan identities are more stable than their religious attachments should be the most responsive to the primes. Empirically, these are individuals in the sample with school-aged children. In contrast, we might not expect a partisan prime to affect those with solidified religious identities, represented in the sample by respondents with grown children. The analyses therefore focus on these two subsamples.[3] Parametric results

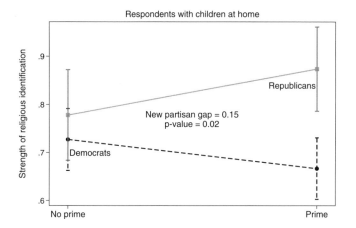

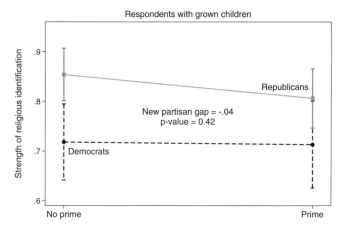

5.1. Partisan primes' effects vary by life-cycle position. The top panel presents the experimental treatment effects for respondents with children at home, and the bottom panel presents the experimental treatment effects for respondents with grown children. The dependent variable is a four-point religious identification scale that ranges from 0 (strong nonidentifier) to 1 (strong identifier). The "new partisan gap" represents the difference-in-difference estimate that compares the treatment effects for Democrats and Republicans.
Source: Priming partisanship experiment.

for the full sample, subsamples, other measures of religiosity, and models that include control variables are in the appendix.

Figure 5.1 presents the average identification scores for those with children at home (top) and those with grown children (bottom). Republicans in the control condition with children at home are stronger religious identifiers compared to Democrats in the control condition.[4] This is unsurprising given that we know that Republicans are, on average, more religious than Democrats. More interesting is that the identification gap between Republicans and Democrats was larger among respondents who rated the political flyers. The average score for the four-point religious identification measure increased from 0.78 to 0.87 for Republicans but decreased from 0.73 to 0.67 among Democrats, thereby increasing the overall partisan gap in religious identification by 0.15 points (p-value = 0.02).[5] The size of the experimental treatment effect is quite large, more than doubling the original identification gap. In contrast, the bottom panel of figure 5.1 shows that stimulus did not affect the identification gap of partisans with grown children (p-value = 0.42). A further test confirms that partisans with children at home and partisans with grown children responded to the primes differently (p-value = 0.02).[6]

The controlled experiment provides a direct test of whether and when partisanship might influence religious identification. Despite being a weak test of politics' influence by relying on self-induced connections between religion and politics, some partisans updated their religious identities in a way that would be consistent with their partisan identities: Republicans systematically became stronger religious identifiers and Democrats became less so. This shift, however, is present only among those at a particular period in their lives in which their religious identities are weaker than their partisan identities.

A key strength of this experiment is that participants can rely on their own assumptions and biases when thinking about what it means to be a partisan. This provides important insight into how different sets of people might respond in a political landscape filled with generic partisan cues, labels, and symbols. This strength, however, raises the possibility that perhaps certain respondents were thinking about other political arenas—economic, racial, or foreign policy—and therefore had no incentive to reconsider their responses to questions about religious identity. The null results among those with grown children may not have occurred because their identities are not open to movement but rather because they simply did not think of issues that would prompt such a change. The next experiment builds on this limitation and explores how Americans respond when they read about the close relationship between conservative religion and the Republican Party.

Faith and Freedom Coalition and the Republican Party

Ralph Reed is synonymous with religion and conservative politics. Tapped by Pat Robertson to head the Christian Coalition in 1989 and dubbed "The Right Hand of God" by *Time* magazine in 1995, Reed is credited with transforming religious conservatives into a core component of the Republican Party and giving their leaders a seat at the political table. Although close dealings with scandal-ridden lobbyist Jack Abramoff resulted in a temporary fall from grace, Reed rose from the political dead in 2009. With a $500,000 donation from undisclosed sources, Ralph Reed founded the Faith and Freedom Coalition (FFC), which he describes as a "21st century version of the Christian Coalition on steroids."[7] With $5 million raised in 2010 and an operating budget of $10 million (Moyers 2012), Reed's influence has become increasingly evident in the electoral arena.

One example of Reed's political reach took place in June 2011—early in the Republican primary season—when six of the seven presidential hopefuls descended upon Washington, DC. However, the event they attended was not a nationally televised debate or a highly anticipated town hall meeting. Instead, the Republican candidates came to "metaphorically kiss the ring of Ralph Reed" and win over the crowd of religious conservatives at the FFC conference (Marrapodi 2011). Candidates emphasized the paramount importance of moral issues like abortion and gay marriage, discussed their personal religious journeys, and peppered their speeches with religious quotes and anecdotes. Newspapers covering the convention reported on the close relationship between the Republican Party and religious conservatives and discussed how important religious voters are to Republican candidates. Headlines from around the country reported that GOP hopefuls "pay homage" to, "court," "compete for," and "woo" the religious right and Christian conservatives. Ralph Reed's FFC highlights the very close and very public relationship between religious conservatives and the Republican Party.

The experiment uses the FFC conference to explore the religious consequences of this public linkage between religion and conservative politics. Some 1,500 respondents, who were randomly selected from the Knowledge Networks (KN) panel, participated in the single-wave study between June 26 and July 6, 2012.[8] Subjects were randomly assigned to either the treatment or the control conditions. Those in the treatment group were told they were participating in a study about how people respond to "everyday issues discussed in the news" and after reading a random newspaper article would answer questions both about what they remembered from the news story and their general opinions about the topic discussed. The experimental treatment, presented in the appendix, is a modified Associated Press (AP) newspaper article about the two-day FFC conference. Though shortened, the newspaper article keeps the language and tone of the initial AP piece unchanged.[9] After reading the newspaper article, respondents in the treatment condition answered three follow-up questions related to the story.[10] The survey concluded by asking all respondents a few questions about their backgrounds, including religious identification and practices. Respondents in the control condition did not read a newspaper article or answer questions about the story. They simply answered the background questions.

Following the literature, the experiment focuses specifically on the relationship between conservative religious organizations and the Republican Party. While secularists represent an important Democratic constituency, Bolce and De Maio (2002) argue that the common assumption is that "traditional religious beliefs motivate people to oppose abortion, back conservative Republican candidates, support conservative social movements, and adopt intolerant attitudes, but that a modernist or secularist outlook apparently had little or no connection to the reasons why someone supports abortion rights, opposes vouchers, joins culturally progressive organizations, expresses antipathy toward evangelical Christians, and votes for liberal Democratic candidates" (16–17).

Despite religious and secular coalitions existing within the party camps, at the elite level the Republican Party is much more closely aligned with religion than the Democratic Party is with secularism or irreligion. For example, Democratic politicians use religion to try to mobilize faith-based voters, and the sharp increase in "God talk" that began in Reagan's presidency did not subside during the Clinton administration (Domke and Coe 2010); Barack Obama also employed religious rhetoric and discussed his religious faith during both his campaigns and his presidency (Kaylor 2011). Moreover, self-proclaimed atheist or agnostic Democratic politicians are quite rare. Abortion is also an issue on which Democrats, even when taking liberal positions, adopt a religious angle. For example, in Bill Clinton's autobiography, he describes his pro-choice position as this: "Still, I believe the ultimate choice should remain a matter for a woman to decide in consultation with her conscience, her doctor, and her God" (1996: 137). Hillary Clinton described abortion in a similar way on the 2008 campaign trail, calling it a wrenching choice for "a young woman, her family, her physician and [her] pastor" (quoted in McGough 2016). Even though Democratic politicians do not reject the notion of religion or faith, the present-day political landscape is marked by a more prominent relationship between the Republican Party and conservative religion (Campbell, Green, and Layman 2011; Hout and Fischer 2014, 2002; Patrikios 2008). One consequence of this asymmetric relationship between the parties and religion is evident in the Pew data presented in chapter 3. While the Republican Party is certainly seen as being "friendlier" to religion than the Democratic Party, the Democratic Party is not seen as wholly "unfriendly" toward religion. The experiment, therefore, mimics elite positions today in which the close relationship between the Republican Party and religious conservatives is more salient.[11]

The dependent variable in this experiment is the same four-point religious identification measure, rescaled to range between 0 and 1, described in the priming partisanship experiment. Using the full sample of respondents, the newspaper article affected both Democrats' and Republicans' responses to the religious identification question, and these shifts are roughly symmetrical. Republicans who read the news story had an average religious identification score that was 0.05 points higher than that of Republicans in the control condition. Democrats who read the news story, on the other hand, had an average religious identification score that was 0.05 points lower than the score of Democrats in the control condition. The resultant religious identification gap between Democrats and Republicans increased by 0.10 points (p-value = 0.07). Whereas the identification gap in the control condition was roughly 0.15 points, the gap increased to approximately 0.25 in the treatment condition. Although the results looking at the full sample of respondents demonstrate a noteworthy shift in reported responses, the life-cycle theory predicts that the treatment effects should vary based on where individuals are within the life cycle.

Similar to the previous set of results, figure 5.2 presents the results separately for Republicans and Democrats who have children at home (top panel) and those with grown children (bottom panel). For respondents with children at home, there is a large shift in responses to the religious identification question. The average Republican response was 0.07 higher in the treatment condition than in the control condition whereas the average Democratic response was 0.10 lower in the treatment condition than in the control condition. The increased size of the identification gap, calculated with a difference-in-difference model, is 0.17 (p-value = 0.04). In contrast, both Democrats and Republicans with grown children remained stable in their responses to the religious identification question.[12] Parametric tests confirm that the treatment effect is statistically different among those with children at home compared to those with grown children.[13]

The two experiments together show that ability of politics to influence religious identity varies. In one experiment, the participants were given no information about the relationship between religion and politics. Instead, the results capture what happens simply when people are encouraged to "think like partisans." The second experiment gives respondents information about the current elite coalition between the Republican Party and the FFC. In this case, the experiment encourages participants to think about

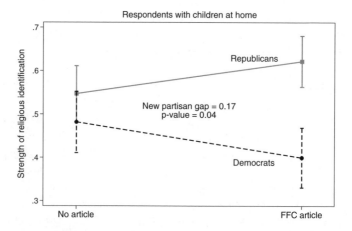

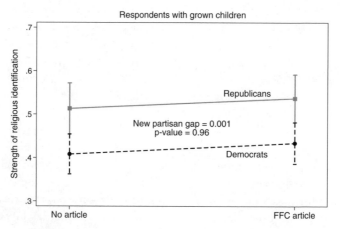

5.2. Partisans' responses to the Faith and Freedom Coalition vary by life-cycle position. The top panel presents the experimental treatment effects for respondents with children at home, and the bottom panel presents the experimental treatment effects for respondents with grown children. The dependent variable is a four-point religious identification scale that ranges from 0 (strong nonidentifier) to 1 (strong identifier). The "new partisan gap" represents the difference-in-difference estimate that compares the treatment effects for Democrats and Republicans.
Source: Faith and Freedom Coalition experiment.

the relationship between religion and politics in a particular way. Despite the differences in these strategies, similar results appear. Among those respondents with children living at home, Republicans moved closer to and Democrats moved further away from religion. Researchers frequently find evidence of people updating an attitude or preference to bring it in line with a preexisting identity or attitude. And this is what both experiments show; however, rather than people bringing their political identities in line with their religious identities, the experiments find evidence of the reverse.

These results indicate that subtle primes and small amounts of information can begin to change how partisans view themselves. The experimental treatments obviously do not have an immediate, real-time effect on partisans' average levels of religious participation and identification. The changes instead reflect shifts in how respondents think about themselves and how they want to present themselves in a survey. The experimental findings therefore offer some indication of how partisans might respond to similar changes to the political landscape in the real world. If an experimental stimulus can change respondents' immediate survey responses, extended exposure to similar information in a natural setting might produce similar results over time. The next section returns to the 2004 election, described at the chapter's outset, and uses four-year panel data to test how Americans responded to an unexpected shift in the salience of morality politics.

2004: An Unexpected Shift in the Religious-Political Landscape

Gay marriage and abortion—two moral issues that frequently have religious undertones—were both salient issues during the lead-up to the 2004 presidential campaign. While scholars have explored whether these issues influenced vote choice in the election (Abramowitz 2004; Campbell and Monson 2008) and evaluations of Bush (Tesler 2015), the increased salience of two religiously laden issues also serves as another opportunity to see how partisans respond to religion and politics being linked at the elite level.

The Partial-Birth Abortion Ban Act in October 2003—a bill that outlaws a particular method of abortion—visibly divided the parties and was frequently discussed in religious terms. For example, a plurality of the extensive floor debate on the bill focused on rights and morality (Schonhardt-Bailey 2008). Moreover, members of Congress voted largely along party lines and President Bush made his views on the matter clear when he signed the bill into law: "Every person, however frail or vulnerable, has a place and a purpose in this world. Every person has a special dignity. This right to life cannot be granted or denied by government, because it does not come from government, it comes from the Creator of life" (Office of the Press Secretary of the White House 2003). Abortion was also a frequently mentioned issue in conservative organizations' direct-mail campaigns during the 2004 election. More mail pieces made reference to abortion than any other issue (Monson and Oliphant 2007).

Gay marriage was also a salient issue in the year leading up to the 2004 election. Gay marriage catapulted to the national stage in November 2003 when the Massachusetts Supreme Court declared that marriage licenses would be granted to same-sex couples. And attention to the issue remained high as San Francisco Mayor Gavin Newsom ordered city officials to issue marriage licenses to couples of the same gender in violation of the California Family Code three months later, in February of 2004. At roughly the same time, President Bush made several statements in support of a constitutional amendment defining marriage as an institution between one man and one woman. In his 2004 State of the Union address he said: "If judges insist on forcing their arbitrary will upon the people, the only alternative left to the people would be the constitutional process. Our nation must defend the sanctity of marriage" (quoted in Oldmixon and Calfano 2007). In a second address, delivered just one month later, President Bush reiterated his position that "the union of a man and woman is the most enduring human institution, honoring—honored and encouraged in all cultures and by every religious faith" (Bush 2004). Republican Senator Alan Wayne Allard of Colorado reintroduced a modified version of the Federal Marriage Amendment in May 2004, and although the amendment stalled in the Senate, public debate about gay marriage continued. Eleven states had anti–gay marriage initiatives on the ballot in November, causing discussion about gay marriage and attempts to mobilize around the issue to continue. In particular, direct mailers supporting Republican candidates emphasized social issues, including gay marriage, throughout the campaign (Putnam and Campbell 2010). Beginning in November of 2003 when the Massachusetts Supreme Court made national headlines until November of 2004 when all eleven gay marriage bans passed, the issue of gay marriage was a salient political issue.

The Democratic and Republican parties differed in their positions on gay marriage in 2004; however, the parties did not take symmetrically opposing positions. For example, John Kerry, the Democratic nominee in 2004, supported civil unions for gay couples but opposed gay marriage. The 2004 Democratic Party platform stated: "We support full inclusion of gay and lesbian families in the life of our nation and seek equal responsibilities, benefits, and protections for these families. In our country, marriage has been defined at the state level for 200 years, and we believe it should continue to be defined there. We repudiate President Bush's divisive effort to politicize the Constitution by pursuing a 'Federal Marriage Amendment.' Our goal is to bring Americans together, not drive them apart." The Democratic language of maintaining the status quo rather than supporting the extension of marriage rights to gay couples highlights that in the instance of gay marriage, the Democratic Party represented the culturally liberal and permissive party by default, not due to active support of a progressive agenda. This comports with the previous discussion in which the Republican Party is seen as being more closely associated with religious values than the Democratic Party is with cultural liberalism despite cultural progressives and secularists making up an important Democratic constituency.

A content analysis on all the newspapers archived at newslibrary.com during President Bush's first three years in office shows the change in the attention paid to gay marriage during this period. The number of newspaper articles that mentioned gay marriage as both a political issue (by referencing "President Bush," "Democrat," or "Republican") and a religious issue (by also mentioning "religion") was always less than 100 per quarter during 2001 and 2002. This number, however, jumped during the second half of 2003 and remained high throughout 2004. There were more than three times the number of stories in 2004 than in the previous three years combined, and the articles in 2004 were more likely to mention gay marriage as both a political and religious issue. The increased salience of gay marriage in 2003–2004 prompted scholars to ask whether the issue influenced the presidential election (Abramowitz 2004; Campbell and Monson 2008).

These policy events coincided with a dramatic shift in how journalists covered the relationship between religion and politics. Bolce and De Maio (2014) counted the number of articles in the *New York Times* and the *Washington Post* that discussed Democrats and Republicans being divided along secular(ist) and religious lines between 1987 and 2012. Figure 5.3, which presents the authors' main findings, shows that trends in media reporting shifted dramatically in 2003 and 2004. The press rarely covered the religious divide between 1987 and 2002, averaging fewer than five articles per year. Instead, readers were sixteen times more likely to find a story about evangelicals and fundamentalist Christians within the Republican Party as they were to see a story about secularists' role in the Democratic Party (Bolce and De Maio 2002). In 2003, however, the number of stories increased slightly before ballooning in 2004. Between 2003 and 2004, the media repeatedly exposed citizens to stories about religious and secular coalitions in the political sphere.

A shift took place, both within the policy arena and reporting practices, in 2003 and 2004. These changes worked together to create a different political landscape, one in which social issues were particularly salient and the media began reporting on religious differences between the parties. The next sections explore whether this unexpected change to the political landscape influenced partisans' relationships with religion soon thereafter. We might

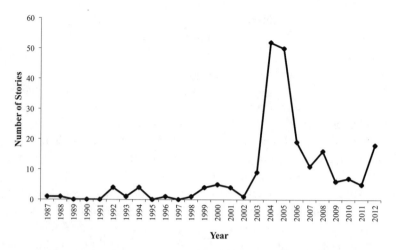

5.3. Trends in media reporting: *New York Times* and *Washington Post* articles that discuss the Democrats and Republicans being divided along secular(ist) and religious lines. *Source*: Bolce and De Maio 2014.

consider this a more difficult test than that using the YPSP and NAES/ISCAP data from chapter 4. Rather than looking at the impact of partisanship over many years—nine in the YPSP and seven in the NAES/ISCAP—here the data span only a two-year window, between 2002 and 2004. In contrast to the previous panel data in which partisanship might slowly exert influence as relevant cues stemming from policy debates and elections accumulate, here the data test whether partisans respond quickly to a change in the political landscape.

Analyses of the ANES panel data, collected in 2000, 2002, and 2004, can assess whether politicized moral issues and a changing media environment affected individual-level survey responses about church attendance between 2002 and 2004. Moreover, analyses of the 2000 and 2002 survey waves can test what happens in the absence of such shifts in the religious-political environment. If the changing landscape affected partisans' religious practices, the gap in church attendance should have widened between 2002 and 2004, but not between 2000 and 2002.

The empirical approach is similar to that used in chapter 4. The dependent variable is church attendance, which ranges between 0 (never attend) and 1 (attend more than once a week), and the main independent variables are lagged partisanship and lagged church attendance. The models include sociodemographic and attitudinal control variables that may influence both partisanship and change in religiosity across survey waves: race, age, age squared, marital status, parental status, education, household income, employment status, region of residence, political ideology, religious identification, views of the economy, feelings toward gays and lesbians, feelings toward feminists, and attitudes on abortion and economic policy.[14] These control variables help rule out common explanations in which sociodemographic traits and attitudes correlate with both partisanship and change in church attendance. And similar to the experiments, the analyses focus on subsamples based on respondents' positions within the life cycle as we should expect partisans with children at home to be more responsive to the political landscape than partisans with grown children.

The top panel of figure 5.4 compares changes between 2000 and 2002. Just as in the previous chapter, the estimates represent the difference between Republicans' and Democrats' religious trajectories over the two-year period. Positive coefficients, therefore, do not indicate that Republicans attend church with greater frequency than Democrats. Instead, a positive coefficient on the variable comparing Republicans and Democrats indicates that the gap in church attendance between Republicans and Democrats grew between 2000 and 2002, with Republicans becoming more frequent attenders relative to Democrats. A negative coefficient, in contrast, indicates the reverse, and a coefficient near zero indicates that whatever gap existed (or did not) exist in 2000 remained in 2002.

The church attendance gap found in 2000 remained stable between 2000 and 2002. The top set of results presents the estimates for the full sample of respondents. Whereas a church attendance gap existed between Republicans and Democrats in 2000—the average rate of church attendance (on a 0–1 scale) was 0.39 among Democrats and 0.54 among Republicans—average rates of church attendance did not change over the two-year period.[15] The estimate (0.005; p-value = 0.86) represents this stability.[16] The second and third estimates reproduce the results for the two subsamples of interest. Among respondents both with children at home and with grown children, Republicans' average rate of church attendance did not change relative to the rate of Democrats between 2000 and 2002.[17]

The linkage between the political parties and religion became more pronounced between the second and third survey waves. The bottom panel of figure 5.4 shows how the church attendance gap changed between 2002 and 2004. Here, there is some evidence of a changing gap between Republicans and Democrats (0.04), but the results are statistically suggestive (p-value = 0.13).[18] These results do not offer compelling evidence that the changes to the political landscape are associated with changes in partisans' levels of religious involvement. After all, the magnitude of the effects is quite small and the results cannot be statistically distinguished from zero

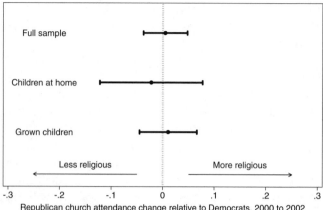

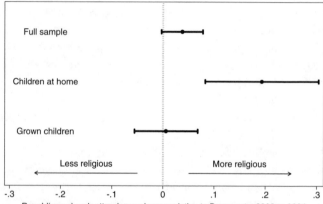

5.4. 2000–2004: Partisans with children at home respond to the changing religious-political environment. The top panel presents partisan differences in changing levels of church attendance between 2000 and 2002. The bottom panel presents the same results between 2002 and 2004. Estimates come from change models that include a lagged dependent variable and control variables described in the text. Positive estimates indicate that Republicans became more frequent church attenders than Democrats over time. Negative estimates indicate that Democrats became more frequent church attenders than Republicans over time. Estimates near zero indicate that neither group became more frequent church attenders relative to the other over time. The top set of results shows changes for the full sample, the middle set of results shows changes for respondents with children at home, and the bottom set of results shows changes for respondents with grown children. *Source*: 2000–2002–2004 American National Election Study.

at conventional levels. The life-cycle theory, however, predicts that people at different points in their lives should respond to the changing political environment differently.

The second and third estimates in the bottom panel of figure 5.4 show the results based on respondents' positions in the life cycle. The middle set of results shows that the existing church attendance gap widened substantially between Republicans and Democrats with children at home (0.19; p-value < 0.01).[19] This gap emerged because Republicans' average level of church attendance increased somewhat while Democrats' average level decreased dramatically. So while partisans of both stripes helped widen the gap, Democrats produced more of the change. The final set of results looks at respondents with grown children. Here, the findings look similar to the 2000–2002 results: the church attendance gap remained stable despite the changing political environment. The full models and tests confirming that the 2002 to 2004 changes for respondents with children at home are statistically different from those with grown children are in the appendix.[20]

Analyses testing partisanship's influence in other areas provide context for these results. First, similar to the issue of gay marriage and partisan divisions along cultural lines, the Iraq War was a salient issue that divided the parties between the 2002 and 2004 survey waves. This allows for a test of how the same group of parents changed their attitudes about another important issue. Here, a partisan gap of approximately 0.32 (on a 0–1 scale) emerged between 2002 and 2004, with Republicans becoming more supportive and Democrats becoming less supportive of the military intervention in Iraq. The magnitude of the church attendance results in relation to the Iraq War attitudes is quite impressive considering that the Iraq War was a new issue, whereas the cultural differences between the parties had existed for many years. Second, elections often make the economy salient and may encourage respondents to answer questions related to the economy as partisan cheerleaders, viewing the economy more positively if the president is a copartisan and more negatively if the president is from the other party. Consistent with this trend, a 0.19 gap emerges between 2002 and 2004 (again on a 0–1 scale), with Republicans coming to view the economy more positively and Democrats coming to view the economy more negatively. Similarly, while Republicans were more likely to approve of how Bush was handling the economy in 2002 and 2004, the gap between Republicans and Democrats widened by 0.28 between 2002 and 2004. Although the relationship between partisanship and changing economic evaluations is likely muted because a Republican was president in both 2002 and 2004, these results show how the salience of a presidential campaign can widen already existing perceptual differences between Republicans and Democrats. More-over, the relative magnitude of partisanship's relationship to attitudes on the Iraq War and the economy offers context to the main findings and shows that the change in reported church attendance is substantively meaningful.

Similar to the YPSP results from chapter 4, religiosity is not correlated with changing political attitudes among partisans with children at home. Despite the increased salience of morality politics and the media empha-sis on Republicans and Democrats differing along cultural lines, there is no evidence that church attendance is associated with a change in party identification, approval of George W. Bush, or a feeling thermometer toward Bush.[21] And also similar to the YPSP results from chapter 4, partisans with children at home did not diverge in nonreligious forms of societal partici-pation between 2002 and 2004. Republicans do not become more likely to attend a political rally or meeting about a community issue compared to Democrats between 2002 and 2004. Further, attitudes about the Iraq War, which began in March of 2003 and was an important campaign issue, do not explain the partisan divergence found in the data. The same results appear among people who approved and disapproved of the war in Iraq.[22]

The ANES, like the NAES/ISCAP data from chapter 4, can also help dis-tinguish between life-cycle and aging effects using models that compare re-spondents with and without children within the same narrow age brackets.[23] Figure 5.5 shows that across six age groupings (under 40, under 35, be-tween 30 and 40, between 25 and 40, between 25 and 35), Republicans and Democrats with children diverged in their reported religious attendance be-tween 2002 and 2004. Among similarly aged respondents without children, however, partisans did not diverge.[24] While the empirical models cannot account for many differences that undoubtedly exist between those with and without children, these results do rule out the possibility that everyone of the same age acted in the same way. Moreover, church attendance also diverged among partisans with children at home, irrespective of respon-dent age, while partisans of all ages with grown children similarly provided stable responses across the time period. Partisans behaved more similarly to those in the same life stage than to those with a similar age but in a dif-ferent life stage. These results, presented in detail in the appendix, indicate that placement in the life cycle does a better job than age in explaining the main results.

The panel data corroborate the two experimental findings from above. Not only can artificial stimuli change reported strength of religious iden-tification, but the ANES data show evidence of this happening in response to an unplanned change in the political arena. The changes in the ANES

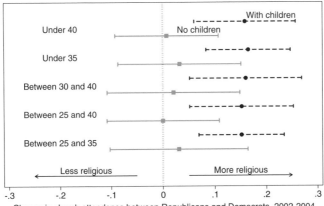

5.5. 2002–2004: Partisans' responses to the changing religious-political environment are not a function of aging. The figure presents partisan differences in changing levels of church attendance between 2002 and 2004 for similarly aged respondents with children (black circles) and without children (gray squares). Estimates come from change models that include a lagged dependent variable. Positive estimates indicate that Republicans became more frequent church attenders than Democrats over time. Negative estimates indicate that Democrats became more frequent church attenders than Republicans over time. Estimates near zero indicate that neither group became more frequent church attenders over time. *Source*: 2000–2002–2004 American National Election Study.

survey responses did not arise from an unrealistic experimental stimulus; rather they arose from the broader political environment. In short, real changes emerge in response to real changes in the political world. The three sets of results together further corroborate the life-cycle theory and provide support for the claim that long-term changes in partisans' levels of religiosity occur as people respond to relevant short-term changes. In particular, Republicans and Democrats update their views such that Republicans become more and Democrats become less religious. The next section looks at what happens when religion is linked with a policy on the political left.

Religious Support for Liberal Immigration Reform

The political landscape has been an important explanation of partisan-driven religious change throughout the last two chapters. When political elites diverged along religious and moral lines, partisans followed suit. In particular, cues linking the Republican Party with religion and the Democratic Party with secularism helped produce religious Republicans and less religious

Democrats. Nevertheless, a growing group of religious leaders is promoting liberal policies, particularly on immigration (Margolis 2018) and the environment (Djupe and Gwiasda 2010). Scholars, however, know virtually nothing about how religious cues on the political left influence partisans' religious identities. This last section begins to fill in this gap with an experiment that takes advantage of the ongoing debate about immigration reform.

Immigration reform is well suited to testing how religious cues associated with different political agendas affect partisans' reported religious responses because religious arguments can justify both liberal and conservative policy positions. In fact, this is precisely what has been happening with the ongoing immigration debate. One side of the debate focuses on the humanitarian justification for immigration reform and points to religious Americans' role in "welcoming the stranger." The other side of the debate emphasizes the rule of law and argues that the Bible requires that immigrants obey the laws and customs of the land they inhabit. The current immigration debate therefore includes religious leaders who both favor and oppose progressive immigration reform, and both sides offer religious justifications for their positions. The goal of this next experiment is to see what happens when partisans are exposed to religious messages about immigration reform coming from either a liberal (pro-reform) or conservative (anti-reform) standpoint.

The experiment took place in August 2014 using a national sample of 3,175 respondents obtained through Survey Sampling International (SSI). Treated respondents were told that the study was about what people remember from news stories and how they respond to new information. These respondents then read one of two experimental stimuli, which were two-page newspaper op-eds on immigration reform dated February 2013. Treated respondents read an op-ed that either favored immigration reform or opposed immigration reform. In both cases, the author of the piece was the fictitious Reverend Gary Chapman, senior pastor at Briarwood Church. The articles discussed the Senate's proposed immigration reform bill; one supported the bill and the other opposed it. Religious rhetoric appeared in both articles. Each article had a title, subtitle, and prominently featured quote that incorporated religious themes. For example, the quote in the pro-reform article read: "For I was hungry and you gave me something to eat. I was thirsty and you gave me something to drink. I was a stranger and you invited me in. —Matthew 25:35." There were also biblical references in the text of the articles that supported the authors' arguments. The op-eds are available in the appendix.[25] Respondents in the control condition did not receive an op-ed on immigration reform but did provide their immigration attitudes. Later in the demographic portion of the survey, all respondents answered the same two-pronged religious identification question discussed earlier in the chapter. The resultant four-point religious identification measure, which ranges between 0 and 1, again serves as the dependent variable.[26]

The results below focus on the subsample of interest—individuals with children living at home—with more detailed findings available in the appendix. The top panel of figure 5.6 plots the experimental treatment effects for Democrats with children living at home. The three experimental conditions are indicated on the x-axis, and the y-axis represents the average religious identification score for each condition. The average religious identification score in the control condition is presented in the center of the graph, approximately 0.80. The average levels for respondents in the pro- and anti-reform conditions are plotted to the left and the right of the control group, respectively. Religious identification remained relatively stable in the pro-reform condition relative to the control group (difference = −0.02; p-value = 0.64). Strength of religious identification in the anti-reform condition, however, decreased dramatically, by roughly 0.13 points, or 13% of the scale (p-value = 0.02). Being exposed to a pro-reform religious message had little effect on Democrats' reported religious identities; however, an anti-reform religious message pushed some Democrats away from religion. The bottom panel of figure 5.6 presents the results for Republicans with children at home. Here, neither treatment produced a change in religious identification.[27]

Both the Democratic and Republican results add to our understanding of how the political landscape shapes, or does not shape, partisans' religious identities. Democrats do not have a knee-jerk reaction against religion, or even the mixing of religion and politics. When religion is linked with a liberal policy position, as it was in the pro-immigration reform piece, there was no change to many Democrats' reported religious identifications. It was only when the religious message was linked to a conservative policy position that stood in contrast to many Democrats' political values that Democrats reacted by distancing themselves from religion. This latter finding is consistent with the previous results from this chapter. Moreover, neither treatment condition changed average levels of religious identification among Republicans. Although policy questions from this particular study reveal that Republicans are much more likely than Democrats to oppose progressive immigration reform, Republican respondents did not respond to a liberal-religious immigration message by shifting away from religion. This piece of evidence does not rule out the possibility that Republicans could distance themselves

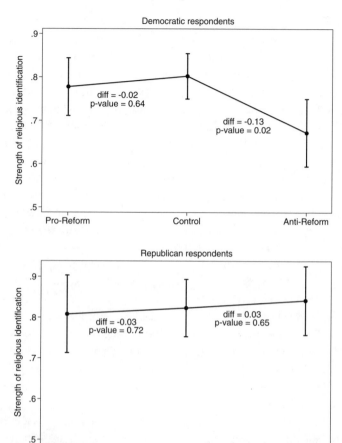

5.6. Religious messages are not always met with backlash among Democrats. The figure presents the experimental treatment effects for Democrats (top panel) and Republicans (bottom panel) with children living at home. The dependent variable is a four-point religious identification scale that ranges from 0 (strong nonidentifier) to 1 (strong identifier).
Source: Immigration rhetoric experiment.

from religion at some point in the future, but it takes more than a single newspaper article to push Republicans away from the institution of religion. Most important, however, religion linked to politics does not always produce a shift away from religion among Democrats. When religion is associated with a liberal position, Democrats' average levels of religious identification remain stable. Instead, the shift appears only when religion is linked to a conservative policy position.

Discussion

The chapter began by describing two possible ways that a link between politics and religion can change religion's role in politics. On the one hand, if religious issues become salient or one party becomes billed as being friendly toward religion, people may rely on their religious identities when making political decisions. On the other hand, people may take the same information as a political cue to guide their religious choices. In doing so, a Democrat might see the Republican Party maintaining a close association with religious groups and taking conservative positions on cultural issues and think, "If this is what religion is, then I must not be very religious." A Republican might see the same political landscape and think, "If this is what religious people support, then I must be religious too." While we commonly assume the first scenario to be true, this chapter looked for evidence in support of the second scenario and tested whether Americans use political information when making religious decisions.

The first two experiments had two aims. The first was to isolate how people's partisan identities influence their reported religious identities. The second was to discover how information linking religious and political issues works in conjunction with partisan identities to affect how religious identities evolve. These questions are difficult to answer using observational data alone. Neither partisan identity nor the political landscape is randomly determined. Thus, when comparing Democrats and Republicans, we do not know whether a difference in religiosity is attributable to partisanship or to some other characteristic on which Democrats and Republicans differ. Similarly, elite coalitions that make up the political landscape do not form at random. Instead, they are often the result of elites' strategic decisions, making it difficult to understand how correlations between party identification, church attendance, and feelings toward politically active religious groups develop. The experiments can circumvent the problems inherent in observational research by measuring what happens when partisanship at the individual level or information about elite-level coalitions is temporarily made more salient.

The priming partisanship experiment tested how partisans answer what we think of as standard demographic religion questions after being encouraged to "think like a partisan." The weak prime, which does not link religion and politics, simply encourages respondents to wear a partisan hat, so to speak, when answering survey questions. The second experiment tests how partisans respond to learning information that links the Republican Party to religious groups and values. While the FFC's close ties with the Republican Party is surely not random, the experiment tests what happens when the relationship is randomly made salient to some and not others. Both experiments find that responses to standard religious questions can change, particularly among those whose religious identities are not yet stable.

A key strength of these findings is the internal validity that comes from running a controlled experiment. Unlike the YPSP and NAES/ISCAP data from chapter 4, unmeasured differences between Democrats and Republicans do not explain the results because the analyses compare treated Democrats and Republicans to untreated Democrats and Republicans. For example, the findings from the last chapter left open the possibility that norms in different religious communities played a role in shaping both partisanship and a return to religion. And while participatory expectations—which vary across religious denominations—may explain why Republicans in the control condition are stronger religious identifiers than Democrats in the control condition, there is less reason to suspect that these norms should correlate with how partisans respond to the political experimental treatments. The experimental results therefore offer an important corroboration of the findings from the long-term panel data because the experiments can account for alternative explanations that the panel data cannot.

Importantly, the sizes of the experimental treatment effects are quite large. In both cases, the existing partisan gaps in religious identification more than doubled in response to the experimental treatments. How should we interpret these results? What do immediate changes in survey responses indicate? An experimental prime and newspaper article are unlikely to immediately and permanently change long-term identities and behaviors. Instead, it is best to think of the experiments as evidence that responses *can* change and that repeated exposure to similar stimuli in the real world might make such a change more long lasting. In fact, the ANES data bracketing the 2004 election finds evidence of this.

While much has been written on the role of religion and morals in the 2004 election, this chapter approaches the topic from a new angle. In particular, this chapter asks whether religion and morality playing a role in the election had the unintended consequence of influencing partisans' levels of religious participation. The panel data from this chapter, in contrast to the YPSP and NAES/ISCAP data, look for religious changes over a short period of time. Instead of measuring how individuals change as they move from one life stage to another, the ANES data measure how individuals within a specific life stage changed in response to a changing political landscape. Moral issues became more salient than usual, and the media reported on the cultural and religious differences between the parties throughout 2003 and 2004. While one might use these two pieces of information to assume that the changing political landscape encouraged church attenders to become more supportive of the Republicans and nonattenders to view the Democrats more favorably, the data show evidence of the reverse. Partisan identification is associated with changes in rates of church attendance. The panel results provide external validation to the experimental results. Outside a laboratory setting, changes in information and exposure to the political landscape can impact the religious involvement of those currently sorting out their religious leanings.

The major strength of the ANES data is that they help make sense of the religiosity gap found in survey research. Both journalists and scholars have written about how people who attend church frequently look different politically from those who do not attend church or attend church infrequently. Analyses showing how answers to this church attendance question changed in response to a shift in the political environment, therefore, offer important insight into these often-discussed correlational relationships. More specifically, the ANES results make it clear that part of why we consistently see strong associations between partisanship and church attendance is because partisans update how they respond to religious survey questions. These results, however, have the inherent limitation that these measures do not capture *actual* behavior but instead *reported* behavior.[28] While the ANES results admittedly do not tell us whether individuals' rates of church attendance actually changed, these results clearly show that politics has helped give rise to the strong correlation between reported church attendance and political outlooks that has garnered so much scholarly and journalistic attention.

The experimental and panel data also build on the results from the previous chapter to show the different pathways that explain how Democrats end up being less religious than Republicans. Chapter 4 showed that Democrats are less likely than Republicans to return to the pews after being on the outskirts of organized religion; partisanship influenced decisions as individuals moved from one life-cycle window to another. The results from this chapter demonstrate that certain Democrats may also respond to the political environment by decreasing their levels of religious engagement. These dual forces increase the likelihood that Democrats end up as less religious than their Republican counterparts. Moreover, the experimental findings indicate that politics may influence Republicans' decisions as well by increasing the likelihood that they return to religion after getting married and having children.

The final part of the chapter offers a further extension to and refinement of our understanding about partisans' responses to the political landscape. Whereas the previous results showed that Democrats have moved away from religion in response to elite-level coalitions between conservative religious groups and the Republican Party, we know little about how partisans might respond when religion is used on the political left. An experiment focused on immigration reform—an issue for which there are religious groups on both sides of the policy aisle—can test what happens when religion is attached to a liberal position as opposed to a conservative position. While Democrats who read a newspaper article that uses a religious justification to take an anti-immigration stance had, on average, weaker religious identities than Democrats who did not read an immigration article, identity strength was the same among those who read a pro-immigration article and those who did not read an immigration article. When religion is linked with policies and groups that Democrats support, Democrats do not dissociate themselves from religion. These results not only reiterate that partisans seem to be taking religious cues from the political world around them, but that the ideological direction of the cues matters.

In addition to showing how partisans at different points in the life cycle respond to a changing political environment, the results from this chapter help address an unresolved concern from chapter 4. Religious denominations emphasize different religious practices and beliefs (see Mockabee, Monson, and Grant 2001; Mockabee, Wald, and Leege 2011), and these differences in expectations may affect the extent to which a person becomes engaged in his or her religious community. For example, members of strict religious communities may be expected to attend services regularly or hold specific religious beliefs. If people who are part of these communities are also more likely to be Republicans, then this could explain why Republicans become more religiously involved as they transition from one life-cycle window to another, a main point from chapter 4. Models that control for the broader religious tradition as well as previous religious practices reduce, but do not altogether eliminate, concerns of this possibility. The results from this chapter—which look at individual-level changes over a short period of time—make it less likely that religious differences across denominations explain partisan-driven religious sorting. Here, individuals are not moving from one position in the life cycle to another, during which time norms of their religious communities may have an influence in religious decision making. Instead, they are responding to changing surroundings, in the form of an experimental stimulus or shifts in the media landscape. Members of conservative Protestant denominations, for example, may identify strongly with their religious faith and be disproportionately Republican. This relationship, however, should not explain why Republicans randomly assigned to be primed with partisan flyers are stronger religious identifiers than Republicans who did not receive such a prime. Similarly, even if Republicans (Democrats) being members of (not) strict religious communities helps explain why Republicans attended church more frequently than Democrats in the 2000 and 2002 waves of the ANES data, there is no reason to assume that these denominational differences account for individual-level changes between 2002 and 2004 after attendance rates were stable between 2000 and 2002. Finding similar results using experimental data and panel data that track changes over a short period of time further assuages concerns that denominational differences explain partisan-driven religious change.

The results from this chapter build on the existing literature that looks at how politics affects religion in three ways. First, Democrats respond to the conservative tilt of religion in politics. While previous research assumed that it was the Republican Party's close connection with religious conservatism that pushed those on the political left out of religion, the FFC experiment confirmed this to be the case. Second, politics not only has the power to push some out of religion but it also has the power to bring others deeper into the religious fold. Hout and Fischer (2014, 2002), who first put forth the religious-political hypothesis, argue that the close relationship between the Republican Party and religious right organizations has pushed liberals and moderates out of organized religion, giving rise to an increase in religious nonidentification in the United States. This argument, however, assumes that religious-political coalitions affect only those on the political left. These people, upon seeing how religion and politics are connected, opt out of organized faith despite retaining certain core religious beliefs regarding the existence of God and the afterlife (Hout and Fischer 2002). But might conservatives have also acted differently in the absence of such right-leaning religious-political coalitions? It is possible that some conservatives would have become nonidentifiers but opted to remain nominal religious affiliates on account of their politics. While we cannot tell from cross-sectional data alone, the experimental results suggest that this may be happening. In both experiments, not only did treated Democrats look less religious than untreated Democrats, but treated Republicans looked more religious than untreated Republicans. In other words, both Democrats and Republicans are producing the religiosity gap in American politics. And third, the political environment and the cues that individuals receive are important drivers of religious change. Hout and Fischer's findings, which rely on repeated cross-sectional data, imply continuous movement over time. The results from this chapter, however, call this assumption into question. The ANES data and the immigration experiment both show that partisans do not update their religious attachments in the absence of a cue that encourages such a change.

Together, these findings not only offer additional evidence in support of the life-cycle theory, but they also show how the political landscape, which has linked the parties with religious groups and values, can influence the religious attachments of some partisans. Making this claim, however, requires the assumption that partisans are aware of religion's current place in politics and can successfully act on this knowledge. This may not be the case for everyone, and politically engaged and knowledgeable partisans may therefore be more likely to align their religious attachments and behaviors with their partisan identities. Political knowledge being a requisite of partisan-driven religious sorting, in turn, may have important consequences. If politically knowledgeable Democrats are selecting out of religion and politically knowledgeable Republicans are selecting into religion, the political makeup of churches will differ not only with respect to partisanship but also with respect to political knowledge and interest. Chapter 6 considers the role of political knowledge in making religious decisions.

SIX

The Religious and Political
Consequences of Political Knowledge

.

The previous chapters showed that religious attachments are not stable
throughout life; rather, identification with and involvement in organized religious life can change over time. One factor shown to influence religiosity and
religious involvement is partisan identity. Partisan identity, in conjunction
with the religious-political environment, encourages Republicans to become
more religious and Democrats to become less so. This explanation, however,
assumes that Americans are aware of the religious and cultural differences
that separate the Democratic and Republican parties. In the absence of such
knowledge, partisans would have little motivation to update their religious
identities to be consistent with their partisan identities. Therefore, an important piece in the argument that the political landscape can influence religious
decisions hinges on partisans' abilities to identify and internalize changes to
the political landscape.

The first part of this chapter shows that political knowledge operates as
an important constraint on partisan-induced religious change. Respondents
with medium and high levels of political knowledge produce the results
presented in the previous chapters. Democrats and Republicans with low
levels of knowledge, in contrast, did not come to be less or more religious,
respectively, unless the information regarding the parties' relationships to
religion were made explicit.

The role of political knowledge in forging relationships between partisanship and religion also has important political consequences. If more knowledgeable Republicans are selecting into religion and more knowledgeable
Democrats are selecting out of religion, America's resultant religious composition will differ along dimensions of both partisanship and political knowledge. The second half of the chapter shows that while political engagement

and religious involvement are positively correlated among Republicans, they are negatively correlated among Democrats. Republicans, therefore, not only attend church more frequently than Democrats, but churchgoing Republicans are more politically engaged than churchgoing Democrats. The chapter concludes by discussing what happens when church attenders differ not only in their partisan attachments but also in their political interest—that is, it explores changes in the ability of churches to influence voters and the potential of political campaigns to mobilize supporters through religious communities.

The Importance of Political Knowledge and Interest

Political elites are in a position to shape opinions and outlooks. Elites not only have the power to disseminate information and frame discussions in the media (Hogg and Reid 2006; T. Lee 2002; Zaller 1992), but they also provide information to citizens, many of whom are not politically knowledgeable (Berelson, Lazarsfeld, and McPhee, 1954; Campbell et al. 1960; Converse 1964; Delli Carpini and Keeter 1996) and want to make political decisions without expending much effort (Miller, Wlezien, and Hildreth 1991; Nisbett and Ross 1980; Sniderman, Brody, and Tetlock 1991). The resultant cues can be very powerful indeed. Politicians' campaign decisions regarding which issues to emphasize and how to talk about these issues allow voters to gain useful information that helps them make sound political judgments despite not being fully informed (Popkin 1991). As Democratic and Republican elites offer distinct viewpoints, the public can, in turn, understand "what goes with what" (Carmines and Stimson 1989; Layman and Carsey 2002; Sniderman, Brody, and Tetlock 1991; Zaller 1992).

Although cues are potentially quite strong, their impact may be limited in the real world. Citizens must first be exposed to the political cues and second be able to properly employ the information. Zaller's (1992) first axiom in his influential book, *The Nature and Origins of Mass Opinion*, reads: "The greater a person's levels of cognitive engagement with an issue, the more likely he or she is to be exposed to and comprehend—in a word, to receive—political messages concerning that issue" (42). Layman and Carsey (2002) found that elite polarization on social welfare, racial, and cultural issues did not produce wholesale polarization among citizens. Instead, only those partisans aware that elites diverged on these issues updated their policy positions. Political knowledge is therefore a prerequisite if citizens are to respond to elite cues and messages. Knowing relevant information is the first step. Knowing how the information relates to one's own attitudes and identities is a crucial second step.

Political information emanating from politicians and the media should therefore not have an equal influence on everyone. More knowledgeable partisans should be more aware of the parties' policy positions and candidates' strategies than their less knowledgeable counterparts. And, armed with this information, informed partisans can subsequently decide whether to update their religious identities, political identities, or both. Without this information, however, religious Democrats and less religious Republicans would not be aware that their identities are unaligned and have no reason to change either.

How do we know whether partisans receive these political cues? In an ideal world, scholars would know the amount and type of political information to which respondents are exposed as well as what they know about related issues and policies. Unfortunately, these data are rarely available. Instead, scholars often rely on proxies. In the next part of the chapter, general political knowledge and levels of education serve as proxy measures of exposure to and understanding of the elite-level divergence along religious and cultural lines. The latter part of the chapter utilizes two measures that more directly tap into current political discussions. The first is an issue-specific knowledge question measuring whether respondents know where the parties stand on abortion. This measure offers a direct assessment of whether respondents can distinguish the parties along the relevant moral and cultural dimension. The second measure—self-reported political interest—does not rely on general levels of knowledge or educational status but rather on respondents' own evaluations. Each proxy has both strengths and limitations; however, it is reassuring that the same pattern of results appears across the different measures. The next section tests whether political information is associated with the partisan-driven religious changes presented in the previous chapters.

Political Knowledge as a Moderator

The YPSP data, presented in chapter 4, offered the first test of partisanship influencing religious decision making. Although the parties did not take distinct positions on religious and cultural issues while members of the student generation were growing up in the late 1950s and early 1960s, the parties began to distinguish themselves in the 1970s. The empirical results showed that both Republicans and Democrats distanced themselves from religion in young adulthood but that Republicans returned to religion at a higher rate than Democrats upon reaching adulthood. This partisan-induced religiosity gap appeared, according to the argument, because the political environment linked the Republican Party with religious conservatives and the Democratic

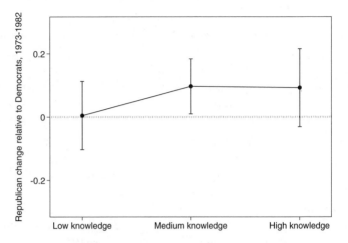

6.1. 1973–1982: Political knowledge facilitates partisan-driven religious change. The figure presents partisan differences in changing levels of church attendance between 1973 and 1982 based on respondents' levels of political knowledge (measured in 1973). Estimates come from a change model that includes a lagged dependent variable and control variables described in chapter 4. Positive estimates indicate that Republicans became more frequent church attenders than Democrats between 1973 and 1982. Negative estimates indicate that Democrats became more frequent church attenders than Republicans between 1973 and 1982. Estimates near zero indicate that neither group became more frequent church attenders relative to the other between 1973 and 1982.
Source: Youth-Parent Socialization Panel Study.

Party with cultural liberals. But not everyone learned about these shifts among political elites, and Democrats' and Republicans' religious behaviors should not differ in the absence of such information.

A composite score of political knowledge based on seven individual items asked in the 1973 survey wave helps test the role of political awareness in producing the main results from chapter 4. The survey asked both civics knowledge (such as the number of Supreme Court justices and the length of a senator's term) and political events knowledge (such as the country of which Tito is the leader and whether the Republicans or Democrats are more con-servative). While there were no questions that directly measured knowledge about the parties' positions on religiously laden issues, the knowledge index serves as a proxy for whether respondents were likely aware of the changing positions of political elites. If elite cues and the political environment explain why Democrats' and Republicans' religious trajectories differed, partisans with higher levels of knowledge should have produced these results.

Table 6.1 Knowledge is an important prerequisite for updating identities

YPSP 1973–1982		Priming partisanship		ANES 2002–2004		Faith and Freedom Coalition	
Full	0.08**	Full	0.15**	Full	0.15**	Full	0.17**
	(0.04)		(0.02)		(0.04)		(0.04)
Low	0.01	Low	−0.01	Low	0.05	Low	0.13
knowledge	(0.07)	education	(0.02)	knowledge	(0.07)	education	(0.09)
	N = 217		N = 114		N = 68		N = 173
Medium	0.10**	Medium	0.32**	Medium	0.23**	Medium	0.31**
knowledge	(0.05)	education	(0.12)	knowledge	(0.06)	education	(0.13)
	N = 196		N = 80		N = 71		N = 124
High	0.09*	High	0.17*	High	0.13**	High	0.13
knowledge	(0.05)	education	(0.08)	knowledge	(0.01)	education	(0.10)
	N = 147		N = 66		N = 104		N = 119

Note: Coefficients represent the partisan difference or partisan change in religiosity for different levels of political knowledge. Standard errors are in parentheses. The dependent variable for the Youth-Parent Socialization Panel Study (YPSP) and American National Election Study (ANES) models is church attendance. The dependent variable for the priming partisanship and Faith and Freedom Coalition experiments is a four-point religious identification measure. Details about the samples, variables, and model specifications are available in the chapters from which the main results are drawn. * $p < 0.10$; ** $p < 0.05$.

Figure 6.1 plots change in church attendance between Republicans and Democrats based on levels of political knowledge, broken into three equally sized knowledge groups.[1] Positive numbers indicate that Republicans became more frequent attenders relative to Democrats between 1973 and 1982. Negative numbers indicate that Democrats became more frequent attenders relative to Republicans between 1973 and 1982. Results near zero indicate that partisans changed (or did not change) at roughly equal rates. In the bottom tercile of political knowledge, both Democrats and Republicans followed the sociological religious life cycle and became more religious between 1973 and 1982, but no partisan gap emerged. Partisan differences, however, are evident among those with middle and high levels of political knowledge. Within these knowledge subgroups, Republicans became more frequent church attenders relative to Democrats between 1973 and 1982. The results using the full sample of respondents presented in chapter 4, therefore, occur primarily because of those with at least moderate levels of political information.[2]

The first two columns of table 6.1 present the YPSP results in table form. The first result, with the coefficient of 0.08, is the main result found in chapter 4. The coefficient indicates that between 1973 and 1982, Republicans returned to the pews at a faster rate than Democrats. The subsequent rows present estimates of the same gap—Republicans versus Democrats between 1973 and 1982—for respondents with low, medium, and high levels of political knowledge.

The second two columns of results take a similar approach for the priming partisanship experiment from chapter 5. As a reminder, the experiment randomly primed some respondents' partisan identities by exposing them to flyers for a political engagement drive. The main dependent variable presented in the chapter was a four-point religious identification scale ranging between 0 (strong nonidentifier) and 1 (strong identifier). Here, education serves as a proxy for political knowledge. Among all respondents with children at home, priming partisan identities produced a 0.15 gap between Republicans and Democrats, with treated Republicans becoming stronger religious identifiers compared to untreated Republicans and treated Democrats becoming weaker religious identifiers compared to untreated Democrats. The results are most pronounced, however, among those with medium and high levels of education. A gap did not emerge among partisans with low levels of education, possibly because the relationships between religion and politics were not well understood and internalized. Interestingly, the results are actually strongest among partisans with moderate levels of education. This is consistent with Zaller's (1992) theory that a certain amount of knowledge is necessary to ensure that people are exposed to relevant information, but that people with high levels of knowledge have firm opinions and are more likely to reject information that is inconsistent with their views. In this case, highly educated partisans may have previously sorted themselves into political and religious camps that suited their needs, limiting the potential for short-term external influence.

The third pair of columns replicates the main ANES findings in which Republicans' and Democrats' reported church attendance moved in opposite directions between 2002 and 2004 in response to the emergence of gay marriage as a salient political issue. Here again, the 0.15 gap that emerged between Republicans and Democrats is most pronounced among both those with medium and high levels of political knowledge. As with the other data, the results are weakest among respondents with low levels of political knowledge, and respondents with moderate levels of knowledge underwent the largest changes.[3]

The final set of columns presents the results for the Faith and Freedom Coalition experiment. Similar to the priming study, the dependent variable is a four-point religious identification measure, and the quantity of interest is the identification gap that emerged between Republicans and Democrats in response to a newspaper article about the FFC. Level of education again serves as a proxy for political knowledge. This experiment differs from the other experimental and observational data in an important way; all treated respondents received relevant information about the religious-political environment, lowering the knowledge barrier. While partisans with a moderate amount of education still responded to the experimental treatment to the largest extent, there is suggestive evidence that respondents with low levels of education also responded to the treatment (p-value = 0.14).[4]

A reanalysis of the empirical findings demonstrates that a certain level of political knowledge or engagement is necessary for partisans to respond to the political environment and update aspects of their religious identities. This relationship between knowledge and religious involvement may, in turn, have important political consequences. Knowledgeable Republicans selecting into religion and knowledgeable Democrats selecting out of religion change not only the partisan makeup of churches but also the political interest and knowledge of church members. The next section explores how partisanship, political knowledge, and religious involvement are correlated today.

Partisanship, Political Knowledge, and Religious Involvement

What are the consequences of political knowledge being a prerequisite of partisan-driven religious change? If partisans need to know relevant information in order to sort themselves religiously, then Republicans with higher levels of political knowledge should, on average, attend church with greater frequency than Republicans with lower levels of political knowledge. Similarly, Democrats with higher levels of political knowledge should, on average, attend church less frequently than Democrats with lower levels of political knowledge. The result is not only a partisan gap in church attendance but also a partisan knowledge gap in church attendance. The 2012 ANES offers a first test of whether political knowledge is associated with partisans' levels of church attendance.

2012 ANES

Two questions asking where the presidential candidates—Barack Obama and Mitt Romney—stand on abortion serve as a measure of political knowledge. Respondents "know" where the candidates stand if they reported that Obama holds a more liberal position on abortion than Romney. This political knowledge measure is particularly telling because it measures specific knowledge about the parties' and their candidates' positions on an issue related to morality and religion. Roughly two-thirds of Americans successfully placed Obama as taking a more liberal position on abortion than Romney. The dependent variable is church attendance, which ranges between 0 (never attend) and 1 (attend weekly or more). In order to understand the overall composition of churches today the sample includes people of all ages and life-cycle stages.[5]

Political knowledge is strongly correlated with levels of religious engagement, but in opposite directions for Democrats and Republicans. Figure 6.2 presents the estimated average levels of church attendance for Republicans and Democrats based on respondents' knowledge. These estimates come from an ordinary least squares (OLS) model that controls for gender, race, age, income, education, religious affiliation, marital status, parental status, level of political interest, and general political knowledge.[6] Among partisans who do not know the candidates' positions on abortion, Republicans attend church more frequently than Democrats (difference = 0.06; p-value < 0.01). This moderately sized gap, however, grows when we look at those who can accurately place the candidates on the abortion issue. Democrats who know the candidates' abortion positions attend church less frequently than Democrats who do not know these positions (difference = −0.06; p-value < 0.01), while Republicans who know the candidates' abortion positions attend church more frequently than Republicans who do not (difference = 0.08; p-value < 0.01). The partisan gap in church attendance is more than three times the size among respondents who know the candidates' positions on abortion than among respondents who do not.[7]

The bottom panel of figure 6.2 uses a different measure—whether a partisan is "conflicted" (1) or not (0)—to answer the same question. A religiosity measure that combines questions on church attendance, biblical literalism, frequency of private prayer, and religious guidance in daily life helps classify respondents.[8] A Democrat is conflicted if his or her religiosity score is one standard deviation or more above the mean, while a Republican is considered conflicted if his or her religiosity score is one standard deviation or more below the mean. About 11% of partisans are classified as conflicted. The results come from a logistic regression model that includes the same control variables described above. Both among those who do and do not know about the candidates' positions on abortion, Republicans are more likely to be conflicted than Democrats, meaning that there are fewer highly religious Democrats today than secular Republicans. The probability of being a conflicted partisan, however, is approximately 5% lower among both Democrats and Republicans who know the candidates' positions on abortion.

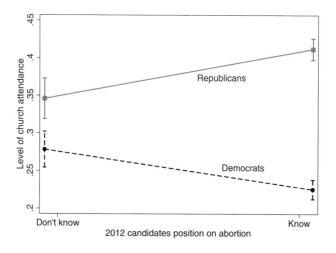

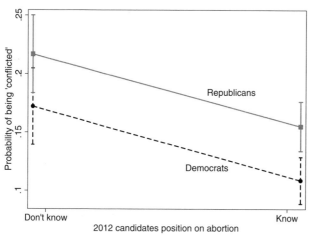

6.2. Partisans' church attendance varies with political knowledge. The top panel presents the estimated levels of church attendance for Democrats (black circles) and Republicans (gray squares) based on whether partisans knew where the 2012 presidential candidates stood on abortion. The bottom panel presents the estimated probabilities of being a "conflicted" partisan—being more than one standard deviation above the mean level of religiosity for Democrats and one standard deviation below the mean level of religiosity for Republicans—based on knowledge about the candidates. Estimates come from an OLS model (top panel) and a logistic regression model (bottom panel) and include control variables described in the text. *Source*: 2012 American National Election Study.

These results come with the caveat that they are descriptive. For example, it is quite likely that people who attend church more frequently are more likely to learn where the candidates stand on abortion. While this alternative explanation highlights that these analyses do not uncover the causal relationship among partisanship, political knowledge, and religious involvement, the correlational results are still informative in showing how these three variables covary. Returning to the example that church attenders might learn where the candidates stand on abortion, the results show that this should only hold true for Republicans. Whereas higher levels of church attendance correspond with Republicans being more likely to know where the candidates stand on abortion, higher levels of church attendance actually correspond with Democrats being less likely to know the same information. Thus, we are left with an explanation that the correlations between church attendance and political knowledge differ for Democrats and Republicans.

These results also do not account for a person's immediate religious environment. Partisans, for example, may behave differently based on whether they believe their religious communities share their political beliefs. Whereas the results above show that there is a negative association between political knowledge and church attendance among Democrats, this may not be the case for Democrats who are part of liberal churches. These individuals may instead have a positive association between knowledge and religious attendance. The ANES results therefore cannot distinguish between partisans in different types of religious communities and present only the weighted average for the entire Democratic population, which includes those not involved in religious communities, those involved in politically liberal religious communities, and those involved in politically conservative religious communities. The next section uses another data set to test how the relationship among partisanship, political knowledge, and religious involvement changes when respondents' religious congregations are also considered.

ELCA/Episcopal Church Study, 1999–2000

Whereas the ANES is a nationally representative survey focused on individual respondents, Paul Djupe and Christopher Gilbert developed a survey focused on what goes on within specific houses of worship. In doing so, the main sampling unit is not the individual, as is the case in many surveys, but rather congregations belonging to the Evangelical Lutheran Church in America (ELCA) and the Episcopal Church, USA. Djupe and Gilbert first surveyed clergy from the two denominations and then surveyed congregants from a subset of the congregations whose clergy had participated. This strategy produced a rich data set that not only captures individual-level information about congregants but also information about their broader religious environments.

The ELCA/Episcopal Church Study measures whether congregants believe they are part of politically like-minded congregations by asking respondents about their fellow church members' political affiliations. Respondents answered whether they thought they were similar to or different from fellow church members on a host of demographic traits, including partisan affiliation. Respondents could answer same as me, Republican, Independent, or Democratic.[9] Level of political interest in the most recent presidential campaign serves as a proxy for political engagement.[10] And consistent with the ANES models, the dependent variable is reported church attendance, rescaled to range between 0 and 1.

The top panel of figure 6.3 presents the correlation between political interest and church attendance for Democrats who report that a majority of their fellow congregants shares their Democratic political viewpoints (gray squares) and those who think they are in the political minority (black circles). Just as above, the points represent predicted estimates from an OLS model that includes socioeconomic control variables, other measures of church involvement, and whether respondents perceive their fellow congregants to be similar to themselves with respect to race, age, religious beliefs, social class, and distance living from the church. Among Democrats in politically like-minded churches, there is a positive correlation between political interest and church attendance. In a religious environment in which Democrats are surrounded by other Democrats, interest in politics is positively associated with religious participation. This result differs from the ANES results, which found a negative association between knowledge and church attendance among Democrats. Among Democrats in politically dissimilar churches—churches in which they feel as though most other members are Republicans—political interest has a mild negative correlation with church attendance. The individual associations between interest and church attendance are statistically significant as is the interaction term testing whether the correlation between political interest and church attendance differs for those in politically similar and dissimilar churches (difference-in-difference estimate = 0.10; p-value = 0.01).

Similar trends appear when looking at Republican respondents (bottom panel of figure 6.3). There is a positive correlation between church attendance and political involvement among Republicans who feel they are on the same political team as other congregants. This is not the case, however, among partisans who feel they are in the political minority in their churches. Again,

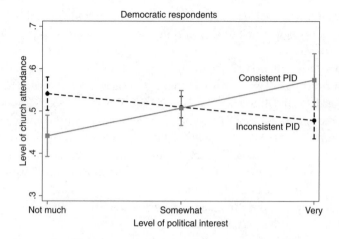

Democratic respondents

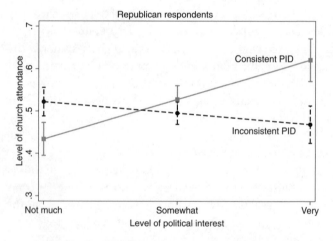

Republican respondents

6.3. Partisans' church attendance varies with political interest and congregational makeup. The top panel presents the estimated levels of church attendance for Democrats based on respondents' levels of political interest and whether they believe others in the congregation are also Democrats (gray squares) or are not also Democrats (black circles). The bottom panel presents the estimates for Republican respondents. Estimates come from OLS models that include control variables described in the text.

Source: Djupe and Gilbert, Evangelical Lutheran Church in America/ Episcopal Church Study, 1999–2000.

the difference between these two slopes is statistically significant (difference-in-difference estimate = 0.12; p-value < 0.01).

These results offer important nuance to the ANES findings. On the one hand, the ELCA/Episcopal Church Study shows a similar trend among Democrats and Republicans. When respondents think their party identifications match those of other congregants, political interest and religious engagement are positively correlated. The reverse relationship appears among those who perceive themselves to be political outsiders. These findings demonstrate that the ANES data overlook relevant congregational factors. On the other hand, looking only at correlations separately for people based on their congregation obscures the wide variation in congregational perceptions. The ELCA/Episcopal Church data show that Democrats and Republicans are not equally likely to belong to politically like-minded churches. Sixty-seven percent of Republicans reported attending churches in which most of the congregants were also Republicans, whereas only 25% of Democrats did so. This unequal balance means that Democrats are far more likely be part of congregations that produce a negative association between political interest and religious involvement, and Republicans are far more likely to be part of congregations that produce a positive association between political interest and religious involvement. The positive correlation between knowledge and church attendance for Republicans and the negative correlation between knowledge and church attendance for Democrats found in the ANES, therefore, reflect the perceived political imbalances that currently exist within churches.

Discussion

Political knowledge and engagement are important in understanding both the causes and the consequences of partisan-driven religious change. The first half of the chapter shows that knowledge is a prerequisite for politics to influence religious decision making. Without being exposed to and internalizing information regarding how the parties and partisans differ, partisans should not align their religious and political identities. A reanalysis of the previous empirical results produces consistent evidence that religious sorting occurs predominantly among those with moderate and high levels of political knowledge.

The second half of the chapter shows that one consequence of political knowledge's role in producing religious change is that the composition of church attenders differs along both partisan and knowledge dimensions. The ANES data show that political knowledge is positively correlated with church attendance among Republicans and negatively correlated with church attendance among Democrats. Further, data collected by Djupe and Gilbert provide additional context to the ANES findings by showing that the correlations likely move in opposite directions because Democrats are more likely to feel like political minorities in church, which yields a negative correlation between political interest and church attendance. In contrast, Republicans are more likely to feel like they are in the political majority, producing a positive correlation between interest and attendance.

While political knowledge is a necessary condition for partisan-driven religious change in the data presented in the previous chapters, this may not always be the case. The two experiments, for example, show that Republicans in the control condition who have low levels of political knowledge or education are still, on average, more religious than control-condition Democrats with a comparable amount of knowledge. Similarly, Republicans with low levels of political knowledge attended church more frequently than Democrats with low levels of political knowledge at the outset of the ANES panel in 2000, and Republicans who did not know the 2012 presidential candidates' positions on abortion still attended church at a higher rate than Democrats who could not correctly place the candidates.[11] In other words, while the priming stimulus and the increased salience of gay marriage did not widen the religious gap between partisans with low levels of political knowledge, a partisan gap still exists.

Homophily—the tendency to associate with others who are similar to themselves (McPherson, Smith-Lovin, and Cook 2001)—can make sense of these results. A person may make religious and political decisions in part based on what family, friends, and neighbors do. In trusting others and looking to them for guidance about how to behave, this person may end up being a not-very-religious Democrat or a religiously involved Republican without knowing anything about his or her religious-political surroundings. While these individuals are not actively making religious decisions based on their partisan affiliations nor are they necessarily able to immediately respond to the political environment, they can nonetheless become sorted over time. The potentially strong influence of social networks means that the overall religiosity gap is not only made up of highly engaged partisans but also of those without much political knowledge.

The compositional differences found in this chapter can have important downstream effects for political campaigns and mobilization strategies. By virtue of being more politically engaged, religious Republicans may be more easily mobilized through religious appeals, making them an ideal audience for Republican candidates. Republican messages that emphasize religious values or policies should be particularly effective as recipients are more likely to be religious, Republican, and politically engaged. Conversely, religious Democrats are less politically knowledgeable and less politically engaged than both their religious Republican counterparts and their nonreligious Democratic counterparts. This means that religious cues and messages—even supporting the Democratic side—may fall flat because the people who would be most receptive to these messages in theory may not care about politics or may not be able to successfully internalize a particular message. These results also raise the question of what approach Democratic politicians should take with respect to religion. One interpretation of the results from this chapter is that the Democrats should employ more of a secularist strategy, emphasizing a strict separation between church and state. In doing so, the party may mobilize Democrats who are not very religious but are politically engaged. But many who are not religious are not hostile toward religion; rather, they just happen not to be involved. It is therefore unclear whether such a strategy would actually energize these religiously uninvolved Democrats. Similarly, we do not know whether a religious strategy deployed by the Democrats would demobilize or dampen support among these politically engaged Democrats who are not very religious. Future research exploring these possibilities would further our understanding of the relationship between religiosity, partisanship, and political engagement.

Finally, the results from this chapter highlight how a church's political makeup constrains its ability to influence congregants. Djupe and Gilbert's book (2009), which uses the data presented in this chapter, provide two such examples. First, the political influence of religious environments is mediated through social interactions. Looking specifically at small groups within churches, Djupe and Gilbert find that social homogeneity allows politically relevant skills to develop. The authors convincingly show that similarities within small church groups increase the likelihood that group members practice civic skills—such as planning a meeting or writing a letter. These civic skills are, in turn, correlated with the likelihood of a group member being recruited for a political activity through the church. Politics is one such dimension on which church members may be similar to one another. While churches can encourage congregants to practice civic skills and become involved in politics, their effects are not uniform. Second, the authors find that clergy speech can motivate political participation, but only under particular circumstances: a congregant must share the party identification of the clergy and the political makeup of the congregation must be similar to the congregant's party identification. Churches do not have direct, unmediated influence on members' attitudes; rather, their influence is highly contingent on the political demographics of the church.

Djupe and Gilbert's findings are important because Democrats and Republicans are not equally likely to be in Democratic- or Republican-majority congregations. Given that fewer Democrats are in Democratically homogeneous churches, they are at a disadvantage for learning civic skills and being recruited into politics by either fellow church members or through their clergy's speeches. The likelihood that these conditions will be met are much higher for Republicans. A church's ability to influence opinion and spur political action will therefore differ for Democrats and Republicans.

The results from this chapter, in conjunction with the previous two, show how the political environment—in which the Republican Party is linked with culturally conservative policy positions and groups—has helped change the religious makeup of the United States by influencing partisans' religious decisions at a certain point in their lives. In doing so, the results help explain the current religious-political environment in which Republicans are more religious than Democrats. The next chapters build on these findings to test the life-cycle theory's reach. Chapter 7 looks at African Americans and utilizes the life-cycle theory as a means of understanding their religious and political outlooks, while chapter 8 uses the life-cycle theory to look for partisan-driven religious change in a different political environment.

SEVEN

Faithful Partisans: A Closer Look at African Americans

African Americans' religious and political attachments demonstrate that the religiosity gap found in American politics does not apply to everyone. Politically, African Americans are solidly Democratic. Although African Americans once identified as Republicans, the party of Abraham Lincoln, their allegiances began to shift during the New Deal Era of the 1930s and solidified in the 1960s during the Civil Rights Era. Today, African Americans are the single most cohesive demographic partisan bloc. In 2016, roughly 87% of African Americans identified as Democrats or leaned Democratic; only 7% identified as or leaned Republican (Pew Research Center 2016b). Based on the preceding chapters, we might incorrectly assume that this strong Democratic constituency is not very religious.

But African Americans are the single most religiously devout racial or ethnic group in the United States. African Americans, particularly those who identify with a black Protestant tradition, attend church more frequently, are more likely to say religion is extremely important to them, are more likely to report that religion plays an important role for them in making personal decisions, and are more likely to believe that the Bible is the word of God than their white counterparts (McDaniel and Ellison 2008; Putnam and Campbell 2010). African Americans' high levels of religiosity are noticeable also in comparison to other racial and ethnic minority groups, such as Hispanic Americans and Asian Americans (Putnam and Campbell 2010). African Americans are therefore simultaneously the most religious and most Democratic demographic group in the United States.

The goal of this chapter is to understand how African Americans' exceptional status matters for politics. The next section provides background on the African American experience with politics and religion. Given African Americans' religious and political histories, identifying as a Democrat and being highly religious may not feel incompatible in the same way that it does for some white Americans. Without such a perceived disconnect between the two identities, the expectations for the life-cycle theory change. Whereas African Americans should experience similar shifts associated with the religious life cycle—decreasing religiosity in young adulthood and subsequently increasing religious involvement in adulthood—African Americans should feel less pressure to update their religious identities to be consistent with their partisan affiliations. This is precisely what the data show. African Americans' religious trajectories look more similar to those of white Republicans than white Democrats.

If politics does not influence black Democrats' religious decisions, how do religious and partisan identities operate among this group? The second part of the chapter considers the political consequences of African Americans' unique set of religious and political attachments. Two experiments show that although African Americans are comfortable with religion and politics mixing in general, as one might expect from a highly religious group, they are less open to Republicans doing the mixing. Together, the chapter adds to the life-cycle theory by considering sociohistorical circumstances and makes political sense of African Americans' unique constellation of identities.

A Unique Relationship between Race, Religion, and Politics

Three interrelated features of black churches' histories and political roles explain how the group's relationship with religion and politics evolved: racial homogeneity, black Protestant theology, and Democratic politicking within the church. These distinguishing markers of the African American religious experience result in religious identities that are more closely tied to racial identities and a distinctive religious view that is highly compatible with many principles of the Democratic Party. These principles are, in turn, reinforced within many politicized black churches.

First, African American Protestantism is the only religious tradition that is categorized explicitly along racial lines. Black churches were not established because of theological divisions with white churches but because African Americans faced racism and discrimination in the United States (Wald and Calhoun-Brown 2011). Black churches allowed African Americans to gather and worship, free from white oversight and oppression. Offering support, aid, and leadership when many social, cultural, and government institutions were unavailable to blacks, the black church became more than a spiritual home; churches served as the social, economic, and political centers of the black community (Brown and Brown 2003; Lincoln 1982; McDaniel 2008; Myrdal 1944). The black church's central role in the broader African American culture and community has created a strong link between African Americans' racial and religious identities. Indeed, Putnam and Campbell (2010) found that black Protestants, compared to those belonging to other religious faiths, are more likely to report that both their religion and ethnicity are important identities. For African Americans, involvement in a religious community may not only be an expression of religious commitment and faith but also an expression of racial identity.

A second distinctive feature of the African American religious experience is black Protestant theology, which is evangelical in its theological orientation. Black Protestants are more likely than white Protestants to believe that the Bible is the literal word of God, Christ physically rose from the dead, and the pathway to salvation requires a "born again" experience (Wilcox 1992b). In this sense, black Protestants, many of whom identify as evangelical, share a common biblical interpretation with white evangelical Protestants. Holding similar overarching beliefs about the Bible, however, obscures important differences in interpretation. On this point, it is worth stepping back and reconsidering what "biblical literalist" means within a broader social context. The Bible is a complicated text with material incorporated from many sources over time, which makes it, according to some, impossible to read "literally" or even consistently (Barr 1981). Instead, its readers must interpret it, and interpretations are inherently socially constructed (Fish 1980). Rather than reading a text in isolation and developing a corresponding set of beliefs, a community imbues the text with meaning. These "interpretive communities" (Fish 1980), in the context of the Bible, allow for a small group of elites— such as theologians and clergy—to rely on common beliefs about why a text exists and what purpose it serves when disseminating a particular interpretation to others in the community. Doing so often also results in certain passages and themes being emphasized and others downplayed (McDaniel and Ellison 2008). People in different religious communities may therefore share the belief that they interpret the Bible literally while simultaneously maintaining different meanings of the text.

Black Protestantism's dogma reflects the struggles African Americans have faced. The theology has a consistent set of themes that has "often expressed resistance and strength in the face of slavery and oppression; has underscored the prophetic concern with issues of injustice, exploitation, and neglect of the less fortunate; and has underscored the imperative of promoting fairness and equality" (McDaniel and Ellison 2008: 183). The collective experience of blacks in the United States has clearly shaped the denomination's theology, with leaders and laypersons alike reading the texts through the lens of their group's history. Importantly, this interpretation differs dramatically from white evangelical theology. Conservative white Protestant theology places a great deal of stress on human sinfulness, divine judgment, and individual repentance and piety (Hunter 1983). Concerns about personal piety and moral conduct (Harvey 1997) lead to strict moral stances on traditional family values and sexual mores. Further, the emphasis on individual behavior produces a biblical interpretation that is largely individualistic rather than communal.[1] In contrast to white conservative Protestants, African Americans' history of social, legal, and religious segregation has allowed for a theological perspective that focuses on predominantly liberal ideas of equality and justice to flourish.

With different theologies, black and white evangelical Protestants are unlikely to have the same interpretation of the Bible despite both groups' supposed literal interpretations of the text. These differences are borne out in policy attitudes. While both white and black biblical literalists are more likely to take conservative positions on moral policies, such as gay rights and abortion, the gap in support for such conservative policies between literalists and nonliteralists is much larger among whites (McDaniel and Ellison 2008). When it comes to social policy preferences, however, the correlations between biblical literalism and preferences run in the opposite direction for whites and blacks. White biblical literalists are generally less likely to think that welfare recipients are in need and less likely to think that the government is spending too little on the poor, compared to whites who are not biblical literalists. The reverse is the case for African Americans. Black biblical literalists are more likely to think that welfare recipients are in need and more likely to think that government is spending too little on the poor, compared to blacks who are not literalists (McDaniel 2008; McDaniel and Ellison 2008). Similar results appear on survey questions relating to the criminal justice system. Biblical literalism among African Americans corresponds to beliefs that the courts should decrease mandatory sentencing and opt for life sentences over the death penalty, whereas biblical literalism among whites corresponds to more conservative positions on crime (McDaniel and Ellison 2008).

A third aspect of the black religious experience that differs from that of many whites is the large role that politics plays within the churches' walls. Studies of black churches frequently note that religious-based activism within the congregation is the norm and is seen in sermons by the clergy, organized activities, and visits from political leaders (Calhoun-Brown 1996; Harris 1994; McAdam 1982; McClerking and McDaniel 2005; McKenzie 2004; Morris 1984; Putnam and Campbell 2010). Black Protestants are more likely than white Protestants and Catholics to hear political sermons, belong to a congregation that organizes voter registration drives, and receive a voter guide at church (Putnam and Campbell 2010; Smidt et al. 2010). Moreover, the political messages, activities, and campaign visits are often tied to liberal policies and Democratic politics. While politicized churches alone do not explain why African Americans are Democrats, the politicization reinforces a naturally occurring relationship based on racial and theological ties to the Democratic Party.[2] The intermingling of black Protestantism and Democratic politics is underscored through Jesse Jackson's 1984 and 1988 presidential bids. Jackson, a Democrat, African American, and minister, showed the centrality of the church as a political mobilization tool for the African American community: "Not only did Jackson go to churches to legitimize his run; his rhetoric consistently fused religion and politics" (Calhoun-Brown 1996: 936). Beyond theology alone, the broader African American religious community provides frequent cues and messages that align with the Democratic Party.

The fused racial-religious identity, black Protestant theology emphasizing social justice and equality, and the active Democratic agenda within black churches make the black experience with religion and politics different from the white majority's. The different histories and experiences, in turn, may change how black Americans internalized Christian conservatism's increased role in politics, particularly Republican politics. The next sections begin to explore the implications of African Americans' dual identities by testing the life-cycle theory on this group.

African Americans within the Life Cycle

The life-cycle theory, presented in chapter 3 and tested in chapters 4 and 5, claims that adolescents and young adults distance themselves from organized religious communities. These same individuals must then decide whether, and to what extent, to be religiously involved as adults, a decision often precipitated by having children. The data showed that partisanship is one factor that affected this decision. The explanation put forth for the findings is that the Republican Party today is seen as the party of religion, friendly to religious values and groups, whereas the Democratic Party is seen as less friendly toward religion and more supportive of secular values and morally liberal policy positions. But not everyone may hold the same associations between the parties and religion.

African Americans, due to their unique social and religious histories in the United States, may not perceive the political landscape in the same way as white Americans. While the Republican Party discusses the importance of marriage being between one man and one woman, an issue on which many African Americans agree with the Republican stance, the Republican Party ignores other religious issues that are important to African Americans, typically related to social justice and equality. On these dimensions, the Democratic Party better serves black Protestants' religious positions. African American Democrats therefore may not perceive their religious and partisan identities as being out of line. Consequently, while African American Democrats should follow the natural pattern of falling away from religion in young adulthood, their Democratic partisan identities should reinforce, rather than weaken, the development of strong religious identities in adulthood.

In an ideal world, it would be possible to replicate all the results presented in previous chapters separately for African Americans. Unfortunately, small sample sizes preclude such an endeavor in all instances. The Youth-Parent Socialization Panel (YPSP), however, allows us to follow African Americans' religious trajectories for a single generation. Although a detailed description of the YPSP data is available in chapter 4, it is worth reiterating important aspects of the data here. The YPSP surveyed a national sample of high school seniors along with their parents in 1965 when respondents were 18 years old and again in 1973 (at 26 years old), 1982 (at 35 years old), and 1997 (at 50 years old). The data therefore offer a test of the life-cycle theory by seeing how individuals' religious trajectories change in young adulthood after leaving home (1965 to 1973) and after getting married, having children, and generally entering adulthood (1973 to 1982). Moreover, data from the parent generation can distinguish between life-cycle effects, in which outside influences are more consequential at a particular stage in one's life, and period effects, in which everyone in the population experiences a similar change. By focusing on one cohort along with cohort members' parents, there are enough African Americans in the data to make meaningful comparisons between African Americans and whites.

The top panel of figure 7.1 shows that church attendance declined in young adulthood among black Democrats (circles and solid line), white Democrats (squares and dashed line), and white Republicans (triangles and dotted line).[3] Chapter 4 showed that Republicans and Democrats both became less religious between 1965 and 1973 and found no partisan difference in these changes over time. Because African Americans are a numerical minority, making up roughly 10% of the original 1965 sample, it would have been possible for African Americans to remain as churchgoers but for the average Democratic church attendance rate to still decline. This is not the case. The vertical axis represents the percentage of respondents who report attend-

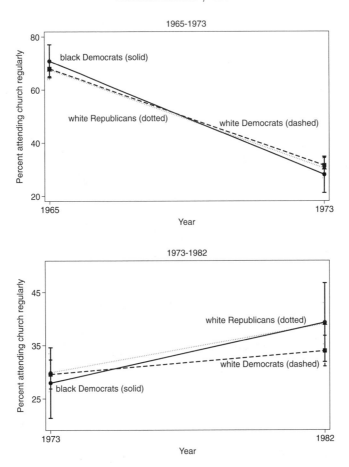

7.1. African Americans' religious trajectories differ from both white Democrats' and white Republicans'. The figure presents raw changes in the percentage of regular church attenders between 1965 and 1973 (top panel) and 1973 and 1982 (bottom panel).
Source: Youth-Parent Socialization Panel Study.

ing church nearly every week, and the horizontal axis represents the first two waves of the YPSP data when the student generation was 18 years old (1965) and again when they were 26 years old (1973). Partisanship is based on self-reports from 1965. In 1965, white Republicans, white Democrats, and black Democrats attended church at roughly the same rate: 68%, 68%, and 71% attended nearly every week, respectively. Further, church attendance for all three groups declined at roughly the same rate. By 1973, only 30% of white Republicans, 31% of white Democrats, and 28% of black Democrats reported

attending church nearly every week or every week. The appendix presents results from parametric change models that include sociodemographic control
variables. These results comport with the religious life-cycle literature that has
focused on African Americans. Even though African American children are
frequently raised in devout households (Petts 2009), rates of measurable religious participation generally decline in young adulthood, including church
attendance and prayer (Smith 2009; Uecker, Regnerus, and Vaaler 2007).

In addition to attending church less frequently, some African American
Democrats also shed their religious affiliations altogether during this time.
While religious nonidentification rates were below 2% for all three groups
in 1965, these numbers increased by 1973, at which time 16% of white
Republicans, 13% of white Democrats, and 10% of black Democrats reportedly did not identify with a religious faith. Importantly, previous research
has shown that nonwhites are less likely to become religious nonidentifiers
compared to whites in young adulthood (Uecker, Regnerus, and Vaaler
2007), even when members of both groups are equally likely to decrease
their levels of outward religious involvement. One reason for this difference
is that when religious affiliations are tied to cultural, ethnic, or racial identities, people are less likely to shed the nominal affiliations despite not being
active community members. This may explain why African American Democrats are slightly more likely to remain religious identifiers in 1973 relative
to white Democrats and white Republicans, although the differences are not
statistically significant (results in the appendix).

African Americans' views about the Bible also changed dramatically between 1965 and 1973. African Americans held the strictest interpretation
of the Bible in 1965: 44% of both white Democrats and white Republicans
reported believing the Bible is the word of God, whereas 58% of African
Americans did so. And yet, despite holding the most dogmatic views on the
Bible as high school seniors, African American Democrats had the largest
change in their beliefs. In 1973, 29% of Republicans, 26% of white Democrats, and 27% of African Americans could be classified as biblical literalists.
Parametric change models (described in detail in chapter 4; presented in the
appendix) that both exclude and include control variables show that African Americans indeed changed their views on the Bible to a greater extent
than white Democrats and white Republicans. Moreover, decreases in religious engagement are limited to this cohort. Across racial lines, members of
the parent generation remained stable in their reported religious practices,
identification, and beliefs between 1965 and 1973.

The decline in religiosity among young African Americans is particularly
striking in the broader societal context. These students were 7 years old when

the Supreme Court ruled that separate is "inherently unequal" in *Brown v. Board of Education of Topeka*, and their formative years occurred during the civil rights movement, during which time black churches played a large role. Ministers and pastors organized boycotts and sit-ins in the South, using their positions as spiritual leaders to encourage civil disobedience, and organizations created to protect and advance African Americans' rights were often structured through local churches and led by clergy (McDaniel 2008). Moreover, feelings that equality and social progress were not occurring quickly enough helped produce black liberation theology in the 1960s, which emphasized Christians' duty to help the oppressed and undo structural inequality (Cone 1997). Yet, even though the church reached far beyond traditional religious boundaries during this time, young African Americans' levels of participation and engagement still declined at this point in their lives.

Chapter 4 showed that Republicans "came back" to organized religion—as measured through church attendance, church-group membership, identification with a denomination, and biblical literalism—to a greater extent than Democrats. The bottom panel of figure 7.1 reproduces the church attendance findings for black Democrats, white Democrats, and white Republicans. In 1973, white Republicans and white Democrats attended church regularly at nearly the same rate, 30% and 31%, respectively, whereas 28% of black Democrats attended church nearly every week. And while Democrats, on average, returned to the pews at a lower rate than Republicans, this trend does not apply to black Democrats. African Americans, despite attending church at a lower rate than both white Democrats and white Republicans in 1973, look identical to white Republicans in 1982, with roughly 40% of both black Democrats and white Republicans reporting that they attend church nearly every week or every week. Parametric change models, presented in the appendix, corroborate these results. The parametric models find that while black Democrats' and white Republicans' religious trajectories were both statistically and substantively the same between 1973 and 1982, white Democrats returned to church at a lower rate. The difference between black Democrats and white Democrats is 0.09 (p-value = 0.07), representing approximately 10% of the church attendance scale and is similar in magnitude to the overall Republican-Democratic gap presented in chapter 4 (change difference = 0.08). Importantly, these results hold when restricting the sample to include only Christian identifiers in 1973.[4]

Other forms of religious belief and involvement also varied across partisan and racial lines. Most notably, whereas black Democrats' views about the Bible's literal interpretation declined sharply between 1965 and 1973, their views rebounded between 1973 and 1982. By 1982, 43% of black

Democrats were once again biblical literalists (up from 27%), compared to 37% of white Republicans (up from 29%), and 25% of white Democrats (stable from 26%). The change between 1973 and 1982 among black Democrats represents a significantly different trajectory from both white Republicans, who also saw an increase in rates of biblical literalism but to a lesser degree, and white Democrats, who saw rates of biblical literalism remain stable over the nine-year period. The YPSP also asked respondents whether they were members of church-connected groups in both 1973 and 1982. Whereas fewer than one in five (18%) were members of such a group in 1973, that number increased by 1982 to 42%, 24%, and 40% for black Democrats, white Democrats, and white Republicans, respectively. Again, black Democrats and white Republicans both increased their levels of religious involvement to a greater extent than white Democrats.

Additionally, the same results appear when looking only at respondents who retained their nominal religious identifications in young adulthood. There were large declines in rates of church attendance and belief that the Bible is the word of God even among those who were religious identifiers in both 1965 and 1973. And when comparing these religious identifiers between 1973 and 1982, the same patterns emerge: black Democrats looked similar in their trajectories to white Republicans. White Democrats, in contrast, returned to religion at a comparatively lower rate. Finally, and consistent with the results presented from chapter 4, these changes took place only among the student generation. Parents, white and black alike, remained stable in their religious participation and beliefs between 1973 and 1982.

While African American Democrats experienced the same decrease in religiosity as their white copartisans, they behaved more similarly to white Republicans than to white Democrats when it came to decisions about returning (or not) to religion. There are many potential explanations for these findings. For example, black Protestant theology, focusing on justice and equality, offers messages consistent with the Democratic policy positions of the 1970s and 1980s. The presence of political messages from both clergy and politicians visiting churches therefore did not place African Americans' religious and political outlooks at odds with each other. In fact, they are likely reinforcing. Moreover, racially segregated churches further reduce the likelihood that black church members hear pro-Republican messages in the pews. Finally, African Americans' social and political histories that have given rise to these dual identities may simply overwhelm whatever influence the political landscape may have on group members' partisan and religious outlooks. While these findings provide insight into one cohort's religious trajectory, the next section looks for similar patterns today.

African Americans Raising Children Today

What about the religious behaviors and identities of African Americans with children today? Does a similar racial-partisan gap emerge among parents of school-aged children? African Americans are more religious than other racial and ethnic groups (Putnam and Campbell 2010; Wald and Calhoun-Brown 2011); however, it is possible that older African Americans, who made religious decisions when religiosity and partisanship were not obviously connected, produce this relationship. Younger African Americans, such as those raising children today, grew up with parties that differentiated themselves along religious lines and may therefore have a different relationship with religion compared to their older counterparts.

Comparing the religiosities of black Democrats who have children at home to white Democrats and white Republicans offers insight into the people who are most likely making or have recently made decisions about religious involvement. The 2012 ANES measures respondents' religious affiliations, involvement in religious communities, and religious beliefs. While the nature of cross-sectional data limits what can be learned about changing levels of religiosity, these data allow for a comparison of religiosity across groups who are otherwise at similar periods in their lives. The top panel of figure 7.2 presents comparisons between white Democrats and black Democrats (gray boxes) and white Republicans and black Democrats (white boxes) while holding constant demographic and socioeconomic variables including gender, age, region of residence, education, income, political knowledge, and political interest. Each dependent variable ranges between 0 and 1, and the black dashed lines represent the confidence intervals surrounding the differences.

Among married respondents with children living at home, black Democrats are more religious than white Democrats on every measure of religiosity. White Democrats, for example, have an average church attendance of 0.38, with approximately 40% saying they never attend and 16% saying they attend weekly. Black Democrats' average church attendance, on the other hand, is 0.63, with just under 15% responding that they never attend and about one-third of respondents reporting that they attend church weekly. The difference in the average level of church attendance is 0.25, which represents one-quarter of the total response scale and over half of one standard deviation. The gap remains virtually unchanged when controls are added into the model (0.23; p-value < 0.01), as shown in figure 7.2. The other dependent variables similarly show that black Democrats are much more religious than their white counterparts. White Democrats are more likely to be religious nonidentifiers

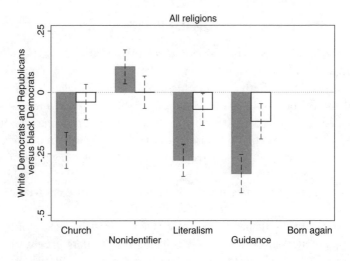

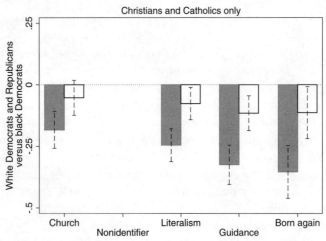

7.2. Racial-political differences in religiosity still exist among partisans raising children today. The sample consists of respondents who are married with children living at home. The gray bars represent the religious differences between white Democrats and black Democrats; the white bars represent the religious differences between white Republicans and black Democrats. *Source*: 2012 American National Election Study.

(nonidentification coded as 1; identification with any faith coded as 0), less likely to believe that the Bible is the word of God (biblical literalism coded as a 1) and less likely to report that religion provides a great deal of guidance in their day-to-day lives (coded as 1). Notably, the religious guidance question is asked only of respondents who previously answered that religion is important in their lives. Even among those respondents who believe religion is important, white Democrats are less likely to report that religion offers "a great deal" of guidance.

One concern with results that include all respondents is that differences in denominational affiliation or a lack of affiliation may be behind the reported associations. For example, religious nonidentifiers attend church with less frequency than identifiers, and Jews are less likely to believe the Bible is the word of God than Christians. Consequently, we may incorrectly infer differences between black Democrats and white Democrats based on certain groups of people, such as nonidentifiers and Jews, who are both Democratic and less religious. To rule out this possibility, the bottom panel of figure 7.2 presents replicated results for Christian and Catholic respondents. The analyses produce the same empirical pattern: black Democrats are more religious than white Democrats. The one measure on which the gap between the groups shrinks noticeably is church attendance, but a gap of 0.18 remains (p-value < 0.01) even among Christian identifiers. Additionally, the right portion of the bottom panel shows that white Democrats—who previously self-identified as Christian—are significantly less likely to call themselves born-again Christians than black Democrats.[5]

In contrast, black Democrats and white Republicans have more similar religious profiles. Roughly one-third of both groups attend church weekly, and while fewer black Democrats are religious nonidentifiers compared to white Republicans (10% versus 14%), the gap disappears after socioeconomic factors are taken into account. To the extent that there are some differences between black Democrats and white Republicans, black Democrats are slightly more religious. In both samples, white Republicans are less likely to believe the Bible is the word of God (difference in full sample = −0.07; p-value = 0.08; difference in Christian and Catholic sample = −0.08; p-value = 0.06), less likely to report that religion provides a great deal of guidance in their daily lives (difference in both samples = −0.12; p-value < 0.01), and less likely to identify as born-again Christians (difference in Christian sample = −0.11; p-value = 0.08) compared to black Democrats.

These results remind us that African Americans, despite being overwhelmingly Democratic, are very religious according to traditional measures of religiosity. Moreover, this trend is unlikely to go away, as it is prominent even among individuals currently raising children. And while the cross-sectional results cannot speak to what sorts of individual-level changes have occurred or will occur, these findings strongly suggest that the YPSP results from above are not anomalous or cohort specific: African American Democrats are raising children in religious households. Despite the religiously charged political environment, African Americans straddle both sides of the religious-political divide by both identifying as Democrats and being highly religious.

African Americans' behaviors do not comport with the conventional explanation that religious Americans have become more Republican over time nor do they follow the life-cycle theory in which their partisan identities influence religious involvement. Instead, sociocultural and historical circumstances add nuance to both explanations and change our expectations about how African Americans' partisan and religious identities influence each other. While the previous results show that African Americans do not feel compelled to update either their partisan or religious identities, they do not address the political consequences of African Americans being both religious and Democratic. The next sections explore whether and how African Americans' partisan and religious identities interact and affect their relationships with today's religiously divided political parties.

How African Americans View and Respond
to the Political Landscape

How much and what type of religion do African Americans want in politics today? Pew Research Center regularly asks about religion's role in politics, most recently in 2014. Three questions in particular shed light on the extent to which African Americans' high levels of personal religiosity translate into attitudes about public religion. The first question asks: "In your opinion, should churches and other houses of worship keep out of political matters or should they express their views on day-to-day social and political questions?" This question taps into general feelings about religious institutions' role in politics, broadly defined. The second question more pointedly asks about churches' role during political campaigns: "During political elections, should churches and other houses of worship come out in favor of one candidate over another, or shouldn't they do this?" These two questions together help us determine how African Americans feel about the separation between politics and religion. For example, do black Democrats want churches talking about politics in general but believe that the discussion should stop before formally endorsing a candidate? Do they want churches going so far as to endorse candidates, or do they want churches out of even day-to-day political discussions? A third question asks about politicians invoking religion: "Do you think there has been too much, too little, or the right amount of expressions of religious faith and prayer by political

Table 7.1 African Americans' views on mixing religion and politics

Churches expressing political views		Churches endorsing candidates		Politicians expressing faith	
Should express	57	Should endorse	41	Too much	29
Should not express	43	Should not endorse	59	Right amount	21
				Too little	51
Total	100%		100%		100%
N	188		187		188

Source: 2014 Pew Research Center.
Note: Cells represent weighted column percentages. The sample includes African American respondents.

leaders?" These questions measure African Americans' views about the intermixing of religion and politics.

African Americans' attitudes on these issues, presented in table 7.1, are divided. While a majority believes churches should express views on general political issues, the majority position is that churches should not endorse candidates running for office. The third question about politicians using religious faith shows that a slight majority of African Americans want to see faith discussed more frequently in politics. These results provide three useful pieces of information about how African Americans perceive religion's role in politics. First, there is general support for church involvement in politics and more expressions of religious faith by politicians. Second, this support, however, is not unconditional: African Americans do not think churches should be in the business of endorsing candidates for elected office. African Americans see a difference between general politicking in churches, which occurs, according to Putnam and Campbell (2010), with greater frequency in African American churches than in other denominations, and overt support for a candidate running for office. And, third, black public opinion is not monolithic. While 57% of African Americans support the idea of churches taking stands on political issues, the remaining 43% think churches should stay out of politics. And while half want to see politicians using more faith than they do, half do not. The divided opinion shows that generalizations should not be made when discussing African American attitudes about the desired role of churches in politics.

Comparisons to others' opinions put these attitudes into context. Similar to the analyses in the previous section, figure 7.3 presents the change in probability of offering a particular response to a survey question when white Democrats and black Democrats (gray bars) and white Republicans and black Democrats (white bars) are compared after socioeconomic factors are

7.3. Racial-political differences exist in attitudes on religion and politics. The gray bars represent the attitudinal differences between white Democrats and black Democrats; the white bars represent the attitudinal differences between white Republicans and black Democrats.
Source: 2014 Pew Research Center.

accounted for.[6] Black Democrats, white Democrats, and white Republicans each have distinctive views on religion's role in politics. On the question of whether churches should express views on political issues, the probability of stating that churches should express opinions on political issues decreases by 0.16 among white Democrats compared to black Democrats. This result is consistent with the religiosity findings from above. If black Democrats are more religious than white Democrats, then it makes sense that African Americans would be more supportive of churches playing a role in politics. In contrast, the probability of believing that churches should express their political views increases by 0.10 among white Republicans compared to black Democrats. Therefore, white Democrats are the least supportive of churches taking political stands, followed by black Democrats, and then white Republicans. Religiosity alone does not determine support for religion's involvement in politics; black Democrats are the most religious of the three groups and the most likely to attend a church in which politics is a salient topic (Putnam and Campbell 2010), and yet white Republicans are the most supportive of churches expressing political views. The second set of bars estimates differences in respondents' beliefs about whether churches should go so far as to endorse candidates for political office. Here again, white Democrats are less likely to support church endorsements compared to black Democrats; however, in this case there is no difference between white Republicans and black Democrats (change in probability = 0.02; p-value = 0.61). Among both white Republicans and black Democrats, about 40% believe churches should endorse candidates. The third and fourth sets of results show two ways of looking at the question asking about politicians expressing religious faith. The third set of results measures differences in the probability of respondents reporting that politicians express "too little" religious faith, and the fourth set captures differences in reports that politicians express "too much." Both measures show that African Americans have attitudes that are neither wholly similar to their white copartisans nor wholly similar to white Republicans whom they resemble on religious dimensions. White Democrats are less likely to say that politicians express too little religious faith and more likely to say that politicians express too much religious faith compared to black Democrats, while white Republicans are more likely than black Democrats to say that politicians express too little religious faith and less likely to say that politicians express too much religious faith.[7]

These results shed light on how race, partisanship, and religion intersect. We might have assumed that because of their high levels of religious commitment and orthodox biblical views black Democrats would be particularly supportive of churches getting involved in politics and politicians using religion. And, to a certain extent, this is what the data show. The baseline attitudes displayed in table 7.1 show that African Americans are generally supportive of this mixing. Black Democrats' enthusiasm, however, has a limit. This is evidenced by white Republicans—despite being less religious than black Democrats across multiple indicators of religiosity—being more supportive of religion entering the political sphere.[8]

While these data indicate that African Americans' partisan and religious attachments translate into a unique set of preferences, they also raise two additional questions. First, what do respondents think about when answering questions about religion's role in politics? The still-segregated nature of religious institutions makes it likely that people of different races interpret the same question differently. Given the high volume of liberal political discussion in black churches, African American respondents may be responding to these questions while thinking of religion as predominantly a tool of the political left. White Democrats, on the other hand, may have conjured up images of religious conservatives or Republican politicians discussing religious values. Borrowing from Zaller (1992), it is possible that the attitudinal gaps just described appear because white and black Democrats have different considerations when answering these questions. A second unanswered question stemming from these results is this: Are African Americans equally supportive of Republican and Democratic leaders bringing religion into politics? While black Democrats are generally supportive of religion entering politics, the results are not evidence that African Americans would respond positively to religion entering right-leaning politics. Instead, the evidence merely suggests that African Americans are supportive of religion entering the political realm generally. The next sections address these questions.

Different Attitudes in Different Contexts

The previous results suggest that black Democrats are not only personally religious but also supportive of mixing religion and politics. White Democrats, on the other hand, look decidedly different on attitudes related to religion and politics. But the results do not tell us *how* black and white Democrats think about religion's role in politics or *why* they hold the attitudes they do. African American Democrats may support mixing religion and politics because religion and Democratic politics are routinely intertwined in their own experiences. White Democrats, on the other hand, may be thinking about the Republican Party's close and public relationship with conservative religious groups, producing different survey responses.

As previously discussed, Pew regularly asks about the amount of faith and prayer used by political leaders. Pew asked this question in 2003, but to only half the sample. The other half answered a question asking specifically about whether then-president George W. Bush used "too little," "the right amount," or "too much" religious faith and prayer. The slight difference in the wording of the question allows for an indirect test of how white Democrats and black Democrats interpret a question about the desirability of political leaders using religion. If black and white Democrats have different considerations—are thinking of different people and ideas—when answering questions about mixing religion and politics, then racial differences in response patterns should emerge. If, for example, white Democrats think about Republican politicians when answering a general question about politicians using religious rhetoric, white Democrats' attitudes should be similar regardless of whether the question asks about leaders in general or the Republican standard-bearer. Both questions would conjure up the same considerations. In contrast, if black Democrats generally think about black churches and politicians using religion on the political left, attitudes should change dramatically when the question asks about President Bush. Heterogeneous effects in which black Democrats change their responses to a larger degree than white Democrats would provide initial evidence that black and white Democrats interpret questions gauging the desire to see politicians using religious faith differently. Pew ran a similar split-question study in 2010, but it asked about President Obama rather than President Bush. Here, we might expect the opposite results. If white Democrats generally think about Republicans using religion when asked about "political leaders," then there might be a larger change in response patterns among white Democrats.[9]

Figure 7.4 presents the predicted probabilities of reporting "too much" religion in 2003 (top panel) and 2010 (bottom panel) separately for white Democrats (gray squares) and black Democrats (black circles). Consistent with the correlational results, white Democrats are much more likely than black Democrats to report that politicians rely "too much" on religious faith in their rhetoric. More pertinent, however, is how black and white Democrats responded to the change in question wording. The probability of white Democrats responding that politicians use "too much" religion increases from 0.32 in the general politicians' category to 0.39 in the Bush-specific category. For black Democrats, the results trend in a similar direction; however, the difference is much more dramatic. The probability of reporting "too much" more than doubles, from 0.12 to 0.29, when the question asks about Bush specifically. While responding "too much" increased among both groups, the increase was much larger among African Americans (p-value = 0.02).[10] The bottom panel presents the same results but asked in 2010 about either political leaders in general or about President Obama specifically. Here, a different picture emerges. While both groups see a decline in the probability of saying "too much" religion, the drop is much steeper among white Democrats. In fact, rates of responding "too much" are statistically indistinguishable between black and white Democrats when the question asks about Obama specifically.[11] The appendix presents the corresponding parametric models, both with and without control variables.

While surveys rarely ask respondents how they interpret a specific question, the pair of Pew studies indirectly measures this, providing further nuance to the cross-sectional results presented in the previous section. The Pew results indicate that black and white Democrats may have been thinking about different aspects of the political arena when answering general questions about religion's role in politics. Black Democrats relative to white Democrats became more likely to report that Bush emphasizes faith too much whereas white Democrats relative to black Democrats became less likely to report that Obama places too much emphasis on faith. These dual results are consistent with the possibility that black Democrats answer these questions by drawing on their own experiences in which liberal politics is

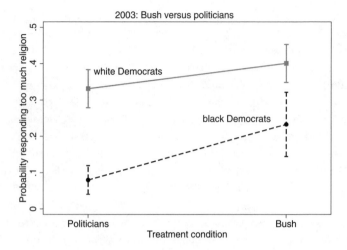

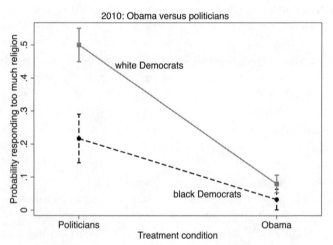

7.4. Views about religion in the political sphere depend on who is using the religion. The points represent the probability that a respondent answered "too much religion." The top panel presents results from 2003 using questions that ask about President George W. Bush or politicians in general. The bottom panel presents results from 2010 using questions that ask about President Barack Obama or politicians in general. *Source*: 2003, 2010 Pew Research Center.

discussed in religious communities and Democratic politicians reach out to black voters, frequently through churches. In contrast, white Democrats may also have been drawing on their own experiences, in which churches are perceived to be more conservative and Republican politicians are thought of as the religious choice. Consequently, white and black Democrats' attitudes about how much is "too much" religion depends, in part, on who is empha-sizing religion. Although African Americans are themselves religious and they want religion to enter politics, the experimental results indicate that their enthusiasm for mixing religion and politics does not extend to Repub-licans' use of religious faith.

These studies also have limits. Asking about politicians in general versus a single politician may muddle the interpretation as people bring strong affective attitudes to bear when answering questions about public figures. This likely explains why the probabilities of answering "the right amount" decrease in the Bush condition and increase the Obama condition for Democrats. Partisans are happy to criticize leaders of the out-party whenever possible whereas they are more hesitant to do so with a member of their own party. Obama's race further heightens the tendency to view leaders of one's own party positively, as black Democrats have been highly supportive of Obama throughout his presi-dency, even when his popularity dipped in the country as a whole (Lederman and Swanson 2015). Additionally, Presidents Bush and Obama used different amounts of religious rhetoric and discussed religious faith differently. Despite these limitations, the findings nevertheless underscore the important point that black and white Democrats seem to conjure up different images when answering questions about religion and politics. A final limitation of these studies is that we still do not know whether the entry of religion into politics can change African Americans' political evaluations apart from their attitudes about mixing religion and politics. How do African Americans' opinions of political candidates change when religion becomes a relevant political consid-eration? The next section uses a final experiment to answer this question.

How Do African Americans Respond to Candidates Receiving Religious Endorsements?

How do African Americans respond when parties inject religion and secu-larism into politics? Since black Democrats are more religious than their white Democratic counterparts and are more supportive of mixing religion and politics, we might wonder how African Americans respond when the Republican (Democratic) Party is linked with religion (secularism). The purpose of this experiment is to explore the political consequences of a religiously infused campaign environment and test whether these cues can influence African Americans' electoral preferences. Doing so builds on the Pew findings from the previous section in two ways. First, the experiment measures feelings toward candidates who are linked with religious or secu-lar values rather than measuring opinions about the mixing of religion and politics. This provides a better indication of how black Democrats' religious and partisan identities operate when they are making political choices. And second, the experiment uses hypothetical candidates, thereby removing concerns associated with asking about specific political leaders.

How might religious and secular cues affect African Americans in a partisan setting? On the one hand, Democrats should support the Democratic candidate and Republicans should support the Republican candidate, regardless of these cues. If this were the case, African Americans' opinions of candidates should remain stable, irrespective of whether they are associated with religious or secular values. On the other hand, black Democrats—by virtue of their strong religious attachments—may respond to religious and secular messages by updating their views of the candidates. In this situation, African American Democrats' preferences may diverge from those of their white copartisans who are, on average, less religious.

Experimental Design

In August 2015, Internet survey participants were told that they were participating in a study about how people make political choices.[12] In particular, respondents learned that the study sought information on how people use voter guides to form opinions about candidates running for local office. Respondents were shown the example of a voter guide created by a local newspaper for a mayoral race in Hidden Hills, Ohio. Figure 7.5 presents the basic voter guide that respondents in the control condition saw. The candidates in the guide are meant to represent average members of their respective parties and have roughly equal amounts of relevant experience and community support. The control version of the voter guide excludes any mention of candidates' religious faiths or positions on moral policy issues. Democratic and Republican respondents in the control condition rated both their own parties' candidates and the opposing parties' candidates at virtually the same level on a seven-point favorability scale.

Respondents were randomly assigned to either the control condition or one of four experimental treatment conditions. Respondents in the control condition saw the mock voter guide presented in figure 7.5. The remaining four conditions are religious Republican, secular Democratic, secular Democratic and religious Republican, and religious Democratic and religious Republican. Respondents in the religious-Republican condition saw the control version of the voter guide with one addition. These respondents saw an additional endorsement for the Republican, John Gibson. Here, the endorsement comes from the Hidden Hills Voters for Faith and reads, "John Gibson is a man of strong

HIDDEN HILLS LEDGER
GUIDE TO THE 2016 MAYORAL ELECTION

Matthew Brown

John Gibson

Personal information
Education: BA (Economics), JD
Current occupation: Lawyer
Age: 52

Personal information
Education: BA (Political Science), MBA
Current occupation: Financial Planner
Age: 55

Politics
Party identification: Democrat
Previous political experience: city council member (2 terms);
school board member (1 term)

Politics
Party identification: Republican
Previous political experience: city council member (2 terms);
water board member (1 term)

Key campaign issues
Develop infrastructure in local communities
Establish task force to help reduce traffic congestion
Initiate community policing programs
Adopt social media strategies to effectively communicate with
local residents

Key campaign issues
Encourage businesses to locate in Hidden Hills
Create community forums to include residents in important
decisions
Ensure our children grow up in a safe community
Increase amount and quality of public transportation

Endorsements
Hidden Hills Teacher's Association: Matthew Brown has a
track record of caring about our schools, students, and
parents.

Retired Persons of Hidden Hills: Matthew Brown is the
candidate who will support the needs of the city's retired
population by prioritizing transportation and community
programming for seniors.

Endorsements
Associated Fire Fighters of Hidden Hills: John Gibson has
demonstrated a commitment to the fire service, firefighters,
and the community's safety.

Hidden Hills Chamber of Commerce: John Gibson is the
candidate who will promote the development and
maintenance of a healthy business climate. As our mayor,
Gibson will encourage economic vitality in Hidden Hills.

7.5. Experimental stimulus (control condition).

principles and unwavering faith. John Gibson's religious values will benefit all
Hidden Hills residents, regardless of religious belief." In this condition, the
Democratic candidate's profile does not mention religion at all. Next, respondents in the secular-Democratic condition saw the basic voter guide but with
an additional endorsement for the Democrat, Matthew Brown. The endorsement comes from the Secular Coalition of Hidden Hills and reads, "Matthew
Brown has shown a commitment to promote a more secular government
and a will to protect the rights of all people, including the nearly 20% of
Americans that do not identify with any particular religion." In this condition, the Republican candidate's profile does not mention religion at all.

Importantly, the secular condition corresponds to political, rather than
personal, secularism. Political secularism is not defined by the absence of
religion or hostility toward religion, but rather *an emphasis that government
institutions should be separate from religious institutions.* Secularist political organizations have grown both in number and size in recent years, but their
influence on public opinion has been largely ignored in the literature. The
Secular Coalition for America, for example, is a nonprofit advocacy group
whose stated mission on its website is to "increase the visibility and respect for nontheistic viewpoints and to protect and strengthen the secular
character of our government as the best guarantee of freedom for all." The

Table 7.2 Experimental treatments

	Secular organization endorsement		Religious organization endorsement	
	Democratic candidate	Republican candidate	Democratic candidate	Republican candidate
Treatments				
Religious Republican	No	Yes	No	No
Secular Democrat	Yes	No	No	No
Secular Democrat, religious Republican	Yes	No	No	Yes
Religious Democrat, religious Republican	No	No	Yes	Yes

Source: Candidate endorsement experiment.

distinction between secular political beliefs and personal secularism is important because there are virtually no federally elected politicians who are openly atheist or agnostic, and very few do not identify with a religious community. Therefore, although some secularist organizations represent nontheistic Americans, secularist organizations' endorsements of candidates usually relate to the politicians' policies and not their private religious stances.

In the secular-Democratic and religious-Republican condition, respondents saw a voter guide that includes both the secular endorsement for Matthew Brown, the Democrat, and the religious endorsement for John Gibson, the Republican. In the final religious-Democrat and religious-Republican condition, both the Democratic and Republican candidates received a religious endorsement. One endorsement is from the Hidden Hills Voters for Faith, described above. The second religious endorsement comes from the Hidden Hills Interfaith Religious Council and reads, "[Candidate's name] respects the diversity of religious traditions in Hidden Hills and has shown a commitment to using religion to bring people together."[13] Which candidate received which religious endorsement is randomized among respondents in this treatment condition.[14] The conditions are detailed in table 7.2 for reference.

After looking at the voter guide, respondents answered a few questions about the guide and their perceptions of the candidates.[15] The main dependent variables are two seven-point ratings, rescaled to range between 0 and 1, which rate the favorability of each candidate. The graphs in figure 7.6 present the results for three groups: black Democrats, white Democrats, and white Republicans. The smaller sample of African Americans—161 in total— means there are about thirty black respondents per treatment condition. The analyses therefore produce noisier estimates, some of which are statistically

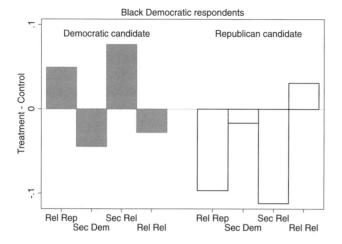

Black Democratic respondents

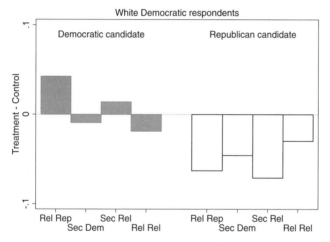

White Democratic respondents

7.6. African Americans do not respond positively to religious endorsements. The gray bars represent the difference in favorability of the Democratic candidate for each treatment condition relative to the control condition. The white bars represent the difference in favorability of the Republican candidate for each treatment condition relative to the control condition. The top panel presents the experimental treatment effects for black Democrats, the bottom panel presents the experimental treatment effects for white Democrats, and the panel on page 172 presents the experimental treatment effects for white Republicans.
Source: Candidate endorsement experiment.

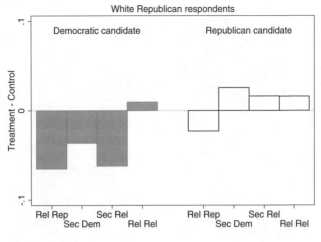

7.6. (*continued*)

suggestive rather than significant at conventional levels. The associated
p-values are noted in the text.

While partisans unsurprisingly prefer their own parties' candidates, they
do not actively dislike the opposition. Black Democrats in the control condition evaluated the Democratic candidate (0.69) more favorably than the
Republican candidate, but they did not provide negative evaluations of the
Republican candidate (0.54). This gap is comparable to that of white Democrats: the average rating for the Democratic candidate was 0.68, whereas the
average rating for the Republican candidate was 0.48.[16] White Republican
respondents in the control condition similarly preferred their own party's
candidate, rating the Republican candidate at 0.70 and the Democratic candidate at 0.51.

Do religious and secular endorsements influence partisans' relative feelings toward the candidates within a partisan context? The first panel of
figure 7.6 presents the results for black Democrats only; the second panel
presents the results for white Democrats only; and the third panel presents
the results for white Republicans only. Each bar in figure 7.6 represents the
difference-in-means between a treatment condition and the control group,
which saw no religious or secular endorsement. The left portion of figure 7.6,
denoted with gray boxes, represents survey respondents' views about the
Democratic candidate. The right side of the graph, denoted with white
boxes, displays the difference-in-means for the Republican candidate.

The experimental analyses answer a few questions about African Americans' responses to the injection of religion and secularism into campaigns.

First, can Republicans benefit when they are billed as the party of religion? While the results from the previous section suggest that black Democrats are not necessarily thinking about the Republican Party when considering religion's place in politics, the religious-Republican condition tests what happens when the linkage between the Republican candidate and organized religion is made explicit. On the one hand, black Democrats evaluated the Democratic candidate more negatively when the Republican candidate received a religious endorsement compared to the control condition (-0.04; p-value = 0.38; first gray bar), but evaluations of the Republican candidate remained virtually unchanged (-0.02; p-value = 0.79; first white bar). These results may suggest that African American respondents want Democratic candidates to be linked with religion; however, these results should not be overstated as they are suggestive at best. Moreover, this slight decrease in Democratic favorability does not correspond to an increase in the Republican candidate's favorability. These results therefore cast doubt on the idea that Republican candidates can effectively use religion to garner support among black voters.

How do these results compare to those for white partisans? The religious-Republican endorsement had no effect on white Democrats' favorability ratings of the Democratic candidate (-0.001; p-value = 0.61), but it decreased favorability toward the Republican candidate (-0.05; p-value = 0.03). Comparing these trends, candidate evaluations changed in different ways for black and white Democrats. Whereas black Democrats did not "punish" the Republican candidate for receiving a religious endorsement, white Democrats did. Moreover, while there is some evidence that black Democrats felt less favorable to the Democratic candidate after learning that the Republican candidate received a religious endorsement, there is no such effect on white Democrats. In contrast, the religious-Republican endorsement both increases the favorability of the Republican candidate slightly (0.03; p-value = 0.38) and decreases the favorability of the Democratic candidate slightly (-0.04; p-value = 0.32) among white Republican respondents, thereby widening the evaluation gap (0.06; p-value = 0.18); however, these results are not statistically significant.

Second, how would African Americans respond if Democrats became known as the party of secularism? Black Democrats straddle the religious-political divide, being both highly religious and highly Democratic. This may be possible, in part, because African Americans' own experiences do not put these identities at odds. If, however, the Democrats become branded as the party of secularism, might this hurt the Democratic Party's relationship with African Americans? The secular-Democratic condition tests this proposition. Black respondents evaluated the Democratic candidate more favorably when the Democratic candidate received a secular endorsement (0.05; p-value = 0.35; second gray bar) and also decreased their evaluations of the Republican candidate (−0.10; p-value = 0.14; second white bar) relative to the control condition. The smaller increase in the Democratic candidate's favorability coupled with the much larger decrease in the Republican candidate's favorability doubles the already sizable favorability gap between the Republican and Democratic candidates (initial gap = 0.15; new gap = 0.30; p-value = 0.10) among African American respondents. These results do not suggest that linking Democratic candidates to secularism weakens the strong ties between African Americans and the Democratic Party. Here, the results for the black subsample mirror the findings for white Democratic respondents. The secular-Democratic endorsement increased favorability toward the Democratic candidate (0.04; p-value = 0.02) and decreased favorability toward the Republican candidate (−0.06; p-value < 0.01) among white Democrats. In contrast, the secular-Democratic endorsement did not have much effect on white Republicans' favorability toward the Republican candidate (−0.02; p-value = 0.40) but produced a sharp decline in favorability toward the Democratic candidate (−0.07; p-value = 0.06).[17] Whereas white and black Democrats responded to the treatment in roughly similar ways, the different response patterns by black Democrats and white Republicans widened the already existing gap in candidate evaluations (0.19; p-value = 0.03). Taken together, black Democrats—despite being more religiously similar to white Republicans than their white copartisans—responded to a secular endorsement in a similar fashion to white Democrats; the secular endorsement actually boosted the Democratic candidate's standing relative to the Republican candidate.

Third, what happens when the candidates are seen as being on opposing sides of the religion-secularism divide? The previous evidence produced inconsistent results among black Democrats: the average favorability rating toward the Democratic candidate decreased when the Republican candidate received a religious endorsement but increased when the Democratic candidate received an endorsement from a secular group (difference between religious-Republican condition and secular-Democratic condition = 0.09; p-value = 0.07). This leaves unanswered the question of how black Democrats respond when the two candidates clearly differ along the religious-secularist dimension. When the Republican candidate received a religious endorsement and the Democratic candidate received a secular endorsement the Democratic candidate's average favorability increased (0.08; p-value = 0.12; third gray bar) while favorability decreased for the Republican candidate

(−0.11; p-value = 0.07; third white bar), dramatically widening the overall favorability between the candidates (0.19; p-value = 0.03).[18] Whatever
slight punishment African American respondents might have imposed on
the Democratic candidate when the Republican candidate received a religious endorsement disappeared when the two candidates provided clear
and distinct cues: not only did favorability toward the Republican candidate
decrease, but favorability toward the Democratic candidate increased. These
results differ from the results of both the white Democratic and white Republican samples. Whereas white Democrats (Republicans) decreased their
evaluations of the Republican (Democratic) candidate, their evaluations of
their own party's candidate remained relatively stable. White Democrats
and Republicans responded similarly to the cues by punishing the political
opposition, while black Democrats updated their evaluations of both candidates. These results suggest that black Democrats are quite loyal to their
party. Even when a Democratic candidate is explicitly linked with a secular
group and the Republican candidate is linked with a religious group, black
Democrats do not abandon their candidate. In fact, their support increases
and attitudes toward the two candidates become further polarized.

And fourth, how do African Americans respond when both candidates
receive a religious endorsement? Within all three subsamples, the same
trend appears: average levels of evaluations remain relatively unchanged.
Among black Democrats, the favorability toward the Democratic candidate
declined somewhat (−0.02; p-value = 0.55) and favorability toward the Republican candidate increased somewhat (0.02; p-value = 0.59). The results,
however, are substantively smaller than other results and statistically indistinguishable from zero. Democrats do not seem to benefit from also being
tied to religion even among one of its largest and most religious voting
blocs. Among both white Democrats and white Republicans, the backlash
seen against the out-party candidate in the other treatment conditions disappears when both candidates receive a religious endorsement. Compared
to Democrats in the control condition, Democrats in the religious-religious
condition offered slightly less favorable ratings of both the Democratic
candidate (−0.02; p-value = 0.30) and the Republican candidate (−0.03;
p-value = 0.17). Additionally, the decline in the Democratic candidate's favorability that was found among white Republicans in the other conditions
disappeared when the Democratic candidate received a religious endorsement (0.01; p-value = 0.79), while evaluations of the Republican candidate
remained stable relative to the control condition (0.02; p-value = 0.57).

These results offer insight into African Americans' responses to today's
religiously polarized environment. While black Democrats may be more

religious and more supportive of religion's introduction into politics than their white copartisans, these differences do not affect how black Democrats respond to a political environment in which both religious and secular values are espoused. African Americans are not persuaded by a Republican candidate of faith and do not seem opposed to a Democratic candidate who is linked to political secularism.

Discussion

Scholars, particularly those interested in studying the relationship between religiosity and partisanship, have long known that African Americans do not conform to many of the current trends found among white Americans. African Americans are often noted as an exception to contemporary patterns and then promptly ignored. The chapter explores whether African Americans' unique set of identities is politically consequential. The first part of the chapter applied the life-cycle theory to black Democrats. African Americans looked like white Republicans rather than white Democrats in the YPSP data, returning to organized religion after a hiatus to a greater extent than their white copartisans. These results, coupled with the 2012 ANES results showing that African American parents today are still much more religious than white Democrats, raise the question of how these dual identities operate in the political realm.

Although African American Democrats are highly devout, they are not the most enthusiastic group in support of religion being brought into politics or politics being brought into churches. Whereas black Democrats are more supportive of this intermixing than white Democrats, white Republicans are even more supportive of churches speaking out on religious issues and politicians drawing on their religious faith. Baseline levels of religiosity therefore do not directly translate into attitudes about religion's role in politics.

The chapter then goes on explore why black Democrats hold these views regarding religion and politics and with what consequence. Two Pew studies support the claim that white and black Democrats have different considerations when answering questions related to religion and politics. In a comparison between those who answered a question about politicians relying on religious rhetoric in general as opposed to a question that asks about President Bush's use of religion in particular, white Democrats reported more similar responses than black Democrats. The reverse trend appears when the question asks about the use of religious rhetoric among politicians in general versus Obama: white Democrats' attitudes shifted more dramatically than did those of black Democrats. The results indicate that when black Democrats report that they want religion to enter the political sphere they may be answering with a specific political leaning in mind.

These experimental results also help explain why black Democrats do not feel that the Republican Party is "friendly" toward religion. Returning to the Pew data discussed in chapter 3, white Democrats and Republicans were in agreement that the Republican Party is "friendly" toward religion in 2014 (62% versus 64%). In contrast, only 25% of black Democrats reported that the Republican Party was friendly toward religion. These results may seem surprising at first given that the Republican Party is seen as the party that relies on religious values in its policymaking; however, this response pattern makes sense if African Americans draw on their own religious values and political experiences within the church when answering these sorts of general questions.

Finally, the endorsement experiment shows that black Democratic respondents do not reward a Republican candidate when he or she receives a religious endorsement, nor do they punish a Democratic candidate who receives a secular endorsement. In fact, the favorability gap between black respondents' views of the Republican candidate and the Democratic candidate is largest in the condition in which the Democratic candidate receives a secular endorsement and the Republican candidate receives a religious endorsement.

African Americans do not seem receptive to Republicans' use of religion and faith. Why? Two explanations, likely working together, are possible. One explanation is religious and one is political. The first explanation returns to the differences between black Protestant and white evangelical theology. Although many black Protestants and white evangelicals are biblical literalists, the meaning of being a literalist depends on the context. Adhering to a literalist interpretation of the Bible may mean holding strong views about social justice and equality for African Americans and personal piety and moral rectitude for white evangelicals. One possible reason that black Democrats do not respond to Republicans' use of religion is that they understand the difference in religious values. Put another way, a white Republican candidate who says "I am religious" may signal something different to religious African Americans than to whites. In this case, the Democratic Party may not be the traditional party of the religious, but it represents many of the religious values emphasized in black churches. Consequently, Republicans cannot use religious rhetoric and emphasize policies that resonate with religious white voters and expect a similar outcome among African American voters. In this interpretation, religious beliefs and commitment can guide political allegiances; however, black Protestantism leads members toward the Democratic Party. Moreover, this explanation also helps us make sense of African American Democrats' religious trajectories relative to those of white Democrats and Republicans. If black Democrats do not feel as if their religious and partisan identities are in conflict, they should see no reason to update either. The result is religiously devout Democrats within the African American community.

A second reason that African Americans are not responsive to the Republican Party's "God" strategy is political in nature. African Americans are the single most cohesive political bloc in the United States. African Americans identify as Democrats and vote for Democratic candidates. A partisan identity, as shown in previous chapters, can be quite powerful. We therefore might not expect African Americans to abandon their partisan identity on a whim, even when faced with religious appeals from the Republican Party. Together, these results confirm African Americans as strongholds within the Democratic Party and cast doubt on the notion that Republican politicians can gain electoral support from black Democrats through a religious strategy.

Finally, the chapter highlights the unique outcomes that arise from African Americans' religious and political attachments. While neither the conventional God gap explanation nor the life-cycle theory adequately encapsulates African Americans' relationship with political parties and religious institutions, the findings demonstrate how the unique social, economic, political, and religious histories of African Americans in the United States impact the way African Americans view and respond to today's political environment.

EIGHT

Generalizing the Life-Cycle Theory: A Reevaluation of the 1960 Election

The analyses in the previous chapters used the life-cycle theory as a way to explain individual-level change in religiosity over time. In particular, the results showed that Republicans have become more religious while the Democrats have become less so. These results comport with expectations derived from the contemporary political environment and help explain the current religious gap found in American politics. The life-cycle theory, however, is silent with respect to the exact ways in which partisanship should influence religious choices. Consequently, the theory should be a useful guide as new issues emerge, new groups form, and the parties change their policy positions and electoral strategies. In other words, the theory should be generalizable to different contexts in which the expectations regarding how politics might affect religion differ. The 1960 presidential election offers an opportunity to see whether partisanship influences religious decision making in a different political environment in which partisans received cues that were quite different from those of today.

The 1960 Presidential Campaign

Religion was a salient issue throughout the 1960 campaign, perpetuated by both political and religious leaders. John F. Kennedy, the Democratic nominee, was only the second Catholic to be a major party nominee for the presidency and the first to be elected president of the United States. Kennedy's Catholicism figured prominently throughout the campaign, visibly linking Catholics and the Democratic Party. The emphasis was not on whether the parties were associated with religious versus secular values; the 1960 campaign instead highlighted the relationship between political parties and specific religious traditions.

Kennedy received a warm, but relatively private, welcome from the Catholic leadership. Catholic leaders supported the Kennedy campaign both behind the scenes and from within the churches (Wilson 2007); however, they made very few public announcements of support. Their limited displays of overt public support were intentional, as the Kennedy campaign worked tirelessly so that Protestant voters would not perceive Kennedy as a "Catholic candidate." These efforts were evident even when Kennedy was campaigning against Hubert Humphrey for the Democratic nomination. The Harris polling firm, hired by the Kennedy campaign in Wisconsin, suggested that Kennedy not make overt attempts to mobilize Catholic support: "Kennedy had to bend over backward not to demonstrate any pro-Catholic bias in his campaigning. No local appearances with Catholic clergy or at Catholic venues must be allowed" (Casey 2009: 65). Despite the hands-off approach, Catholics supported Kennedy over Humphrey four to one in the days leading up to the Wisconsin primary.

Kennedy's religion was also a major issue for many Protestants. Protestant leaders expressed concern about whether Kennedy could act in the best interest of America or whether the Oval Office would become a pawn of the Vatican. One such expression took place before Kennedy even formally announced his candidacy for president. The editor of the *Christian Herald*, a Protestant newspaper with a circulation of more than 400,000, ran Reverend Daniel Poling's story about his son, a Protestant chaplain, who died along with a Jewish, a Catholic, and another Protestant chaplain after they gave their life vests to others aboard the sinking *USS Dorchester* during World War II. After raising funds to build a memorial chapel in honor of these fallen chaplains, Reverend Poling invited then-representative John Kennedy to speak at a dinner in Philadelphia in honor of the chapel's completion. According to Poling, Kennedy withdrew from the event at the request of the Catholic bishop of Philadelphia. This, according to Poling, was evidence that Kennedy responded to orders from the Catholic hierarchy (Casey 2009).

This anecdote illustrates the uphill battle that Kennedy faced in winning Protestant support, particularly among Protestant clergy. On the same day Kennedy announced he was running for the Democratic nomination, Methodist Episcopal Bishop G. Bromley Oxnam's response to the Poling story was quoted in the *New York Times*: "I had thought he could exercise independent judgment as an American citizen until I saw a report that he had cancelled an interfaith speaking engagement because a Cardinal had insisted he do it." The editor of *Christianity and Crises*, another prominent Protestant newspaper of the time, summed up the Protestant response to Kennedy's Catholicism succinctly in March 1960:

> The issue raised by the possibility of a Roman Catholic candidate for the Presidency is the most significant and immediate problem that grows out of the confrontation of Roman Catholicism with other religious communities in the United States. There are a great many Protestants of influence who are inclined to say that they would never vote for a Roman Catholic for President. Many of them refuse to say this with finality, but there is a strong trend in this direction. Our guess is that it may be stronger among clergy and among official Protestant spokesmen than among laity. (Bennett 1960: 17–19)

Kennedy combated the "Catholic issue" head-on in public statements, such as his acceptance speech for the Democratic Party's nomination for president:

> I am fully aware of the fact that the Democratic Party, by nominating someone of my faith, has taken on what many regard as a new and hazardous risk—new, at least since 1928. But I look at it this way: the Democratic Party has once again placed its confidence in the American people, and in their ability to render a free, fair judgment. And you have, at the same time, placed your confidence in me, and in my ability to render a free, fair judgment—to uphold the Constitution and my oath of office—and to reject any kind of religious pressure or obligation that might directly or indirectly interfere with my conduct of the Presidency in the national interest. My record of fourteen years supporting public education—supporting complete separation of church and state—and resisting pressure from any source on any issue should be clear by now to everyone. (Kennedy 1960a)

Kennedy made similar comments in his famous speech to the Greater Houston Ministerial Association: "I am not the Catholic candidate for president. I am the Democratic Party's candidate for president, who happens also to be a Catholic. I do not speak for my church on public matters, and the church does not speak for me" (Kennedy 1960b). These public statements were coupled with an intensive campaign strategy to win support from non-Catholics, including educational television programs answering questions about the Catholic faith, letters from Kennedy to Protestant ministers, and campaign advertisements addressing Kennedy's religion (Casey 2009).

Importantly, most voters were aware of Kennedy's Catholicism. In February of 1960, just one month after Kennedy officially announced his candidacy for the Democratic nomination, 64% of Americans successfully identified Kennedy as Catholic, and this number increased to 91% as the election drew near. By way of comparison, only 36% were able to do the same for John Kerry in 2004 (Tesler 2015). Further, despite "signs that some Protestant respondents were struggling to avoid mention of it [religion] although it was a matter of concern," 40% of ANES respondents voluntarily mentioned Kennedy's Catholicism as a salient issue during the campaign (Converse et al. 1961: 276). The large number of respondents mentioning religion without prompting "testifies rather eloquently to the importance of the [religious] factor in conscious political motivations during the fall campaign" (Converse et al. 1961: 276).

Religious Responses to the 1960 Election

How did Catholics and non-Catholics respond to the Kennedy campaign? Wilson (2007) uses the 1960 ANES to measure electoral support both across and within religions. Looking across religions, Catholics supported Kennedy at a much higher rate than non-Catholics, most of whom were Protestant. And looking within religions, church attendance is correlated with support for Kennedy among both Catholics and non-Catholics, but in opposite directions. Church attendance is positively correlated with a Kennedy vote among Catholics and negatively correlated with a Kennedy vote among non-Catholics. Wilson uses these results as evidence that ethnocultural group identity exerted a strong influence on behavior during the 1960 campaign; Catholics who were most entrenched in their religious communities were the most likely to support Kennedy. Conversely, non-Catholics well ensconced in their religious communities were less likely to support the Catholic candidate than were non-Catholics who had weaker ties with their religious communities.

The life-cycle theory offers an alternative interpretation of the findings described above. Rather than church attendance or involvement in the Catholic community creating a unified voting bloc in support of Kennedy, perhaps Catholics who were less supportive of Kennedy decreased their levels of religious involvement. Given the enthusiasm for Kennedy's campaign among both Catholic leaders and laypersons, Catholics who supported Nixon may have felt less comfortable being in the pews on Sunday. Similarly, perhaps Protestants—whose elites vocally opposed electing a Catholic president— who supported Kennedy also felt uncomfortable in church. For both Catholics and Protestants, preferences about Kennedy may have generated either ease or discomfort within their religious communities. Additionally, Wilson notes that the relationship between religiosity and Kennedy support was most pronounced among younger respondents. These are the same people who were likely married with school-aged children and making decisions about religious involvement. Based on expectations stemming from the life-cycle theory, attitudes toward Kennedy may have systematically encouraged some and discouraged others from being involved in their religious communities.

1956–1958–1960 American National Election Study

Although the life-cycle theory presents a plausible alternative to the ethnocultural explanation, the 1960 ANES alone cannot adjudicate between the two. Luckily, the 1960 election is actually the third wave of a panel study, with the first two waves collected in 1956 and 1958. As a result, it is possible to trace how levels of church attendance among Catholic and Protestant partisans varied in response to Kennedy's campaign for president using a series of change models, similar to those used in previous chapters. Just as with the 2000–2002–2004 ANES results presented in chapter 5, church attendance serves as the dependent variable and lagged partisanship and church attendance operate as the main independent variables.[1] Additionally, the models control for factors that may influence partisanship and changing religiosity: gender, race, age, education, income, region of residence, and belonging to a union.

The political landscape and the life-cycle theory together help shape our empirical expectations. First, the discussions and debates surrounding Kennedy's religion created an environment in which Catholic and Protestant partisans should have responded differently. Catholic supporters of Kennedy should have felt more comfortable in the pews than Catholic Nixon supporters, while the reverse should have been the case for Protestants. In other words, the expectations run in different directions for Catholics and Protestants. Second, the life-cycle theory holds that individuals in a certain life stage are more likely to respond to the political environment by updating aspects of their religious identities. Taken together, among Catholics with children at home, the 1960 election should have encouraged Republicans to be less religiously involved than their Democratic counterparts. Conversely, among Protestants with children at home, the election should have encouraged Republicans to be more religiously involved than their Democratic counterparts. And finally, among both Catholics and Protestants with grown children, religious involvement should have remained relatively stable in response to the 1960 election.

The top panel of figure 8.1 begins by presenting changing levels of church attendance between 1956 and 1958. The stable political landscape means

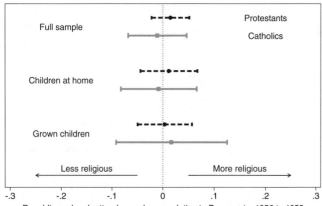

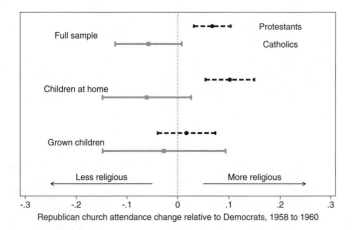

8.1. Protestant and Catholic partisans with children at home respond to the 1960 election differently. The top panel presents partisan differences in changing levels of church attendance between 1956 and 1958 for Protestants (black circles) and Catholics (gray squares). The bottom panel presents the same results between 1958 and 1960. Estimates come from change models that include a lagged dependent variable and control variables described in the text. Positive estimates indicate that Republicans became more frequent church attenders than Democrats over time. Negative estimates indicate that Democrats became more frequent church attenders than Republicans over time. Estimates near zero indicate that neither group became more frequent church attenders relative to the other over time. The top set of results shows changes for the full sample, the middle set of results shows changes for respondents with children at home, and the bottom set of results shows changes for respondents with grown children. *Source*: 1956–1958–1960 American National Election Study.

that there should not be any partisan-driven changes in religious involvement over the two-year period. The black circles represent the difference between Protestant Republicans' and Protestant Democrats' levels of church attendance over the two-year period. The gray squares represent the same partisan difference among Catholics. Similar to the results from earlier chapters, these coefficients test whether partisans' levels of religiosity changed at similar or different rates. In the absence of a change to the political environment, rates of religious involvement remained stable between 1956 and 1958 among both Protestants and Catholics. This is the case in the full sample (top set of results) as well as subsamples of respondents with children at home (middle set of results) and grown children (bottom set of results).

The bottom panel of figure 8.1 shows how Catholic and Protestant partisans' levels of religious involvement changed in different ways between 1958 and 1960. In the full sample of respondents (top set of results), Republican Protestants became more frequent attenders relative to Democratic Protestants (0.07; p-value < 0.01). Republican Catholics, on the other hand, became less frequent attenders relative to Democratic Catholics (difference = −0.06; p-value = 0.15). And similar to the analyses in previous chapters, respondents with children at home drive these results (second set of results). When looking at Protestants with children at home, Republican Protestants became more frequent church attenders than Democratic Protestants (0.10; p-value < 0.01), while Catholic Republicans became less religiously involved over time compared to Catholic Democrats (−0.06; p-value = 0.25). Importantly, these Catholic results—despite being substantively meaningful—are statistically suggestive and not significant at conventional levels. This is likely due to the fact that a large majority of Catholics identified as Democrats in 1958, and the relatively small number of Catholic Republicans produces higher levels of uncertainty around the estimate. Additionally, partisan-driven change in religious attendance differed for Protestants and Catholics (difference-in-difference = −0.17; p-value < 0.01).[2] In other words, the political landscape influenced both Catholic and Protestant partisans, but in different directions. Moreover, religiosity rates are again stable among partisans with grown children. The bottom set of results shows no evidence of partisan-driven change in church attendance among both Catholics (−0.02; p-value = 0.72) and Protestants (0.02; p-value = 0.62) with grown children. And finally, church attendance in 1958 is not correlated with a change in seven-point party identification between 1958 and 1960. Among Catholics and Protestants with children at home, partisans' religious ties changed but their political attachments remained stable.

Discussion

The results from this chapter are different from those of previous chapters. Earlier chapters used the life-cycle theory as a way of explaining an important empirical regularity in American politics today, namely, that Republicans are more religious than Democrats. By showing that partisans diverge in their levels of religiosity in systematic ways, the results cast doubt on the explanation that today's God gap appeared solely because religious voters gravitated toward the Republican Party while less devout voters moved into the Democratic camp. But how generalizable is the life-cycle theory? This chapter helps answer this question.

The 1960 campaign and Kennedy's election as the first Catholic president offer a very different religious-political landscape from that of today. In 1960, a social schism existed between Protestants and Catholics, making Kennedy's religion a salient political issue. This environment changes the expectations surrounding the relationship between religious and political attachments. While religiosity may be correlated with partisanship and vote choice, the relationship is moderated by religious identification. More specifically, the direction of church attendance's relationship with politics depends on whether the individual is a Catholic or a Protestant. The distinct political environment, along with its corresponding expectations, allows me to test the generalizability of the life-cycle theory outside the present-day context.

Changes between the 1956 and the 1958 survey waves provide a baseline understanding of change over time. The 1960 election had not yet claimed center stage, and religious elites were not discussing the presidential election. In this environment, church attendance remained stable. Two trends, however, appeared between 1958 and 1960. First, Protestant Democrats became less frequent church attenders compared to Protestant Republicans. More specifically, whereas Protestant Republicans' church attendance rates remained stable between 1958 and 1960, Protestant Democrats' attendance declined. Second, Catholic Republicans became less frequent church attenders than Catholic Democrats. Here, Catholic Democrats' church attendance rates remained stable over the two-year period while Catholic Republicans' attendance decreased. In both cases, feeling like the political outsider may have resulted in decreased religious involvement. And, consistent with the life-cycle theory, the results are most prominent among respondents with children living at home whereas levels of religious attendance are stable among older individuals without children at home.

The results—due to differences in sample size—are more definitive for the Protestant subsample than the Catholic subsample. The Catholic results, however, are still suggestive and trend in the direction of the life-cycle predictions. These results also comport with Wilson's (2007) findings that the relationship between strength of religious ties—measured by church attendance—correlates to political attitudes differently for Protestants and Catholics. The over-time results offered by the panel data, however, change how we should interpret these correlations. Rather than assume that the strength of religious ties is wholly fixed, thereby causing changes in political preferences, partisan identities—for some—can affect the strength of these religious ties. The life-cycle theory helps explain how partisan-driven religious change occurred during the 1960 campaign.

These results demonstrate that the life-cycle theory can explain more than a single case of religious change. Despite a different political context leading to different expectations, the evidence supports the underlying theory. The life-cycle theory, therefore, can generally be thought of as a vehicle for understanding religious behaviors in a variety of contexts.

NINE

The Religious Sort

Identifying with a social group and interacting with other members of that group set the stage for group-centered politics. By virtue of their shared outlooks and priorities, group members can unite politically in support of a policy, party, or candidate. This potential for political cohesion serves as the starting point for a rich literature exploring the consequences of politicized identities. This book revisits this starting point by asking how people initially form attachments to these social groups that lie at the heart of politics.

This book does not dispute the idea that identification with a social group can influence group members and even produce cohesive political blocs. Rather, one goal of this book has been to think about the origins of these social groups. How do these social identities develop, and what causes variation in identity strength? American politics scholars often ignore these first-order questions because we do not think that politics contributes to the development of social identities or the strength with which individuals identify with a group. If we assume that the factors shaping someone's depth of group identification are unrelated to politics, then political scientists can proceed to use strength of identification and involvement in a community as independent variables that explain differences in political attitudes. Having long taken this approach, scholars have found that strong group identifiers and group members who are deeply enmeshed in their social groups are most likely to hold partisan identities and policy preferences that are perceived to benefit their groups or are advocated by their groups' leaders. In short, this assumption that group membership is causally prior to politics has led researchers to find strong support for group-centered theories of public opinion formation. But if politics plays at least some role in explaining why and how social identities evolve, then we would have to reevaluate the power of social groups to influence politics.

The preceding chapters address this possibility by focusing on religion. Over the past forty years, religion has come to play a new role in American politics. This book has examined how citizens have responded to the changing presence of religion in politics. Do Americans promote their religious beliefs and values by evaluating political parties based on their own religious attachments? Or, rather, do they look to the parties and adopt religious viewpoints that are consistent with their preferred party's positions on religion?

Returning to Karen and Fran, whose stories opened the book, we are left wondering why Karen is a religious Republican and Fran is a religiously uninvolved Democrat. Years of research have assumed that Karen and Fran rely on their religious attachments when formulating political preferences, particularly partisan identification and vote choice. This explanation assumes that once the parties distinguished themselves along a cultural dimension and provided the women with a choice in terms of policies related to religion and religious values, then voters like Karen and Fran would draw on their religious outlooks when making political choices. This explanation makes the reasonable assumption that religious attachments, which are often linked to fundamental beliefs about one's soul and eternity, are strong enough to change one's party affiliation in the mundane world of secular politics. Having made this assumption, scholars have then shown that religiosity, measured by involvement in a religious community, has become increasingly correlated with party identification and vote choice in recent years. From this perspective, Karen and Fran understood the choices provided by the parties and responded accordingly. This book, however, advances an alternative perspective and has argued that the increasing correlation between religiosity and party identification during the latter part of the last century occurred, in part, because people like Karen and Fran updated aspects of their religious attachments in response to politics.

After briefly revisiting the book's main argument, the chapter explores the implications of politics' influence on religious decisions. Partisan-driven religious sorting has consequences for how scholars and journalists think about religion and politics, both separately and together. The chapter then goes on to discuss different trends that may make it more or less likely to see religious sorting continue in the future and concludes by offering guidance to scholars interested in exploring the role and consequences of identities.

When Might Politics Affect Religion?

Considering how religious identities develop can help identify when politics and partisanship can shape key aspects of a person's relationship with religion. Sociologists of religion have shown that levels of religious commitment change over the life course; religiosity and religious involvement decrease in adolescence and young adulthood and later increase for some as they transition into adulthood, which is often marked by marrying and having children. In particular, having school-aged children motivates parents to consider what kind of religious upbringing, if any, they want for their children. During this critical juncture, religious decision making is open to external influences.

One such external influence is politics, specifically partisanship. Individuals' partisan identities develop and crystallize in adolescence and young adulthood during the very time that religion is peripheral to many people's lives. The resultant partisan identities are stable and internalized by the time people make choices about their religious involvement in adulthood. The different windows during which different identities form give rise to the possibility that at some points partisan identities are more stable and salient than religious identities and can therefore influence religious choices.

While the religious and political socialization literatures identify a window during which partisanship is most likely to impact religious behavior, the particular political landscape linking religion to political parties generates specific expectations about how Democrats and Republicans should behave. In the absence of any perceived difference between the parties on issues related to religion, partisanship should not exert a meaningful influence over religious decisions even at a time when partisanship is stable and religious attachments are open to outside influences.

Beginning in the 1970s, however, America's parties increasingly offered voters different choices on the religious dimension. Whereas the parties had not previously distinguished themselves on policies related to morality, the separation of church and state, or the use of religious rhetoric and religious campaign strategies, political elites began staking out different positions at this time. The result is striking: religiosity, measured by religious involvement and commitment, has become strongly associated with the Republican Party over the past forty years. The corresponding cleavage between religious Republicans and less religious Democrats is one of the most profound sociocultural political divisions in American politics today.

Armed with the life-cycle theory, this book presents evidence that the religiosity gap has emerged, in part, because of partisans selecting into or out of religion based on their preexisting partisan identities. Once the parties and party elites were seen as distinct on questions related to religion, partisans could draw on their partisanship when making religious decisions. The elite-level changes to positions and strategies not only made religiosity a salient dimension on which Americans can make political decisions but also a dimension on which partisans can distinguish themselves. Moreover, partisanship's influence on religious decision making is not merely a small statistical finding. Rather, partisanship produces substantively meaningful changes in religious attachments that are evident years later.

The Consequences of Politics Affecting Religion: Implications for Religion and Politics

Understanding America's Religious Makeup

The findings in this book offer a new way for scholars to think about Americans' relationships with the largest social institution in the United States. Scholars and journalists have long been interested in Americans' unusually high levels of religiosity relative to citizens of other Western democracies (Barber 2011; Berger, Davie, and Fokas 2008; Bruce 2002; Holifield 2014; Norris and Inglehart 2011; Wald and Calhoun-Brown 2011) as well as changes in Americans' levels of religiosity over time (Lamb 2015; Lipka 2015; Main 2015; Marler and Hadaway 2002). The results strongly suggest that scholars should take the political environment into account when trying to understand religiosity and religious identification in America. Additionally, scholars must consider a political explanation for the recent emergence of the religiosity gap. The simple explanation that secular and less religious people moved toward the Democrats while the devout made a home within the Republican camp excludes the important reality that Democrats and Republicans also alter their religious attachments and outlooks to better fit with their chosen political party. Therefore, one of the largest and most enduring social divisions present in American electoral politics has developed, in part, because of politics.

Rethinking Religion's Role in Politics

While this book does not argue that religion has no influence on politics, the findings should change how we think about the impact of religion on political attitudes and mobilization. In particular, religion's influence may appear to be larger than it actually is due to partisan-influenced selection into religion. Consider, for example, a woman who becomes mobilized into the pro-life movement through her church. Perhaps through clergy speeches, study groups, or informal conversations with other congregants, she acts politically in support of the pro-life movement despite not having done so before. This example would seem to highlight the ability of religious communities to influence their members' involvement with politics. But how would the story change if this hypothetical church member had selected into her church because of her identification with the Republican Party in the first place? Knowing that this hypothetical Republican became more involved in her religious community because of politics might indicate that she was more susceptible to political mobilization through church activities, particularly since the cause she mobilized in support of is also aligned with her Republican partisan identification. If the same person were a Democrat, she may have ignored conversations about upcoming pro-life rallies at church. In this example, partisanship not only drives the person's selection into religion but also changes the likelihood that the individual will respond to political messages received in church.

The book's findings similarly suggest that religious campaign strategies may be better suited for mobilization than for persuasion. If partisans not only adopt their party's policy positions (Lenz 2012) but also update their levels of religiosity accordingly, Republican politicians' religious messages will resonate with Republican voters—who are already more likely to be religious—and fall flat with less religious Democratic voters. Partisan-driven religious sorting, therefore, decreases the likelihood that religious values can successfully be used to win new supporters and instead may play an important role in energizing and mobilizing already existing ones. Taken together, the ability of religion to politically influence and mobilize voters is now different on account of politics affecting religion.

Self-selection into religion also has different implications for the Republican and Democratic parties. On the one hand, religious voters represent a doubly captive audience for the Republican Party. Ralph Reed, one-time executive director of the Christian Coalition, founder of the Faith and Freedom Coalition, and key figure on the religious right, once quipped that religious people have a distinct electoral advantage because they are in church three days before an election. Reed is right that churches represent fertile grounds for political mobilization and activism (Djupe and Gilbert 2009; Verba, Schlozman, and Brady 1995). Based on the findings in this book, however, Reed may be understating the potential political influence of membership in religious groups. Not only do religious voters' values align with the Republican Party, but these religious voters may have become more involved in religion because they were Republicans.

Inactivity in religion, on the other hand, does not ignite the same levels of political fervor. Although secular humanist and atheist organizations exist, their membership and reach are minuscule compared to those of organized religion. Most nonidentifiers and nonreligious people are not necessarily opposed to religion, nor do they have strong antireligious tendencies. Rather, they simply happen not to be involved (Lim, MacGregor, and Putnam 2010). In contrast to Republicans who can rally people under the banner of religion, Democrats cannot use secularism to mobilize their members. Because politics affects religion, the two parties' bases—as well as each party's ability to energize its base—are now different.

New Interpretations of Existing Religion and Politics Research

Building on the practical implications regarding religion's role in the political sphere, the findings from this book should encourage scholars to reconsider the extensive correlational research demonstrating religion's various effects on politics. In the face of partisan-driven religious sorting, we should expect personal religiosity—however measured—to be strongly correlated with partisan identification, policy preferences, and vote choice. If those who are most (least) receptive to religious cues are also more likely to have opted into (out of) religion in the first place, religion's influence may appear stronger than it actually is. Correlational results using cross-sectional regressions can accurately measure how religion affects political attitudes only if we assume that the religious independent variable is an "unmoved mover" (Campbell et al. 1960; Johnston 2006; Miller and Shanks 1996)—itself stable but affecting political dependent variables. The findings presented in the previous chapters show that scholars must be cautious when designing studies aimed at understanding religion's influence on political outlooks and seriously consider religion's ability to be both an explanatory and outcome variable.

Contributions of the Life-Cycle Theory

The life-cycle theory described in this book also contributes to previous research exploring how politics shapes individuals' religious involvement. Others have shown that the politically polarized religious environment—one that links the Republican Party with evangelical Protestants and religious conservatives—influences Americans' religious identifications (Hout and Fischer 2014, 2002), evangelicals' rates of church attendance (Patrikios 2008), and partisans' religious and secular orientations (Campbell et al., forthcoming). Recent work by Djupe, Neiheisel, and Sokhey (forthcoming) also shows how the political makeup of congregations coupled with individuals' attitudes toward religious groups in the political sphere can affect church attendance and church affiliation. This book therefore builds on prior research but substantially broadens our understanding of how and why politics affects religion. First, the life-cycle theory predicts *when* politics is most likely to impact individuals' religious identities, abandoning the perhaps implausible assumption that politics should have a uniform effect across different types of people. Second, the life-cycle theory takes the rather counterintuitive claim that politics can affect religion and offers a more intuitive explanation of when and why this reverse relationship might appear. While it is unlikely that partisanship and the political environment can affect religious attachments at all points during the life cycle, the life-cycle theory identifies a window during which partisan identities are more likely to influence religious decisions. And third, the theory and empirics show how partisanship and the political environment can influence Republicans and Democrats alike. Democrats not only respond to the political environment by distancing themselves from organized religion, Republicans also respond by strengthening their religious attachments.

Another important feature of the life-cycle theory is that it is generalizable, offering researchers a way to look for religious divergence among partisans in different contexts. While the life-cycle theory identifies a certain point when political cues should be more likely to influence individuals' religious decisions, it does not make any assumptions about how politics necessarily affects religion. The theory is not specific to the religiosity gap that has emerged over the past forty years. Rather, it is capable of shedding light on the nexus of politics and religion in other contexts. Chapter 8 provides one example of this by looking to the past: Attendance at church changed among Catholic and Protestant partisans in response to the 1960 presidential election in which John F. Kennedy, a Catholic, was the Democratic nominee. As the parties evolve, new issues emerge, and politicians experiment with different ways of reaching voters, the religious-political environment will likely change as well. When this occurs, the life-cycle theory can provide researchers a means of exploring whether and to what extent the political environment affects the religious makeup of the country.

And finally, the life-cycle theory can also help researchers better predict how the relationship between religious and partisan attachments may change in the future. The religious socialization literature tells us that religious attachments are open to outside influences when individuals are making religious choices for themselves and their families. After making these decisions, however, religious attachments are generally stable throughout adulthood. On the other hand, we know from the political socialization literature that partisan identities are largely stable once they crystallize in young adulthood. Taking these theories together, we should not expect to see large, dramatic changes in the correlation between religiosity and partisanship over short periods of time. After all, many individuals have stable religious and political attachments. Instead, cohort replacement should produce gradual change. For instance, the YPSP data from chapter 4 showed partisan-induced changes in religiosity among the student generation but not the parent generation. Additionally, in a nationally representative survey conducted around the same time, there is little evidence of any religious-political connection. After all, the student cohort—among whom identifying as a Republican correlates with church attendance—represents a small segment of the national sample. However, a correlation appears years later once the student and subsequent cohorts make up a larger proportion of the sample. The life-cycle theory can therefore offer researchers a place to identify new trends as well as the ability to better predict how the religious-political landscape may change in the future.

In addition to offering a new way to think about religion and politics, this book also provides broader lessons related to identity politics and public opinion.

The Consequences of Politics Affecting Religion: Broader Implications

This book also provides broader lessons related to how politically relevant identities and opinions form.

The Importance of Party Identification

This book demonstrates that partisanship's power can be felt outside the political sphere, extending so far as to affect apolitical behaviors and aspects of a social identity commonly assumed to shape political outlooks. Importantly, partisanship's influence is not only seen among strong partisans. While data limitations preclude separate analyses of weak and strong partisans, the empirical results suggest that strong partisans are not the only source of the religious divergence. Although the small sample sizes mean that the results should be interpreted with caution, the effects of partisanship on religious outcomes among strong partisans were never statistically different from those same effects among weak partisans. While out-party hostility and bias are most concentrated among the strongest partisans (Huddy, Mason, and Aarøe 2015; Iyengar, Sood, and Lelkes 2012; Miller and Conover 2015), partisan-induced religious updating—in both the experimental and observational data—occurs among weak partisans as well. One explanation for this finding is that weak Democrats, for example, may not be actively eschewing religion on account of their partisan identities but rather are becoming less religious because others in their social circles, some of whom may be strong partisans, have become less religious. Therefore, homophily, the desire to associate with others who are similar, may result in weak partisans becoming religiously sorted as well.

Partisan-induced social cleavages have important implications related to polarization within the American political system. Affective polarization—that is, partisans' attitudes toward the political out-party and its members—has increased dramatically in recent decades. Knowing that partisans have created out-groups that differ on multiple dimensions—in this case, political and religious—an in-group mentality, along with associated biases and even hostility toward those outside the group, is more likely to arise (see Brewer and Pierce 2005; Roccas and Brewer 2002). The results from this book therefore may not bring comfort to those concerned about the normative implications of out-party dislike and distrust as politically sorted social groups may further fuel the out-party animosity that currently exists in American politics.

Citizen Competence and Democratic Accountability

The ability of partisanship to influence involvement and identification with social groups raises questions as to whether group cues can serve as efficient and effective shortcuts when individuals are forming opinions. Identifying with a group can offer members a way to hold elected officials accountable even in the absence of extensive political knowledge. By utilizing cues from group leaders and other group members, otherwise uninformed voters can act as if they are informed without exerting much effort. Social group membership can potentially constitute a reassuring response to those concerned about citizen competence and whether elected officials represent constituents' preferences. If, however, group membership develops in response to politics, group cues and identity-based evaluations would not necessarily help voters overcome informational deficits when they are forming political judgments. Instead, these politically relevant social identities are just another consequence of partisan identities. Consequently, voters' social group memberships and identities may not offer an easy way for otherwise unengaged voters to reward and punish politicians.

Rethinking the Role of Social Group Influence

This book's findings also encourage scholars to rethink how to measure group influence. Scholars take cohesive political behaviors and attitudes among strong group identifiers as evidence of social group influence; the more strongly a person identifies with a group, the more likely he or she is to internalize group norms and adopt the group's preferences. If, however, a person's political surroundings influence depth of identification or involvement within a social community, the correlations researchers have found between identity strength and various political outcomes may be misleading. Group influence may not be as strong as previously thought, and these correlations may be partially a function of who chooses to be strongly affiliated with a group.

How Coherent Worldviews Form and Why They Are Slow to Change

Political scientists have long been interested in how people come to hold their beliefs and develop political worldviews. The theory and results in the book explain how multiple identities work together to create an overarching belief structure. For example, if Democrats' partisanship pushes them away from religion, they become less likely to hear religious messages that may comport with Republican ideology or policies. Consequently, both their religious and political attachments strengthen in the absence of countervailing information. The relationship between social and political identities is strong, in part, because many people's social and political identities continuously reinforce one another. A similar logic explains why identities are slow to change. Initially choosing identities that are consistent with one another reduces subsequent internal pressure to update membership in or affect toward groups associated with the chosen identities. When identities develop in conjunction with preexisting identities and beliefs, a cohesive worldview also develops, which should be difficult to change.

Will Politics Continue to Affect Religion?

Having discussed the implications of the book's theory and findings, it is worth exploring what the future may have in store. Of course, any speculation about the future comes with the caveat that that there are so many unknowns about what is to come, particularly involving politics, that it is difficult to predict whether the patterns observed over the past decades will continue. Nevertheless, the sections below make informed predictions by considering trends that may make sorting more or less likely to continue in the future.

Why We Might Continue to See a Sorted Electorate

Politics Drives Religious Socialization

Though the focus of this book has been on understanding how Americans engage with religion, their decisions affect more than just their own identities. Children with Democratic parents are raised in less religious households than children with Republican parents. Consequently, entire generations have been religiously socialized based partly on politics. Religious socialization experiences matter when the time comes for the next generation to make religious decisions for themselves and their families, as religious upbringing is an important influence on religiosity and religious involvement in adulthood (Wilson and Sherkat 1994).

A religiously sorted electorate is likely to persist among more recent generations, particularly among children whose party identifications match those of their parents. Imagine a scenario in which two Republican parents raise their child in a religious household and their child comes to identify as a Republican in young adulthood. When this child grows up and makes her own religious decisions, her party identification and religious upbringing apply twin pressures in the same direction. In this case, referring to her decision as politically driven religious sorting may be a mistake since she is maintaining the status quo of being both religious and a Republican. In the absence of any cross-pressure, members of future generations will likely reproduce the religiosity gap. In short, religiously sorted parents increase the likelihood that future generations of partisans will also be religiously sorted.

Social and Demographic Changes

Changing trends related to marriage and childbearing may increase the ability of partisanship to influence religious decisions. In postponing life-cycle events that traditionally bring people back into the religious fold, young people now remain on the outskirts of religion for longer than previous generations. Increasing education rates and delays in becoming financially independent have corresponded to an increase in the average age at which people marry and have children, the two primary reasons for returning to religion (Wuthnow 2007). The Centers for Disease Control found that the average age of first-time mothers in the United States rose from 24.9 in 2000 to 26.3 in 2014. Although this change is partially attributable to fewer teenagers having babies, it is also because the proportion of women 35 and older having their first child increased by 23%. Jeffrey Jensen Arnett (2000) argues that these changes have brought about a new life-cycle window called "emerging adulthood." Emerging adulthood, which falls between young adulthood and adulthood, is marked by the personal independence that comes with being an adult but without the corresponding responsibilities.

Delays in entering adulthood, in turn, delay decisions about religious involvement. Being on the periphery of religion for longer allows other identities to further crystallize and strengthen. When other nonreligious identities, including partisan identities, are stronger, they are more likely to impact future religious decisions. As individuals postpone the life-cycle transitions that encourage a return to religion, we can continue to expect partisanship to shape religious decisions.

Growth of Affective Polarization

The presence and growth of affective polarization may encourage partisans to continue relying on their political outlooks when making religious decisions. Polarization has occurred in the American electorate over the last three decades, not along policy lines (Fiorina, Abrams, and Pope 2006) but in changing feelings toward the political parties. Distrust and dislike toward the political out-party have grown in recent years (Iyengar, Sood, and Lelkes 2012), and these feelings have had a big impact on how partisans view and treat members of the opposing party (Iyengar and Westwood 2015). This increase in affective polarization may be partially a consequence of partisans selecting into and out of religious institutions, but it can also affect the likelihood of seeing partisan-driven religious sorting in the future. If partisans' dislike for out-party members persists, religious sorting will continue as partisans will want to select into politically like-minded social groups, both religious and otherwise.

Homophily

Homophily—or the tendency to associate with similar others—can also exacerbate religious sorting. Chapter 6 showed that partisans require information and knowledge to respond to the political environment in short order; however, partisan-driven religious sorting can also occur indirectly through social relationships. Partisans, for example, are more likely to be romantically interested in people who share their political identities and outlooks (Huber and

Malhotra 2017). Assortive mating creates households with shared political identities, and this can influence the couple when they make religious decisions. Similarly, selecting friends based on politics (Huber and Malhotra 2017; Iyengar, Sood, and Lelkes 2012) creates politically homogeneous social environments, which can also ultimately impact religious choices. Even without extensive political knowledge, Republicans (Democrats) may still end up religiously (un)involved by virtue of their friends' and loved ones' religiosities. Political homophily helps explain why the religiosity gap is so large, why it exists even among the less politically aware, and why the gap is likely to remain.

Limits to Religious Sorting
The Presence of Liberal Churches

It is not a foregone conclusion that partisanship will produce the religious divergence seen throughout the book, and there are reasons that the religiosity gap may not continue to grow or may even begin to shrink. Liberal churches represent one bulwark against a growing religiosity gap. Democrats should not feel uncomfortable attending a liberal church. If a church espouses principles consistent with those of the Democratic Party and partisans' fellow congregants are similarly politically inclined, partisanship should not discourage Democrats from membership in such a religious congregation. This book does not address church shopping or the idea that people select into specific religious communities. In fact, chapters 4 and 5 show that Republicans become more frequent church attenders than Democrats despite the possibility that people choose congregations that suit their needs. Even though many Democrats have the option to join politically liberal churches, Democrats are still less religiously involved than Republicans.

Nevertheless, Democrats can still make their way back to religion—a specific type of religion. If Democrats return to politically liberal religious communities, we may see the church attendance gap that currently exists between Republicans and Democrats shrink. If so, then the religious participation gap that has been so prominent in recent elections would also wane. Although this trend would diminish the religious sorting described in this book, these changes would constitute an important new form of religious sorting, sorting into specific congregations. If partisanship drives decisions about which churches people attend, then it would be fair to say that politically driven religious change is still occurring, just in a different form than it previously had.

Political Independents

Political Independents were neither pulled into religion nor pushed out of religion. These findings remind us that an affective or psychological attachment to a party is necessary for the political-religious landscape to influence Americans' relationships with religion. Though there is certainly room for more research on the causes and consequences of Independents' religious behaviors, the findings from this book suggest that if the number of pure political Independents grows, aggregate levels of partisan-driven religious sorting should decrease.

Changing Demographics of America

America's shifting demographic landscape may also limit, or at the very least change, patterns of religious sorting. Chapter 7 showed that African Americans' patterns of religious involvement largely reflect the religious life cycle—decreasing religiosity in young adulthood followed by increasing religiosity upon reaching adulthood—but politics plays virtually no role. Explanations for politics' limited influence in the black community include the black community's unique social history in the United States and African American Protestantism's distinctive theological outlook compared to that of white Protestantism. Consequently, when religious identities are closely linked to other salient social identities, such as race, the power of politics may shrink. As the United States becomes more racially, ethnically, and religiously diverse through immigration, particularly from Latin America and Asia, more Americans may have religious identities that are closely tied to ethnic or cultural groups, causing politics' influence to wane or change.

Partisan Cues

A final, albeit obvious, requirement for sorting to continue is that the parties must differ along lines related to religion. Often, we are tempted to think of the current political landscape as permanent. But a brief look at history shows how quickly politics can change. As recently as the mid-1960s, the parties were indistinguishable on issues related to religious values. Today's differences could disappear or new issues on which the parties look similar could emerge. Partisans can respond only when the parties offer distinct choices. If Democrats and Republicans espouse similar views on issues related to religion, morality, and culture, partisans will not have cues to follow. Consequently, we would expect to see less partisan-driven sorting.

What Would It Take to Become "Unsorted"?

Having discussed the factors that would make it more or less likely for sorting to continue in the future, it is also worth considering what it would take for partisans to become religiously "unsorted" at the mass level. Just as it took many years for partisan-driven religious sorting to occur, unsorting would also likely be a slow process. Consistent with the life-cycle theory, the empirical results in this book show that certain people—namely, those with school-aged children—are the most likely to bring their religious identities into alignment with their partisan identities. In contrast, both partisan and religious identities generally remain stable over time among those in other life stages. Changes among small subsets of people eventually produce large-scale changes noticeable in aggregate data; however, the shifts are not evident immediately. Thinking back to chapter 4, a God gap was evident in YPSP student data a decade before nationally representative surveys found the same pattern. This lag occurred because it took time for the YPSP student generation, as well as subsequent cohorts, to replace older generations whose religious identities were stable by the time the parties diverged on positions related to religion and morality.

We should expect a similarly slow transition if partisans were eventually to become religiously unsorted. For example, if the parties became indistinguishable on religious issues, the life-cycle theory predicts that this would not affect the religious identities of partisans who have already made religious decisions. Among the younger generations, however, we may expect the God gap to weaken. Republicans with school-aged children, for instance, may not feel any added political pressure to attend church frequently. Instead, these Republicans would rely on other considerations when deciding their levels of religious involvement. This should mean that some Republicans within this life stage would continue to be religiously active while others would be less so but that partisan identities would play a diminishing role in that choice.

There is also reason to believe that unsorting may actually be more difficult than sorting. Returning to the hypothetical situation in which the parties are identical in the cultural, religious, and moral arenas, the potential for a person's religious and partisan identities to be in conflict also disappears. A Democrat, for example, would feel no pressure either to attend or not attend church. Consequently, he or she is likely to behave in a manner long predicted by sociologists of religion: Those raised in more religious households are likely to be more religiously involved in adulthood and those raised in less religious households are likely to be less religious in adulthood. This means that even in the absence of partisan-driven religious sorting, younger Democrats—by virtue of being raised in less religious households—are less likely to be religious in adulthood than Republicans who were raised in more religious households. This trend, coupled with the tendency for people with similar partisan identities to marry (Alford et al. 2011; Hersh and Ghitza 2016; Huber and Malhotra 2017), indicates that convergence at the elite level alone is not sufficient to undo sorting in the mass electorate.

Where Does This Leave Us?

The preceding chapters not only tell a specific story about the relationship between religion and politics, but they also provide guidance to researchers interested in the role of social identities and group membership in politics. First, more attention must be paid to the causes of group identification and the reasons that strength of identification varies. Knowing politics' role in the development of group attachments is not only important for understanding politics' and partisanship's reach but also for understanding social group influence on political attitudes and behaviors. Second, and relatedly, scholars interested in how social group membership can impact political attitudes should not rely on correlational analyses alone and should develop experimental and observational research designs to establish the direction of causality. Third, drawing on theories of political science and related disciplines is a useful way to develop theoretically based, testable hypotheses about individuals' identities, attitudes, and behaviors. Researchers can use the fact that identities do not form at random but rather through socialization processes when developing theories and research strategies. And finally, identity scholars should explore how different identities relate to one another or what happens when people hold multiple politically relevant identities simultaneously. Research that considers how identities reinforce or compete with one another will offer a more complete understanding of public opinion and political behavior.

APPENDIX

Youth-Parent Socialization Panel

Table A.1 1965–1973: Republicans and Democrats did not diverge in church attendance

	1973 church attendance		
	(1)	(2)	(3)
1965 partisanship			
Republican	−0.02	−0.01	0.02
	(0.04)	(0.04)	(0.05)
Independent	−0.07*	−0.07*	−0.04
	(0.04)	(0.04)	(0.04)
1965 church attendance			
A few times a year	0.13	0.14*	0.13
	(0.09)	(0.08)	(0.10)
Once or twice a month	0.19**	0.19**	0.12
	(0.09)	(0.09)	(0.10)
Almost every week	0.42**	0.42**	0.29**
	(0.08)	(0.08)	(0.10)
Intercept	0.21**	0.13	0.07
	(0.08)	(0.10)	(0.11)
Demographic controls	No	Yes	Yes
Upbringing controls	No	No	Yes
N	558	558	558

Source: Youth-Parent Socialization Panel Study.
Note: Estimates are OLS coefficients with clustered standard errors in parentheses. The dependent variable of 1973 church attendance ranges between 0 (never attend) and 1 (attend almost weekly or more). Democratic identification in 1965 is the partisan reference category. Rarely or never attend religious services in 1965 is the church attendance reference category. Demographic controls include 1965 measures of the student's religious affiliation and beliefs, region of residence, gender, race, high school curriculum (college preparatory track or not), and stated closeness with parents as well as 1973 measures of whether the student had attended college, was married, had children, or served in the Vietnam War between 1965 and 1973. The model also controls for student's income, measured in 1973. Upbringing controls include 1965 parent responses regarding average church attendance, mother's and father's party identifications, education of the household head, and family income.
* $p < 0.10$, ** $p < 0.05$.

Table A.2 1973–1982: Republicans and Democrats diverged in church attendance

	1982 church attendance			
	(1)	(2)	(3)	(4)
1973 partisanship				
Republican	0.05*	0.07**	0.08**	0.08**
	(0.03)	(0.03)	(0.04)	(0.04)
Independent	0.03	0.05	0.06	0.07
	(0.05)	(0.05)	(0.05)	(0.05)
1973 church attendance				
A few times a year	0.14**	0.14**	0.11**	0.11**
	(0.04)	(0.04)	(0.04)	(0.04)
Once or twice a month	0.30**	0.28**	0.21**	0.21**
	(0.05)	(0.05)	(0.06)	(0.06)
Almost every week	0.49**	0.47**	0.38**	0.38**
	(0.05)	(0.05)	(0.06)	(0.06)
Every week	0.59**	0.57**	0.48**	0.48**
	(0.05)	(0.05)	(0.06)	(0.06)
Intercept	0.19**	0.15**	−0.01	−0.01
	(0.03)	(0.06)	(0.11)	(0.11)
Demographic controls	No	Yes	Yes	Yes
Upbringing controls	No	No	Yes	Yes
Attitudinal controls	No	No	No	Yes
R^2	0.33	0.35	0.40	0.41
N	461	461	461	461

Source: Youth-Parent Socialization Panel Study.
Note: Estimates are OLS coefficients with clustered standard errors in parentheses. The dependent variable of 1982 church attendance ranges between 0 (never attend) and 1 (attend weekly). Democratic identification in 1973 is the partisan reference category. Rarely or never attend religious services in 1973 is the church attendance reference category. Demographic controls include 1973 measures of the student's region of residence, education, income, marital and parental status, gender, race, service in Vietnam, and stated closeness with parents as well as 1965 measures of the student's religious affiliation and beliefs and high school curriculum (college preparatory track or not). Upbringing controls include 1965 parent responses regarding average church attendance, mother's and father's party identifications, education of the household head, and family income. Attitudinal controls include 1973 opinions about the Vietnam War, school busing, marijuana legalization, government aid to minorities, equal rights for women, and economic liberalism. * $p < 0.10$, ** $p < 0.05$.

Table A.3 1973–1997: Partisan divergence in church attendance remains present fifteen years later

	(1)	(2)	(3)	(4)
	1997 church attendance			
1973 partisanship				
Republican	0.07*	0.10**	0.11**	0.11**
	(0.04)	(0.04)	(0.04)	(0.04)
Independent	0.01	0.03	0.04	0.05
	(0.05)	(0.05)	(0.05)	(0.05)
1973 church attendance				
A few times a year	0.14**	0.14**	0.12**	0.12**
	(0.04)	(0.04)	(0.04)	(0.04)
Once or twice a month	0.23**	0.22**	0.17**	0.18**
	(0.06)	(0.06)	(0.06)	(0.06)
Almost every week	0.44**	0.41**	0.35**	0.35**
	(0.06)	(0.06)	(0.06)	(0.06)
Every week	0.45**	0.45**	0.39**	0.39**
	(0.05)	(0.05)	(0.06)	(0.06)
Intercept	0.27**	0.24**	0.05	0.07
	(0.04)	(0.06)	(0.11)	(0.12)
Demographic controls	No	Yes	Yes	Yes
Upbringing controls	No	No	Yes	Yes
Attitudinal controls	No	No	No	Yes
R^2	0.21	0.25	0.29	0.31
N	460	460	460	460

Source: Youth-Parent Socialization Panel Study.
Note: Estimates are OLS coefficients with clustered standard errors in parentheses. The dependent variable of 1997 church attendance ranges between 0 (never attend) and 1 (attend weekly). Democratic identification in 1973 is the partisan reference category. Rarely or never attend religious services in 1973 is the church attendance reference category. Demographic controls include 1973 measures of the student's region of residence, education, income, marital and parental status, gender, race, service in Vietnam, and stated closeness with parents as well as 1965 measures of the student's religious affiliation and beliefs and high school curriculum (college preparatory track or not). Upbringing controls include 1965 parent responses regarding average church attendance, mother's and father's party identifications, education of the household head, and family income. Attitudinal controls include 1973 opinions about the Vietnam War, school busing, marijuana legalization, government aid to minorities, equal rights for women, and economic liberalism. * $p < 0.10$, ** $p < 0.05$.

Table A.4 1973–1982: Republicans and Democrats did not diverge in church attendance among the parent generation

	1982 church attendance		
	(1)	(2)	(3)
1973 partisanship			
Republican	−0.02	−0.02	−0.03
	(0.02)	(0.03)	(0.03)
Independent	−0.02	−0.02	−0.02
	(0.04)	(0.05)	(0.05)
1973 church attendance			
A few times a year	0.15**	0.15**	0.15**
	(0.04)	(0.04)	(0.04)
Once or twice a month	0.35**	0.35**	0.34**
	(0.05)	(0.05)	(0.05)
Almost every week	0.57**	0.57**	0.55**
	(0.05)	(0.05)	(0.05)
Every week	0.70**	0.70**	0.69**
	(0.03)	(0.03)	(0.04)
Intercept	0.21**	0.15**	0.08
	(0.04)	(0.07)	(0.08)
Demographic controls	No	Yes	Yes
Attitudinal controls	No	No	Yes
R^2	0.52	0.53	0.54
N	480	480	480

Source: Youth-Parent Socialization Panel Study.
Note: The sample consists of the parent generation. Estimates are OLS coefficients with clustered standard errors in parentheses. The dependent variable of 1982 church attendance ranges between 0 (never attend) and 1 (attend weekly). Democratic identification in 1973 is the partisan reference category. Rarely or never attend religious services in 1973 is the church attendance reference category. Demographic controls include 1973 measures of the parent's region of residence, education, income, marital status, gender, race, as well as 1965 measures of the parent's religious affiliation and beliefs and education. Attitudinal controls include 1973 opinions about the Vietnam War, school busing, marijuana legalization, government aid to minorities, equal rights for women, and economic liberalism. * $p < 0.10$, ** $p < 0.05$.

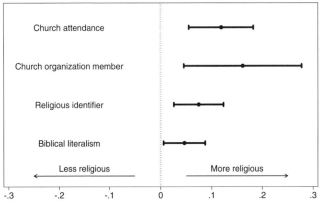

Republican religious change relative to Democrats (non-South), 1973 to 1982

A.1. Similar results appear among nonsouthern respondents. The figure presents partisan differences in changing levels of religiosity between 1973 and 1982 among nonsoutherners (region measured in 1973). Estimates come from change models that include a lagged dependent variable and control variables described in chapter 4. Positive estimates indicate that Republicans became relatively more religious than Democrats between 1973 and 1982. Negative estimates indicate that Democrats became relatively more religious than Republicans between 1973 and 1982. Estimates near zero indicate that neither group became relatively more religious than the other between 1973 and 1982.

Source: Youth-Parent Socialization Panel Study.

Table A.5 1973–1982: Republicans and Democrats diverged in church attendance (same party identification in 1973 and 1982)

| | 1982 church attendance | | | |
	(1)	(2)	(3)	(4)
1973 partisanship				
Republican	0.07*	0.10**	0.12**	0.12**
	(0.03)	(0.04)	(0.05)	(0.05)
Independent	0.03	0.05	0.04	0.03
	(0.06)	(0.07)	(0.07)	(0.08)
1973 church attendance				
A few times a year	0.15**	0.15**	0.11**	0.12**
	(0.04)	(0.04)	(0.05)	(0.05)
Once or twice a month	0.27**	0.25**	0.16**	0.15**
	(0.05)	(0.06)	(0.07)	(0.07)
Almost every week	0.52**	0.48**	0.38**	0.39**
	(0.06)	(0.06)	(0.07)	(0.07)
Every week	0.59**	0.57**	0.48**	0.47**
	(0.05)	(0.05)	(0.06)	(0.06)
Intercept	0.19**	0.23**	0.03	0.01
	(0.04)	(0.07)	(0.11)	(0.12)
Demographic controls	No	Yes	Yes	Yes
Upbringing controls	No	No	Yes	Yes
Attitudinal controls	No	No	No	Yes
R^2	0.37	0.39	0.44	0.47
N	318	318	318	318

Source: Youth-Parent Socialization Panel Study.
Note: The sample consists of respondents who had the same three-point party identification in 1973 and 1982. Estimates are OLS coefficients with clustered standard errors in parentheses. The dependent variable of 1982 church attendance ranges between 0 (never attend) and 1 (attend weekly). Democratic identification in 1973 is the partisan reference category. Rarely or never attend religious services in 1973 is the church attendance reference category. Demographic controls include 1973 measures of the student's region of residence, education, income, marital and parental status, gender, race, service in Vietnam, and stated closeness with parents as well as 1965 measures of the student's religious affiliation and beliefs and high school curriculum (college preparatory track or not). Upbringing controls include 1965 parent responses regarding average church attendance, mother's and father's party identifications, education of the household head, and family income. Attitudinal controls include 1973 opinions about the Vietnam War, school busing, marijuana legalization, government aid to minorities, equal rights for women, and economic liberalism. * $p < 0.10$, ** $p < 0.05$.

Table A.6 1973–1982: Republicans and Democrats diverged in church attendance (1973 partisanship as an instrument for 1982 partisanship)

	(1)	(2)	(3)	(4)
	\multicolumn{4}{c}{1982 church attendance}			
1982 partisanship (instrumented)				
Republican	0.09*	0.11**	0.13**	0.13**
	(0.05)	(0.05)	(0.06)	(0.06)
Independent	0.07	0.15	0.19	0.20
	(0.16)	(0.17)	(0.17)	(0.17)
1973 church attendance				
A few times a year	0.14**	0.12**	0.09**	0.09**
	(0.04)	(0.04)	(0.04)	(0.04)
Once or twice a month	0.30**	0.27**	0.21**	0.21**
	(0.05)	(0.05)	(0.05)	(0.05)
Almost every week	0.49**	0.47**	0.39**	0.39**
	(0.05)	(0.05)	(0.05)	(0.05)
Every week	0.59**	0.57**	0.48**	0.48**
	(0.05)	(0.04)	(0.05)	(0.05)
Intercept	0.17**	0.14**	−0.10	−0.11
	(0.04)	(0.06)	(0.10)	(0.11)
Demographic controls	No	Yes	Yes	Yes
Upbringing controls	No	No	Yes	Yes
Attitudinal controls	No	No	No	Yes
R^2	0.32	0.33	0.37	0.38
N	460	460	460	460

Source: Youth-Parent Socialization Panel Study.
Note: Estimates are the second stage of a two-stage least squares model in which 1973 party identification is an instrument for 1982 partisanship. Estimates are OLS coefficients with clustered standard errors in parentheses. The dependent variable of 1982 church attendance ranges between 0 (never attend) and 1 (attend weekly). Democratic identification in 1973 is the partisan reference category. Rarely or never attend religious services in 1973 is the church attendance reference category. Demographic controls include 1973 measures of the student's region of residence, education, income, marital and parental status, gender, race, service in Vietnam, and stated closeness with parents as well as 1965 measures of the student's religious affiliation and beliefs and high school curriculum (college preparatory track or not). Upbringing controls include 1965 parent responses regarding average church attendance, mother's and father's party identifications, education of the household head, and family income. Attitudinal controls include 1973 opinions about the Vietnam War, school busing, marijuana legalization, government aid to minorities, equal rights for women, and economic liberalism. * $p < 0.10$, ** $p < 0.05$.

Priming Partisanship Experiment

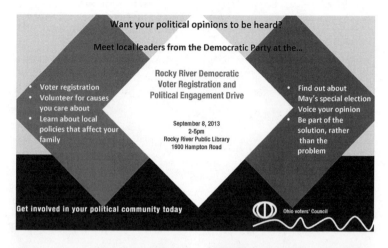

A.2. Democratic priming stimuli.
Source: Priming partisanship experiment.

Are you new to Rocky River? Unsure how to register to vote? Want your political opinions to be heard? Come to the....

Rocky River Democratic Voter Registration and Political Engagement Drive

meet local leaders from the Democratic Party.

September 8, 2013 from 2-5pm.
Rocky River Public Library.
1600 Hampton Road

Ohio voters' council

The registration drive goes beyond just registering new voters, come to...

* meet local leaders
* learn about policies that affect your family
* voice your opinion

* volunteer about issues you care about
* be part of the solution, rather than the problem
* find out about the upcoming special election in May

Get involved in your political community today!

A.2. (*continued*)

Table A.7 Distribution of religious identification (%)

Strong nonidentifier	16
Weak nonidentifier	5
Weak identifier	30
Strong identifier	48
Total	100

Source: Priming partisanship experiment.
Note: Cells include raw percentages for respondents in control condition.

Table A.8 Priming partisanship experimental results

Religious identification	Full sample		Children at home		Grown children		Life-cycle tests	
	(1)	(2)	(3)	(4)	(5)	(6)	(7)	(8)
Treatment	0.06	0.18	−0.49	−0.51	0.05	0.14	0.04	0.21
	(0.15)	(0.17)	(0.30)	(0.36)	(0.43)	(0.50)	(0.38)	(0.44)
Republican	0.97**	0.46*	0.27	−0.48	1.06**	0.84	1.02**	0.74
	(0.18)	(0.24)	(0.40)	(0.49)	(0.40)	(0.57)	(0.37)	(0.46)
Independent	−0.19	−0.30	−0.42	−1.26**	0.54	0.89	0.51	0.91
	(0.22)	(0.30)	(0.44)	(0.64)	(0.61)	(0.89)	(0.73)	(1.09)
Treat * Rep	0.02	−0.03	1.46**	1.67**	−0.46	−0.59	−0.45	−0.70
	(0.27)	(0.29)	(0.65)	(0.72)	(0.57)	(0.65)	(0.53)	(0.60)
Treat * Ind	−0.44	−0.77*	−0.49	−0.02	−0.76	−1.24	−0.72	−1.32
	(0.32)	(0.42)	(0.63)	(1.00)	(0.86)	(1.14)	(0.94)	(1.28)
Kids (1) vs. Grown (0)							0.30	0.51
							(0.35)	(0.48)
Treat * Kids							−0.56	−0.62
							(0.50)	(0.57)
Rep * Kids							−0.74	−0.96
							(0.56)	(0.63)
Ind * Kids							−0.94	−2.20*
							(0.85)	(1.21)
Treat * Rep * Kids							1.95**	2.21**
							(0.87)	(0.95)
Treat * Ind * Kids							0.20	1.14
							(1.13)	(1.76)
cut1 Intercept	−1.50**	−0.48	−2.02**	−2.66	−2.00**	−1.12	−1.83**	0.85
	(0.12)	(0.62)	(0.26)	(2.76)	(0.35)	(4.63)	(0.27)	(1.59)
cut2 Intercept	−1.07**	−0.01	−1.60**	−2.21	−1.50**	−0.51	−1.39**	1.36
	(0.12)	(0.61)	(0.24)	(2.76)	(0.32)	(4.63)	(0.26)	(1.59)
cut3 Intercept	0.42**	1.66**	−0.03	−0.33	0.36	1.50	0.30	3.25**
	(0.11)	(0.62)	(0.22)	(2.74)	(0.30)	(4.62)	(0.26)	(1.61)
Controls	No	Yes	No	Yes	No	Yes	No	Yes
N	1,097	921	260	217	216	195	476	412

Source: Priming partisanship experiment.
Note: Estimates are from ordered logistic regression models. The dependent variable is a four-point religious identification measure that ranges between 0 (strong nonidentifier) and 3 (strong identifier). Democratic identification is the partisan reference category. Treatment is a binary measure indicating whether the respondent is in the treatment condition (1) or not (0). The coefficient *Treat * Rep * Kids* is the relevant coefficient testing whether the partisan treatment effects found among respondents with children at home (coefficient *Treat * Rep* in columns 3 and 4) are different from the null results found among respondents with grown children (columns 5 and 6). * $p < 0.10$, ** $p < 0.05$.

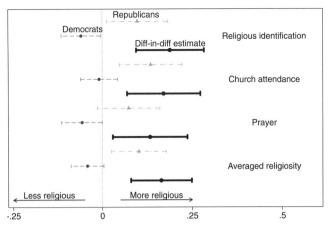

A.3. Replication of priming partisanship results for other dependent variables. The figure presents treatment effects for respondents with children at home, separately for Republicans (gray triangles) and Democrats (small black circles). Positive estimates indicate that the treated respondents report being more religious than respondents in the control condition. Negative estimates indicate that treated respondents report being less religious than respondents in the control condition. And estimates near zero indicate that the treatment and control groups look the same. The thick black circles represent the difference-in-difference estimates testing whether the partisan prime affected Republicans and Democrats differently. The first dependent variable is a replication of the four-point religious identification measure presented in the main text in which treated Republicans (Democrats) reported being stronger (weaker) religious identifiers than untreated Republicans (Democrats). The positive difference-in-difference estimate means that partisan prime caused the religious identification gap between Republicans and Democrats to grow. The second dependent variable measures church attendance, which ranges from never attend (0) to attend more than once a week (1), and the third dependent variable measures frequency of personal prayer, which ranges from never (0) to multiple times per day (1). A final dependent variable takes the average of the four religious measures and also ranges between 0 and 1. Given that frequency of church attendance and prayer cannot change immediately, these results are best interpreted as subjective attitudes about religion rather than actual behaviors. *Source*: Priming partisanship experiment.

Faith and Freedom Coalition Experiment

National News

2012 Republican Hopefuls Court Religious Right

By Charles Babington, Associated Press
June 4, 2011

WASHINGTON (AP): A Washington gathering of religious conservatives this weekend did something a South Carolina Republican debate and a well-publicized forum in New Hampshire couldn't do a few weeks ago. It drew nearly all the GOP presidential hopefuls to one stage.

The Faith and Freedom Coalition's two-day conference proved that the religious right still plays a major role in the Republican nominating process, even if it's somewhat less organized than it was in the Christian Coalition's heyday.

The gathering was a tryout, of sorts, for candidates hoping to fill a void left by former Arkansas Gov. Mike Huckabee. The Southern Baptist minister won the 2008 Iowa caucus but is not running this time.

National News

2012 Republican Hopefuls Court Religious Right

On the opening day of the conference, most of the candidates spent more time on fiscal issues than on spiritual matters. But they generally portrayed the federal debt and health care policies as moral concerns. They also paid tribute to religious conservatives who often place social issues ahead of questions such as taxes and spending. Candidates bypassed mainstream journalists in order to give interviews to the Christian-oriented CBN network and peppered their speeches with Biblical quotes and personal religious anecdotes.

The audience members sat silently when Mississippi Gov. Haley Barbour urged them to embrace the eventual Republican nominee. The crowd warmed up when Barbour said the overriding goal, regardless of who is nominated, is to make Obama a one-term president.

A.4. Faith and Freedom Coalition experimental stimulus.
Source: Faith and Freedom Coalition experiment.

Table A.9 Faith and Freedom Coalition experimental results

Religious identification	Children at home		Grown children		Life-cycle tests	
	(1)	(2)	(3)	(4)	(5)	(6)
Treatment	-0.53	-0.89**	0.10	0.06	0.11	0.06
	(0.32)	(0.37)	(0.20)	(0.21)	(0.20)	(0.21)
Republican	0.28	-0.18	0.48**	0.01	0.51**	0.05
	(0.30)	(0.40)	(0.24)	(0.26)	(0.25)	(0.26)
Independent	-0.71**	-0.84**	0.03	-0.14	0.03	-0.11
	(0.32)	(0.38)	(0.20)	(0.22)	(0.21)	(0.22)
Treat * Rep	0.92**	1.28**	-0.00	0.09	-0.00	0.11
	(0.42)	(0.45)	(0.32)	(0.33)	(0.34)	(0.34)
Treat * Ind	0.61	0.94*	-0.17	-0.15	-0.18	-0.18
	(0.44)	(0.49)	(0.28)	(0.30)	(0.29)	(0.31)
Kids (1) vs. Grown (0)					0.39	0.77**
					(0.25)	(0.30)
Treat * Kids					-0.61*	-0.82**
					(0.37)	(0.40)
Rep * Kids					-0.27	-0.19
					(0.37)	(0.40)
Ind * Kids					-0.72**	-0.61
					(0.36)	(0.40)
Treat * Rep * Kids					0.87*	1.02*
					(0.51)	(0.54)
Treat * Ind * Kids					0.76	1.00*
					(0.51)	(0.55)
cut1 Intercept	-1.53**	-0.05	-1.08**	5.50**	-1.10**	1.94**
	(0.24)	(0.98)	(0.15)	(1.44)	(0.15)	(0.62)
cut2 Intercept	-0.67**	0.90	-0.18	6.50**	-0.21	2.91**
	(0.23)	(0.98)	(0.14)	(1.45)	(0.14)	(0.62)
cut3 Intercept	0.04	1.68*	0.49**	7.23**	0.48**	3.65**
	(0.23)	(0.99)	(0.14)	(1.46)	(0.15)	(0.63)
cut4 Intercept	0.45**	2.14**	0.82**	7.59**	0.83**	4.04**
	(0.23)	(1.00)	(0.15)	(1.46)	(0.15)	(0.63)
Controls	No	Yes	No	Yes	No	Yes
N	416	415	803	796	1,219	1,211

Source: Faith and Freedom Coalition experiment.
Note: Estimates are from ordered logistic regression models. The dependent variable is a four-point religious identification measure that ranges between 0 (strong nonidentifier) and 3 (strong identifier). Democratic identification is the partisan reference category. Treatment is a binary measure indicating whether the respondent is in the treatment condition (1) or not (0). The coefficient *Treat * Rep * Kids* is the relevant coefficient testing whether the partisan treatment effects found among respondents with children at home (coefficient *Treat * Rep* in columns 1 and 2) are different from the null results found among respondents with grown children (columns 3 and 4). * $p < 0.10$, ** $p < 0.05$.

2000–2002–2004 ANES

Table A.10 Partisan church attendance diverged after gay marriage became salient

	2002 church attendance		
	(1)	(2)	(3)
2000 partisanship			
Republican	−0.01	0.00	0.00
	(0.03)	(0.03)	(0.03)
Independent	−0.05*	−0.03	−0.02
	(0.03)	(0.03)	(0.03)
2000 church attendance			
A few times a year	0.15**	0.08*	0.08*
	(0.04)	(0.04)	(0.04)
Once or twice a month	0.34**	0.27**	0.26**
	(0.04)	(0.04)	(0.04)
Almost every week	0.53**	0.44**	0.43**
	(0.03)	(0.04)	(0.04)
Every week	0.83**	0.72**	0.69**
	(0.03)	(0.05)	(0.05)
More than once a week	0.63**	0.53**	0.51**
	(0.04)	(0.05)	(0.05)
Intercept	0.12**	0.04	0.06
	(0.04)	(0.14)	(0.16)
Demographic controls	No	Yes	Yes
Attitudinal controls	No	No	Yes
R^2	0.67	0.73	0.74
N	579	579	579

Table A.10 (*continued*)

	2004 church attendance		
	(1)	(2)	(3)
2002 partisanship			
Republican	0.06**	0.05**	0.04
	(0.02)	(0.02)	(0.02)
Independent	−0.02	−0.03	−0.03
	(0.02)	(0.02)	(0.02)
2002 church attendance			
A few times a year	0.14**	0.12**	0.13**
	(0.03)	(0.03)	(0.03)
Once or twice a month	0.32**	0.30**	0.29**
	(0.02)	(0.03)	(0.03)
Almost every week	0.49**	0.44**	0.43**
	(0.03)	(0.03)	(0.03)
Every week	0.62**	0.58**	0.56**
	(0.02)	(0.03)	(0.03)
More than once a week	0.80**	0.72**	0.70**
	(0.03)	(0.03)	(0.03)
Intercept	0.05**	−0.06	−0.07
	(0.02)	(0.08)	(0.09)
Demographic controls	No	Yes	Yes
Attitudinal controls	No	No	Yes
R^2	0.73	0.75	0.76
N	559	559	559

Source: 2000–2002–2004 American National Election Study.
Note: Estimates are OLS coefficients with robust standard errors in parentheses. The dependent variable of church attendance ranges between 0 (never attend) and 1 (attend more than once a week). When the dependent variable is church attendance in 2002 (top panel), independent variables are measured in 2000. When the dependent variable is measured in 2004 (bottom panel), independent variables are measured in 2002. Democratic identification is the partisan reference category. Never attend religious services is the church attendance reference category. Demographic controls include gender, race, age, age squared, education, income, employment status, region of residence, and religious affiliation (measured in 2000). Attitudinal controls include views of the economy, feelings toward feminists, feelings toward gays and lesbians, economic liberalism, attitudes on abortion (measured in 2000), political ideology, and support for the Iraq War (2002–2004 models only).
* $p < 0.10$, ** $p < 0.05$.

Table A.11 Respondents with children at home drive the results

	Children at home			Grown children			Life-cycle effect		
2002 church attendance	(1)	(2)	(3)	(4)	(5)	(6)	(7)	(8)	(9)
2000 partisanship									
Republican	-0.00	-0.04	-0.03	-0.00	0.02	0.01	-0.01	-0.02	-0.02
	(0.05)	(0.06)	(0.05)	(0.05)	(0.03)	(0.03)	(0.07)	(0.06)	(0.06)
Independent	-0.01	-0.06	-0.03	-0.02	-0.00	-0.00			
	(0.07)	(0.07)	(0.06)	(0.03)	(0.03)	(0.03)			
2000 church attendance									
A few times a year	0.20*	0.16*	0.25**	0.09**	-0.00	-0.01			
	(0.10)	(0.09)	(0.08)	(0.04)	(0.05)	(0.05)			
Once or twice a month	0.31**	0.37**	0.41**	0.34**	0.21**	0.21**			
	(0.08)	(0.07)	(0.07)	(0.04)	(0.06)	(0.06)			
Almost every week	0.59**	0.54**	0.53**	0.52**	0.40**	0.40**			
	(0.05)	(0.07)	(0.07)	(0.04)	(0.06)	(0.05)			
Every week	0.86**	0.77**	0.76**	0.85**	0.68**	0.68**			
	(0.04)	(0.07)	(0.07)	(0.04)	(0.06)	(0.05)			
More than once a week	0.66**	0.59**	0.63**	0.62**	0.48**	0.48**			
	(0.06)	(0.06)	(0.06)	(0.06)	(0.06)	(0.06)			
Intercept	0.07	-0.76**	-0.90**	0.10**	0.08	0.04			
	(0.05)	(0.34)	(0.34)	(0.03)	(0.46)	(0.46)			
Demographic controls	No	Yes	Yes	No	Yes	Yes	No	Yes	Yes
Attitudinal controls	No	No	Yes	No	No	Yes	No	No	Yes
R^2	0.69	0.81	0.84	0.73	0.81	0.82	0.71	0.75	0.76
N	133	133	133	266	266	266	399	399	399

2004 church attendance	Children at home			Grown children			Life-cycle effect		
	(1)	(2)	(3)	(4)	(5)	(6)	(7)	(8)	(9)
2002 partisanship									
Republican	0.15**	0.17**	0.19**	-0.01	-0.02	0.00	0.14**	0.14**	0.16**
	(0.05)	(0.06)	(0.07)	(0.03)	(0.03)	(0.04)	(0.05)	(0.05)	(0.05)
Independent	0.08	0.10	0.13**	-0.04	-0.03	-0.01			
	(0.05)	(0.06)	(0.06)	(0.03)	(0.03)	(0.03)			
2002 church attendance									
A few times a year	0.21**	0.19**	0.18**	0.15**	0.13**	0.12**			
	(0.07)	(0.08)	(0.08)	(0.04)	(0.04)	(0.04)			
Once or twice a month	0.38**	0.35**	0.35**	0.32**	0.31**	0.30**			
	(0.06)	(0.07)	(0.07)	(0.04)	(0.04)	(0.04)			
Almost every week	0.54**	0.50**	0.48**	0.48**	0.44**	0.43**			
	(0.05)	(0.07)	(0.06)	(0.04)	(0.04)	(0.04)			
Every week	0.64**	0.60**	0.54**	0.69**	0.66**	0.66**			
	(0.05)	(0.06)	(0.07)	(0.03)	(0.04)	(0.04)			
More than once a week	0.79**	0.72**	0.68**	0.86**	0.81**	0.78**			
	(0.05)	(0.07)	(0.08)	(0.04)	(0.05)	(0.05)			
Intercept	-0.03	0.56	0.31	0.06**	0.05	0.09			
	(0.05)	(0.51)	(0.58)	(0.03)	(0.32)	(0.34)			
Demographic controls	No	Yes	Yes	No	Yes	Yes	No	Yes	Yes
Attitudinal controls	No	No	Yes	No	No	Yes	No	No	Yes
R^2	0.74	0.79	0.81	0.74	0.78	0.80	0.74	0.77	0.79
N	128	128	128	256	256	256	384	384	384

Source: 2000–2002–2004 American National Election Study.

Note: Estimates are OLS coefficients with robust standard errors in parentheses. The dependent variable of church attendance ranges between 0 (never attend) and 1 (attend more than once a week). When the dependent variable is church attendance in 2002 (top panel), independent variables are measured in 2000. When the dependent variable is measured in 2004 (bottom panel), independent variables are measured in 2002. Democratic identification is the partisan reference category. Never attend religious services is the church attendance reference category. Demographic controls include gender, race, age, age squared, education, income, employment status, region of residence, and religious affiliation (measured in 2000). Attitudinal controls include views of the economy, feelings toward feminists, feelings toward gays and lesbians, economic liberalism, attitudes on abortion (measured in 2000), political ideology, and support for the Iraq War (2002–2004 models only). Columns 7, 8, and 9 test whether the change over time is different for partisan parents with children at home (columns 1, 2, and 3) and partisan parents with grown children (columns 4, 5, and 6). * $p < 0.10$, ** $p < 0.05$.

Table A.12 2002–2004: Republicans and Democrats diverged in opinions (marginal effects)

	Iraq attitude (04) (1)	Economic support (04) (2)	Bush approval on economy (04) (3)
2002 partisanship			
Republican	0.32**	0.19**	0.28**
	(0.04)	(0.03)	(0.07)
Independent	0.13**	0.06**	0.13**
	(0.04)	(0.03)	(0.06)
2002 dependent variables			
Iraq attitude	0.34**		
	(0.04)		
Economic support		0.22**	
		(0.04)	
Bush approval on economy			0.50**
			(0.05)
Controls	Yes	Yes	Yes
N	634	782	75

Source: 2000–2002–2004 American National Election Study.
Note: The sample consists of married respondents with children living at home. Estimates are marginal effects after logit models (columns 1 and 3) and an ordered logit model (column 2). Democratic identification is the partisan reference category. Control variables include age, age squared, gender, education, income, employment status, region of residence, race, political ideology, and religious affiliation (measured in 2000). * $p < 0.10$, ** $p < 0.05$.

Table A.13 2002–2004: No church-driven divergence in political attitudes

	Party id (04) (1)	Bush approval (04) (2)	Bush eval (04) (3)
2002 church attendance			
Attend a few times a year	−0.08	0.05	−0.03
	(0.07)	(0.12)	(0.08)
Attend once or twice a month	0.03	0.04	−0.01
	(0.06)	(0.11)	(0.07)
Attend almost every week	−0.11**	−0.07	−0.07
	(0.05)	(0.10)	(0.07)
Attend every week	0.01	−0.02	0.01
	(0.06)	(0.10)	(0.07)
Attend more than once a week	−0.07	−0.12	−0.09
	(0.06)	(0.12)	(0.08)
2002 dependent variables			
Seven-point party id	0.75**	0.06	0.02
	(0.07)	(0.13)	(0.10)

Table A.13 (*continued*)

	Party id (04) (1)	Bush approval (04) (2)	Bush eval (04) (3)
Bush approval		0.44** (0.15)	
Bush eval			0.44** (0.12)
Intercept	0.49 (0.46)	1.23 (0.82)	1.27** (0.56)
Controls	Yes	Yes	Yes
N	127	126	128

Source: 2000–2002–2004 American National Election Study.
Note: The sample consists of married respondents with children living at home. Estimates are OLS coefficients with robust standard errors in parentheses. All dependent variables range between 0 (strong Democrat, strongly disapprove of Bush, cold feeling thermometer for Bush) and 1 (strong Republican, strongly approve of Bush, warm feeling thermometer for Bush). Never attend religious services is the church attendance reference category. Control variables include age, age squared, gender, education, income, employment status, region of residence, race, political ideology, and religious affiliation (measured in 2000). $* p < 0.10$, $** p < 0.05$.

Table A.14 2002–2004: Position in life cycle, rather than age, produce the main results

	Children at home		Grown children	
2004 church attendance	Younger half (1)	Older half (2)	Younger half (3)	Older half (4)
2002 partisanship				
Republican	0.16** (0.07)	0.15** (0.07)	−0.01 (0.04)	−0.00 (0.05)
Independent	0.09 (0.08)	0.05 (0.08)	−0.07* (0.03)	0.01 (0.05)
2002 church attendance				
A few times a year	0.20* (0.10)	0.26** (0.10)	0.13** (0.04)	0.24** (0.08)
Once or twice a month	0.33** (0.08)	0.47** (0.09)	0.36** (0.05)	0.27** (0.06)
Almost every week	0.51** (0.08)	0.61** (0.08)	0.46** (0.05)	0.51** (0.07)
Every week	0.58** (0.07)	0.75** (0.08)	0.73** (0.04)	0.68** (0.06)
More than once a week	0.77** (0.07)	0.82** (0.10)	0.87** (0.05)	0.81** (0.08)
Intercept	−0.01 (0.07)	−0.10 (0.08)	0.08** (0.03)	0.03 (0.05)

Table A.14 (*continued*)

2004 church attendance	Children at home		Grown children	
	Younger half (1)	Older half (2)	Younger half (3)	Older half (4)
R^2	0.77	0.72	0.80	0.67
N	64	64	144	112

Source: 2000–2002–2004 American National Election Study.
Note: Estimates are OLS coefficients with robust standard errors in parentheses. The dependent variable of 2004 church attendance ranges between 0 (never attend) and 1 (attend more than once a week). Democratic identification is the partisan reference category. Never attend religious services is the church attendance reference category. Columns 1 and 2 include married respondents with children at home, and columns 3 and 4 include married respondents with grown children. Within each life-cycle window, respondents are classified into two equally sized age categories. Columns 1 and 3 include respondents who are below the median age of respondents with children living at home and grown children, respectively. Columns 3 and 4 include respondents who are above the median age of respondents with children living at home and grown children, respectively. These models do not include control variables due to sample size constraints. * $p < 0.10$, ** $p < 0.05$.

Table A.15   2002–2004: Republicans do not become more likely to be politically involved

	Attend community rally (2004)		Attend community meeting (2004)	
2002 partisanship				
Republican	−0.13*	−0.15*	0.08	−0.01
	(0.07)	(0.09)	(0.09)	(0.10)
Independent	−0.16**	−0.17*	0.08	0.04
	(0.07)	(0.09)	(0.10)	(0.11)
2002 dependent variables				
Attend community rally	0.29	0.19		
	(0.19)	(0.19)		
Attend community meeting			0.31**	0.28**
			(0.07)	(0.08)
Controls	No	Yes	No	Yes
Intercept	0.20**	0.37	0.26**	0.09
	(0.07)	(0.58)	(0.08)	(0.93)
R^2	0.09	0.19	0.10	0.21
N	178	178	178	178

Source: 2000–2002–2004 American National Election Study.
Note: The sample consists of married respondents with children living at home. Estimates are OLS coefficients with robust standard errors in parentheses. The dependent variables are measured in 2004 and are coded as attended (1) or not (0). Democratic identification is the partisan reference category. Control variables include race, age, age squared, gender, education, employment status, household income, and region of residence. The negative coefficient on *Republican* indicates that Republicans became *less* likely to attend a rally between 2002 and 2004 relative to Democrats.
* $p < 0.10$, ** $p < 0.05$.

Table A.16 2002–2004: Support for Iraq War does not explain
results

2004 church attendance	Iraq not worth it (1)	Iraq worth it (2)
2002 partisanship		
Republican	0.16**	0.14**
	(0.07)	(0.07)
Independent	0.07	0.18**
	(0.05)	(0.08)
2002 church attendance		
A few times a year	0.18**	−0.04
	(0.08)	(0.08)
Once or twice a month	0.31**	0.25**
	(0.08)	(0.07)
Almost every week	0.54**	0.48**
	(0.06)	(0.07)
Every week	0.57**	0.61**
	(0.08)	(0.06)
More than once a week	0.52**	0.82**
	(0.09)	(0.06)
Intercept	−0.02	0.02
	(0.06)	(0.07)
R^2	0.62	0.75
N	79	100

Source: 2000–2002–2004 American National Election Study.
Note: The sample consists of married respondents with children living
at home. Estimates are OLS coefficients with robust standard errors in
parentheses. The dependent variable of 2004 church attendance ranges
between 0 (never attend) and 1 (attend more than once a week). Democratic identification is the partisan reference category. Never attend religious services is the church attendance reference category. These models
do not include control variables due to sample size constraints. * $p < 0.10$,
** $p < 0.05$.

Table A.17 2002–2004: Republicans and Democrats with children at home diverged in church attendance (same party identification in 2002 and 2004)

	Children at home			Grown children		
2004 church attendance	(1)	(2)	(3)	(4)	(5)	(6)
2002 partisanship						
Republican	0.18**	0.19**	0.22**	0.01	-0.00	0.06
	(0.06)	(0.07)	(0.10)	(0.03)	(0.04)	(0.04)
Independent	0.09	0.07	0.13	-0.03	-0.01	0.03
	(0.07)	(0.08)	(0.09)	(0.03)	(0.04)	(0.04)
2002 church attendance						
A few times a year	0.20**	0.17*	0.16*	0.21**	0.18**	0.16**
	(0.08)	(0.09)	(0.09)	(0.05)	(0.05)	(0.05)
Once or twice a month	0.39**	0.31**	0.31**	0.34**	0.34**	0.32**
	(0.06)	(0.08)	(0.09)	(0.04)	(0.05)	(0.05)
Almost every week	0.54**	0.45**	0.42**	0.50**	0.47**	0.45**
	(0.06)	(0.08)	(0.08)	(0.04)	(0.05)	(0.05)
Every week	0.62**	0.52**	0.45**	0.70**	0.67**	0.65**
	(0.06)	(0.08)	(0.09)	(0.04)	(0.05)	(0.05)
More than once a week	0.77**	0.67**	0.63**	0.83**	0.78**	0.74**
	(0.06)	(0.09)	(0.09)	(0.05)	(0.06)	(0.06)
Intercept	-0.05	0.76	0.66	0.05	-0.06	-0.09
	(0.06)	(0.60)	(0.69)	(0.03)	(0.40)	(0.40)
Demographic controls	No	Yes	Yes	No	Yes	Yes
Attitudinal controls	No	No	Yes	No	No	Yes
R^2	0.70	0.78	0.81	0.73	0.78	0.81
N	105	105	105	205	205	205

Source: 2000–2002–2004 American National Election Study.

Note: The sample consists of married respondents with children at home who had the same three-point party identification in 2002 and 2004. Estimates are OLS coefficients with robust standard errors in parentheses. The dependent variable of 2004 church attendance ranges between 0 (never attend) and 1 (attend more than once a week). Democratic identification is the partisan reference category. Never attend religious services is the church attendance reference category. Demographic controls include gender, race, age, age squared, education, income, employment status, region of residence, and religious affiliation (measured in 2000). Attitudinal controls include views of the economy, feelings toward feminists, feelings toward gays and lesbians, economic liberalism, attitudes on abortion (measured in 2000), political ideology, and support for the Iraq War. $* p < 0.10$. $** p < 0.05$.

Table A.18 2002–2004: Republicans and Democrats with children at home
diverged in church attendance (2002 partisanship as an instrument for
2004 partisanship)

Church attendance (2004)	Children at home	
	(1)	(2)
2004 partisanship (instrumented)		
Republican	0.19**	0.22**
	(0.06)	(0.08)
Independent	0.11	0.12
	(0.07)	(0.08)
2002 church attendance		
Attend a few times a year	0.21**	0.19**
	(0.08)	(0.08)
Attend once or twice a month	0.39**	0.38**
	(0.06)	(0.07)
Attend almost every week	0.58**	0.52**
	(0.06)	(0.06)
Attend every week	0.63**	0.56**
	(0.05)	(0.06)
Attend more than once a week	0.79**	0.76**
	(0.06)	(0.07)
Intercept	−0.07	0.52
	(0.06)	(0.55)
Controls	No	Yes
R^2	0.70	0.76
N	120	120

Source: 2000–2002–2004 American National Election Study.
Note: The sample consists of married respondents with children at home. Estimates are the second stage of a two-stage least squares model in which 2002 party identification is an instrument for 2004 partisanship. The dependent variable of 2004 church attendance ranges between 0 (never attend) and 1 (attend more than once a week). Democratic identification is the partisan reference category. Never attend religious services is the church attendance reference category. Demographic controls include gender, race, age, age squared, education, income, employment status, region of residence, and religious affiliation (measured in 2000). Attitudinal controls include views of the economy, feelings toward feminists, feelings toward gays and lesbians, economic liberalism, attitudes on abortion (measured in 2000), political ideology, and support for the Iraq War. * $p < 0.10$, ** $p < 0.05$.

Immigration Rhetoric Experiment

The Opinion Pages

Let every person be subject to the governing authorities
Immigration reform plan places interests of illegal immigrants ahead of Americans

By REVEREND GARY CHAPMAN
Published: February 16, 2013

(PAGE 1 of 2)

The United States Congress is currently drafting and debating a law that could potentially overhaul our immigration system. In addition to changing border security, rehabbing the legal immigration system, and establishing a stronger employment verification system, a major component of the legislation is a pathway to citizenship for the 11.1 million individuals currently living in the United States illegally.

But legalizing everyone who is in the country illegally is not the answer. The Bible requires that the immigrant obey the law and customs of her inhabited land. These immigrants broke the law when they entered the country illegally, and it is the government's role to act as an agent of justice.

The Opinion Pages

Let every person be subject to the governing authorities
(PAGE 2 of 2)

The discussion surrounding the fairness and compassion of allowing the estimated 11 million illegal immigrants to remain in the country ignores the need to have fairness and compassion for the people who have been waiting in lines for years to come legally. To reward those who broke the law we are saying to the law-abiding immigrant, "You were dumb to wait. Why didn't you enter illegally?" The result of a legalization program would not only be an increase in illegal immigration but a new precedent whereby we, as Americans and Christians, reward illegal behavior.

> *"For there is no authority except from God, and those that exist have been instituted by God. Therefore whoever resists the authorities resists what God has appointed, and those who resist will incur judgment". – Romans 13-1*

As Congress wrestles with immigration reform, I urge you to contact your representative and make sure she knows that immigration reform is not only an economic and security issue; it also is an issue of fairness and rule of law. It reveals our character as a people and our values as a nation.

Reverend Gary Chapman is the senior Pastor at Briarwood Church.

A.5. Anti-immigration reform stimulus.
Source: Immigration rhetoric experiment.

The Opinion Pages

You shall not wrong a foreigner or oppress him, for you were foreigners in the land of Egypt

Do we finally have the moral vision and courage to do what is right for immigrant families?

By REVEREND GARY CHAPMAN
Published: February 16, 2013

(PAGE 1 of 2)

The United States Congress is currently debating a law that could potentially overhaul our immigration system. In addition to changing border security and establishing a stronger employment verification system, a major component of the legislation is a pathway to citizenship for the 11.1 million individuals currently living in the United States without legal documents.

Now is the time for comprehensive immigration reform. There is an inconsistency in how immigrants are currently treated and how the Bible says to treat newcomers. Verse after verse, the Bible instructs us to care for and welcome the alien, the stranger, the sojourner among us. Yet we have passed laws that force our neighbors to live in the shadows of society. The result is these immigrants—whom the Bible requires us to care for—are among the most marginalized and vulnerable in the population.

The Opinion Pages

You shall not wrong a foreigner or oppress him, for you were foreigners in the land of Egypt

(PAGE 2 of 2)

Undocumented immigrants are particularly susceptible to human rights abuses, such as trafficking, rape, and exploitation in the workplace. These crimes often go unreported out of fear of deportation. Immigration reform will allow victims to come forward and criminals to be prosecuted for their crimes. Immigration reform will also protect the unity of the immediate family. Keeping families intact and safe strengthens both the families and the community as a whole.

> *"For I was hungry and you gave me something to eat. I was thirsty and you gave me something to drink. I was a stranger and you invited me in." - MATTHEW 25:35*

We must respect the God-given dignity of every person, including the millions of individuals who leave their homeland in search of a better life in the United States. As Congress wrestles with immigration reform, I urge you to contact your representative and make sure she knows that immigration reform is not only an economic and security issue; it also is a moral issue. It reveals our character as a people and our values as a nation.

Reverend Gary Chapman is the senior Pastor at Briarwood Church.

A.6. Pro-immigration reform stimulus.
Source: Immigration rhetoric experiment.

Table A.19 Anti- and pro-reform messages had different effects on Democratic parents

| | Children at home | | | |
| | Democrats | | Republicans | |
Strength of religious identification	(1)	(2)	(3)	(4)
Pro-reform message	−0.02	−0.04	−0.03	0.01
	(0.05)	(0.06)	(0.07)	(0.07)
Anti-reform message	−0.13**	−0.20**	0.03	−0.01
	(0.06)	(0.06)	(0.07)	(0.06)
Intercept	0.80**	0.88**	0.83**	1.42**
	(0.04)	(0.30)	(0.05)	(0.50)
Controls	No	Yes	No	Yes
R^2	0.03	0.14	0.01	0.11
N	208	182	113	103

| | Grown children | | | |
| | Democrats | | Republicans | |
Strength of religious identification	(1)	(2)	(3)	(4)
Pro-reform message	0.06	0.05	0.06	−0.00
	(0.06)	(0.07)	(0.06)	(0.06)
Anti-reform message	0.06	0.05	0.08	0.02
	(0.06)	(0.06)	(0.06)	(0.06)
Intercept	0.76**	1.06	0.79**	1.07
	(0.04)	(0.85)	(0.04)	(0.90)
Controls	No	Yes	No	Yes
R^2	0.01	0.15	0.02	0.07
N	122	108	135	129

Source: Immigration rhetoric experiment.
Note: Estimates are OLS coefficients. The dependent variable is a four-point religious identification measure that ranges between 0 (strong nonidentifier) and 1 (strong identifier). No newspaper article is the experimental reference category. The results in the top panel come from analyses that look at respondents with children at home. The results in the bottom panel come from analyses that look at respondents with grown children. Control variables include gender, race, age, age squared, education, income, and political ideology. The results from the main text use the models without control variables. * $p < 0.10$, ** $p < 0.05$.

Consequences of Religious Sorting: Political Knowledge

ıble A.20 Political knowledge, church attendance, and partisanship

	Democrats		Republicans		Full sample	
ᴴurch attendance	(1)	(2)	(3)	(4)	(5)	(6)
ᴴow candidates'	-0.12**	-0.06**	0.14**	0.08**	-0.12**	-0.06**
positions on abortion	(0.02)	(0.02)	(0.02)	(0.02)	(0.02)	(0.02)
ᴇpublican (1) vs.					0.05**	0.06**
Democrat (0)					(0.02)	(0.02)
ᴴow candidates'					0.26**	0.16**
positions * Republican					(0.03)	(0.03)
ᴵtercept	0.44**	-0.01	0.39**	-0.10	0.44**	-0.03
	(0.01)	(0.04)	(0.02)	(0.07)	(0.01)	(0.03)
ᴼntrols	No	Yes	No	Yes	No	Yes
	0.02	0.28	0.02	0.23	0.05	0.26
	2,481	2,481	1,755	1,755	4,236	4,236

ᴜrce: 2012 American National Election Study.

ᴛe: Estimates are OLS coefficients with robust standard errors in parentheses. The dependent variable of church at ᴺdance ranges between 0 (never attend) and 1 (almost weekly or more). Control variables include gender, region of ᴺidence, age, age squared, income, education, race, denominational affiliation, marital status, parental status, politi ᴬ interest, and general political knowledge. * $p < 0.10$, ** $p < 0.05$.

Table A.21 Political interest, church attendance, and congregational factors

Church attendance	Democrats		Republicans	
	(1)	(2)	(3)	(4)
Congregation same party id (1) or not (0)	−0.08** (0.04)	−0.10** (0.04)	0.05 (0.04)	0.09** (0.04)
Political interest	−0.00 (0.03)	−0.03 (0.03)	−0.05** (0.03)	−0.03 (0.02)
Congregation same party id * Political interest	0.09** (0.04)	0.10** (0.04)	0.10** (0.04)	0.12** (0.04)
Intercept	0.51** (0.03)	0.21 (0.24)	0.44** (0.03)	0.66** (0.26)
Controls	No	Yes	No	Yes
R^2	0.02	0.13	0.03	0.17
N	257	257	283	283

Source: Djupe and Gilbert, Evangelical Lutheran Church in America (ELCA)/Episcopal Church Study, 1999–2000.
Note: Estimates are OLS coefficients with clustered standard errors in parentheses. The dependent variable of church attendance ranges between 0 (never attend) and 1 (almost weekly or more). Control variables include gender; race; age; income; education; marital status; employment status; denominational affiliation; involvement in church groups; and how other members of the congregation compare to the respondent with respect to race, age, religious beliefs, class, and distance living from church. * $p < 0.10$, ** $p < 0.05$.

African Americans' Unique Relationship with Religion and Politics: Youth-Parent Socialization Panel

Table A.22 1965–1973: Black Democrats also fell away from organized religion between 1965 and 1973

	Church attendance		Religious identification		Biblical literalism	
	(1)	(2)	(3)	(4)	(5)	(6)
1965 partisanship						
White Democrat	0.01	0.05	−0.20	−0.01	0.32	0.59*
	(0.04)	(0.04)	(0.44)	(0.39)	(0.33)	(0.30)
White Republican	−0.01	0.04	−0.50	−0.23	0.60*	1.04**
	(0.04)	(0.05)	(0.46)	(0.43)	(0.34)	(0.35)
1965 church attendance						
A few times a year	0.08	0.06				
	(0.08)	(0.08)				
A few times a month	0.15**	0.09				
	(0.07)	(0.08)				
Almost weekly	0.26**	0.17**				
	(0.07)	(0.08)				
1965 religious identifier			0.57	0.30		
			(0.65)	(0.50)		
1965 biblical literalism					1.40**	1.26**
					(0.16)	(0.16)
Intercept	0.30**	0.33**	1.61**	1.69**	−2.12**	−1.91**
	(0.08)	(0.09)	(0.75)	(0.69)	(0.34)	(0.42)
Controls	No	Yes	No	Yes	No	Yes
N	1,039	1,039	1,084	1,084	1,057	1,057

Source: Youth-Parent Socialization Panel Study.

Note: Estimates are OLS coefficients for the church attendance dependent variable and logistic regression coefficients for religious identification and biblical literalism dependent variables. Black Democrats are excluded as the racial/partisan reference category. Rarely or never attend religious services in 1965 is the church attendance reference category. Demographic controls include 1965 measures of the student's religious affiliation, region of residence, gender, race, high school curriculum (college preparatory track or not), and stated closeness with parents as well as 1973 measures of whether the student had attended college, was married, and had children. Upbringing controls include 1965 parent responses regarding average church attendance, mother's and father's party identifications, education of the household head, and family income. * $p < 0.10$, ** $p < 0.05$.

Table A.23 1973–1982: Black Democrats do not follow same pattern as white Democrats or white Republicans

	Church attendance		Religious identification		Biblical literalism		Membership in org	
	(1)	(2)	(3)	(4)	(5)	(6)	(7)	(8)
1973 partisanship								
White Democrat	-0.13**	-0.09*	-0.32	-0.14	-1.74**	-1.47**	-0.97*	-0.92*
	(0.05)	(0.05)	(0.51)	(0.55)	(0.44)	(0.56)	(0.55)	(0.57)
White Republican	-0.05	0.02	0.31	0.67	-1.47**	-1.10*	-0.41	-0.16
	(0.05)	(0.05)	(0.54)	(0.69)	(0.44)	(0.56)	(0.54)	(0.60)
1973 church attendance								
A few times a year	0.19**	0.15**						
	(0.04)	(0.04)						
A few times a month	0.32**	0.26**						
	(0.05)	(0.05)						
Almost weekly	0.52**	0.43**						
	(0.05)	(0.05)						
Weekly or more	0.60**	0.50**						
	(0.04)	(0.05)						
1973 religious identifier			2.20**	2.32**				
			(0.32)	(0.33)				

	(1)	(2)	(3)	(4)	(5)	(6)	(7)	(8)
1973 biblical literalism	0.28**	0.05	0.56	−1.97*	2.91**	2.81**	1.40**	0.97**
	(0.05)	(0.08)	(0.53)	(1.06)	(0.26)	(0.31)	(0.24)	(0.28)
1973 church org member								
Intercept					−0.21	−0.66	−0.39	−3.55**
					(0.39)	(0.89)	(0.52)	(0.97)
Controls	No	Yes	No	Yes	No	Yes	No	Yes
N	512	512	513	513	513	513	400	400

Source: Youth-Parent Socialization Panel Study.

Note: Estimates are OLS coefficients for the church attendance dependent variable and logistic regression coefficients for religious identification, biblical literalism, and membership in a church organization dependent variables. Black Democrats are excluded as the racial/partisan reference category. Rarely or never attend religious services in 1973 is the church attendance reference category. For the church attendance, biblical literalism, and church organization membership dependent variables, the sample only includes Christian identifiers in order to compare African American Democrats—who are overwhelmingly Christian—with other Christians. The results are statistically and substantively similar when using the full sample of respondents. Demographic controls include 1973 measures of the student's region of residence, education, income, marital and parental status, gender, service in Vietnam, and stated closeness with parents as well as 1965 measures of the student's religious affiliation and high school curriculum (college preparatory track or not). Upbringing controls include 1965 parent responses regarding average church attendance, mother's and father's party identifications, education of the household head, and family income. * $p < 0.10$, ** $p < 0.05$.

Table A.24 Black Democrats' attitudes on church-state relations differ from both white Democrats' and white Republicans' attitudes

	Churches express			Churches endorse			Politicians express too little			Politicians express too much		
	(1)	(2)	(3)	(4)	(5)	(6)	(7)	(8)	(9)	(10)	(11)	(12)
White Democrats	-0.15**	-0.16**	-0.09*	-0.17**	-0.15**	-0.13**	-0.28**	-0.24**	-0.15**	0.23**	0.21**	0.12**
	(0.05)	(0.05)	(0.05)	(0.04)	(0.05)	(0.05)	(0.05)	(0.05)	(0.05)	(0.04)	(0.05)	(0.04)
White Republicans	0.09**	0.10**	0.11**	0.00	0.02	0.02	0.08*	0.12**	0.14**	-0.13**	-0.17**	-0.18**
	(0.05)	(0.05)	(0.05)	(0.05)	(0.05)	(0.05)	(0.05)	(0.05)	(0.05)	(0.04)	(0.04)	(0.04)
Intercept	0.54**	0.37**	0.30**	0.39**	0.41**	0.43**	0.49**	0.21**	0.11	0.29**	0.38**	0.40**
	(0.04)	(0.11)	(0.12)	(0.04)	(0.11)	(0.12)	(0.04)	(0.11)	(0.11)	(0.04)	(0.10)	(0.10)
SES controls	No	Yes	Yes	No	Yes	Yes	No	Yes	Yes	No	Yes	Yes
Religious controls	No	No	Yes	No	No	Yes	No	No	Yes	No	No	Yes
N	1,270	1,270	1,270	1,253	1,253	1,253	1,237	1,237	1,237	1,237	1,237	1,237

Source: 2014 Pew Research Center.

Note: Estimates are OLS coefficients with robust standard errors. Black Democrats are excluded as the racial/partisan reference category. First, the survey asks whether churches and other houses of worship should keep out of political matters (0) or express their views on day-to-day social and political questions (1). Second, the survey asks whether churches should endorse political candidates (1) or not (0). And third, the survey asks whether there has been too much, too little, or the right amount of expressions of religious faith and prayer by political leaders. Columns 7–9 measure whether the respondent reports that politicians express too little faith (1) or not (0), while columns 10–12 measure whether the respondent reports that politicians express too much faith (1) or not (0). The SES control variables include gender, age, age squared, region of residence, education, and income. The religious control variables include a measure of religious nonidentification and church attendance. * $p < 0.10$, ** $p < 0.05$.

Table A.25 Black and white Democrats responded to changes in question wording differently

	White Democrats		Black Democrats		All Democrats	
	(1)	(2)	(3)	(4)	(5)	(6)
Bush (1) vs. politician (0)	-0.31**	-0.31**	-1.11**	-1.11**	-1.25**	-1.25**
	(0.16)	(0.16)	(0.35)	(0.35)	(0.36)	(0.36)
White Democrat (1) vs. Black Democrat (0)					-1.73**	-1.73**
					(0.29)	(0.29)
Question wording Bush * White Democrat					0.94**	0.94**
					(0.39)	(0.39)
Control variables	No	Yes	No	Yes	No	Yes
cut1 Intercept	-0.74**	-0.74**	-2.02**	-2.02**	-2.43**	-2.43**
	(0.12)	(0.12)	(0.32)	(0.32)	(0.27)	(0.27)
cut2 Intercept	1.28**	1.28**	-0.56**	-0.56**	-0.50*	-0.50*
	(0.13)	(0.13)	(0.26)	(0.26)	(0.26)	(0.26)
N	565	565	125	125	690	690

(continued)

Table A.25 (*continued*)

	White Democrats		Black Democrats		All Democrats	
	(1)	(2)	(3)	(4)	(5)	(6)
Obama (1) vs. politician (0)	0.97**	0.95**	-0.92**	-1.05**		
	(0.16)	(0.16)	(0.28)	(0.31)		
White Democrat (1) vs. Black Democrat (0)					-2.12**	-1.53**
					(0.25)	(0.26)
Question wording Obama * White Democrat					1.87**	2.01**
					(0.32)	(0.33)
Control variables	No	Yes	No	Yes	No	Yes
cut1 Intercept	-0.37**	0.84**	-2.62**	2.53	-2.50**	-0.65*
	(0.12)	(0.36)	(0.29)	(1.76)	(0.23)	(0.39)
cut2 Intercept	2.24**	3.85**	0.17	5.84**	0.15	2.32**
	(0.15)	(0.39)	(0.21)	(1.80)	(0.21)	(0.40)
N	664	664	209	209	873	873

Source: 2003, 2010 Pew Research Center.

Note: Estimates are coefficients from ordered logistic regression models. The dependent variable measures whether respondents think politicians in general or the specific politician expresses "too much" faith (0), "the right amount of" faith (1), or "too little" faith (2). The results in the top panel come from a 2003 experiment that asked respondents about politicians in general or about George W. Bush. The results in the bottom panel come from a 2010 experiment that asked respondents about politicians in general or about Barack Obama. Control variables include gender, age, age squared, education, income, region of residence, church attendance, and whether religion is important. * $p < 0.10$, ** $p < 0.05$.

Candidate Endorsement Experiment

Table A.26 Experimental treatment effects among black Democrats and relative to white Democrats

	Black Democrats		Democrats	
	Favorability toward Democratic candidate (1)	Favorability toward Republican candidate (2)	Favorability toward Democratic candidate (3)	Favorability toward Republican candidate (4)
Secular Democrat (Sec Dem)	0.05 (0.05)	-0.10 (0.06)	0.04** (0.02)	-0.06** (0.02)
Religious Republican (Rel Rep)	-0.04 (0.05)	-0.02 (0.06)	-0.01 (0.02)	-0.05** (0.02)
Rel Rep and Sec Dem (Rel Sec)	0.08* (0.04)	-0.11* (0.06)	0.01 (0.02)	-0.07** (0.02)
Rel Rep and Rel Dem (Rel Rel)	-0.03 (0.05)	0.03 (0.06)	-0.02 (0.02)	-0.03 (0.02)
Black Dem (1) vs. white Dem (0)			0.01 (0.03)	0.05 (0.05)
Sec Dem * Black Dem			0.01 (0.05)	-0.03 (0.06)
Rel Rep * Black Dem			-0.04 (0.05)	0.03 (0.07)
Rel Sec * Black Dem			0.06 (0.05)	-0.04 (0.06)
Rel Rel * Black Dem			-0.01 (0.05)	0.06 (0.06)
Intercept	0.69** (0.03)	0.54** (0.04)	0.69** (0.01)	0.49** (0.01)
N	161	161	1,261	1,261

Source: Candidate endorsement experiment.

Note: The sample consists of black Democrats (columns 1 and 2) and Democrats (columns 3 and 4). Coefficients are from OLS models. The dependent variables are seven-point favorability ratings of the Democratic (columns 1 and 3) and Republican (columns 2 and 4) candidates and range between 0 (very unfavorable) and 1 (very favorable). The control condition is excluded as the reference category. Columns 3 and 4 test whether self-identified white and black Democratic respondents responded in a similar manner to the experimental treatments. $p < 0.10$, ** $p < 0.05$.

ANES 1956–1958–1960

Table A.27 Suggestive evidence that church attendance among Republican Catholics with children at home dropped between 1958 and 1960 relative to Democratic Catholics

	Full sample		Children at home		Grown children	
1958 church attendance	(1)	(2)	(3)	(4)	(5)	(6)
1956 partisanship						
Republican	−0.02	−0.01	−0.03	−0.01	0.01	0.02
	(0.03)	(0.04)	(0.04)	(0.05)	(0.06)	(0.07)
Independent	0.01	0.01	0.01	0.01	−0.02	−0.01
	(0.03)	(0.03)	(0.03)	(0.04)	(0.05)	(0.07)
1956 church attendance	0.79**	0.78**	0.71**	0.70**	0.96**	0.88*
	(0.06)	(0.07)	(0.07)	(0.08)	(0.14)	(0.18)
Intercept	0.15**	−0.13	0.23**	0.07	−0.00	−0.24
	(0.06)	(0.16)	(0.07)	(0.19)	(0.13)	(0.35)
Controls	No	Yes	No	Yes	No	Yes
R^2	0.51	0.55	0.45	0.49	0.63	0.70
N	223	223	149	149	74	74

	Full sample		Children at home		Grown children	
1960 church attendance	(1)	(2)	(3)	(4)	(5)	(6)
1958 partisanship						
Republican	−0.06	−0.06	−0.05	−0.06	−0.03	−0.02
	(0.04)	(0.04)	(0.04)	(0.04)	(0.07)	(0.07)
Independent	0.04	0.04	0.02	0.02	0.05	0.06
	(0.03)	(0.03)	(0.04)	(0.04)	(0.06)	(0.06)
1958 church attendance	0.61**	0.59**	0.62**	0.60**	0.69**	0.58*
	(0.07)	(0.07)	(0.09)	(0.09)	(0.12)	(0.11)
Intercept	0.34**	0.37**	0.35**	0.34*	0.27**	0.36
	(0.07)	(0.15)	(0.09)	(0.20)	(0.11)	(0.35)
Controls	No	Yes	No	Yes	No	Yes
R^2	0.42	0.46	0.39	0.43	0.60	0.75
N	204	204	143	143	61	61

Source: 1956–1958–1960 American National Election Study.
Note: The sample consists of Catholic respondents. Estimates are OLS coefficients with robust standard errors in parentheses. The dependent variable of church attendance ranges between 0 (never attend) and 1 (attend more than once a week). When the dependent variable is church attendance in 1958 (top panel), party identification and lagged church attendance are measured in 1956. When the dependent variable is measured in 1960 (bottom panel), party identification and lagged church attendance are measured in 1958. Control variables include race, gender, age, age squared, education, income, region of residence, and union member status. * $p < 0.10$, ** $p < 0.05$.

able A.28 Church attendance among Republican Protestants with children at home increased between
958 and 1960 relative to Democratic Protestants

958 church attendance	Full sample		Children at home		Grown children	
	(1)	(2)	(3)	(4)	(5)	(6)
956 partisanship						
epublican	0.02	0.01	0.03	0.01	−0.02	0.00
	(0.02)	(0.02)	(0.03)	(0.03)	(0.03)	(0.03)
ndependent	0.04	0.04	0.03	0.03	0.04	0.04
	(0.02)	(0.03)	(0.03)	(0.03)	(0.04)	(0.05)
956 church attendance	0.67**	0.66**	0.63**	0.62**	0.72**	0.71**
	(0.03)	(0.03)	(0.04)	(0.04)	(0.04)	(0.04)
ntercept	0.20**	−0.02	0.22**	0.16	0.18**	−0.08
	(0.02)	(0.11)	(0.04)	(0.19)	(0.03)	(0.18)
ontrols	No	Yes	No	Yes	No	Yes
²	0.44	0.46	0.38	0.40	0.53	0.56
	691	691	377	377	260	260

60 church attendance	Full sample		Children at home		Grown children	
	(1)	(2)	(3)	(4)	(5)	(6)
58 partisanship						
epublican	0.06**	0.07**	0.10**	0.10**	0.00	0.02
	(0.02)	(0.02)	(0.03)	(0.03)	(0.03)	(0.03)
dependent	−0.03	−0.03	−0.04	−0.02	0.01	−0.00
	(0.03)	(0.03)	(0.03)	(0.03)	(0.05)	(0.05)
58 church attendance	0.69**	0.67**	0.64**	0.61**	0.78**	0.75**
	(0.03)	(0.03)	(0.04)	(0.04)	(0.04)	(0.04)
tercept	0.18**	−0.03	0.21**	−0.04	0.12**	−0.03
	(0.02)	(0.11)	(0.03)	(0.21)	(0.04)	(0.26)
ontrols	No	Yes	No	Yes	No	Yes
	0.49	0.52	0.48	0.52	0.52	0.57
	652	652	360	360	243	243

urce: 1956–1958–1960 American National Election Study.
te: The sample consists of Protestant respondents. Estimates are OLS coefficients with robust standard errors in
renetheses. The dependent variable of church attendance ranges between 0 (never attend) and 1 (attend more than
ce a week). When the dependent variable is church attendance in 1958 (top panel), party identification and lagged
urch attendance are measured in 1956. When the dependent variable is measured in 1960 (bottom panel), party
ntification and lagged church attendance are measured in 1958. Control variables include race, gender, age, age
nared, education, income, region of residence, and union member status. * $p < 0.10$, ** $p < 0.05$.

Table A.29 Religious involvement of Protestants and Catholics with children at home diverged between 1958 and 1960

1958 church attendance	Catholics		Protestants		Full sample	
	(1)	(2)	(3)	(4)	(5)	(6)
1956 partisanship						
Republican	−0.03	−0.01	0.03	0.01	0.03	0.02
	(0.04)	(0.05)	(0.03)	(0.03)	(0.03)	(0.03)
Independent	0.01	0.01	0.03	0.03	0.03	0.03
	(0.03)	(0.04)	(0.03)	(0.03)	(0.03)	(0.03)
1965 church attendance	0.71**	0.70**	0.63**	0.62**	0.65**	0.64*
	(0.07)	(0.08)	(0.04)	(0.04)	(0.04)	(0.04)
Catholic (1) vs. Protestant (0)					0.08**	0.07*
					(0.03)	(0.04)
1956 Rep * Catholic					−0.06	−0.04
					(0.05)	(0.05)
1956 Ind * Catholic					−0.02	−0.01
					(0.05)	(0.05)
Intercept	0.23**	0.07	0.22**	0.16	0.21**	0.11
	(0.07)	(0.19)	(0.04)	(0.19)	(0.03)	(0.15)
Controls	No	Yes	No	Yes	No	Yes
R^2	0.45	0.49	0.38	0.40	0.44	0.46
N	149	149	377	377	526	526

1960 church attendance	Catholics		Protestants		Full sample	
	(1)	(2)	(3)	(4)	(5)	(6)
1958 partisanship						
Republican	−0.05	−0.06	0.10**	0.10**	0.10**	0.10*
	(0.04)	(0.04)	(0.03)	(0.03)	(0.03)	(0.03)
Independent	0.02	0.02	−0.04	−0.02	−0.04	−0.02
	(0.04)	(0.04)	(0.03)	(0.03)	(0.03)	(0.03)
1958 church attendance	0.62**	0.60**	0.64**	0.61**	0.64**	0.61*
	(0.09)	(0.09)	(0.04)	(0.04)	(0.04)	(0.04)
Catholic (1) vs. Protestant (0)					0.12**	0.15*
					(0.03)	(0.03)
1958 Rep * Catholic					−0.16**	−0.17
					(0.06)	(0.05)
1958 Ind * Catholic					0.06	0.04
					(0.05)	(0.05)
Intercept	0.35**	0.34*	0.21**	−0.04	0.21**	0.02
	(0.09)	(0.20)	(0.03)	(0.21)	(0.03)	(0.15)
Controls	No	Yes	No	Yes	No	Yes
R^2	0.39	0.43	0.48	0.52	0.51	0.55
N	143	143	360	360	503	503

Source: 1956–1958–1960 American National Election Study.
Note: The sample consists of married respondents with children at home. Estimates are OLS coefficients with robust standard errors in parentheses. The dependent variable of church attendance ranges between 0 (never attend) and 1 (attend more than once a week). When the dependent variable is church attendance in 1958 (top panel), party identification and lagged church attendance are measured in 1956. When the dependent variable is measured in 1960 (bottom panel), party identification and lagged church attendance are measured in 1958. Control variables include race, gender, age, age squared, education, income, region of residence, and union member status. * $p < 0.1$; ** $p < 0.05$.

NOTES

CHAPTER ONE

1. Karen and Fran, introduced in the next paragraph, are real people whose names have been changed to protect their privacy.
2. The official name for the program frequently referred to as food stamps is the Supplemental Nutrition Assistance Program (SNAP).
3. Other common measures of religious beliefs include questions related to the afterlife, the devil, and God. Mockabee, Wald, and Leege (2011) argue that many of these common measures of religious beliefs are more closely held by certain religious denominations than others and advocate for additional measures of religiosity that tap into the communitarian-sacramental dimension of religion.
4. This perspective therefore stresses a cognitive approach to forming opinions, in which a person wants internal consistency between sets of private beliefs.
5. Utilizing the "3 B" conceptualization of religion, the focus of this book will be on *belonging* and *behaving*, with less focus on *believing*.
6. This does not mean, however, that members of different religious denominations attend religious services at the same rate. The empirical chapters take into account the fact that members of certain religious traditions may attend religious services with greater frequency than others.

CHAPTER TWO

1. Portions of this discussion appear in the online appendix to the paper "How Politics Affects Religion: Partisanship, Socialization, and Religiosity in America" (2018) published in the *Journal of Politics*.
2. While many assume that social issues like abortion spurred political action among religious conservatives, there is evidence suggesting that race relations and racially segregated private schools are what first prompted political engagement among religious leaders (Crespino 2008; Edsall and Edsall 1992; Reichley 1986). Understanding what motivated religious elites to become politically involved is less important for the book's main argument than the positions and strategies they adopted afterward.
3. Religious organizations that focus on social and moral issues had previously existed locally (Bruce 1988), but the 1970s marked the first time that these sorts of organizations existed on a state or national level.

4. See Noel (2013) for a more thorough discussion of how today's liberal-conservative ideologies came to be mapped onto the political parties in the United States.

5. As noted previously in the chapter, nonwhite and non-Christian Americans are more likely to have racial, ethnic, or religious ties to one of the two major parties resulting in cohesive political blocs that look more like the *ethnoreligious* model of politics rather than the *restructuring* model. Chapter 3 discusses the empirical implications of these differences.

CHAPTER THREE

1. The survey, conducted through Knowledge Networks, includes a nationally representative online sample of 18- to 29-year-olds interviewed between December 2010 and January 2011. The Barna Group, a private, nonpartisan, for-profit organization under the umbrella of the Issachar Companies, commissioned the data collection. The Barna Group conducts research on cultural trends related to values, beliefs, attitudes, and behaviors.

2. Moreover, a full majority—55%—reported being less active in church today than when they were 15 years old, while 25% reported the same level of activity and 18% reported being more active.

3. Religious traditions were determined using Steensland et al.'s (2000) classification scheme.

4. Importantly, the research does not explain why we observe religious stability in adulthood. One possible reason is that people in later life stages are more resistant to change. A second reason is that older individuals are part of more stable social structures, which encourage their identities to be regularly reinforced. While understanding the reason is not essential for the life-cycle theory, if religious stability in adulthood comes from environmental stability, then shocks to the political and social system that change these stabilizing structures could mean that politics may affect religious identities later in life.

5. The hypothesis is distinguished from previous socialization theories by recognizing that core beliefs are largely stable over the course of one's adult life, while also conceding that attitudes can change a great deal during childhood and early adolescence (Jennings and Niemi 1981, 1974; Vaillancourt 1973).

6. A third potential factor explaining political identities is genetics. Recent research has shown that genes influence political ideologies (Alford, Funk, and Hibbing 2005; Hatemi et al. 2010), turnout (Hatemi et al. 2007), and strength of partisanship (Settle, Dawes, and Fowler 2009). Although biology appears to play a role in the development of politically relevant attitudes, there is debate as to whether a "party gene" exists (see Hatemi et al. 2009a and Settle, Dawes, and Fowler 2009 for discussion of why partisanship is not genetically determined and Fazekas and Littvay 2015 for how a party gene can be expressed in certain contexts). Whether a genetic component to partisanship exists does not change the timing of the political life course. Scholars have found that genetic influences on social attitudes and behaviors are weak among children and adolescents, with the genetic influence becoming stronger after these people leave home in young adulthood (Hatemi et al. 2011; Hatemi and McDermott 2012; Kendler and Myers 2009). In this case, a genetic explanation offers one additional avenue of influence in the development of party identification during the period in people's lives that scholars have already pinpointed as a key time when partisan identities crystallize and stabilize.

7. Mael and Tetrick (1992) first created the full ten-item scale, which Brewer and Silver (2000) later showed to be broadly applicable to many different types of groups in society.

8. The life-cycle theory helps explain how partisan identities shape religious decisions when the parties have unique relationships with religious issues and groups. And while this book focuses on the changing religious and political environments from the 1960s until today, the theory does not rely on political divergence in which Republicans are perceived as being more religious and culturally conservative than Democrats. An alternative political-religious environment would simply generate different expectations as to how partisanship might influence a person's religious identity. Chapter 8 shows evidence supporting the life-cycle theory using a different political environment and different expectations.

9. The study did not assess whether a single secular-Democratic identity exists.

10. The empirical chapters offer additional discussion about the political differences across religious faiths and how these differences may impact the interpretation of various results.

11. A total of 94% of Americans aged 18 to 40 either have children or would like to have children in the future, and 86% of Americans aged 45 or older have children (Newport and Wilke 2013).

CHAPTER FOUR

1. Gregory Markus and Laura Stoker were also principal investigators on the later YPSP waves.

2. In 1965 the most frequent attendance category was "almost every week." The 1973 survey included an additional category for weekly attendance. Collapsing the top two categories in 1973 allows for comparisons across the two waves using a consistent scale.

3. In fact, these data may underestimate the size of the change if church attendance rates started to decline before 1965.

4. The college preparatory curriculum question is an education measure from 1965, which minimizes concerns that a person may have chosen to go to college *after* or *as a consequence of* becoming less religious. Using a measure from 1973 that identifies whether the respondent attended college, however, produces similar trends. Among those who had not attended college at any point between 1965 and 1973, the average level of church attendance dropped from 0.81 to 0.54. The average level of church attendance dropped from 0.82 to 0.50 among those who had attended college.

5. Although these raw percentages include the full sample of respondents, the rates are unchanged for white respondents. In 1973, 13% of white Democrats were religious nonidentifiers.

6. Political Independents similarly underwent a shift away from religion. Average rates of church attendance declined from 0.80 in 1965 to 0.49 in 1973. Independents' rates of religious nonidentification also increased from about 1% to 13%, and rates of biblical literalism declined from 45% in 1965 to 33% in 1973.

7. Another empirical strategy would be to use a differenced dependent variable. This specification assumes that the lagged dependent variable (Y_{t-1}) does not influence either the dependent variable at time t (Y_t) or the change in dependent variable across the survey waves (ΔY) (Finkel 1995; Morgan and Winship 2007). Given the nature of the dependent variables used throughout the book, it is highly improbable that

partisanship or church attendance at one point in time is uncorrelated with a change in these variables over time. Models that use a differenced dependent variable approach, however, produce similar results.

8. More formally, the model $\Delta Y = \beta_0 + \beta_1 X_{t-1} + (\beta_2 - 1)Y_{t-1} + \varepsilon_t$ can be interpreted as the effect of $\beta_1 X_{t-1}$ on ΔY while controlling for previous measures of Y (Finkel 1995).

9. Standard errors are clustered at the school level.

10. The regression tables are available in the appendix.

11. Point estimates come from logistic regression models and represent the change in the probability of being a religious identifier or biblical literalist for Republicans as opposed to Democrats.

12. Biblical literalism rates dropped among Mainline Protestants from 34% in 1965 to 25% in 1973. Catholic rates of literalism dropped from 44% to 19%. Evangelical rates of literalism dropped from 66% to 45%.

13. Similarly, Jewish respondents had the lowest rates of biblical literalism in 1965, 19%, which dropped to 13% in 1973. This relatively small gap, however, has less of an effect on the broader results because Jews make up only 6% of the Democratic subsample despite 77% of Jewish respondents identifying as Democrats.

14. Political Independents' declining levels of church attendance, religious affiliation, and biblical literalism between 1965 and 1973 looked similar to the trajectories of both Democrats and Republicans.

15. Finding different results in the student and parent generations does not mean that the broader environment played no role in weakening religious ties among the students. It is possible, likely even, that the changing societal values described in chapter 2 exacerbated a trend that would have taken place regardless among the student cohort.

16. Chapter 2 offers a more detailed discussion of the changes that took place during this time.

17. While a reasonable alternative explanation that highlights the need to control for religious identification, the YPSP data do not support either of these claims. First, evangelical Christians were not more likely to return to religion between 1973 and 1982 than mainline Protestants or Catholics. Second, only 35% of evangelicals identified as Republicans in 1973, making up 26% of the Republican subsample in 1973.

18. The parent-level control variables include average church attendance, mother's and father's party identifications, education of the household head, and family income. Responses to these questions come from the 1965 parent interviews.

19. Including policy attitudes as control variables raises concerns about whether individuals choose their party identifications to match their policy positions (which would make it important to control for policy preferences) or whether partisans adopt policy positions to match their partisanship (which might result in posttreatment bias on the partisanship variable). Models that include and exclude attitudinal control variables produce the same relationship between partisanship and changing religiosity.

20. In 1973, respondents who reported that they did not identify with any religious tradition did not answer the church attendance question and were automatically coded as never attending church. In 1982, all respondents reported their attendance at religious services irrespective of their reported religious affiliations. Because even religious nonidentifiers may attend religious services on occasion, the 1982 question represents a more accurate measure of church attendance. It is possible that these slight differences may affect the overall results; however, a close inspection of the data mitigates concerns. First, an examination of nonidentifiers in 1982 shows that 78% report never

attending church, and the cumulative percentage increases to 95% when those who report going a few times per year are also included. It is therefore not wholly incorrect to assume that nonidentifiers do not attend religious services. Second, analyses that exclude religious nonidentifiers produce the same pattern of results; religious nonidentifiers do not drive the overall findings.

21. There is a question of exactly which control variables to include and exclude given that the independent variable of interest—parents' church attendance—is measured in 1965 and likely has an effect on other control variables in the model. The results described above include the demographic and background control variables but exclude the attitudinal control variables measured in 1973. Including the attitudinal control variables, however, only modestly changes the results (regularly attend versus never attend = 0.13; p-value = 0.06; regularly attend versus infrequently attend = 0.08; p-value = 0.07; regularly attend versus attend somewhat frequently = 0.07; p-value = 0.07). The variables included in the model do not dramatically change the magnitude of the relationships.

22. Correlation between 1973 party identification and 1973 economic liberalism = −0.03; correlation between 1973 party identification and 1982 economic liberalism = 0.29; correlation between 1982 party identification and 1982 economic liberalism = 0.32.

23. In contrast, there is not much evidence that economically conservative (liberal) respondents in 1973 became more Republican (Democratic) between 1973 and 1982. In fact, certain model specifications show that economically conservative respondents were *less* likely to become Republicans over time relative to economically liberal respondents. Partisanship seems to be driving economic attitudes rather than the other way around.

24. While there are some gender differences in group membership rates, both men and women reported being members of these smaller groups (44% and 50%, respectively).

25. Biblical literalism rates also remained stable across religious traditions. In both 1973 and 1982, 19% of Catholics were biblical literalists. Forty-four percent and 47% of evangelical Protestants were biblical literalists in 1973 and 1982, respectively, whereas 25% and 28% of mainline Protestants were. Additional analyses reveal high levels of individual stability over time. And while biblical literalism is more closely associated with certain religious traditions than others, the data suggest that partisanship helps explain variation in biblical beliefs within religious traditions as well. Black Protestants are the only group for whom there was a large uptick in rates of biblical literalism, increasing from 27% in 1973 to 43% in 1982. Replicating the analyses from above using the white subsample, however, produces the same results (Republican versus Democrat = 0.03; p-value = 0.10), likely because African American Democrats make up a relatively small portion of the sample.

26. Independents returned to the pews to a greater extent than Democrats (0.07) but the difference is not statistically significant at conventional levels (p-value = 0.16). Because Independents attended church less frequently in 1973 than both Democrats and Republicans, Independents and Democrats had virtually identical levels of church attendance in 1982. Republicans, by contrast, attended more frequently than both Democrats and Independents.

27. The results are statistically and substantively similar with and without control variables.

28. Religious identification (measured in both 1965 and 1973) also has limited influence on changing political views. There is suggestive evidence that mainline (p-value = 0.10)

and evangelical (*p*-value = 0.17) Protestants were more likely to become Republicans between 1973 and 1982 compared to Catholics; however, there is no relationship between identification with a religious tradition and changing voting patterns between 1973 and 1982. These findings do not contradict the existence of partisan differences across religious traditions. Catholics were more likely to identify as Democrats and support the Democratic presidential candidates in both 1973 and 1982 compared to both mainline and evangelical Protestant families. The size of the gaps, however, did not grow between the two waves.

29. Membership in fraternal organizations was almost exclusively men. Analyses looking at just the male subsample produce the same results. Men also made up a large majority of the professional group members. Again, the results are the same when looking just at male respondents.

30. The relationship holds for both the full sample of respondents and the white subsample.

31. This is the case for the full sample of respondents as well as the white subsample.

32. While there is consistent evidence of a genetic component for private religious beliefs, the results are mixed as it relates to church attendance. Some scholars have found evidence of a genetic component (Bradshaw and Ellison 2008; Kirk et al. 1999); however, most have shown that one's social environment is the primary driver of church attendance (Eaves et al. 2008; Friesen and Ksiazkiewicz 2015; Truett et al. 1992).

33. In fact, in a situation in which there is a genetic component to religiosity but there is not a genetic component to partisanship, it should be more difficult to find the results presented above. If certain Democrats are genetically predisposed to be religiously involved and some Republicans are genetically predisposed to not be, then partisanship may not be powerful enough to push these Democrats away from religion and Republicans toward religion. In this scenario, the results appear despite a genetic component of religiosity, not because of it.

34. The overwhelming majority of both Republicans and Democrats had children by 1982, and there is no statistical difference between Republicans and Democrats in these data with respect to having children.

35. Control variables include gender, race, education, income, age, region of residence, and religious tradition in 2007.

36. There was a 0.12 church attendance gap in 2007 between Republicans and Democrats.

37. The smaller coefficients associated with the grown-children category occurs despite the grown-children group being the largest numeric subsample.

38. Additionally, the religious measures from 2007 are not correlated with changes in party identification between 2007 and 2014 among parents of school-aged children.

39. Among NAES/ISCAP respondents with school-aged children in 2014, the mean age is 36, with 75% of the respondents ranging between 30 and 45 years of age.

40. The results comport with those of Hout and Fischer (2014, 2002) who found that religious nonidentification does not necessitate holding certain views about God or the afterlife.

CHAPTER FIVE

1. Other religion and politics work has isolated religion's impact on political attitudes using priming designs (e.g., Calfano and Oldmixon 2016, 2015; Chapp 2012; Hollander 1998; Weber and Norton 2012). This experiment is different, however, by looking at the reverse relationship and identifying partisanship's effect on religious attitudes.

2. The sample was obtained through Survey Sampling International (SSI). SSI recruits participants through online communities, social networks, and website ads and makes efforts to recruit hard-to-reach groups, such as ethnic minorities and seniors. Potential participants are then screened and invited into the panel. When deploying a particular survey, SSI randomly selects panel participants for survey invitations. There are no quotas, but SSI recruits a target population that matches the (18 and over) census population on education, gender, age, geography, and income. The resulting sample is not a probability sample but is a diverse national sample.

3. By comparing individuals with school-aged children and grown children, the decision to have children is held constant across groups.

4. Among Republicans, 65% reported that they were strong identifiers, compared to 48% of Democrats.

5. The religious identification gap and corresponding p-value come from a model that includes an interaction term testing whether the treatment affected Republicans and Democrats differently.

6. The parametric test involves a triple interaction model that includes treatment condition, partisanship, and parental status.

7. Because the FFC is a nonprofit 501(c)3 organization, the identities of donors do not need to be released.

8. The KN panel is based on probability sampling that covers both the online and offline populations in the United States. Panel members are recruited through national random samples (telephone and postal mail), and members without Internet access are given the hardware to complete the Internet surveys. Previous research has shown that the demographics of KN panel members closely approximate the broader population (Chang and Krosnick 2009).

9. Multiple local papers throughout the country, as well as USA Today and abcnews .com, published the AP article. The shortened article does not contain any mention of specific presidential candidates in order to minimize the possibility that feelings about an individual candidate could affect respondents' reported religious attitudes.

10. In addition to a recall question, respondents in the treatment group were asked whether they thought politicians pay too much or too little attention to religion and whether churches and religious groups have too much or too little power.

11. An exception to this trend occurred in late 2003 and 2004 when there was an uptick in media reports distinguishing the Republican and Democratic parties along religious and secularist lines. I discuss this exception in detail later in the chapter.

12. For both Democrats and Republicans, the average identification measures increased by 0.02 and are statistically insignificant, with p-values of 0.61 and 0.63, respectively. The p-value corresponding to the difference-in-difference estimate is 0.96.

13. Independents did not respond to the treatment. Among both those with children at home and those with grown children, Independents' levels of religious identification were stable across treatment conditions. Whereas partisans, including weak and leaning partisans, reacted to the information linking the Republican Party to the FFC, pure Independents did not respond to the information.

14. Variables measured in 2000 serve as controls in the analyses measuring change between 2000 and 2002, whereas variables measured in 2002 serve as controls in the analyses measuring change between 2002 and 2004 with two exceptions. Religious identification and abortion attitudes are not measured in 2002. The 2002–2004 analyses therefore use respondents' religious identifications and abortion attitudes from

2000. The 2002–2004 analyses also include a control variable measuring support for the Iraq War, also measured in 2002.

15. Church attendance was 0.38 among Democrats and 0.54 among Republicans in 2002.

16. Terror management theory (TMT) may lead us to assume that church attendance increased between 2000 and 2002 on account of the terrorist attacks of September 11, 2001 (Dezutter et al. 2008; Jonas and Fischer 2006; Vail et al. 2010). Consistent with TMT, church attendance increased in the immediate wake of the attacks (Wakin 2001); however, these increases were short-lived and rates returned to normal by the end of the year (Goodstein 2001). Consequently, we should not expect to see evidence of increased religious participation between 2000 and 2002 on account of September 11, as the 2002 wave took place thirteen months after the attacks.

17. Difference among respondents with children at home = −0.02; p-value = 0.67. Difference among respondents with grown children = 0.01; p-value = 0.77.

18. The changing gap between Republicans and Democrats is 0.06 (p-value < 0.01) in a model that only includes lagged partisanship, lagged church attendance, and marital and parental status as independent variables. The changing gap between Republicans and Democrats is 0.05 (p-value = 0.02) in a model that also includes demographic and religious control variables. The statistically suggestive results appear once the model controls for policy preferences and attitudes, which may not be appropriate to include in the model if partisanship influences these attitudes. The result presented in the main text, therefore, is a conservative estimate of partisanship's relationship with changing rates of church attendance.

19. The magnitude of the results is usually unchanged in models without and with control variables. In this case, a model that includes only lagged partisanship and church attendance produces slightly different substantive results (0.15; p-value < 0.01). A model that also includes demographic and religious control variables produces a partisan gap of 0.17 (p-value < 0.01).

20. Just as in the experiments, Independents with children at home did not respond to the changing political environment; however, a church attendance gap emerged between Independents and Democrats (0.13; p-value = 0.04) between 2002 and 2004. Whereas Independents attended church less frequently than Democrats in both 2000 and 2002, Independents' average rates of church attendance remained stable between 2002 and 2004 (0.38 and 0.37, respectively). The decline among Democrats resulted in Independents being more frequent attenders than Democrats by 2004, reversing the trend from both 2000 and 2002.

21. In fact, comparisons of weekly attenders and nonattenders trend in the wrong direction: the political gaps between these two groups shrink somewhat between 2002 and 2004.

22. Full results are available in the appendix.

23. See chapter 4 for a detailed discussion of this strategy, including limitations. While possible that some childless individuals have made the active decision to forgo having children, Newport and Wilke (2013) find that 87% of individuals aged 18–40 without children plan to have them in the future. It is still the overwhelming norm to plan on having children and therefore reasonable to assume that the majority in this subsample will try to become parents in the future.

24. These models include partisanship and church attendance, both measured in 2002, as independent variables. The small number of respondents in each age bracket makes it difficult to run models with a full set of control variables. While certainly a limitation, it is comforting to know that the inclusion or exclusion of control vari-

ables did not have a large impact on the magnitude or statistical significance of any of the previous results.

25. Pretests showed that people perceived the two newspaper articles to be similar with respect to how convincing and ideologically extreme they were. Pretest respondents also rated the article's author as having a similar level of competence and ideological extremity in both articles. After reading the newspaper article, treated respondents answered questions about the story and then reported their attitudes on immigration reform.

26. Given that political discussions about immigration reform frequently focus on immigration from Latin America, Hispanic respondents may respond differently to the experimental conditions than white respondents. The results, however, are statistically and substantively unchanged in models that include the full sample of respondents as well as a subsample that excludes Hispanic respondents.

27. The difference between Republicans in the anti-reform versus pro-reform conditions has a p-value of 0.41.

28. The asymmetrical results do offer one piece of evidence suggesting that the church attendance question does measure real behavior to some extent. In the experiments, which measure purely subjective attitudes, partisan divergence is symmetrical. Treated Republicans come to feel closer to religion while treated Democrats come to feel less so. In the ANES data, however, the results are concentrated among Democrats reportedly attending church less frequently over time. Given that church attendance is costly—it requires time and there are opportunity costs associated with attending—increasing and decreasing attendance should not be equally likely to occur. Although there are other reasons to explain the asymmetrical results, the large change among Democrats relative to Republicans is consistent with a story in which the church attendance variable measures behaviors rather than a purely subjective religious attachment.

CHAPTER SIX

1. Chapter 4 provides a detailed description of the models used.

2. Similar results emerge on all the religious dependent variables and when using level of formal education instead of political knowledge as a measure of awareness about the changing political environment.

3. The statistical model includes partisanship and church attendance, both measured in 2002, as independent variables. The small number of respondents in each political knowledge classification means it is not possible to run the models with the full set of control variables. For consistency, the 0.15 coefficient in table 6.1 comes from a model that also excludes control variables, meaning that the coefficient is slightly different from the result in chapter 5 (0.19).

4. The NAES/ISCAP data also suggest similar trends; however, the results should be taken with caution due to the small number of respondents within each education category. Similar analyses run on the parent generation (YPSP panel) and respondents with grown children (priming experiment, ANES panel, and FFC experiment) show no differences across different levels of political knowledge or education. These group members are homogeneously stable in their religious attachments.

5. Analyses that look at respondents who have children at home produce the same results.

6. Analyses that look only at white respondents produce the same statistical and substantive results.

7. A model that interacts identifying as a Republican (1) versus Democrat (0) with knowing the candidates' positions on abortion (1) or not (0) produces a substantively large (0.16) and statistically significant (p-value < 0.01) estimate.

8. The religiosity measure comes from a factor analysis. All four variables load onto a single dimension, with the first eigenvalue being 2.3 and the second eigenvalue being −0.02.

9. A second way of measuring whether individuals are part of a church with similar political leanings is to compare a respondent's reported partisan affiliation to the average partisan identification for the other congregants in the sample. Both measures produce statistically and substantively similar results.

10. Unfortunately, no political knowledge questions were asked on the survey.

11. There is not a religiosity gap between Democrats and Republicans with low levels of political knowledge in the 1973 YPSP data. Unlike the other data sets in which the relationship between the political parties and religion were well established when the data were first collected, this was not the case in 1973.

CHAPTER SEVEN

1. This theological understanding of white evangelical Protestantism has also changed over time, further highlighting not only that there might be multiple interpretations of the same text but also that the interpretation within a religious faith can change. Evangelical Protestantism in the nineteenth century focused on the social gospel, which emphasized improving social conditions. In the early twentieth century, however, an emphasis on otherworldliness and political withdrawal became the dominant biblical interpretation (Moberg 1977). It was not until the 1970s that a new evangelical interpretation of the Bible encouraged evangelicals to become politically active.

2. There are counterexamples to this claim, however, such as California's Proposition 8 which would outlaw same-sex marriages. African Americans, clergy and laypersons alike, tended to support the proposition (Wald and Calhoun-Brown 2011). And while originally pro-life, African Americans have become increasingly supportive of pro-choice policies in recent years. In the 2012 ANES, 53% of African Americans gave the most permissive response of "by law, a woman should always be able to receive an abortion."

3. Because African Americans overwhelmingly identify as Democrats, there are not enough African American Republicans in the sample for this group to be analyzed separately.

4. Looking specifically at Christian identifiers reduces concerns that the behaviors of a specific religious group drive the overall trends. For example, Jewish Americans are disproportionately Democratic, and Jews, on average, attend religious services at a lower rate than members of Christian faiths. Further, biblical literalism is not a major tenet of Judaism in the same way that it is for Christianity. Thus, these compositional differences could influence the overall trends across the groups. Models that control for religious affiliation and models that exclude non-Christian respondents produce the same substantive and statistical results.

5. Only self-identified Christians answered the born-again Christian question.

6. Control variables include gender, age, age squared, region of residence, education, and income.

7. One might be tempted to include religious control variables—such as church attendance and religious identification—in order to see how the groups differ while

holding religious identity constant. But, this difference in religiosity is precisely what we think matters for politics. If black Democrats are more religious than white Democrats and religiosity is correlated with specific views about how religion and politics should mix (or not), it is important to allow these differences to remain. Importantly, however, the results do not disappear when religious controls are included. Models that include religious controls produce smaller estimated differences between white Democrats and black Democrats; however, the same general patterns appear, and the results remain statistically significant. Including religious control variables makes very little difference when comparing white Republicans and black Democrats, likely because they have similar religious profiles. In fact, to the extent that there is any difference between models that include and exclude religious controls, the results are slightly larger in the models that include the additional control variables.

8. Importantly, the cross-sectional nature of the data cannot identify the independent effects of race, party identification, and religiosity on views about religion's involvement in politics. Instead, these results provide a broad understanding of how people holding different identities view the political landscape today.

9. The analyses that follow focus on differences between white and black Democrats. Doing so holds partisanship constant and increases the likelihood that differences found between the groups stem from respondents' perceptions of the political landscape. Whereas white and black Democrats are similar in partisanship but may differ in their opinions and perceptions of politicians using religion, white Republicans likely differ from black Democrats on both dimensions. Consequently, it is more difficult to attribute differences between black Democrats and white Republicans to their views of the political landscape as they also differ in their evaluations of both President Bush and President Obama, leaving us to wonder what is the driving force behind the results.

10. The rate at which white Republicans reported that there is "too much" religion actually declined slightly from the general politicians' condition (0.11) to the condition that asks about Bush specifically (0.07). Importantly, however, it is unclear what drives the results among Republican respondents. It may be that Republican respondents conjure up images of white Republican politicians utilizing religion to advance a conservative policy agenda, that Republican respondents are unlikely to criticize their party's standard-bearer, or some combination of both. While the experimental results for the Republican subsample do not provide additional insight into the main results presented above, the difference in trends is noteworthy. Whereas black Democrats and white Republicans looked roughly similar in their assessments of political leaders using religion, their attitudes diverged when asked specifically about Bush: Republicans became slightly less likely to report that there is "too much" religion while black Democrats became much more likely to report that there is "too much" religion. These results build on the correlational data presented in figure 7.3 by showing that the conditions differ under which black Democrats and white Republicans support mixing religion and politics.

11. In 2010, there was no difference between white Republicans' views of political leaders (0.19) versus Obama (0.20) using "too much" religious rhetoric. Given that Republicans are generally supportive of political leaders emphasizing religion, it seems unlikely that Republicans would think that Obama uses "too much" religion relative to political leaders in general. Consistent with this, rates of saying "too little" religion

are higher among white Republicans in the Obama condition than in the general political leader condition.

12. The survey was conducted using Amazon's Mechanical Turk (MTurk). Respondents all had American Internet Service Providers (ISP). While the respondents were not a representative sample, common experimental results have been replicated on MTurk samples (Berinsky, Huber, and Lenz 2012), and liberals and conservatives on MTurk look similar to their counterparts in the public (Clifford, Jewell, and Waggoner 2015). Even though the experimental sample is disproportionately liberal and highly educated relative to the population as a whole, there are still stark religious differences between black and white Democratic respondents; black Democrats in the sample are much more religious than their white copartisans.

13. Although the emphasis is frequently on Republicans being linked to religious groups and values, the Democratic Party tries to use religion to its electoral advantage as well. For example, the increase in "God talk," in which presidents, beginning with Reagan, regularly employ religious rhetoric, did not subside during the Clinton administration (Domke and Coe 2010). Many Democratic politicians continue to discuss their religious views and reach out to religious voters (Kaylor 2011). This is particularly true in the African American community in which there is a great deal of political mobilization within churches (Calhoun-Brown 1996; McClerking and McDaniel 2005; Putnam and Campbell 2010). And finally, as previously mentioned, self-proclaimed atheistic or agnostic Democratic politicians are quite rare, and many large Democratic campaigns also try to mobilize religious communities.

14. The results below combine the two conditions in which both candidates received a religious endorsement. There are no differences based on which religious endorsement is associated with which candidate.

15. It seems as though respondents read the voter guide; 92% of respondents were able to identify the town where the election is taking place as Hidden Hills, 65% of respondents knew that the election was for mayor, and only 5% of respondents could not successfully answer either question. Additionally, respondents rated how religious they thought the candidates were. The experimental stimuli operated as expected, with treated respondents and control-condition respondents viewing the candidates differently: Respondents who read a secular endorsement of the Democratic candidate viewed the Democratic candidate as less religious, respondents who read a religious endorsement of the Republican candidate viewed the Republican candidate as more religious, and respondents who read a religious endorsement of the Democratic candidate viewed the Democratic candidate as more religious. A more detailed description of these results is available in the appendix.

16. While white and black Democrats evaluated the Democratic candidate similarly, black Democrats evaluated the Republican candidate slightly more favorably than white Democrats (0.05; p-value = 0.23).

17. Interaction models show that black and white Democrats responded to the secular-Democratic endorsement in roughly the same manner. There are no substantive or statistically significant differences in the Democratic and Republican evaluations. Black Democrats and white Republicans, however, responded to the endorsement differently. Black Democrats in the treatment condition came to view the Democratic candidate more favorably than did white Republicans in the treatment condition (0.11; p-value = 0.10). There is also suggestive evidence that black Democrats in the

treatment condition also came to view the Republican candidate less favorably than did white Republicans in the treatment condition (–0.07; *p*-value = 0.20).

18. Initial gap = 0.15; new gap = 0.34.

CHAPTER EIGHT

1. Partisanship serves as a proxy for electoral support as views of Kennedy and Nixon are not available in the 1956 and 1958 survey waves.

2. Statistical models presented in the appendix.

REFERENCES

Abadie, Alberto. 2003. "Semiparametric Instrumental Variable Estimation of Treatment Response Models." *Journal of Econometrics* 113(2): 231–63.

Abdelal, Rawi, Yoshiko M. Herrera, Alastair Iain Johnston, and Rose McDermott. 2009. "Identity as a Variable." In *Measuring Identity: A Guide for Social Scientists*, edited by Rawi Abdelal, Yoshiko M. Herrera, Alastair Iain Johnston, and Rose McDermott, 17–32. New York: Cambridge University Press.

Abelman, Robert, and Kimberly Neuendorf. 1987. "Themes and Topics in Religious Television Programming." *Review of Religious Research* 29(2): 152–74.

"About the Secular Coalition for America." N.d. Accessed September 7, 2017. https://www.secular.org/about/main.

Abramowitz, Alan I. 2004. "Terrorism, Gay Marriage, and Incumbency: Explaining the Republican Victory in the 2004 Presidential Election." *Forum* 2(4): 1540–84.

Abramowitz, Alan I., and Kyle L. Saunders. 1998. "Ideological Realignment in the U.S. Electorate." *Journal of Politics* 60(3): 634–52.

Abramson, Paul R. 1979. "Developing Party Identification: A Further Examination of Life-Cycle, Generational, and Period Effects." *American Journal of Political Science* 23(1): 78–96.

Adams, Greg D. 1997. "Abortion: Evidence of an Issue Evolution." *American Journal of Political Science* 41(3): 718–37.

Adkins, Todd, Geoffrey C. Layman, David E. Campbell, and John C. Green. 2013. "Religious Group Cues and Citizen Policy Attitudes in the United States." *Politics and Religion* 6(2): 235–63.

Ahmed, Ali M., and Osvaldo Salas. 2008. "In the Back of Your Mind: Subliminal Influences of Religious Concepts on Prosocial Behavior." Working Papers in Economics 331. University of Gothenburg.

Albertson, Bethany L. 2015. "Dog-Whistle Politics: Multivocal Communication and Religious Appeals." *Political Behavior* 37(1): 3–26.

———. 2011. "Religious Language and Implicit Attitudes." *Political Psychology* 32(1): 109–30.

Albrecht, Stan L., Marie Cornwall, and Perry H. Cunningham. 1998. "Religious Leave-Taking: Disengagement and Disaffiliation among Mormons." In *Fall from the Faith: The Causes, Course, and Consequences of Religious Apostasy*, edited by David G. Bromley, 62–80. Newbury Park, CA: Sage.

Alford, John R., Carolyn L. Funk, and John R. Hibbing. 2005. "Are Political Orientations Genetically Transmitted?" *American Political Science Review* 99(2): 153–67.

Alford, John. R., Peter K. Hatemi, John R. Hibbing, Nicholas G. Martin, and Lindon J. Eaves. 2011. "The Politics of Mate Choice." *Journal of Politics* 73(2): 362–79.

Alwin, Duane F. 1986. "Religion and Parental Child-Rearing Orientations: Evidence of a Catholic-Protestant Convergence." *American Journal of Sociology* 92(2): 412–40.

Alwin, Duane F., Ronald L. Cohen, and Theodore M. Newcomb. 1991. *Political Attitudes over the Life Span: The Bennington Women after Fifty Years.* Madison: University of Wisconsin Press.

Ansolabehere, Stephen, Jonathan J. Rodden, and James M. Snyder Jr. 2008. "The Strength of Issues: Using Multiple Measures to Gauge Preference Stability, Ideological Constraint, and Issue Voting." *American Political Science Review* 102(2): 215–32.

Arceneaux, Kevin, and Robin Kolodny. 2009a. "Educating the Least Informed: Group Endorsements in a Grassroots Campaign." *American Journal of Political Science* 53(4): 755–70.

———. 2009b. "The Effects of Grassroots Campaigning on Issue Preferences and Issue Salience." *Journal of Elections, Public Opinion, and Parties* 19(3): 235–49.

Argue, Amy, David R. Johnson, and Lynn K. White. 1999. "Age and Religiosity: Evidence from a Three-Wave Panel Analysis." *Journal for the Scientific Study of Religion* 38(3): 423–35.

Arnett, Jeffrey J. 2000. "Emerging Adulthood: A Theory of Development from the Late Teens through the Twenties." *American Psychologist* 55(5): 469–80.

———. 1998. "Learning to Stand Alone: The Contemporary American Transition to Adulthood in Cultural and Historical Context." *Human Development* 41(5): 295–315.

Arnett, Jeffrey J., and Lene A. Jensen. 2002. "A Congregation of One: Individualized Religious Beliefs among Emerging Adults." *Journal of Adolescent Research* 17(5): 451–67.

Asch, Solomon E. 1951. "Effects of Group Pressure upon the Modification and Distortion of Judgment." In *Groups, Leadership, and Men: Research in Human Relations*, edited by Harold S. Guetzkow, 117–90. Pittsburgh, PA: Carnegie Press.

Bafumi, Joseph, and Robert Y. Shapiro. 2009. "A New Partisan Voter." *Journal of Politics* 71(1): 1–24.

Baldassarri, Delia, and Andrew Gelman. 2008. "Partisans without Constraint: Political Polarization and Trends in American Public Opinion." *American Journal of Sociology* 114(2): 408–46.

Barber, Nigel. 2011. "Why Americans Are So Religious." *Psychology Today*, January 19.

Barker, David C., Jon Hurwitz, and Traci L. Nelson. 2008. "Of Crusades and Culture Wars: 'Messianic' Militarism and Political Conflict in the United States." *Journal of Politics* 70(2): 307–22.

Barna Group. 2007. "Barna's Annual Tracking Study Shows Americans Stay Spiritually Active, but Biblical Views Wane," May 21.

Barr, James. 1981. *The Scope and Authority of the Bible.* Atlanta: Westminster John Knox Press.

Bartels, Larry. 2006. "Priming and Persuasion in Presidential Campaigns." In *Capturing Campaign Effects*, edited by Henry E. Brady and Richard Johnston, 78–112. Ann Arbor: University of Michigan Press.

———. 2002. "Beyond the Running Tally: Partisan Bias in Political Perceptions." *Political Behavior* 24(2): 117–50.

———. 2000. "Partisanship and Voting Behavior 1952–1996." *American Journal of Political Science* 44(1): 35–50.

Beatty, Kathleen M., and Oliver Walter. 1989. "A Group Theory of Religion and Politics: The Clergy as Group Leaders." *Western Political Quarterly* 42(1): 129–46.

Beck, Paul Allen. 1974. "A Socialization Theory of Partisan Realignment." In *The Politics of Future Citizens: New Dimensions in Socialization*, edited by Richard G. Niemi, 199–219. San Francisco: Jossey-Bass.

Beck, Paul Allen, and M. Kent Jennings. 1991. "Family Traditions, Political Periods, and the Development of Partisan Orientations." *Journal of Politics* 53(3): 742–63.

———. 1975. "Parents as 'Middlepersons' in Political Socialization." *Journal of Politics* 37(1): 83–107.

Becker, Penny Edgell, and Heather Hofmeister. 2001. "Work, Family, and Religious Involvement for Men and Women." *Journal for the Scientific Study of Religion* 40(4): 707–22.

Belenko, Steven R. 2000. *Drugs and Drug Policy in America: A Documentary History*. Westport, CT: Greenwood Press.

Bendyna, Mary E., and Celinda Lake. 1994. "Gender and Voting in the 1992 Presidential Election." In *The Year of the Woman: Myths and Realities*, edited by Elizabeth Adell Cook, Sue Thomas, and Clyde Wilcox, 237–54. New York: West View Press.

Bennett, John C. 1960. "A Roman Catholic for President?" *Christianity and Crisis* 20(3): 17–19.

Benson, John M. 2001. "Heard Enough: When Is an Opinion Really an Opinion." *Public Perspectives* 12 (October): 40–41.

Bercovitch, Sacvan. 1976. "How the Puritans Won the American Revolution." *Massachusetts Review* 17(4): 597–630.

Berelson, Bernard R., Paul F. Lazarsfeld, and William N. McPhee. 1954. *Voting: A Study of Opinion Formation in a Presidential Election*. Chicago: University of Chicago Press.

Berger, Peter L. 1967. *The Sacred Canopy*. Garden City, NY: Anchor.

Berger, Peter L., Grace Davie, and Effie Fokas. 2008. *Religious America, Secular Europe? A Theme and Variation*. New York: Ashgate.

Berinsky, Adam J., Gregory A. Huber, and Gabriel S. Lenz. 2012. "Evaluating Online Labor Markets for Experimental Research: Amazon.com's Mechanical Turk." *Political Analysis* 20(3): 351–68.

Berinsky, Adam J., Michele F. Margolis, and Michael W. Sances. 2014. "Separating the Shirkers from the Workers? Making Sure Respondents Pay Attention on Self-Administered Surveys." *American Journal of Political Science* 58(3): 739–53.

Billing, Michael, and Henri Tajfel. 1973. "Social Categorization and Similarity in Intergroup Behaviour." *European Journal of Social Psychology* 3(1): 27–51.

Bishop, George F., Robert W. Oldendick, Alfred J. Tuchfarber, and Stephen E. Bennett. 1980. "Pseudo-Opinions on Public Affairs." *Public Opinion Quarterly* 44(2): 198–209.

Bishop, George F., Alfred J. Tuchfarber, Robert W. Oldendick. 1986. "Opinions on Fictitious Issues: The Pressure to Answer Survey Questions." *Public Opinion Quarterly* 50(2): 240–50.

Bjarnason, Thoroddur, and Michael R. Welch. 2004. "Father Knows Best: Parishes, Priests, and American Catholic Parishioners' Attitudes toward Capital Punishment." *Journal for Scientific Study of Religion* 43(1): 103–18.

Bolce, Louis, and Gerald De Maio. 2014. "The Evolution of the Religion Gap Metaphor in the Language of American Political Journalists: 1987–2012." *Geolinguistics* 39: 45–62.

———. 2008. "A Prejudice for the Thinking Class." *American Politics Research* 36(1): 155–85.

———. 2002. "Our Secularist Democratic Party." *Public Interest* 149(3): 3–20.

———. 1999a. "The Anti-Christian Fundamentalist Factor in Contemporary Politics." *Public Opinion Quarterly* 63(4): 508–42.

———. 1999b. "Religious Outlook, Culture War Politics, and Antipathy toward Christian Fundamentalists." *Public Opinion Quarterly* 63(1): 29–61.

Boorstein, Michelle. 2016. "Why the March for Life Is Becoming a Destination for More Evangelicals." *Washington Post*, January 21.

Box-Steffensmeier, Janet M., Suzanna De Boef, and Tse-Min Lin. 2004. "The Dynamics of the Partisan Gender Gap." *American Political Science Review* 98(3): 515–28.

Boyd, Heather Hartwig. 1999. "Christianity and the Environment in the American Public." *Journal for the Scientific Study of Religion* 38(1): 36–44.

Boyer, Paul. 2008. "The Evangelical Resurgence in 1970s American Protestantism." In *Rightward Bound: Making America Conservative in the 1970s*, edited by Bruce J. Schulman and Julian E. Zelizer, 29–51. Cambridge, MA: Harvard University Press.

Brader, Ted, Nicholas A. Valentino, and Elizabeth Suhay. 2008. "What Triggers Public Opposition to Immigration?" *American Journal of Political Science* 52(4): 959–78.

Bradshaw, Matt, and Christopher G. Ellison. 2008. "Do Genetic Factors Influence Religious Life? Findings from a Behavioral Genetics Analysis of Twin Siblings." *Journal for the Scientific Study of Religion* 47(4): 529–44.

Brenner, Philip S. 2011. "Identity Importance and the Overreporting of Religious Service Attendance: Multiple Imputation of Religious Attendance Using American Time Use Study and the General Social Survey." *Journal for the Scientific Study of Religion* 50(1): 103–15.

Brewer, Marilynn B. 2001. "Ingroup Identification and Intergroup Conflict: When Does Ingroup Love Become Outgroup Hate?" In *Social Identity, Intergroup Conflict, and Conflict Reduction*, edited by Richard D. Ashmore, Lee Jussim, and David Wilder, 17–41. New York: Oxford University Press.

Brewer, Marilynn B., and Rupert J. Brown. 1998. "Intergroup Relations." In *The Handbook of Social Psychology*, edited by Daniel T. Gilbert, Susan T. Fiske, and Gardner Linzey, 554–94. Boston: McGraw-Hill.

Brewer, Marilynn, and Kathleen P. Pierce. 2005. "Social Identity Complexity and Outgroup Tolerance." *Personality and Social Psychology Bulletin* 31(3): 428–37.

Brewer, Marilynn B., and Michael D. Silver. 2000. "Group Distinctiveness, Social Identification, and Collective Mobilization." In *Self, Identity, and Social Movements*, edited by Sheldon Stryker, Timothy J. Owens, and Robert W. White, 153–71. Minneapolis: University of Minnesota Press.

Brewer, Mark D., and Jeffrey M. Stonecash. 2007. *Split: Class and Cultural Conflict in American Politics*. Washington, DC: Congressional Quarterly Press.

Brinkerhoff, Merlin B., and Marlene M. Mackie. 1993. "Casting Off the Bonds of Organized Religion: A Religious-Careers Approach to the Study of Apostasy." *Review of Religious Research* 34(3): 235–58.

Brown, Ernest J. 1963. "Quis Custodiet Ipsos Custodes?—The School-Prayer Cases." *Supreme Court Review* 1963: 1–33.

Brown, R. Khari, and Ronald E. Brown. 2003. "Faith and Works: Church-Based Social Capital Resources and African American Political Activism." *Social Forces* 82(2): 617–41.

Bruce, Steve. 2002. *God Is Dead: Secularization in the West*. Vol. 3. Oxford: Blackwell.

———. 1988. *The Rise and Fall of the New Christian Right: Conservative Protestant Politics in America, 1978–1988*. Oxford: Clarendon Press.

Brudney, Jeffrey L., and Gary W. Copeland. 1984. "Evangelicals as a Political Force: Reagan and the 1980 Religious Vote." *Social Science Quarterly* 65(4): 1072–79.

Bryant, Alyssa N., Jeung Yun Choi, and Maiko Yasuno. 2003. "Understanding the Religious and Spiritual Dimensions of Students' Lives in the First Year of College." *Journal of College Student Development* 44(6): 723–45.

Burns, Peter, and James G. Gimpel. 2000. "Economic Insecurity, Prejudicial Stereotypes and Public Opinion on Immigration Policy." *Political Science Quarterly* 115(2): 201–25.

Bush, George W. 2004. "Remarks Calling for a Constitutional Amendment Defining and Protecting Marriage, February 24, 2004." In *Public Papers of the President of the United States: George W. Bush, 2004*. Book I, *January 1–June 30, 2004*, 263–64. Washington, DC: Government Printing Office, 2007.

Calfano, Brian R., and Paul A. Djupe. 2009. "God Talk: Religious Cues and Electoral Support." *Political Research Quarterly* 62(2): 329–39.

Calfano, Brian R., and Elizabeth A. Oldmixon. 2016. "Remember to Ask the Boss: Priming and the Political Dynamics of Priest Reliance on Bishop Cues." *Religions* 7(21): 1–18.

———. 2015. "Primed Parsons: Reference Groups and Clergy Political Attitudes." *Journal of Religion and Society* 17: 1–10.

Calhoun-Brown, Allison. 1996. "African American Churches and Political Mobilization." *Journal of Politics* 58(4): 935–53.

Campbell, Angus. 1960. "Surge and Decline: A Study of Electoral Change." *Public Opinion Quarterly* 24(3): 397–418.

Campbell, Angus, Philip E. Converse, Warren E. Miller, and Donald E. Stokes. 1960. *The American Voter*. Chicago: University of Chicago Press.

Campbell, Angus, Gerald Gurin, and Warren E. Miller. 1954. *The Voter Decides*. Evanston, IL: Row, Peterson.

Campbell, David E., John C. Green, and Geoffrey C. Layman. 2011. "The Party Faithful: Partisan Images, Candidate Religion, and the Electoral Impact of Party Identification." *American Journal of Political Science* 55(1): 42–58.

Campbell, David E., Geoffrey C. Layman, and John C. Green. 2012. "A Jump to the Right, a Step to the Left. Religion and Public Opinion." In *New Directions in Public Opinion*, edited by Adam J. Berinsky, 168–92. New York: Routledge.

Campbell, David E., Geoffrey C. Layman, John C. Green, and Nathanael G. Sumaktoyo. Forthcoming. "Putting Politics First: The Impact of Politics on American Religious and Secular Orientations." *American Journal of Political Science*.

Campbell, David E., and J. Quin Monson. 2008. "The Religion Card: Gay Marriage and the 2004 Election." *Public Opinion Quarterly* 72(3): 399–419.

———. 2003. "Follow the Leader: Mormon Voting on Ballot Propositions." *Journal for the Scientific Study of Religion* 42(2): 605–19.

Caplovitz, David, and Fred Sherrow. 1977. *The Religious Drop-Outs: Apostasy among College Graduates*. Beverly Hills, CA: Sage.

Carleton, William G. 1964. "Kennedy in History: An Early Appraisal." *Antioch Review* 24(3): 277–99.

Carmines, Edward G., and Harold W. Stanley. 1992. "The Transformation of the New Deal Party System: Social Groups, Political Ideology, and Changing Partisanship among Northern Whites, 1972–1988." *Political Behavior* 14(3): 213–37.

Carmines, Edward G., and James A. Stimson. 1989. *Issue Evolution: Race and the Transformation of American Politics*. Princeton, NJ: Princeton University Press.

Carmines, Edward G., and James Woods. 2002. "The Role of Party Activists in the Evolution of the Abortion Issue." *Political Behavior* 24(4): 361–77.

Carroll, Jackson W., and Wade Clark Roof, eds. 1993. *Beyond Establishment: Protestant Identity in a Post-Protestant Age*. Louisville, KY: Westminster John Knox Press.

Carwardine, Richard. 1993. *Evangelicals and Politics in Antebellum America*. New Haven, CT: Yale University Press.

Casey, Shaun A. 2009. *The Making of a Catholic President: Kennedy vs. Nixon 1960*. New York: Oxford University Press.

Chaffee, Steven H., Jack M. McLeod, and Daniel B. Wackman. 1973. "Family Communication Patterns and Adolescent Political Participation." In *Socialization to Politics: A
Reader*, edited by John L. Dennis, 349–64. New York: Wiley.

Chang, Linchiat, and Jon A. Krosnick. 2009. "National Surveys via RDD Telephone Interviewing versus the Internet." *Public Opinion Quarterly* 73(4): 641–78.

Chapp, Christopher B. 2012. *Religious Rhetoric and American Politics: The Endurance of Civil
Religion in Electoral Campaigns*. Ithaca, NY: Cornell University Press.

Chaves, Mark A. 2011. *American Religion: Contemporary Trends*. Princeton, NJ: Princeton University Press.

———. 1991. "Family Structure and Protestant Church Attendance: The Sociological Basis
of Cohort and Age Effects." *Journal for the Scientific Study of Religion* 30(4): 501–14.

Claassen, Ryan L. 2015. *Godless Democrats and Pious Republicans? Party Activists, Party Capture, and the "God Gap."* New York: Cambridge University Press.

Clark, Cynthia A., and Everett L. Worthington. 1987. "Family Variables Affecting the Transmission of Religious Values from Parents to Adolescents: A Review." *Family Perspectives*
21(1): 1–21.

Clark, Norman H. 1976. *Deliver Us from Evil: An Interpretation of American Prohibition.*
Vol. 2. New York: W. W. Norton.

Clifford, Scott, Ryan M. Jewell, and Philip D. Waggoner. 2015. "Are Samples Drawn from
Mechanical Turk Valid for Research on Political Ideology?" *Research & Politics* 2(4): 1–9.

Clinton, Bill. 1996. *Between Hope and History: Meeting America's Challenges for the 21st Century*. New York: Random House.

Cobble, Dorothy S. 2004. *The Other Women's Movement: Workplace Justice and Social Rights
in Modern America*. Princeton, NJ: Princeton University Press.

Cohen, Geoffrey L. 2003. "Party over Policy: The Dominating Impact of Group Influence
on Political Beliefs." *Journal of Personality and Social Psychology* 85(5): 808–22.

Cone, James H. 1997. *Black Theology and Black Power*. New York: Orbis Books.

Conover, Pamela Johnston. 1988. "The Role of Social Groups in Political Thinking." *British Journal of Political Science* 18(1): 51–76.

———. 1984. "The Influence of Group Identifications on Political Perception and Evaluation." *Journal of Politics* 46(3): 760–85.

Conover, Pamela Johnston, and Stanley Feldman. 1984. "How People Organize the Political World: A Schematic Model." *American Journal of Political Science* 28(1): 95–126.

Converse, Philip E. 1964. "The Nature of Belief Systems in Mass Publics." In *Ideology and
Discontent*, edited by David E. Apter, 206–61. New York: Free Press.

Converse, Philip E., Angus Campbell, Warren E. Miller, and Donald E. Stokes. 1961. "Stability and Change in 1960: A Reinstating Election." *American Political Science Review*
55(2): 269–80.

Converse, Philip E., and Gregory B. Markus. 1979. "Plus Ca Change. . . . The New CPS
Election Study Panel." *American Political Science Review* 73(1): 32–49.

Crawford, Sue E. S., and Laura R. Olson. 2001. *Christian Clergy in American Politics*. Baltimore, MD: Johns Hopkins University Press.

Crespino, Joseph. 2008. "Civil Rights and the Religious Right." In *Rightward Bound: Making America Conservative in the 1970s*, edited by Bruce J. Schulman and Julian E. Zelizer,
90–105. Cambridge, MA: Harvard University Press.

Curry, Lerond. 2015. *Protestant-Catholic Relations in America: World War I through Vatican II*.
Lexington: University Press of Kentucky.

Dalton, Russell J. 2007. "Partisan Mobilization, Cognitive Mobilization and the Changing
American Electorate." *Electoral Studies* 26(2): 274–86.

———. 1984. "Cognitive Mobilization and Partisan Dealignment in Advanced Industrial Democracies." *Journal of Politics* 46(1): 264–84.

Daniels, Joseph P., and Marc Von Der Ruhr. 2005. "God and the Global Economy: Religion and Attitudes towards Trade and Immigration in the United States." *Socio-Economic Review* 3(3): 467–89.

Dean, Kenda Creasy. 2010. *Almost Christian. What the Faith of Our Teenagers Is Telling the American Church.* New York: Oxford University Press.

Deaux, Kay, Anne Reid, Kim Mizrahi, and Kathleen A. Ethier. 1995. "Parameters of Social Identity." *Journal of Personality and Social Psychology* 68(2): 280–91.

Delli Carpini, Michael X. 1989. "Age and History: Generations and Sociopolitical Change." In *Political Learning in Adulthood: A Sourcebook of Theory and Research,* edited by Roberta S. Sigal, 11–55. Chicago: University of Chicago Press.

Delli Carpini, Michael X., and Scott Keeter. 1996. *What Americans Know about Politics and Why It Matters.* New Haven, CT: Yale University Press.

———. 1991. "Stability and Change in the U.S. Public's Knowledge of Politics." *Public Opinion Quarterly* 55(4): 583–612.

Democratic Party Platform. 2004. "2004 Democratic Party Platform," July 27. Gerhard Peters and John T. Woolley, *The American Presidency Project.* http://www.presidency.ucsb.edu/ws/?pid=29613.

———. 1980. "1980 Democratic Party Platform," August 11. Gerhard Peters and John T. Woolley, *The American Presidency Project.* http://www.presidency.ucsb.edu/ws/?pid=29607.

———. 1976. "1976 Democratic Party Platform," July 12. Gerhard Peters and John T. Woolley, *The American Presidency Project.* http://www.presidency.ucsb.edu/ws/?pid=29606.

Desmond, Scott A., Kristopher H. Morgan, and George Kikuchi. 2010. "Religious Development: How (and Why) Does Religiosity Change from Adolescence to Adulthood?" *Sociological Perspectives* 53(2): 247–70.

De Vaus, David, and Ian McAllister. 1987. "Gender Differences in Religion: A Test of the Structural Location Theory." *American Sociological Review* 52(4): 472–81.

Dezutter, Jessie, Bart Soenens, Koen Luyckx, Sabrina Bruyneel, Maarten Vansteenkiste, Bart Duriez, and Dirk Hutsebaut. 2008. "The Role of Religion in Death Attitudes: Distinguishing between Religious Belief and Style of Processing Religious Contents." *Death Studies* 33(1): 73–92.

Dijksterhuis, Ap, Jesse Preston, Daniel M. Wegner, and Aarts Henk. 2008. "Effects of Subliminal Priming of Self and God on Self-Attribution of Authorship for Events." *Journal of Experimental Social Psychology* 44(1): 2–9.

Dijksterhuis, Ap, and Ad van Knippenberg. 1998. "The Relation between Perception and Behavior, or How to Win a Game of Trivial Pursuit." *Journal of Personality and Social Psychology* 74(4): 865–77.

Dillon, Michele, and Paul Wink. 2007. *In the Course of a Lifetime: Tracing Religious Belief, Practice, and Change.* Berkeley: University of California Press.

Dinas, Elias. 2014. "Why Does the Apple Fall Far from the Tree? How Early Political Socialization Prompts Parent-Child Dissimilarity." *British Journal of Political Science* 44(4): 827–52.

———. 2013. "Opening 'Openness to Change': Political Events and Increased Sensitivity of Young Adults." *Political Research Quarterly* 66(4): 868–82.

Dinges, William, Dean R. Hoge, Mary Johnson, and Juan L. Gonzales Jr. 1998. "A Faith Loosely Held: The Institutional Allegiance of Young Catholics." *Commonwealth* 17(1): 13–18.

Djupe, Paul A., and Brian R. Calfano. 2013. *God Talk: Experimenting with the Religious Causes of Public Opinion.* Philadelphia: Temple University Press.

Djupe, Paul A., and Christopher P. Gilbert. 2009. *The Political Influence of Churches*. New York: Cambridge University Press.

———. 2006. "The Resourceful Believer: Generating Civic Skills in Church." *Journal of Politics* 68(1): 116–27.

———. 2003. *The Prophetic Pulpit: Clergy, Churches, and Communities in American Politics*. Lanham, MD: Rowman and Littlefield.

———. 2002. "The Political Voice of Clergy." *Journal of Politics* 64(2): 466–90.

Djupe, Paul A., and Gregory W. Gwiasda. 2010. "Evangelizing the Environment: Decision Process Effects in Political Persuasion." *Journal for the Scientific Study of Religion* 49(1): 73–86.

Djupe, Paul A., Jacob R. Neiheisel, and Anand E. Sokhey. Forthcoming. "Reconsidering the Role of Politics in Leaving Religion: The Importance of Affiliation." *American Journal of Political Science*.

Domke, David, and Kevin Coe. 2010. *The God Strategy: How Religion Became a Political Weapon in America*. New York: Oxford University Press.

Duck, Robert J., and Bruce Hunsberger. 1999. "Religious Orientation and Prejudice: The Role of Religious Proscription, Right-Wing Authoritarianism and Social Desirability." *International Journal for the Psychology of Religion* 9(3): 157–79.

Dumenil, Lynn. 1991. "The Tribal Twenties: 'Assimilated' Catholics' Response to Anti-Catholicism in the 1920s." *Journal of American Ethnic History* 11(1): 21–49.

Eaves, Lindon J., and Peter K. Hatemi. 2008. "Transmission of Attitudes toward Abortion and Gay Rights." *Behavior Genetics* 38(3): 247–56.

Eaves, Lindon J., Peter K. Hatemi, Elizabeth C. Prom-Womley, and Lenn Murrelle. 2008. "Social and Genetic Influences on Adolescent Religious Attitudes and Practices." *Social Forces* 86(4): 1621–46.

Ebaugh, Helen R. F., and C. Allen Haney. 1978. "Church Attendance and Attitudes toward Abortion: Differentials in Liberal and Conservative Churches." *Journal for the Scientific Study of Religion* 17(4): 407–13.

Eckberg, Douglas Lee, and T. Jean Blocker. 1989. "Varieties of Religious Involvement and Environmental Concerns: Testing the Lynn White Thesis." *Journal for the Scientific Study of Religion* 28(4): 509–17.

Ecklund, Elaine Howard, and Kristen Shultz Lee. 2011. "Atheists and Agnostics Negotiate Religion and Family." *Journal for the Scientific Study of Religion* 50(4): 728–43.

Edsall, Thomas B., and Mary D. Edsall. 1992. *Chain Reaction: The Impact of Race, Rights, and Taxes on American Politics*. New York: W. W. Norton.

Engs, Ruth C., and Kenneth Mullen. 1999. "The Effect of Religion and Religiosity on Drug Use among a Selected Sample of Post Secondary Students in Scotland." *Addiction Research and Theory* 7(2): 149–70.

Erickson, Joseph A. 1992. "Adolescent Religious Development and Commitment: A Structural Equation Model of the Role of Family, Peer Group, and Educational Influences." *Journal for the Scientific Study of Religion* 31(2): 131–52.

Erikson, Robert S., and Kent L. Tedin. 2007. *American Public Opinion: Its Origins, Content, and Impact*. 7th ed. Boston: Allyn and Bacon.

Fawcett, Jennifer, Vicki Andrews, and David Lester. 2000. "Religiosity and Attitudes about Abortion." *Psychological Reports* 87(3): 980.

Fazekas, Zoltàn, and Levente Littvay. 2015. "The Importance of Context in the Genetic Transmission of U.S. Party Affiliation." *Political Psychology* 36(4): 361–77.

Fejes, Fred. 2016. *Gay Rights and Moral Panic: The Origins of America's Debate on Homosexuality*. New York: Palgrave Macmillan.

Ferree, Myra M. 2003. "Resonance and Radicalism: Feminist Framing in the Abortion Debates of the United States and Germany." *American Journal of Sociology* 109(2): 304–44.

Festinger, Leon. 1957. *A Theory of Cognitive Dissonance*. Redwood City, CA: Stanford University Press.

Fetzer, Joel. 2000. *Public Attitudes toward Immigration in the United States, France, and Germany*. New York: Cambridge University Press.

Finkel, Steven E. 1995. *Causal Analysis with Panel Data*. Thousand Oaks, CA: Sage.

Fiorina, Morris P. 1981. *Retrospective Voting in American National Elections*. New Haven, CT: Yale University Press.

Fiorina, Morris P., Sam Abrams, and Jeremy Pope. 2006. *Culture War? The Myth of the Polarized America*. 2nd ed. New York: Longman.

Firebaugh, Glen, and Kevin Chen. 1995. "Vote Turnout of Nineteenth Amendment Women: The Enduring Effect of Disenfranchisement." *American Journal of Sociology* 100(4): 972–96.

Fish, Stanley E. 1980. *Is There a Text in This Class: The Authority of Interpretive Communities*. Cambridge, MA: Harvard University Press.

Fowler, Anthony, and Michele Margolis. 2014. "The Political Consequences of Uninformed Voters." *Electoral Studies* 34: 100–110.

Fowler, Robert, Allen D. Hertzke, Laura R. Olson, and Kevin Den Dulk. 2004. *Religion and Politics in America*. 3rd ed. Boulder, CO: Westview Press.

Frankl, Razelle. 1987. *Televangelism: The Marketing of Popular Religion*. Carbondale: Southern Illinois University Press.

Friesen, Amanda, and Aleksander Ksiazkiewicz. 2015. "Do Political Attitudes and Religiosity Share a Genetic Path?" *Political Behavior* 37(4): 791–818.

Friesen, Amanda, and Michael W. Wagner. 2012. "Beyond the 'Three Bs': How American Christians Approach Faith and Politics." *Politics and Religion* 5(2): 224–52.

Funk, Richard B., and Fern K. Willits. 1987. "College Attendance and Attitude Change: A Panel Study, 1970–81." *Sociology of Education* 60(3): 224–31.

Gallup, George Jr., and Jim Castelli. 1989. *The People's Religion: American Faith in the '90s*. New York: Macmillan.

Gelman, Andrew, David Park, Boris Shor, Joseph Bafumi, and Jeronimo Cortina. 2009. *Red State, Blue State, Rich State, Poor State: Why Americans Vote the Way They Do*. Princeton, NJ: Princeton University Press.

Gerber, Alan S., and Donald P. Green 1998. "Rational Learning and Partisan Attitudes." *American Journal of Political Science* 42(3): 794–818.

Gerber, Alan S., and Gregory A. Huber. 2010. "Partisanship, Political Control, and Economic Assessments." *American Journal of Political Science* 54(1): 153–73.

———. 2009. "Partisanship and Economic Behavior: Do Partisan Differences in Economic Forecasts Predict Real Economic Behavior?" *American Political Science Review* 103(3): 407–26.

Gerber, Alan S., Gregory A. Huber, David Doherty, Conor M. Dowling, and Shang E. Ha. 2010. "Personality and Political Attitudes: Relationships across Issue Domains and Political Contexts." *American Political Science Review* 104(1): 111–33.

Gerber, Alan S., Gregory A. Huber, David Doherty, Conor M. Dowling, Connor Raso, and Shang E. Ha. 2011. "Personality Traits and Participation in Political Processes." *Journal of Politics* 74(3): 692–706.

Gerber, Alan S., Gregory A. Huber, and Ebonya Washington. 2010. "Party Affiliation, Partisanship, and Political Beliefs: A Field Experiment." *American Political Science Review* 104(4): 720–44.

Gilbert, Christopher P. 1993. *The Impact of Churches on Political Behavior*. Westport, CT: Greenwood Press.

Gilbert, Christopher P., David A. M. Peterson, Timothy R. Johnson, and Paul A. Djupe. 1999. *Religious Institutions and Minor Parties in the United States*. Westport, CT: Greenwood Publishing Group.

Giuliano, Paola, and Antonio Spilimbergo. 2014. "Growing Up in a Recession." *Review of Economic Studies* 81(2): 787–817.

Glass, Jennifer, Vern L. Bengston, and Charlotte Chorn Dunham. 1986. "Attitude Similarity in Three-Generation Families: Socialization, Status Inheritance, or Reciprocal Influence." *American Sociological Review* 51(5): 685–98.

Goldscheider, Frances, and Calvin Goldscheider. 1999. *The Changing Transition to Adulthood: Leaving and Returning Home*. Thousand Oaks, CA: Sage.

Goodstein, Laurie. 2001. "As Attacks' Impact Recedes, a Return to Religion as Usual." *New York Times*, November 26.

Greeley, Andrew. 1993. "Religion and Attitudes toward the Environment." *Journal for the Scientific Study of Religion* 32(1): 19–28.

Green, Donald, Bradley Palmquist, and Eric Schickler. 2002. *Partisan Hearts and Minds: Political Parties and the Social Identities of Voters*. New Haven, CT: Yale University Press.

Green, John C. 2010. *The Faith Factor: How Religion Influences American Elections*. Washington, DC: Potomac Books.

———. 2007. *The Faith Factor: How Religion Influences American Elections*. Westport, CT: Praeger.

———. 2004. "Two Faces of Pluralism in American Politics." In *One Electorate under God? A Dialogue on Religion and American Politics*, edited by E. J. Dionne, Jean B. Elshtain, and Kayla M. Drogosz, 189–211. Washington, DC: Congressional Quarterly Press.

Green, John C., and E. J. Dionne Jr. 2008. "Religion and American Politics: More Secular, More Evangelical or Both?" In *Red, Blue and Purple America: The Future of Election Demographics*, edited by Ruy Teixeira, 194–224. Washington, DC: Brookings Institution Press.

Green, John C., and James L. Guth. 1993. "From Lambs to Sheep: Denominational Change and Political Behavior." In *Rediscovering the Religious Factor in American Politics*, edited by David C. Leege and Lyman A. Kellstedt, 100–117. Armonk, NY: M. E. Sharpe.

———. 1991. "The Bible and the Ballot Box: The Shape of Things to Come." In *The Bible and the Ballot Box: The Shape of Things to Come*, edited by James L. Guth and John C. Green, 207–25. Boulder, CO: Westview.

———. 1988. "The Christian Right in the Republican Party: The Case of Pat Robertson's Supporters." *Journal of Politics* 50(1): 150–65.

———. 1986. "Big Bucks and Petty Cash: Party and Interest Group Activists in American Politics." *Interest Group Politics* 2: 91–113.

Green, John C., James L. Guth, Lyman A. Kellstedt, and Corwin E. Smidt. 1996. *Religion and the Culture Wars. Dispatches from the Front*. Lanham, MD: Rowman and Littlefield.

Green, John C., Mark J. Rozell, and Clyde Wilcox, eds. 2006. *The Values Campaign? The Christian Right and the 2004 Elections*. Washington, DC: Georgetown University Press.

Green, John, and Mark Silk. 2004. "Gendering the Religion Gap." *Religion in the News* 7(1): 11–13.

Greene, Steven. 2004. "Social Identity Theory and Party Identification." *Social Science Quarterly* 85(1): 136–53.

———. 1999. "Understanding Party Identification: A Social Identity Approach." *Political Psychology* 20(2): 393–403.

Greenfield, Emily A., and Nadine F. Marks. 2008. "Religious Social Identity as an Explanatory Factor for Associations between More Frequent Formal Religious Participation and Psychological Well-Being." *International Journal for the Psychology of Religion* 17(3): 245–59.

Gurin, Patricia, Arthur H. Miller, and Gerald Gurin. 1980. "Stratum Identification and Consciousness." *Social Psychology Quarterly* 43(1): 30–47.

Guth, James L. 1983. "The New Christian Right," In *The New Christian Right: Mobilization and Legitimation*, edited by Robert C. Liebman and Robert Wuthnow, 31–45. New York: Aldine.

Guth, James L., and John C. Green. 1986. "Faith and Politics: Religion and Ideology among Political Contributors." *American Politics Quarterly* 14(3): 186–200.

Guth, James L., John C. Green, Lyman A. Kellstedt, and Corwin E. Smidt. 1995. "Faith and the Environment: Religious Beliefs and Attitudes on Environmental Policy." *American Journal of Political Science* 39(2): 364–82.

Guth, James L., John C. Green, Corwin E. Smidt, Lyman A. Kellstedt, and Margaret Poloma. 1997. *The Bully Pulpit: The Politics of Protestant Clergy*. Lawrence: University of Kansas Press.

Guth, James L., Lyman A. Kellstedt, John C. Green, and Corwin Smidt. 2007. "Getting the Spirit? Religious and Partisan Mobilization in the 2004 Elections." In *Interest Group Politics*, 7th ed., edited by Allan J. Cigler and Burdett A. Loomis, 157–81. Washington, DC: Congressional Quarterly Press.

Guth, James L., Lyman A. Kellstedt, Corwin E. Smidt, and John C. Green. 2006. "Religious Influences in the 2004 Presidential Election." *Presidential Studies Quarterly* 36(2): 223–42.

Hadaway, Kirk C., and Wade C. Roof. 1988. "Apostasy in American Churches: Evidence from National Survey Data." In *Falling from the Faith: Causes and Consequences of Religious Apostasy*, edited by David Bromley, 29–46. Thousand Oaks, CA: Sage.

Hadden, Jeffery K. 1987. "Religious Broadcasting and the Mobilization of the New Christian Right." *Journal for the Scientific Study of Religion* 26(1): 1–24.

Haidt, Jonathan, and Marc J. Hetherington. 2012. "Look How Far We've Come Apart." *New York Times Blog*, September 17.

Hammond, Phillip E. 1983. "In Search of a Protestant Twentieth Century: American Religion and Power Since 1900." *Review of Religious Research* 24(4): 281–94.

Harper, Marcel. 2007. "The Stereotyping of Nonreligious People by Religious Students: Contents and Subtypes." *Journal for the Scientific Study of Religion* 46(4): 539–52.

Harris, Frederick C. 1994. "Something Within: Religion as a Mobilizer of African-American Political Activism." *Journal of Politics* 56(1): 42–68.

Hart, Stephen. 1996. *What Does the Lord Require? How American Christians Think about Economic Justice*. New Brunswick, NJ: Rutgers.

Hartman, Andrew. 2015. *A War for the Soul of America: A History of the Culture Wars*. Chicago: University of Chicago Press.

Harvey, Paul. 1997. "'These Untutored Masses': The Campaign for Respectability among White and Black Evangelicals in the American South, 1870–1930." *Journal of Religious History* 21(3): 302–17.

Hatemi, Peter K., John R. Alford, John R. Hibbing, Nicholas G. Martin, and London J. Eaves. 2009a. "Is There a 'Party' in Your Genes?" *Political Research Quarterly* 62(3): 584–600.

Hatemi, Peter K., Christopher T. Dawes, Amanda Fros-Keller, Jaime E. Settle, and Brad Verhulst. 2011. "Integrating Social Science and Genetics: News from the Political Front." *Biodemography and Social Biology* 57(1): 67–87.

Hatemi, Peter K., Carolyn L. Funk, Sarah E. Madland, Hermine M. Maes, Judy L. Silberg, Nicholas G. Martin, and London J. Eaves. 2009b. "Genetic and Environmental Transmission of Political Attitudes over a Life Time." *Journal of Politics* 71(3): 1141–56.

Hatemi, Peter K., John R. Hibbing, Sarah E. Medland, Matthew C. Keller, John R. Alford, Kevin B. Smith, Nicholas G. Martin, and Lindon J. Eaves. 2010. "Not by Twins Alone: Using the Extended Family Design to Investigate Genetic Influence on Political Beliefs." *American Journal of Political Science* 54(3): 798–814.

Hatemi, Peter K., and Rose McDermott. 2012. "The Genetics of Politics: Discovery, Challenges, and Progress." *Trends in Genetics* 28(10): 525–33.

Hatemi, Peter K., Sarah E. Medland, Katherine I. Morley, Andrew C. Heath, and Nicholas G. Martin. 2007. "The Genetics of Voting: An Australian Twin Study." *Behavioral Genetics* 37(3): 435–48.

Hersh, Eitan, and Yair Ghitza. 2016. "Mixed Partisan Households and Electoral Participation in the United States." Working Paper. Yale University and Catalist, LLC.

Hetherington, Marc J. 2001. "Resurgent Mass Partisanship: The Role of Elite Polarization." *American Political Science Review* 95(3): 619–31.

Hewstone, Miles. 1990. "The 'Ultimate Attribution Error'? A Review of the Literature on Intergroup Causal Attribution." *European Journal of Social Psychology* 20(4): 311–35.

Hewstone, Miles, Mark Rubin, and Hazel Willis. 2002. "Intergroup Bias." *Annual Review of Psychology* 53(4): 575–604.

Hillygus, D. Sunshine, and Todd G. Shields. 2005. "Moral Issues and Voter Decision Making in the 2004 Presidential Election." *Political Science and Politics* 38(2): 201–9.

Himmelstein, Jerome L. 1983. "The New Right." In *The New Christian Right: Mobilization and Legitimation*, edited by Robert C. Liebman and Robert Wuthnow, 13–30. New York: Aldine.

Hoge, Dean R. 1981. *Converts, Dropouts, and Returnees*. New York: Pilgrim Press.

Hoge, Dean R., Benton Johnson, and Donald A. Luidens. 1993. "Determinants of Church Involvement of Young Adults Who Grew Up in Presbyterian Churches." *Journal for the Scientific Study of Religion* 32(3): 242–55.

Hoge, Dean R., Greg H. Petrillo, and Ella I. Smith. 1982. "Transmission of Religious and Social Values from Parents to Teenage Children." *Journal of Marriage and the Family* 44(3): 569–80.

Hogg, Michael A., and Scott A. Reid. 2006. "Social Identity, Self-Categorization, and the Communication of Group Norms." *Communication Theory* 16(1): 7–30.

Hogg, Michael A., and John C. Turner. 1987. "Intergroup Behaviour, Self-Stereotyping and the Salience of Social Categories." *British Journal of Social Psychology* 26(4): 325–40.

Hojnacki, Marie, and Lawrence Baum. 1992. "'New-Style' Judicial Campaigns and the Voters: Economic Issues and Union Members in Ohio." *Western Political Quarterly* 45(4): 921–48.

Holifield, E. Brooks. 2014. "Understanding Why Americans Seem More Religious Than Other Western Powers." *Huffington Post*, February 15.

Hollander, Barry A. 1998. "The Priming of Religion in Political Attitudes: The Role of Religious Programming." *Journal of Communication & Religion* 21(1): 67–83.

Hout, Michael, and Claude S. Fischer. 2014. "Explaining Why More Americans Have No Religious Preference: Political Backlash and Generational Succession, 1987–2012." *Sociological Science* 1(9): 423–47.

———. 2002. "Why More Americans Have No Religious Preference: Politics and Generations." *American Sociological Review* 67(2): 165–90.

Huber, Gregory A., and Neil Malhotra. 2017. "Political Homophily in Social Relationships: Evidence from Online Dating Behavior." *Journal of Politics* 79(1): 269–83.

Huckfeldt, Robert, Eric Plutzer, and John Sprague. 1993. "Alternative Contexts of Political Behavior: Churches, Neighborhoods, and Individuals." *Journal of Politics* 55(2): 365–81.

Huddy, Leonie. 2011. "From Group Identity to Political Cohesion and Commitment." In *Oxford Handbook of Political Psychology*, 2nd ed., edited by David Sears, Leonie Huddy, and Jack S. Levy, 737–73. New York: Oxford University Press.

———. 2003. "Group Identity and Political Cohesion." In *Oxford Handbook of Political Psychology*, edited by David Sears, Leonie Huddy, and Robert Jervis, 511–58. New York: Oxford University Press.

———. 2001. "From Social to Political Identity: A Critical Examination of Social Identity Theory." *Political Psychology* 22(1): 127–56.

Huddy, Leonie, Lilliana Mason, and Lene Aarøe. 2015. "Expressive Partisanship: Campaign Involvement, Political Emotion, and Partisan Identity." *American Political Science Review* 109(1): 1–17.

Hunsberger, Bruce, and Laurence B. Brown. 1984. "Religious Socialization, Apostasy, and the Impact of Family Background." *Journal for the Scientific Study of Religion* 23(3): 239–51.

Hunter, James D. 2006. "The Enduring Culture War." In *Is There a Culture War? A Dialogue on Values and American Public Life*, edited by James D. Hunter and Alan Wolfe, 10–40. Washington. DC: Brookings Institution Press.

———. 1991. *Culture Wars: The Struggle to Define America*. New York: Basic Books.

———. 1983. *American Evangelicalism: Conservative Religion and the Quandary of Modernity*. New Brunswick, NJ: Rutgers University Press.

Hunter, James Davison, and Alan Wolfe. 2006. *Is There a Culture War? A Dialogue on Values and American Public Life*. Washington, DC: Brookings Institution Press.

Iannaccone, Laurence R. 1994. "Why Strict Churches Are Strong." *American Journal of Sociology* 99(5): 1180–1211.

Ingersoll-Dayton, Berit, Neal Krause, and David Morgan. 2002. "Religious Trajectories and Transitions over the Life Course." *International Journal of Aging and Human Development* 55(1): 51–70.

Islam, Mir R., and Miles Hewstone 1993. "Intergroup Attributions and Affective Consequences in Majority and Minority Groups." *Journal of Personality and Social Psychology* 64(6): 936–50.

Iyengar, Shanto, Gaurav Sood, and Yphtach Lelkes. 2012. "Affect, Not Ideology. A Social Identity Perspective on Polarization." *Public Opinion Quarterly* 76(3): 405–31.

Iyengar, Shanto, and Sean J. Westwood. 2015. "Fear and Loathing across Party Lines: New Evidence on Group Polarization." *American Journal of Political Science* 59(3): 690–707.

Jackson, Lynne M., and Bruce Hunsberger. 1999. "An Intergroup Perspective on Religion and Prejudice." *Journal for the Scientific Study of Religion* 38(4): 509–23.

Jackson, Melinda S. 2011. "Priming the Sleeping Giant: The Dynamics of Latino Political Identity and Vote Choice." *Political Psychology* 32(4): 691–716.

Jacobson, Gary C. 2010. "Perception, Memory, and Partisan Polarization on the Iraq War." *Political Science Quarterly* 125(1): 31–56.

Jelen, Ted G. 1993. "The Political Consequences of Religious Group Attitudes." *Journal of Politics* 55(1): 178–90.

———. 1992. "Political Christianity: A Contextual Analysis." *American Journal of Political Science* 36(3): 178–90.

———. 1991. *The Political Mobilization of Religious Beliefs*. New York: Praeger.

————. 1988. "Changes in the Attitudinal Correlations of Opposition to Abortion, 1977–1985." *Journal for the Scientific Study of Religion* 27(2): 211–28.

————. 1984. "Respect for Life, Sexual Morality, and Opposition to Abortion." *Review of Religious Research* 25(3): 220–31.

Jennings, M. Kent, and Gregory B. Markus. 1984. "Partisan Orientations over the Long Haul: Results from the Three-Wave Political Socialization Study." *American Political Science Review* 78(4): 1000–1018.

Jennings, M. Kent, Gregory B. Markus, Richard G. Niemi, and Laura Stoker. 2005. *Youth-Parent Socialization Panel Study, 1965–1997, Four Waves Combined.* Ann Arbor: University of Michigan, Center for Political Studies/Survey Research Center.

Jennings, M. Kent, and Richard G. Niemi. 1981. *Generations and Politics.* Princeton, NJ: Princeton University Press.

————. 1975. "Continuity and Change in Political Orientations: A Longitudinal Study of Two Generations." *American Political Science Review* 69(4): 1316–35.

————. 1974. *The Political Character of Adolescence: The Influence of Families and Schools.* Princeton, NJ: Princeton University Press.

————. 1968. "The Transmission of Political Values from Parent to Child." *American Political Science Review* 62(1): 169–84.

Jennings, M. Kent, Laura Stoker, and Jake Bowers. 2009. "Politics across Generations: Family Transmission Reexamined." *Journal of Politics* 71(3): 782–99.

Johnson, Jason. 1972. *Econometric Methods.* New York: McGraw-Hill.

Johnson, Megan K., Wade C. Rowatt, and Jordan P. LaBouff. 2012. "Religiosity and Prejudice Revisited: In-Group Favoritism, Out-Group Derogation, or Both?" *Psychology of Religion and Spirituality* 4(2): 154–68.

Johnson, Stephen D., Joseph B. Tamney, and Ronald Burton. 1989. "Pat Robertson: Who Supported His Candidacy for President?" *Journal for the Scientific Study of Religion* 28(4): 387–99.

Johnston, Richard. 2006. "Party Identification: Unmoved Mover or Sum of Preferences?" *Annual Review of Political Science* 9: 329–51.

Jonas, Eva, and Peter Fischer. 2006. "Terror Management and Religion: Evidence that Intrinsic Religiousness Mitigates Worldview Defense Following Mortality Salience." *Journal of Personality and Social Psychology* 91(3): 553–67.

Kam, Cindy D. 2012. "Risk Attitudes and Political Participation." *American Journal of Political Science* 44(4): 750–67.

Kaufmann, Karen M., and John R. Petrocik. 1999. "The Changing Politics of American Men: Understanding the Sources of the Gender Gap." *American Journal of Political Science* 43(3): 864–87.

Kauper, Paul G. 1968. "The Warren Court: Religious Liberty and Church-State Relations." *Michigan Law Review* 67(2): 269–88.

Kaylor, Brian T. 2011. *Presidential Campaign Rhetoric in an Age of Confessional Politics.* Lanham, MD: Lexington Books.

Keele, Luke J. 2005. "The Partisan Roots of Trust in Government." *Journal of Politics* 67(3): 432–51.

Keith, Bruce E., David B. Magelby, Candice J. Nelson, Elizabeth Orr, Mark C. Westlye, and Raymond E. Wolfinger. 1992. *The Myth of the Independent Voter.* Berkeley: University of California Press.

Kellstedt, Lyman. 1988. "The Falwell Issue Agenda: Sources of Support among White Protestant Evangelicals." In *Research in the Social Scientific Study of Religion,* vol. 1, edited by M. Lynn and D. Moberg, 68–92. New York: JAI Press.

Kellstedt, Lyman A., and John C. Green. 1993. "Knowing God's Many People: Denominational Preference and Political Behavior." In *Rediscovering the Religious Factor in American Politics*, edited by David C. Leege and Lyman A. Kellstedt, 53–71. Armonk, NY: M. E. Sharpe.

Kellstedt, Lyman A., John C. Green, James L. Guth, and Corwin E. Smidt. 1996. "Grasping the Essentials: The Social Embodiment of Religion and Political Behavior." In *Religion and the Culture Wars: Dispatches from the Front*, edited by John C. Green, James L. Guth, Corwin E. Smidt and Lyman A. Kellstedt, 174–92. Lanham, MD: Rowman and Littlefield.

———. 1994. "Religion Voting Blocs in the 1992 Election: The Year of the Evangelical." *Sociology of Religion* 55(3): 307–25.

Kellstedt, Lyman A., John C. Green, Corwin E. Smidt, and James L. Guth. 2007. "Faith Transformed: Religion and American Politics from FDR to George W. Bush." In *Religion and American Politics*, 2nd ed., edited by Mark A. Noll and Luke E. Harlow, 269–95. New York: Oxford University Press.

Kellstedt, Lyman A., and Mark A. Noll. 1990. "Religion, Voting for President, and Party Identification, 1948–1984." In *Religion and American Politics*, edited by Mark A. Noll, 355–79. New York: Oxford University Press.

Kellstedt, Lyman A., and Corwin E. Smidt. 1993. "Doctrinal Beliefs and Political Behavior: Views of the Bible." In *Rediscovering the Religious Factor in American Politics*, edited by David C. Leege and Lyman A. Kellstedt, 177–98. Armonk, NY: M. E. Sharpe.

Kendler, Kenneth K., and John Myers. 2009. "A Developmental Twin Study of Church Attendance and Alcohol and Nicotine Consumption: A Model for Analyzing the Changing Impact of Genes and Environment." *American Journal of Psychiatry* 166(10): 1150–55.

Kennedy, John F. 1960a. "Address of Senator John F. Kennedy Accepting the Democratic Party Nomination for the Presidency of the United States—Memorial Coliseum, Los Angeles." July 15. Gerhard Peters and John T. Woolley, *The American Presidency Project*. http://www.presidency.ucsb.edu/ws/?pid=25966.

———. 1960b. "Transcript: JFK's Speech on His Religion." September 12. http://www.npr.org/templates/story/story.php?storyId=16920600.

Kenski, Henry C. 1988. "The Gender Factor in a Changing Electorate." In *The Politics of the Gender Gap: The Social Construction of Political Influence*, edited by Carol McClurg Mueller, 38–60. Newbury Park, CA: Sage.

Kenski, Henry, C., and William Lockwood. 1991. "Catholic Voting Behavior in 1988: A Critical Swing Vote." In *The Bible and the Ballot Box: Religion and Politics in the 1988 Election*, edited by James L. Guth and John C. Green, 173–87. Boulder, CO: Westview Press.

Kinder, Donald R. 1983. "Diversity and Complexity in American Public Opinion." In *Political Science: The State of the Discipline*, edited by A. W. Finifter. Washington, DC: American Political Science Association.

Kinder, Donald R., and Cindy D. Kam. 2010. *Us against Them: Ethnocentric Foundations of American Opinion.* Chicago: University of Chicago Press.

Kirk, Kathy M., Hermine H. Maes, Michael C. Neale, Andrew C. Heath, Nicholas G. Martin, and Lindon J. Eaves. 1999. "Frequency of Church Attendance in Australia and the United States: Models of Family Resemblance." *Twin Research* 2(2): 99–107.

Kirkpatrick, Jeanne. 1976. *The New Presidential Elite: Men and Women in National Politics.* New York: Sage.

Klar, Samara. 2013. "The Influence of Competing Identity Primes on Political Preferences." *Journal of Politics* 75(4): 1108–24.

Klar, Samara, and Yanna Krupnikov. 2016. *Independent Politics*. New York: Cambridge University Press.

Knoll, Benjamin R. 2009. "And Who Is My Neighbor? Religion and Immigration Policy Attitudes." *Journal for the Scientific Study of Religion* 48(2): 313–31.

Koenig, Laura B., Matt McGue, and William G. Iacono. 2008. "Stability and Change in Religiousness during Emerging Adulthood." *Developmental Psychology* 44(2): 532–43.

Koenig, Laura B., Matt McGue, Robert F. Krueger, and Thomas J. Bouchard. 2005. "Genetic and Environmental Influences on Religiousness: Findings for Retrospective and Current Religiousness Ratings." *Journal of Personality* 73(2): 471–88.

Kohut, Andrew, John C. Green, Scott Keeter, and Robert C. Toth. 2000. *The Diminishing Divide. Religion's Changing Role in American Politics*. Washington, DC: Brookings Institution Press.

Kuklinski, James H., and Paul J. Quirk. 2000. "Reconsidering the Rational Public: Cognition, Heuristics, and Mass Opinion." In *Elements of Reason: Cognition, Choice, and the Bounds of Rationality*, edited by Arthur Lupia, Matthew D. McCubbins, and Samuel L. Popkin, 153–82. New York: Cambridge University Press.

Kuo, David. 2006. *Tempting Faith. An Inside Story of Political Seduction*. New York: Free Press.

LaBouff, Jordan P., Wade C. Rowatt, Megan K. Johnson, and Callie Finkle. 2012. "Differences in Attitudes toward Outgroups in Religious and Nonreligious Contexts in a Multinational Sample: A Situational Context Priming Study." *International Journal for the Psychology of Religion* 22(1): 1–9.

Lamb, W. Scott. 2015. "Are Americans Becoming More Religious or More Secular?" *Washington Times*, November 3.

Lassiter, Matthew D. 2008. "Inventing Family Values." In *Rightward Bound: Making America Conservative in the 1970s*, edited by Bruce J. Schulman and Julian E. Zelizer, 13–28. Cambridge, MA: Harvard University Press.

Layman, Geoffrey C. 2001. *The Great Divide: Religious and Cultural Conflict in American Party Politics*. New York: Columbia University Press.

———. 1997. "Religion and Political Behavior in the United States: The Impact of Beliefs, Affiliations, and Commitment from 1980–1994." *Public Opinion Quarterly* 61(2): 288–316.

Layman, Geoffrey C., and Thomas M. Carsey. 2002. "Party Polarization and 'Conflict Extension' in the American Electorate." *American Journal of Political Science* 46(4): 786–802.

Laythe, Brian, Deborah G. Finkel, Robert G. Bringle, and Lee A. Kirkpatrick. 2002. "Religious Fundamentalism as a Predictor of Prejudice: A Two-Component Model." *Journal for the Scientific Study of Religion* 41(4): 623–35.

Lederman, Josh, and Emily Swanson. 2015. "Minorities, Young Americans Still Support Obama, Poll Finds." *The Rundown* (blog), PBS *Newshour*, July 17.

Lee, Jenny J. 2002. "Religion and College Attendance: Change among Students." *Review of Higher Education* 25(4): 369–84.

Lee, Taeku. 2009. "Between Social Theory and Social Science Practice: Toward a New Approach to the Survey Measurement of Race." In *Measuring Identity. A Guide for Social Scientists*, edited by Rawi Abdelal, Yoshiko M. Herrera, Alastair Iain Johnston, and Rose McDermott, 113–44. New York: Cambridge University Press.

———. 2008. "Race, Immigration, and the Identity-to-Politics Link." *Annual Review of Political Science* 11: 457–78.

———. 2002. *Mobilizing Public Opinion. Black Insurgency and Racial Attitudes in the Civil Rights Era*. Chicago: University of Chicago Press.

Leege, David C., and Lyman A. Kellstedt. 1993. *Rediscovering the Religious Factor in American Politics*. Armonk, NY: M. E. Sharpe.

Leege, David C., Kenneth D. Wald, Brian S. Krueger, and Paul D. Mueller. 2002. *The Politics of Cultural Differences: Social Change and Voter Mobilization Strategies in the Post New Deal Period*. Princeton, NJ: Princeton University Press.

Lenski, Gerhard E. 1963. *The Religious Factor: A Sociological Study of Religion's Impact on Politics, Economics, and Family Life*. Garden City, NY: Doubleday.

Lenz, Gabriel S. 2012. *Follow the Leader? How Voters Respond to Politicians' Performance and Policies*. Chicago: University of Chicago Press.

Levendusky, Matthew. 2009. *The Partisan Sort: How Liberals Became Democrats and Conservatives Became Republicans*. Chicago: University of Chicago Press.

Liebman, Robert C., and Robert Wuthnow, eds. 1983. *The New Christian Right: Mobilization and Legitimation*. Hawthorne, NY: Aldine.

Lim, Chaeyoon, Carol Ann MacGregor, and Robert D. Putnam. 2010. "Secular and Liminal: Discovering Heterogeneity among Religious Nones." *Journal for the Scientific Study of Religion* 49(4): 596–618.

Lincoln, Charles E., and Lawrence H. Mamiya. 1990. *The Black Church in the African American Experience*. Durham, NC: Duke University Press.

Lincoln, James R. 1982. "Intra- (and Inter-)Organizational Networks." *Research in the Sociology of Organizations* 1(1): 1–38.

Lipka, Michael. 2015. "5 Key Findings about Religiosity in the U.S.—and How It's Changing." Washington, DC: Pew Research Center, November 3.

Littell, Joseph F. 1976. *Coping with the Mass Media*. Evanston, IL: McDougal.

Lupia, Arthur. 1994. "Shortcuts versus Encyclopedias: Information and Voting Behavior in California Insurance Reform Elections." *American Political Science Review* 88(1): 63–76.

MacCoun, Robert J., James P. Kahan, James Gillespie, and Jeeyang Rhee. 1993. "A Content Analysis of the Drug Legalization Debate." *Journal of Drug Issues* 23(4): 615–29.

Mael, Fred A., and Lois E. Tetrick. 1992. "Identifying Organizational Identification." *Educational and Psychological Measurement* 52(4): 813–24.

Main, Douglas. 2015. "Study: America Becoming More Christian, More Secular." *Newsweek*, May 12.

Malhotra, Neil, and Yotam Margalit. 2010. "Short-Term Communication Effects of Longstanding Dispositions? The Public's Response to the Financial Crisis of 2008." *Journal of Politics* 72(3): 852–67.

Malhotra, Neil, Yotam Margalit, and Cecilia H. Mo. 2013. "Economic Explanations for Opposition to Immigration: Distinguishing between Prevalence and Conditional Impact." *American Journal of Political Science* 57(2): 391–410.

Manheim, Karl. 1952. "The Problem of Generations." In *Essays on the Sociology of Knowledge*, edited by Paul Kecskemeti, 276–320. London: Routledge.

Manza, Jeff K., and Clem Brooks. 1997. "The Religious Factor in U.S. Presidential Elections 1960–1992." *American Journal of Sociology* 130(1): 38–81.

Margolis, Michele F. 2018. "How Far Does Social Group Influence Reach? Elites, Evangelicals, and Immigration Attitudes." *Journal of Politics* 80(3).

———. 2016. "Cognitive Dissonance, Elections, and Religion: How Partisanship and the Political Landscape Shape Religious Behaviors." *Public Opinion Quarterly* 80(3): 717–40.

Markus, Gregory B. 1979. "The Political Environment and the Dynamics of Public Attitudes: A Panel Study." *American Journal of Political Science* 23(3): 338–59.

Markus, Gregory B., and Philip E. Converse. 1979. "A Dynamic Simultaneous Equation Model of Electoral Choice." *American Political Science Review* 73(4): 1055–70.

Marler, Penny Long, and C. Kirk Hadaway. 2002. "'Being Religious' or 'Being Spiritual' in America: A Zero-Sum Proposition?" *Journal for the Scientific Study of Religion* 41(2): 289–300.

Marrapodi, Erin. 2011. "Why Ralph Reed Matters." CNN.com, June 3.

Mason, Liliana. 2015. "'I Disrespectfully Agree': The Differential Effects of Partisan Sorting on Social and Issue Polarization." *American Journal of Political Science* 59(1): 128–45.

Masuoka, Natalie. 2006. "Together They Become One: Examining the Predictors of Panethnic Group Consciousness among Asian Americans and Latinos." *Social Science Quarterly* 87(5): 993–1011.

McAdam, Doug. 1982. *Political Process and the Development of Black Insurgency, 1930–1970.* Chicago: University of Chicago Press.

McBride, Dorothy E., and Janine A. Parry. 2016. *Women's Rights in the USA: Policy Debates and Gender Roles.* 5th ed. New York: Routledge.

McCaffrey, Dawn. 2000. "Competitive Framing Processes in the Abortion Debate: Polarization-Vilification, Frame Saving, and Frame Debunking." *Sociological Quarterly* 41(1): 41–61.

McClerking, Harwood K., and Eric L. McDaniel. 2005. "Belonging and Doing: Political Churches and Black Political Participation." *Political Psychology* 26(5): 721–34.

McCormick, Richard L. 1986. *The Party Period and Public Policy: American Politics from the Age of Jackson to the Progressive Era.* New York: Oxford University Press.

McDaniel, Eric L. 2008. *Politics in the Pews. The Political Mobilization of Black Churches.* Ann Arbor: University of Michigan Press.

McDaniel, Eric L., and Christopher G. Ellison. 2008. "God's Party? Race, Religion and Partisanship over Time." *Political Research Quarterly* 61(2): 180–91.

McDermott, Monika L. 2007. "Voting for Catholic Candidates: The Evolution of a Stereotype." *Social Science Quarterly* 88(4): 953–69.

McGough, Michael. 2016. "Hillary Clinton Tweaks Her 'Safe, Legal, and Rare' Abortion Mantra." *Los Angeles Times*, February 9.

McGreevy, John T. 1997. "Thinking on One's Own: Catholicism in the American Intellectual Imagination, 1928–1960." *Journal of American History* 84(1): 97–131.

McKenzie, Brian D. 2004. "Religious Social Networks, Indirect Mobilization, and African-American Political Participation." *Political Research Quarterly* 57(4): 621–32.

McKenzie, Brian D., and Stella M. Rouse. 2013. "Shades of Faith: Religious Foundations of Political Attitudes among African Americans, Latinos, and Whites." *American Journal of Political Science* 57(1): 218–35.

McLeish, Kendra N., and Robert J. Oxoby. 2009. "Stereotypes in Intertemporal Choice." *Journal of Economic Behavior and Organization* 70(1–2): 135–41.

McPherson, Miller, Lynn Smith-Lovin, and James M. Cook. 2001. "Birds of a Feather: Homophily in Social Networks." *Annual Review of Sociology* 27(1): 415–44.

McQuillan, Kevin. 2004. "When Does Religion Influence Fertility?" *Population and Development Review* 30(1): 25–56.

Messick, David M., and Marilynn B. Brewer. 1983. "Solving Social Dilemmas: A Review." *Review of Personality and Social Psychology* 4(1): 11–44.

Meyer, David S. 2004. "Protest and Political Opportunities." *Annual Review of Sociology* 30: 125–45.

Miller, Alan S., and Takashi Nakamura. 1996. "On the Stability of Church Attendance Patterns during a Time of Demographic Change: 1965–1988." *Journal for the Scientific Study of Religion* 35(3): 275–84.

Miller, Arthur H., Patricia Gurin, Gerald Gurin, and Oksana Malanchuk. 1981. "Group Consciousness and Political Participation." *American Journal of Political Science* 25(3): 494–511.

Miller, Arthur H., and Martin P. Wattenberg. 1984. "Politics from the Pulpit: Religiosity and the 1980 Elections." *Public Opinion Quarterly* 48(1B): 301–17.

Miller, Arthur H., Christopher Wlezien, and Anne Hildreth. 1991. "A Reference Group Theory of Partisan Coalitions." *Journal of Politics* 53(4): 1134–49.

Miller, Monica K., and David R. Hayward. 2008. "Religious Characteristics and the Death Penalty." *Law and Human Behavior* 32(2): 113–23.

Miller, Patrick R., and Pamela Johnston Conover. 2015. "Red and Blue States of Mind Partisan Hostility and Voting in the United States." *Political Research Quarterly* 68(2): 225–39.

Miller, Steven P. 2014. *The Age of Evangelicalism: America's Born-Again Year*. New York: Oxford University Press.

Miller, Warren E. 1991. "Party Identification, Realignment, and Party Voting: Back to the Basics." *American Political Science Review* 85(2): 557–68.

Miller, Warren E., and J. Merrill Shanks. 1996. *The New American Voter*. Cambridge, MA: Harvard University Press.

Moberg, David O. 1977. *The Great Reversal: Evangelism and Social Concern*. Philadelphia: Lippincott.

Mockabee, Stephen T. 2007. "The Political Behavior of American Catholics: Change and Continuity." In *From Pews to Polling Places: Faith and Politics in the American Religious Mosaic*, edited by J. Matthew Wilson, 81–104. Washington, DC: Georgetown University Press.

Mockabee, Stephen T., Joseph Quin Monson, and J. Tobin Grant. 2001. "Measuring Religious Commitment among Catholics and Protestants: A New Approach." *Journal for the Scientific Study of Religion* 40(4): 675–90.

Mockabee, Stephen T., Kenneth D. Wald, and David C. Leege. 2011. "In Search of a Religious Left." In *Improving Public Opinion Surveys: Interdisciplinary Innovation and the American National Election Studies*, edited by John H. Aldrich and Kathleen M. McGraw, 278–98. Princeton, NJ: Princeton University Press.

Mondak, Jeffrey J. 1993. "Source Cues and Policy Approval: The Cognitive Dynamics of Public Support for the Reagan Agenda." *American Journal of Political Science* 37(1): 186–212.

Monson, J. Quin, and John B. Oliphant. 2007. "Microtargeting and the Instrumental Mobilization of Religious Conservatives." In *A Matter of Faith: Religion in the 2004 Presidential Election*, edited by David E. Campbell, 95–119. Washington, DC: Brookings Institution Press.

Morgan, Edmund S. 1967. "The Puritan Ethic and the American Revolution." *William and Mary Quarterly* 24(1): 3–43.

Morgan, Stephen L., and Christopher Winship. 2007. *Counterfactuals and Causal Inference*. New York: Cambridge University Press.

Morone, James A. 2003. *Hellfire Nation: The Politics of Sin in American History*. New Haven, CT: Yale University Press.

Morris, Aldon D. 1984. *The Origin of the Civil Rights Movement: Black Communities Organizing for Change*. New York: Free Press.

Moyers, Bill. 2012. "The Resurrection of Ralph Reed." *Moyers and Company*, August 15.

Mullainathan, Sendhil, and Ebonya Washington. 2009. "Sticking with Your Vote: Cognitive Dissonance and Political Attitudes." *American Economic Journal: Applied Economics* 1(1): 86–111.

Mulligan, Kenneth. 2006. "Pope John II and Catholic Opinion toward the Death Penalty and Abortion." *Social Science Quarterly* 87(3): 739–53.

Munger, Michael, and Thomas Schaller. 1997. "The Prohibition-Repeal Amendments: A Natural Experiment in Interest Group Influence." *Public Choice* 90(1): 139–63.

Munro, Geoffrey D., Carrie Weih, and Jeffrey Tsai. 2010. "Motivated Suspicion. Asymmetrical Attributions of the Behavior of Political Ingroup and Outgroup Members." *Basic and Applied Social Psychology* 32(2): 173–84.

Myers, Scott M. 1996. "An Interactive Model of Religiosity Inheritance: The Importance of Family Context." *American Sociological Review* 61(3): 858–66.

Myrdal, Gunnar. 1944. *An American Dilemma: The Negro Problem and American Democracy.* New York: Harper and Row.

National Center for Health Statistics. "Births by Age and Race of Mother." *National Vital Statistics Reports* 64(1).

Newport, Frank. 2014. "Mississippi Most Religious State, Vermont Least Religious." Gallup Poll, February 3.

———. 1979. "The Religious Switcher in the United States." *American Sociological Review* 44(4): 528–52.

Newport, Frank, and Joy Wilke. 2013. "Desire for Children Still Norm in U.S." *Gallup*, September 25.

Niemi, Richard G., and M. Kent Jennings. 1991. "Issues and Inheritance in the Formation of Party Identification." *American Journal of Political Science* 35(4): 970–88.

Niemi, Richard G., and Herbert F. Weisberg. 2001. *Controversies in Voting Behavior.* 4th ed. Washington, DC: Congressional Quarterly Press.

Nisbett, Richard E., and Lee Ross. 1980. *Human Inference: Strategies and Shortcomings of Social Judgment.* Englewood Cliffs, NJ: Prentice Hall.

Noel, Hans. 2013. *Political Ideologies and Political Parties in America.* New York: Cambridge University Press.

Norrander, Barbara. 1999. "The Evolution of the Gender Gap." *Public Opinion Quarterly* 63(4): 566–76.

———. 1997. "The Independence Gap and the Gender Gap." *Public Opinion Quarterly* 61(3): 464–76.

Norris, Pippa, and Ronald Inglehart. 2011. *Sacred and Secular: Religion and Politics Worldwide.* New York: Cambridge University Press.

Nteta, Tatishe M., and Jill S. Greenlee. 2013. "A Change Is Gonna Come: Generational Membership and White Racial Attitudes in the 21st Century." *Political Psychology* 34(6): 877–97.

Nteta, Tatishe M., and Kevin J. Wallsten. 2012. "Preaching to the Choir? Religious Leaders and American Opinion on Immigration Reform." *Social Science Quarterly* 93(4): 891–910.

Office of the Press Secretary of the White House. 2003. "President Bush Signs Partial Birth Abortion Ban Act of 2003." https://georgewbush-whitehouse.archives.gov/news/releases/2003/11/20031105-1.html.

Oldfield, Duane M. 1996. *The Right and the Righteous: The Christian Right Confronts the Republican Party.* Lanham, MD: Rowan and Littlefield.

———. 1986. *The Right and the Righteous: The Christian Right Confronts the Republican Party.* Lanham, MD: Rowman and Littlefield.

Oldmixon, Elizabeth Anne, and Brian Robert Calfano. 2007. "The Religious Dynamics of Decision Making on Gay Rights Issues in the US House of Representatives." *Journal for the Scientific Study of Religion* 46(1): 55–70.

Olson, Laura R., Wendy Cadge, and James T. Harrison. 2006. "Religion and Public Opinion about Same-Sex Marriage." *Social Science Quarterly* 87(2): 340–60.

Olson, Laura R., and John C. Green. 2006. "The Religion Gap." *Political Science & Politics* 39(3): 455–59.

Osborne, Danny, David O. Sears, and Nicholas A. Valentino. 2011. "The End of the Solidly Democratic South: The Impressionable-Years Hypothesis." *Political Psychology* 32(1): 81–108.

Page, Benjamin, and Robert Y. Shapiro. 2010. *The Rational Public: Fifty Years of Trends in Americans' Policy Preferences*. Chicago: University of Chicago Press.

Page, Benjamin, Robert Y. Shapiro, and Glenn Dempsey. 1987. "What Moves Public Opinion?" *American Political Science Review* 81(1): 23–44.

Patrikios, Stratos. 2013. "Self-Stereotyping as 'Evangelical Republican': An Empirical Test." *Politics and Religion* 6(4): 800–822.

———. 2008. "American Republican Religion? Disentangling the Causal Link between Religion and Politics in the US." *Political Behavior* 30(3): 367–89.

Perkins, Wesley, H. 1987. "Parental Religion and Alcohol Use Problems as Intergenerational Predictors of Problem Drinking among College Students." *Journal for the Scientific Study of Religion* 26(3): 340–57.

Perl, Paul, and Mary E. Bendyna. 2002. "Perceptions of Anti-Catholic Bias and Political Party Identification among US Catholics." *Journal for the Scientific Study of Religion* 41(4): 653–68.

Pettigrew, Thomas F. 1979. "The Ultimate Attribution Error: Extending Allport's Cognitive Analysis of Prejudice." *Personality and Social Psychology Bulletin* 5(4): 461–76.

Petts, Richard J. 2009. "Trajectories of Religious Participation from Adolescence to Young Adulthood." *Journal for the Scientific Study of Religion* 48(3): 552–71.

Pew Research Center. 2016a. "How the Faithful Voted: A Preliminary 2016 Analysis." November 9.

———. 2016b. "The Parties on the Eve of the 2016 Election: Two Coalitions, Moving Further Apart." September 13.

———. 2012. "How the Faithful Voted." November 7.

———. 2009. "Faith in Flux." April 27.

———. 2008. "How the Faithful Voted." November 10.

Pichon, Isabelle, Giulio Boccato, and Vassilis Saroglou. 2007. "Nonconscious Influences of Religion on Prosociality: A Priming Study." *European Journal of Social Psychology* 37(5): 1032–45.

Ploch, Donald R., and Donald W. Hastings. 1998. "Effects of Parental Church Attendance, Current Family Status, and Religious Salience on Church Attendance." *Review of Religious Research* 39(4): 309–20.

Popkin, Samuel L. 1991. *The Reasoning Voter: Communication and Persuasion in Presidential Campaigns*. Chicago: University of Chicago Press.

Preston, Jesse Lee, and Ryan S. Ritter. 2013. "Different Effects of Religion and God on Prosociality with the Ingroup and Outgroup." *Personality and Social Psychology Bulletin* 39(11): 1471–83.

Preston, Jesse Lee, Ryan S. Ritter, and J. Ivan Hernandez. 2010. "Principles of Religious Prosociality: A Review and Reformulation." *Social and Personality Compass* 4(8): 574–90.

Putnam, Robert D., and David E. Campbell. 2010. *American Grace: How Religion Divides and Unites Us*. New York: Simon and Schuster.

Randolph-Seng, Brandon, and Michael E. Nielsen. 2007. "Honesty: One Effect of Primed Religious Representations." *International Journal for the Psychology of Religion* 17(4): 303–15.

Reichley, James A. 1987. "The Evangelical and Fundamentalist Revolt." In *Piety and Politics: Evangelicals and Fundamentalists Confront the World*, edited by Richard J. Neuhaus and Michael Cromartie, 69–95. Washington, DC: Ethics and Public Policy Center.

———. 1986. "Religion and the Future of American Politics." *Political Science Quarterly* 101(1): 23–47.

Republican Party Platform. 1984. "Republican Party Platform of 1984," August 20. Gerhard Peters and John T. Woolley, *The American Presidency Project*. http://www.presidency.ucsb.edu/ws/?pid=25845.

———. 1980. "Republican Party Platform of 1980," July 15. Gerhard Peters and John T. Woolley, *The American Presidency Project*. http://www.presidency.ucsb.edu/ws/?pid=25844.

———. 1976. "Republican Party Platform of 1976," August 18. Gerhard Peters and John T. Woolley, *The American Presidency Project*. http://www.presidency.ucsb.edu/ws/?pid=25843.

Rinalta, Marvin. 1968. "Generations in Politics." In *Encyclopedia of the Social Sciences*, edited by David L. Sills, 69–95. New York: Macmillan.

Roccas, Sonia, and Marilynn Brewer. 2002. "Social Identity Complexity." *Personality and Social Psychology Review* 6(1): 88–106.

Roof, Wade C. 1993. *A Generation of Seekers: The Spiritual Journeys of the Baby Boom Generation*. New York: Harper Collins.

———. 1979. "Concepts and Indicators of Religious Commitment: A Critical Review." In *The Religious Dimension: New Directions in Quantitative Research*, edited by Robert Wuthnow, 17–45. New York: Elsevier.

Rosenbaum, Paul R. 2002. *Design of Observational Studies*. New York: Springer.

Rotolo, Thomas. 2000. "A Time to Join, a Time to Quit: The Influence of Life Cycle Transitions on Voluntary Association Membership." *Social Forces* 78(3): 1133–61.

Rounding, Kevin, Albert Lee, Jill A. Jacobson, and Li-Jun Ji. 2012. "Religion Replenishes Self-Control." *Psychological Science* 23(6): 635–42.

Rowatt, Wade C., Lewis M. Franklin, and Marla Cotton. 2005. "Patterns and Personality Correlates of Implicit and Explicit Attitudes toward Christians and Muslims." *Journal for the Scientific Study of Religion* 44(1): 29–43.

Rowatt, Wade C., Jordan LaBouff, Megan K. Johnson, Paul Froese, and Jo-Ann Tsang. 2009. "Associations among Religiousness, Social Attitudes, and Prejudice in a National Random Sample of American Adults." *Psychology of Religion and Spirituality* 1(1): 14–24.

Sances, Michael, and Charles Stewart III. 2015. "Partisanship and Voter Confidence, 2000–2010." *Electoral Studies* (40): 176–88.

Sandomirsky, Sharon, and John Wilson. 1990. "Processes of Disaffiliation: Religious Mobility among Men and Women." *Social Forces* 68(4): 1211–29.

Saroglou, Vassilis, Olivier Corneille, and Patty Van Cappellen. 2009. "'Speak, Lord, Your Servant Is Listening': Religious Priming Activates Submissive Thoughts and Behaviors." *International Journal for the Psychology of Religion* 19(3): 143–54.

Schaffner, Brian F., and Matthew J. Streb. 2002. "The Partisan Heuristic in Low Information Elections." *Public Opinion Quarterly* 66(4): 559–81.

Schleifer, Cyrus, and Mark Chaves. 2017. "Family Formation and Religious Service Attendance: Untangling Marital and Parental Effects." *Sociological Methods and Research* 46(1): 125–52.

Schonhardt-Bailey, Cheryl. 2008. "The Congressional Debate on Partial-Birth Abortion: Constitutional Gravitas and Moral Passion." *British Journal of Political Science* 38(3): 383–410.

Sears, David O. 1990. "Whither Political Socialization Research? The Question of Persistence." In *Political Socialization, Citizenship, Education, and Democracy*, edited by Orit Ichikov, 69–97. New York: Teachers College Press.

———. 1983. "The Persistence of Early Political Predispositions: The Roles of Attitude Object and Life Stage." In *Review of Personality and Social Psychology*, vol. 4, edited by Ladd Wheeler and Phillip Shaver, 79–116. Thousand Oaks, CA: Sage.

———. 1975. "Political Socialization." In *Handbook of Political Science*, vol. 2, edited by Fred I. Greenstein and Nelson W. Polsby, 93–153. Reading, MA: Addison-Wesley.

Sears, David O., and Carolyn L. Funk. 1999. "Evidence of Long-Term Persistence of Adults' Political Predispositions." *Journal of Politics* 61(1): 1–28.

———. 1990. "The Limited Effect of Economic Self-Interest on the Political Attitudes of the Mass Public." *Journal of Behavioral Economics* 19(3): 247–71.

Sears, David O., and Nicholas A. Valentino. 1997. "Politics Matters: Political Events as Catalysts for Preadult Socialization." *American Political Science Review* 91(1): 45–65.

Settle, Jaime E., Christopher T. Dawes, and James H. Fowler. 2009. "The Heritability of Partisan Attachment." *Political Research Quarterly* 62(3): 601–13.

Seul, Jeffrey R. 1999. "Ours Is the Way of God': Religion, Identity, and Intergroup Conflict." *Journal of Peace Research* 36(5): 553–69.

Shariff, Azim F., and Ara Norenzayan. 2007. "God Is Watching You: Priming God Concepts Increases Prosocial Behavior in an Anonymous Economic Game." *Psychological Science* 18(9): 803–9.

Sharot, Stephan, Hannah Ayalon, and Eliezer Ben-Rafael. 1986. "Secularization and the Diminishing Decline of Religion." *Review of Religious Research* 27(3): 193–207.

Sherkat, Darren E. 1998. "Counterculture or Continuity? Competing Influences on Baby Boomers' Religious Orientations and Participation." *Social Forces* 76(3): 1087–1115.

Sherkat, Darren E., and T. Jean Blocker. 1997. "Explaining the Political and Personal Consequences of Protest." *Social Forces* 75(3): 1049–70.

Sherkat, Darren E., and John Wilson. 1995. "Preferences, Constraints, and Choices in Religious Switching and Apostasy." *Social Forces* 73(3): 993–1026.

Shih, Margaret, Todd L. Pittinsky, and Nalini Ambady. 1999. "Stereotype Susceptibility: Identity Salience and Shifts in Quantitative Performance." *Psychological Science* 10(1): 80–83.

Shingles, Richard D. 1981. "Black Consciousness and Political Participation: The Missing Link." *American Political Science Review* 75(1): 76–91.

Shively, W. Phillips. 1979. "The Development of Party Identification among Adults: Exploration of a Functional Model." *American Political Science Review* 73(4): 1039–54.

Shupe, Anson, and William Stacey. 1983. "The Moral Majority Constituency." In *The New Christian Right: Mobilization and Legitimation*, edited by Robert C. Liebman and Robert Wuthnow, 104–16. New York: Aldine.

Sigelman, Lee. 1991. "Jews and the 1988 Election: More of the Same?" In *The Bible and the Ballot Box: Religion and Politics in the 1988 Election*, edited by John C. Green and James L. Guth, 188–203. Boulder, CO: Westview Press.

Simon, Bernd, and Bert Klandermans. 2001. "Politicized Collective Identity: A Social Psychological Analysis." *American Psychologist* 56(4): 319–31.

Sinclair, Betsy. 2012. *The Social Citizen*. Chicago: University of Chicago Press.

Smidt, Corwin E., Kevin R. den Dulk, Bryan T. Froehle, James M. Penning, Stephen V. Monsma, and Douglas L. Koopman. 2010. *The Disappearing God Gap? Religion in the 2008 Presidential Election*. New York: Oxford University Press.

Smidt, Corwin E., Lyman A. Kellstedt, and James L. Guth. 2009. "The Role of Religion in American Politics: Explanatory Theories and Associated Analytical and Measurement Issues." In *The Oxford Handbook of Religion and American Politics*, edited by Corwin E. Smidt, Lyman A. Kellstedt, and James L. Guth, 3–42. New York: Oxford University Press.

Smith, Christian. 2009. *Souls in Transition: The Religions and Spiritual Lives of Emerging Adults*. New York: Oxford University Press.

———. 2005. *Soul Searching: The Religious and Spiritual Lives of American Teenagers*. New York: Oxford University Press.

Smith, Christian, Melinda Lundquist Denton, Robert Faris, and Mark D. Regnerus. 2002. "Mapping American Adolescent Religious Participation." *Journal for the Scientific Study of Religion* 41(4): 597–612.

Smith, Christian, David Sikkink, and Jason Bailey. 1998. "Devotion in Dixie and Beyond: A Test of the 'Shibley Thesis' on the Effects of Regional Origin and Migration on Individual Religiosity." *Journal for the Scientific Study of Religion* 37(3): 494–506.

Smith, Gregory A. 2008. *Politics in the Parish: The Political Influence of Catholic Priests*. Washington, DC: Georgetown University Press.

Smith, Kevin B., Douglas R. Oxley, Matthew V. Hibbing, John R. Alford, and John R. Hibbing. 2011. "Linking Genetics and Political Attitudes: Reconceptualizing Political Ideology." *Political Psychology* 32(3): 369–97.

Smith, Mark A. 2015. *Secular Faith: How Culture Has Trumped Religion in American Politics*. Chicago: University of Chicago Press.

Sniderman, Paul M. 1993. "The New Look in Public Opinion Research." In *The State of the Discipline II*, edited by Ada W. Finifter, 219–45. Washington, DC: American Political Science Association.

Sniderman, Paul M., Richard A. Brody, and Philip E. Tetlock. 1991. *Reasoning and Choice: Explorations in Political Psychology*. Cambridge: Cambridge University Press.

Sniderman, Paul M., and Louk Hagendoorn. 2007. *When Ways of Life Collide: Multiculturalism and Its Discontents in the Netherlands*. Princeton, NJ: Princeton University Press.

Sniderman, Paul M., and Matthew S. Levendusky. 2007. "An Institutional Theory of Political Choice." In *Oxford Handbook of Political Behavior*, edited by Russell J. Dalton and Hans-Dieter Klingemann, 437–56. New York: Oxford University Press.

Srull, Thomas K., and Robert S. Wyer Jr. 1979. "The Role of Category Accessibility in the Interpretation of Information about Persons: Some Determinants and Implications." *Journal of Personality and Social Psychology* 37(10): 1660–72.

Stanley, Harold W., William T. Bianco, and Richard G. Niemi. 1986. "Partisanship and Group Support over Time: A Multivariate Analysis." *American Political Science Review* 80(3): 969–76.

Stanley, Harold W., and Richard G. Niemi. 1991 "Partisanship and Group Support, 1952–1988." *American Politics Quarterly* 19(2): 189–210.

Stark, Rodney, and William S. Bainbridge. 1985. *The Future of Religion: Secularization, Revival, and Cult Formation*. Berkeley: University of California Press.

Steensland, Brian, Jerry Z. Park, Mark D. Regnerus, Lynn D. Robinson, W. Bradford Wilcox, and Robert D. Woodberry. 2000. "The Measure of American Religion: Toward Improving the State of the Art." *Social Forces* 79(1): 291–318.

Stewart, Abigail J., Isis H. Settles, and Nicholas J. G. Winters. 1998. "Women and Social Movements of the 1960s: Activists, Engaged Observers, and Nonparticipants." *Political Psychology* 19(1): 63–94.

Stolzenberg, Ross, M., Mary Blair-Loy, and Linda L. Waite. 1995. "Religious Participation in Early Adulthood: Age and Family Life Cycle Effects on Church Membership." *American Sociological Review* 60(1): 84–104.

Stump, Roger W. 1984. "Regional Migration and Religious Commitment in the United States." *Journal for the Scientific Study of Religion* 23(3): 292–303.

Swierenga, Robert P. 2009. "Religion and American Voting Behavior, 1830s to 1930s." In *The Oxford Handbook of Religion and American Politics*, edited by James L. Guth, Lyman, A. Kellstedt, and Corwin E. Smidt, 69–94. New York: Oxford University Press.

———. 1990. "Ethnoreligious Political Behavior in the Mid-Nineteenth Century: Voting, Values, and Cultures." In *Religion and American Politics*, edited by Mark A. Noll. New York: Oxford University Press.

Tajfel, Henri. 1982. "Social Psychology of Intergroup Relations." *Annual Review of Psychology* 33(1): 1–39.

———. 1981. *Human Groups and Social Categories: Studies in Social Psychology.* Cambridge: Cambridge University Press.

———. 1979. "An Integrative Theory of Intergroup Conflict." In *The Social Psychology of Intergroup Relations*, edited by William G. Austin and Stephen Worchel, 33–47. Monterey, CA: Brooks-Cole.

———. 1970. "Experiments in Intergroup Discrimination." *Scientific American* 223(5): 96–102.

Tajfel, Henri, and John C. Turner. 1986. "The Social Identity Theory of Intergroup Behaviour." In *Psychology of Intergroup Relations*, edited by Stephen Worchel and William G. Austin, 7–24. Chicago: Nelson.

Tate, Katherine. 1994. *From Protest to Politics: The New Black Voters in American Elections.* Cambridge, MA: Harvard University Press and Russell Sage Foundation.

Taylor, Robert J., and Linda M. Chatters. 1988. "Church Members as a Source of Informal Social Support." *Review of Religious Research* 30(2): 193–204.

Tedin, Kent L. 1974. "The Influence of Parents on the Political Attitudes of Adolescents." *American Political Science Review* 68(4): 1579–92.

Tesler, Michael. 2015. "Priming Dispositions and Changing Policy Positions: An Account of When Mass Opinion Is Primed or Changed." *American Journal of Political Science* 59(4): 806–24.

Thornton, Arland, William G. Axinn, and Daniel H. Hill. 1992. "Reciprocal Effects of Religiosity, Cohabitation, and Marriage." *American Journal of Sociology* 98(3): 628–51.

Tourangeau, Roger J., Lance Rips, and Kenneth Rasinski. 2000. *The Psychology of Survey Response.* Cambridge, MA: Harvard University Press.

Truett, K. R., L. J. Eaves, J. M. Meyer, A. C. Heath, and N. G Martin. 1992. "Religion and Education as Mediators of Attitudes: A Multivariate Analysis." *Behavioral Genetics* 22(1): 43–62.

Turner, John C., Michael A. Hogg, Penelope J. Oakes, Stephen D. Reicher, and Margaret S. Wetherell. 1987. *Rediscovering the Social Group: A Self-Categorization Theory.* Oxford: Basil Blackwell.

Uecker, Jeremy E., Mark D. Regnerus, and Margaret L. Vaaler. 2007. "Losing My Religion: The Social Sources of Religious Decline in Early Adulthood." *Social Forces* 85(4): 1667–92.

Vail, Kenneth E., Zachary K. Rothschild, Dave R. Weise, Sheldon Solomon, Tom Pyszczynski, and Jeff Greenberg. 2010. "A Terror Management Analysis of the Psychological Functions of Religion." *Personality and Social Psychology Review* 14(1): 84–94.

Vaillancourt, Pauline M. 1973. "Stability of Children's Survey Responses." *Public Opinion Quarterly* 37(3): 373–87.

Valentino, Nicholas, and David O. Sears. 1998. "Event-Driven Political Socialization and the Preadult Socialization of Partisanship." *Political Behavior* 20(2): 127–54.

Valenzuela, Ali Adam. 2014. "Tending the Flock. Latino Religious Commitments and Political Preferences." *Political Research Quarterly* 67(4): 930–42.

Vance, Todd, Hermine H. Maes, and Kenneth S. Kendler. 2010. "Genetic and Environmental Influences on Multiple Dimensions of Religiosity: A Twin Study." *Journal of Nervous and Mental Disease* 198(1): 755–61.

Van Tyne, Claude H. 1913. "Influence of the Clergy, and of Religious and Sectarian Forces, on the American Revolution." *American Historical Review* 19(1): 44–64.

Verba, Sidney, Kay L. Schlozman, and Henry E. Brady. 1995. *Voice and Equality: Civic Voluntarism in American Politics*. Cambridge, MA: Harvard University Press.

Wakin, Daniel. 2001. "Attacks Spur a Surge of Interest in Religion; As Attendance at Services Rises, Clerics Hope for a General Moral Uplift." *New York Times*, September 30.

Wald, Kenneth D. 1992. *Religion and Politics in the United States*. 2nd ed. Washington, DC: Congressional Quarterly Press.

Wald, Kenneth D., James W. Button, and Barbara A. Rienzo. 1996. "The Politics of Gay Rights in American Communities: Explaining Antidiscrimination Ordinances and Policies." *American Journal of Political Science* 40(4): 1152–78.

Wald, Kenneth D., and Allison Calhoun-Brown. 2011. *Religion and Politics in the United States*. Washington, DC: Congressional Quarterly Press.

Wald, Kenneth D., Dennis E. Owen, and Samuel S. Hill Jr. 1988. "Churches as Political Communities." *American Political Science Review* 82(2): 531–48.

Wald, Kenneth D., and Corwin E. Smidt. 1993. "Measurement Strategies in the Study of Religion and Politics." In *Rediscovering the Religious Factor in American Politics*, edited by David C. Leege and Lyman A. Kellstedt, 26–49. New York: M. E. Sharpe.

Walsh, Andrew D. 2000. *Religion, Economics, and Public Policy. Ironies, Tragedies, and Absurdities of the Contemporary Culture Wars*. Westport, CT: Praeger.

Wasserman, Ira M. 1989. "Prohibition and Ethnocultural Conflict: The Missouri Prohibition Referendum of 1918." *Social Science Quarterly* 70(4): 886–901.

Wattenberg, Martin P. 1986. *The Decline of American Political Parties: 1952–1984*. Cambridge, MA: Harvard University Press.

Weber, Christopher, and Matthew Norton. 2012. "Courting Christians: How Political Candidates Prime Religious Considerations in Campaign Ads." *Journal of Politics* 74(2): 400–413.

Westholm, Anders. 1999. "The Perceptual Pathway: Tracing the Mechanism of Political Value Transfer across Generations." *Political Psychology* 20(3): 525–52.

Westholm, Anders, and Richard G. Niemi. 1998. "Political Institutions and Political Socialization." *Comparative Politics* 25(1): 25–41.

White, Theodore H. 1973. *The Making of the President, 1972*. New York: Atheneum.

Whitley, Bernard E. 2009. "Religiosity and Attitudes toward Lesbians and Gay Men: A Meta-Analysis." *International Journal for the Psychology of Religion* 19(1): 21–38.

Wilcox, Clyde. 1992a. *God's Warriors: The Christian Right in Twentieth-Century America*. Baltimore, MD: Johns Hopkins University Press.

———. 1992b. "Race, Religion, Region, and Abortion Attitudes." *Sociology of Religion* 53(1): 97–105.

———. 1988. "The Christian Right in Twentieth Century America: Continuity and Change." *Review of Politics* 50(4): 659–81.

Wilcox, Clyde, Mark J. Rozell, and Roland Gunn. 1996. "Religious Coalitions in the New Christian Right." *Social Science Quarterly* 77(3): 543–58.

Wilcox, W. Bradford. 1998. "Conservative Protestant Childrearing: Authoritarian or Authoritative?" *American Sociological Review* 63(6): 796–809.

Wilcox, W. Bradford, and Nicholas H. Wolfinger. 2007. "Then Comes Marriage? Religion, Race, and Marriage in Urban America." *Social Science Research* 36(2): 569–89.

Williams, Daniel K. 2010. "Jerry Falwell's Sunbelt Politics: The Regional Origins of the Moral Majority." *Journal of Policy History* 22(2): 125–47.

Willits, Fern K., and Donald M. Crider. 1989. "Church Attendance and Traditional Religious Beliefs in Adolescence and Young Adulthood: A Panel Study." *Review of Religious Research* 31(1): 68–81.

Wilson, J. Matthew. 2007. "The Changing Catholic Voter: Comparing Responses to John Kennedy in 1960 and John Kerry in 2004." In *A Matter of Faith? Religion in the 2004 Presidential Election*, edited by David E. Campbell, 163–79. Washington, DC: Brookings Institution Press.

Wilson, John, and Darren E. Sherkat. 1994. "Returning to the Fold." *Journal for the Scientific Study of Religion* 33(2): 148–61.

Wolfe, Alan. 2006. "The Culture War that Never Came." In *Is There a Culture War? A Dialogue on Values and American Public Life*, edited by James D. Hunter and Alan Wolfe, 41–73. Washington, DC: Brookings Institution Press.

Wuthnow, Robert. 2007. *After the Baby Boomers: How Twenty- and Thirty-Somethings Are Shaping the Future of American Religion.* Princeton, NJ: Princeton University Press.

———. 1989. *The Struggle for America's Soul: Evangelicals, Liberals, and Secularism.* Grand Rapids, MI: Eerdmans.

———. 1988. *The Restructuring of American Religion: Society and Faith since World War II.* Princeton, NJ: Princeton University Press.

Young, Robert L. 1992. "Religious Orientation, Race and Support for the Death Penalty." *Journal for the Scientific Study of Religion* 31(1): 76–87.

Ysseldyk, Renate, Kimberly Matheson, and Hymie Anisman. 2010. "Religiosity as Identity: Toward an Understanding of Religion from a Social Identity Perspective." *Personality and Social Psychology Review* 14(1): 60–71.

Zaleski, Ellen H., and Kathleen M. Schiaffino. 2000. "Religiosity and Sexual Risk-Taking Behavior during the Transition to College." *Journal of Adolescence* 23(2): 223–27.

Zaller, John. 1992. *The Nature and Origins of Mass Opinion.* New York: Cambridge University Press.

Zaller, John, and Stanley Feldman. 1992. "A Simple Theory of Survey Response: Answering Questions versus Revealing Preferences." *American Journal of Political Science* 36(3): 579–616.

Zezima, Katie. 2008. "More Women than Ever Are Childless, Census Finds." *New York Times*, August 18.

Zuckerman, Alan S., Nicholas A. Valentino, and Ezra W. Zuckerman. 1994. "A Structural Theory of Vote Choice: Social and Political Networks and Electoral Flows in Britain and the United States." *Journal of Politics* 56(4): 1008–33.

INDEX

pact on, 6, 85, 87, 97, 101, 108, 124–25, 143, 190, 194–95; religiously sorted electorate, 199; religious socialization, 199; social group influence, 5; social identity, 189; as tangential to people's lives, 36
Presbyterians, 42
presidential campaign (1960), 179–81, 186; religious responses to, 182–83, 185
presidential election (2004), 103–4, 129, 136; issues of, 113–17, 119–20; religion and morals in, 126
Prohibition, 27
Protestants, 128, 150, 202; interpretive communities, 149; religious denomination, 61. *See also* evangelical Protestants; mainline Protestants
public religion, 12
public sphere, 29, 35, 59; conservative Christianity, emphasis on, 12–13; and religion, 2
Puritans, 28
Putnam, Robert D., 28, 58, 149, 161

Reagan, Ronald, 30–31, 34, 110; religious voters, appeal to, 32–33; Year of the Bible, 32
Reed, Ralph, 108–9, 193
Regnerus, Mark D., 42–43
religion: as family activity, 39; God gap, 2, 20; group interest, 36; as hereditary trait, 35–36; indoctrination, business of, 36; as mental phenomenon, 10; and morals, 126; partisan identities, 2–3; as political threat, 32–33; politicization of, 27; and politics, 2–3, 5, 31, 58–59, 100, 111, 167–68, 192, 204; shared identity, 10–11; social framework, 54; as social identity, 12; as social phenomenon, 10–12; stable identity of, 58
religiosity, 2, 88, 96, 99, 104, 191–92, 194, 202; and children, 63; partisan identification, 24, 36–37; and partisanship, 86, 176, 196; political decisions, effect on, 85; and politics, 24, 87; religious upbringing, 80; social aspects of, 101
religiosity gap, 22–23, 35, 59–60, 88–89, 100, 127, 147, 195, 199; in American politics, 129; culture wars, 25; elite-level changes, 191–92; ethnoreligious model, 24–25; and homophily, 201;

life-cycle theory, 191; as relatively new, 24–25, 27; restructuring principle, 25
religious broadcasting, 30
religious fold: family formation and increased religious participation, 47; return to, 46–48, 75–78; traditional family, as part of, 47
religious identification, 74–77, 82, 85, 97, 123–24, 136; ebbing and flowing of, 40; as not static, 40; religious attachment, 45; religious involvement, 39; social and personal dimensions of, 84
religious identity, 48, 60, 100, 102, 106, 190; as changeable, 37–38; church attendance, 12; complexity of, 12; group norms, adhering to, 61; as less stable, 37; meaning of, 9–13; older adults and stable levels of, 47; parents of teenagers, 47–48; and partisanship, 190–91; and politics, 20; religious attachment, 48; religious faith, identifying with, 12, 47; stabilization of, 52–53, 104; strength of, 61; as unique, 12
religious life-course model, 48
religious nonidentification, 83; growth of, 20–21, 42
Religious Roundtable, 30; National Affairs Briefing, 32
religious socialization, 39
religious socialization theory, 63, 66, 75, 80, 89
religious sorting: changing demographics, 202; homophily, exacerbating of, 200–201; liberal churches, presence of, 201; limits to, 201–2; partisan cues, 202; partisan driven, 130, 190, 204; political Independents, 202
Republicans, 4, 19, 38, 50, 52, 55, 59, 65–66, 71–74, 78, 83–85, 88–89, 93–94, 101–2, 107, 109, 123–24, 132, 141, 148, 190, 193, 195, 198–99, 201, 203–4; abortion, stance on, 33–34; African Americans, 16, 22, 147, 152; biblical literalists, identification with, 20; Christian conservatism, 59, 76; church attendance, 27, 35, 86–87, 143–44; church attendance gap, 80; churchgoers, identification with, 1; as conservative, 7–9, 12; as culturally conservative, 146; Democratic South's, shift toward Republican Party, 90–91; and Democrats, religious difference

changing, 71; religious involvement,
drop in, 67–69, 75
Youth-Parent Socialization Panel Study
(YPSP), 65–67, 71–72, 74–76, 80–85,
92, 94, 95, 102, 116, 120, 126, 133,
135, 196; African American study,

152–53, 156, 159–60, 176, 203; drawback of, 99–100; parametric tests, 73,
77; strength of, 99–100; time lag problem, 78, 100–101

Zaller, John, 132, 136, 163

Chicago Studies in American Politics

*A series edited by Benjamin I. Page, Susan Herbst,
Lawrence R. Jacobs, and Adam J. Berinsky*

Series titles, continued from front matter: